Just Health

In this new book by the award-winning author of *Just Health Care*, Norman Daniels develops a comprehensive theory of justice for health that answers three key questions: What is the special moral importance of health? When are health inequalities unjust? How can we meet health needs fairly when we cannot meet them all? The theory has implications for national and global health policy: Can we meet health needs fairly in aging societies? Or protect health in the workplace while respecting individual liberty? Or meet professional obligations and obligations of justice without conflict? When is health reform or the selection of patients for treatment for HIV or coverage for catastrophic health benefits fair? When is an effort to reduce health disparities or to set priorities in realizing a human right to health fair? What do richer, healthier societies owe poorer, sicker societies? *Just Health: Meeting Health Needs Fairly* explores the many ways that social justice is good for the health of populations in developed and developing countries.

Norman Daniels is Mary B. Saltonstall Professor and Professor of Ethics and Populations Health at Harvard School of Public Health. A member of the Institute of Medicine, a Fellow of the Hastings Center, a Founding Member of the National Academy of Social Insurance and of the International Society for Equity in Health, he has consulted for organizations, commissions, and governments, including the United Nations, WHO, and the President's Commission for the Study of Ethical Problems in Medicine, on issues of justice and health policy. Dr. Daniels is the author of numerous books. He has received fellowships and grants from the National Endowment for the Humanities, the National Science Foundation, and the Robert Wood Johnson Foundation, and he has held a Robert Wood Johnson Investigator's Award as well as a Rockefeller Foundation grant for the international adaptation of the Benchmarks of Fairness for health reform.

For Anne
My constant guide

Just Health

Meeting Health Needs Fairly

NORMAN DANIELS

Harvard School of Public Health

CAMBRIDGE UNIVERSITY PRESS
Cambridge, New York, Melbourne, Madrid, Cape Town, Singapore, São Paulo, Delhi

Cambridge University Press
32 Avenue of the Americas, New York, NY 10013-2473, USA

www.cambridge.org
Information on this title: www.cambridge.org/9780521876322

First published 2008

Printed in the United States of America

A catalog record for this publication is available from the British Library.

Library of Congress Cataloging in Publication Data
Daniels, Norman, 1942–
Just health : meeting health needs fairly / Norman Daniels.
p. ; cm.
Includes bibliographical references and index.
ISBN 978-0-521-87632-2 (hardback) – ISBN 978-0-521-69998-3 (pbk.)
1. Medical policy – Moral and ethical aspects.   2. Health services accessibility.
3. Right to health care.   4. Equality – Health aspects.   5. Justice (Philosophy)
6. Medical ethics.   I. Title.
[DNLM: 1. Health Services Accessibility.   2. Health Policy.   3. Social Justice.
4. World Health.   W 76 D186j 2008]
RA394.D27   2008
362.1–dc22   2007011711

ISBN   978-0-521-87632-2 hardback
ISBN   978-0-521-69998-3 paperback

HEALTH NEEDS AND OPPORTUNITY

In order to show that meeting health needs promotes health, health promotes opportunity, and therefore meeting health needs promotes opportunity, I will need to define these terms carefully.

Needs

Why do we need to talk about "needs"? While the concept is common for most people and is prominent in public health and political discourse, some philosophers and many economists think that it is vague and problematic[2] and should be replaced by talk about "preferences" and their strength, as in welfare economics. Rather than invoking health-care needs, for example, some propose that we simply consider what preferences for health care people would express in an insurance market if they all had a fair share of income.[3] This proposal fails for two reasons.

First, needs and preferences are not equivalent. Most of us learn the difference when we discover that we have lacked insight or acted like fools. As fools, either we are unaware of our real needs, and thus do not desire to meet them, or we desire and chase after things that do not meet our real needs. Being clear about what is wise or foolish, however, requires an evaluative framework. One objection to talking about needs is the claim that we lack the kinds of agreement that would allow us to converge on such a framework and develop an account of needs. Absent such a framework, insisting that people need something when they do not even want it, or that they do not need what they strongly desire, sounds dogmatic and unjustifiably paternalistic to some (see footnote 2). I will suggest in what follows that we do, in fact, have such a framework.

Second, the proposal to substitute preferences for needs, assuming that people have fair income shares, will not work. Suppose that we define a reasonable health-care insurance package as one that meets the health-care needs or covers the risks that an informed, prudent person would rationally insure against. Though we know little else about "fair income shares," it seems plausible that an income share is *fair* only if it allows the person to buy a reasonable insurance package. If an income share is too small to cover the premium for reasonable insurance coverage, then the share is

---

[2] For a helpful discussion of the grounds for disrepute and an important attempt to rescue the concept of needs, see Braybrook (1987: Ch. 1); see also the rigorous discussion in Wiggins (1988: Ch. 1) and his effort to rescue the concept.

[3] I paraphrase Charles Fried (1978: 126ff.), though others over several decades have expressed similar views (Havighurst 1977). Fried was concerned about paternalism in specifying needs independently of preferences. Paternalism is also an issue once fair shares are clearly large enough for individuals to purchase a reasonable insurance package: Should this purchase be compulsory?

inadequate: It is *unfair* that whoever has it cannot buy reasonable insurance.[4] Accordingly, we cannot eliminate talk about justly meeting health needs in favor of talk about income distribution alone, for the latter presupposes income adequate to meet reasonable needs.[5]

This response to the proposal about fair income shares faces an objection: There is no insurance level that is "prudent" for all persons. What is prudent for an individual depends on his resources, needs, and preferences. The rich will not insure against all risks, and the poor will prudently accept greater risks. So there is no sense to the notion of a "reasonable" health-care insurance package since there is no one package that every prudent person would want to buy.

The kernel of truth to this objection is that prudent choices vary with resource limits, though not as drastically as is claimed. Our notion of prudence has a structure that reflects our concern for meeting certain basic needs. We cannot use that notion in a way that ignores the difference between being able to participate in a market for meeting those needs and being excluded from it. Indeed, we can reasonably claim that exclusion from the market for meeting those needs denies people the chance to act prudently. The notion of a fair income share presupposes income adequate to meet reasonable health-care needs.

Because we cannot easily eliminate the concept of needs, we should be clear about what we mean when we appeal to them, especially given obvious worries about the concept.[6] One worry is that the concept seems both too weak and too strong to get us very far in thinking about what we owe each other. Too many things become needs: Without abuse of language, we refer to the means necessary to reach any of our goals as needs. If I want to go to the opera, I need a ticket; I do not need to go to the opera, however much I want to. Also, too few things become needs: If I act foolishly, I fail to recognize what I really need. Finding a middle ground seems to involve many of the problems of distributive justice one might hope to solve by appeal to a clear notion of needs, including the connection of needs to egalitarian concerns (cf. Wiggins 1988: Ch. 1).

---

[4] How big the basic or reasonable package would be presumably depends on the wealth of the society, for there might be poor societies in which no one can insure against needs that would reasonably covered be in a wealthier society. But however we relativize the reasonable package, we will require some account of the needs it must meet at different levels of wealth.

[5] I have addressed an argument in the policy literature, not the philosophical literature. With a much more sophisticated philosophical approach involving much stronger assumptions about egalitarian requirements for distribution, an insurance approach might be crafted that avoids the force of my previous reply. For example, if we could assume that insurance was being bought by people with equal entitlements to resources across a broad array of resources (talents, skills, capabilities, income, wealth), then we may have built enough into the concept of "fair shares" to avoid having to talk about needs. Cf. Dworkin (2000: Chs. 2, 8.). These strong assumptions would not appeal, however, to those who make the policy argument paraphrased from Fried earlier, and the two arguments should not be confused.

[6] See footnote 2.

Still, certain things we say we need, including health-care needs, play a special role and are given special moral weight in a variety of moral contexts. If my friend tells me that he needs money to see a therapist, I will not hesitate to help him. If he says that he needs the money to buy a Hiroshige woodcut he greatly admires, I will hesitate. A gift of money for the woodcut would come not from my duty to help a friend in need, but from the generosity associated with long friendship. Similarly, a social welfare agency responding to my friend's two requests would doubtless appeal to criteria other than the strength of his preference in assessing his need, ignoring his stronger desire for the Japanese print.

In many relationships, both personal and public, the specific reasons people have for making claims on others for assistance matter, not their own subjective assessments of how badly off they are without what they want (Scanlon 1975, 1998). In distributive justice and other moral contexts, we appeal to various objective criteria – including various unmet needs – in determining the strength of people's claims for assistance. It is not just a question of rejecting subjective criteria in favor of objective ones, say on the grounds that we have better knowledge of them. What counts is the *kind* of objective criteria we invoke.[7]

We can recast this point as a claim about the structure of the scale (or scales) we use for assessing the strength of people's claims for assistance in diverse moral practices, whether individual or social. The scale does not include or reflect all of people's preferences. Rather, it is a selective scale with a moral structure that gives weight to some kinds of deficits in well-being and not to others. It favors some reasons for assisting people and considers others irrelevant.[8] The satisfaction of preferences falling into certain categories, such as certain needs, weighs heavily in the truncated scale; the satisfaction

---

[7] Scanlon (1998) argues, persuasively in my view, that a global notion of well-being does not and should not play a role in the practical reasoning of individuals. It is not, in that sense, a "master value" for individuals. Even for third-party benefactors, such as parents or friends, or for purposes of moral reasoning about societal obligations, where it might seem that we need to include the overall assessment of the well-being of people we interact with and may owe things to, we appropriately restrict ourselves to more focused concerns about specific kinds of deficits in well-being on which there is agreement about their moral importance. For example, Rawls's appeal to primary social goods and Sen's to capabilities are specific versions of this narrower focus on morally specified components of well-being. The argument that follows is compatible with this approach.

[8] What is important is the content of the scale. Suppose that we construct a welfare scale in which some categories of desires or preferences are lexically primary to others. On such a scale, preferences that are generally not included on the more selective scale we actually use enter only to break ties among those equally well off on the satisfaction of key preferences. Such a scale may avoid the worries I expressed earlier, but we now need a rationale for its ranking or structure of the preferences. Such a rationale would have to build a moral content into the scale of well-being. This scale would then no longer have the structure many consequentialists require, for it would already embody moral values and not simply be the ground for determining what they are.

of certain other preferences may not be counted or viewed as relevant at all. And some deficits, – for example, some needs – that matter very much may not be reflected in actual preferences. The scale will vary with the moral context: What is relevant to a parent in evaluating what is needed to improve the well-being of a child will differ from the scale used by a friend or a coworker, and all of these will differ from the scale society uses in designing basic social institutions. For example, helping my friend get a therapist meets a need, but helping him buy the woodcut does not. In short, some of the things we want and claim to need fall into special categories that give them a weightier moral claim in contexts involving the distribution of resources, depending, of course, on how well off we already are within those categories of need (Scanlon 1975: 660, 1998).

For a scale to function as a framework for assessing claims we make on each other, we must be able to assess objectively the deficit that exists in each of those special categories. In addition, we need widespread agreement on the importance and relevance of the categories (or reasons). Can we characterize a set of needs that have these two key features and that arguably should be included on such a scale? If we can, we can avoid the complaint that we initially encountered: that needs are so expansive that they give us little guidance about what we owe each other.

The needs we are seeking are those required for normal species functioning.[9] This characterization specifies the nature of the "harm" that results from a deficiency in a need, providing a bridge to Wiggins's (1988) account.[10] Such needs are objectively ascribable, assuming that we can specify the appropriate notion of species-typical functioning. There is also widespread public agreement that these needs should be met, whether through the "thin" social safety net that provides food, medical, and housing assistance to the poorest people in the United States or through more robust programs elsewhere.

What explains the widespread agreement on the importance of these needs? One tempting answer is that these needs are prerequisites for

---

9 This characterization has its origins in David Braybrook's (1968, 1987) suggestion that a deficiency in "course-of-life needs" "endangers the normal functioning of the subject of need considered as a member of a natural species" (Braybrook 1968: 90). Course-of-life needs are ones we have throughout our lives or at stages of life through which we all must pass, while "adventitious needs" arise because of specific projects we undertake. Personal medical services do not count as course-of-life needs by this criterion, but they do in that a deficiency of such services can endanger the individual's normal functioning. McCloskey (1976: 2f) makes a similar suggestion when he says that needs "relate to what it would be detrimental for us to lack where detrimental is explained by reference to our natures as men and specific persons."

10 Wiggins's (1988) analysis builds on the claim that our needs are necessary to prevent harms to us. We should, however, distinguish between the harm to my friend who suffers disappointment at not getting the woodblock print and the harm he suffers if he fails to solve the problems that the therapist could solve. I focus on the harm that comes from departures from normal functioning.

happiness. Our ability to achieve our chosen goals, and consequently our happiness, will be diminished without normal species functioning. For example, it is sometimes said that whatever our chosen goals or tasks, we need our health and, therefore, appropriate health care.

This claim, however, is not, strictly speaking, true. Some of our most important goals are not necessarily undermined by ill health or disability. Moreover, many people adjust their goals to fit better with their dysfunction or long-term disability, at least for some kinds of disability, and thus achieve happiness or satisfaction in life comparable to that of people who are functioning normally, a fact supported by survey results of judgments about being in various health states. This point has ethical implications for the development and use of population measures of health.[11]

Nevertheless, meeting needs that are necessary for normal functioning may have a definite *tendency* to promote happiness or the satisfaction of preferences. This tendency may be all the utilitarian requires to guide public policy, and it may explain why there is wide agreement on the importance of meeting these needs. I offer no conclusive response to this position: It is a generalized and more satisfactory version of the view that health care, for example, is special because it reduces pain and suffering, which much of it no doubt does.[12] Instead, I sketch an account that better explains our wide agreement on meeting needs essential to normal functioning and that does not depend on an empirical claim about the relationship between happiness and normal functioning.

The alternative account builds on the fact that impairments of normal functioning reduce the range of exercisable opportunities from which individuals may construct their "plans of life"[13] or "conceptions of the good." This range of exercisable opportunities is reduced because some of our capabilities are reduced when normal functioning is impaired. These opportunities may be diminished even when society has made reasonable efforts to include people with disabilities (Buchanan et al. 2000: Ch. 7).

Life plans for which we are otherwise suited, and that we reasonably hope to find satisfying or happiness-producing, are rendered unreasonable by some impairments of normal functioning. Consequently, if people have a fundamental interest in preserving the opportunity to revise their

---

[11] A considerable literature has developed about these ethical implications. See Harris (1987), Gold et al. (1996), Brock (1998), Daniels (1998a), Nord (1999).

[12] Advocates of this view must be willing to weigh the reduction of pain and suffering against the satisfaction of all other kinds of preferences. It is this empirical estimate of the strength of the tendency that makes health care special: The specialness disappears when the estimate changes.

[13] A life plan is a long-term plan in which an individual selects and revises her goals or ends and schedules activities to achieve them harmoniously. The good for an individual is defined by reference to this plan and the choice of goals, projects, and the means for achieving them that it contains (Rawls 1971: 92ff.). I leave aside how much of an idealization the idea of a plan of life is and how happiness is related to successful pursuit of a life plan.

conceptions of the good over time (Buchanan 1975), then they will have a pressing interest in meeting whatever needs are required for normal species functioning. (They also have a fundamental interest in making sure that social institutions are structured to reasonably include of them, even if they have long-term disabilities [Buchanan et al. 2000: Ch. 7]. In sum, there is wide agreement on the importance of meeting needs required for normal functioning because people have a fundamental interest in maintaining a normal range of opportunities.

To better see the relationship between this account of important needs and health needs specifically, we must specify what we mean by "health."

Health

I begin with the basic, if somewhat misleading, idea that "health is the absence of disease," both physical and mental, the core of the much-criticized "biomedical" conception of health.

This idea is misleading because "disease" is too narrow a notion to provide the full contrast with health. It captures neither our ordinary usage nor the even broader theoretical notion of pathology. For example, we do not consider people healthy when they have injuries from trauma or from environmental hazards or toxins, none of which are diseases. Similarly, we do not say that people are healthy when they suffer from a broad range of birth defects, whether genetic or developmental. Functional deficits, such as blindness or deafness or quadriplegia, as well as cognitive deficits, are more complex. We might say that someone is quadriplegic, though "otherwise" healthy, signaling that the loss of function from the condition has not undermined other aspects of the person's health. Some people find that qualification redundant, even insulting; for them, the functional deficit does not compromise health at all, even though it clearly involves what medicine considers pathology. Similarly, the parents of a child with a specific cognitive dysfunction, such as dyslexia, might insist that their child is "perfectly healthy." And the child, like the quadriplegic, is clearly "not sick."

Our ordinary usage thus includes conflicting tendencies, a situation not present in the more theoretical notion of pathology. A broadening tendency widens the scope of health to include the absence of injuries and other deficits. A narrowing tendency connects health to a more literal and narrower notion of disease or sickness, counting some people as healthy despite having permanent functional deficits. In *Just Health Care* I broadened the term "disease" to include disability and injury,[14] but to avoid confusion here,

---

[14] In that usage, I agreed with Boorse (1975, 1976, 1977), who had also used a broad notion of disease to capture what he views as a "theoretical" (as opposed to a clinical) concept in the medical sciences. Boorse himself (1997 and personal communication) cites approvingly the convergence of his own view with the more explicitly normative approach taken by Wakefield (1997a, 1997b, 1999), to which I return later.

I shall follow Boorse's (1997) suggestion and say that health is the absence of pathology. (Admittedly, "health is the absence of pathology" has neither the ring nor the familiarity of "health is the absence of disease.") We may understand "pathology" to refer to any deviation from the natural functional organization of a typical member of a species.[15] Pathology, viewed as disrupted part function, takes place at various levels (genetic, organelle, cell, tissue, organ, systemic) with different consequences, ranging from innocuous to fatal. Much pathology is not clinically detectable, and much is not worthy of treatment.[16] In short, pathology is a departure from normal functioning.

This modification of the (misleading) idea that health is the absence of disease leads us to the view that health is normal functioning for our species. Health needs, and thus the narrower class of health-care needs, are things we need to maintain normal functioning – or health – over the course of our lives. Health needs are objectively ascribable, on this approach, since we can ultimately rely on the scientific methods of the biomedical sciences to characterize pathology, as well as on our growing understanding of epidemiology, including social epidemiology, to clarify what we need to function normally. This extension of the original intuition thus draws a tight connection between "course-of-life" needs and their objectivity (see footnote 9) and health needs. This tight connection may help account for the convergence that I suggested exists in our moral beliefs and practices regarding what we owe each other to meet health needs and sustain health.

Before saying more about understanding health as normal functioning, I want to forestall a common misunderstanding about the narrowness of this biomedical conception. The *conceptual* narrowness is required. Health is not all there is to well-being or happiness, contrary to the famous World Health Organization (WHO) definition: "Health is a state of complete physical, mental, and social well-being, and not merely the absence of disease or infirmity."[17] The WHO definition risks turning all of social philosophy and social policy into health care. Moreover, health as normal functioning is what epidemiologists and public health practitioners actually measure, for example when they quantify the global burden of disease.[18] Nevertheless,

---

[15] Boorse (1997) suggests that function is relative to a relevant species subgroup, such as an age group within the males or females of a species.

[16] Much pathology is compatible with the colloquial judgment that a person is still healthy. The point is obvious when the pathology is localized and innocuous, as in a small area of injured skin. The point remains controversial when the pathology is a serious functional loss, such as blindness or quadriplegia.

[17] From the Preamble to the Constitution of the World Health Organization. Adopted by the International Health Conference held in New York, 19 June–22 July 1946, and signed on 22 July 1946. Official Record of World Health Organization 2, no. 100.

[18] The disability-adjusted life year (DALY), for example, combines a measure of premature death with morbidity. Another measure used in cost-effectiveness analysis, the

that conceptual focus is completely compatible with the broad view of the determinants of health mentioned earlier and elaborated on in Chapter 4. It is crucial not to confuse cause with effect.

The central intuitive idea that health should be understood as normal functioning can be made more precise in several ways. In *Just Health Care*, I was attracted to the thoroughgoing "naturalism" (or nonnormativity) of Boorse's (1975, 1976, 1977) "biostatistical" account. On his view, a biological function can be defined as a causal contribution to a species-typical goal, such as survival or reproduction, and it is the task of the biomedical sciences, broadly conceived, to characterize these functions of organisms and their parts. A departure from normal functioning is then simply a statistical deviation from the causal contribution of the relevant part. I remain attracted to the idea that we are to read departures from normal functioning "off the biological facts of nature without value judgments" (Boorse 1997). This makes ascribing health or departures from it as objective and value-free as the biomedical sciences themselves. A claim on others based on health needs is thus an objective claim. Of course, our response to those needs and those claims, in clinical medicine or public health, is not at all value-free. Judging their relative importance in deciding what we owe each other is a normative task that can be illuminated by seeing what is of special moral importance about meeting health needs. What attracts me about Boorse's account is *where* it locates normative judgments about health, not that it avoids them altogether.

This approach to making the notion of normal functioning precise remains controversial in two ways: its avoidance of an etiological or "natural selection" account of biological function[19] and its avoidance of all normative judgments in identifying departures from normal functioning. Fortunately, for our purposes in bioethics and political philosophy, we do not have to resolve all disputes in the philosophy of biology before we can safely employ a widely used notion such as "normal functioning." By sidestepping the first controversy completely and making a modest concession to the second, we can still arrive at an account of normal functioning that suits our purposes well. Indeed, it is Boorse (1997) who suggests that we can combine

---

quality-adjusted life year (QALY), combines life years with a weighting function for health states to quantify the health benefit produced by an intervention. Both measures of health sacrificed and health gained quantify a normal functioning conception of health.

[19] One alternative to Boorse's causal contribution approach takes a function of something to be those of its effects that explain its presence through its causal history, in particular through a history of selection (for artifacts) by the designer's intentions or (for organisms) Darwinian selection (cf. Wright 1973; Neander 1983, 1991a,b; Millikan 1984; Godfrey-Smith 1994). Yet another kind of alternative analysis is "value-centered" in that it takes a function to be an effect that is useful or good for some beneficiary (Bedau 1992). Each of these general approaches has difficulty with certain counterexamples, as does the causal contribution view. In some cases, they are too broad, counting the wrong things as functions; in others, they are too narrow, failing to recognize certain functions; in some cases, they are both.

an etiological account of biological function with the weak normative judgment that we shall count something as a dysfunction when it is a harmful departure from species-typical functioning and still have an account that converges with his on nearly all judgments about normal or abnormal functioning. He cites Wakefield (1992, 1997a,b) as doing just that when he provides an account of mental disorders.[20]

Because he states that dysfunctions must be "harmful," Wakefield abandons the stricter naturalism of Boorse's view, which simply refers to subtypical efficiency of a part-function – a statistical, not normative, view of pathology. This contrast allows us to assess how important naturalism is for my argument. I shall argue that Boorse's strict naturalism is not important to my argument and that Wakefield, because he incorporates a nonnormative notion of normal functioning and departures from it, distances himself adequately from the extreme normative views I avoided by invoking Boorse's naturalism. Wakefield's appeal to the harmfulness of objectively specified dysfunctions is not a threat to the public agreement I consider central to the moral argument. After all, we must make normative judgments about which dysfunctions are worthy of treatment. The opportunity-based account I later defend provides a normative framework for just such judgments (though it must be supplemented with an account of fair decision-making process, as developed in Chapter 4).

There is initial plausibility to a view, like Wakefield's, that makes disease or pathology a normative notion. People seek medical attention, we may suppose, because they suffer from a condition they do not want to have. To capture the concept of disease, we might then think, we should start with all instances in which that salient reason for seeking help is present and then find the conditions that increase their probability of occurring. Perhaps some such view motivates Wakefield, but his restriction to dysfunctions – departures from (etiologically analyzed) biological functions – works in an opposing way, for it is not an abstraction from unwanted conditions. The problem with the initially plausible idea is that there are simply *too many*

---

[20] The etiological and causal accounts tend to converge because the two main goals considered in Boorse's causal contribution view, survival and reproduction, are also the central elements in a natural selection approach (Boorse 1997). The accounts may diverge where a trait was established by an effect that no longer promotes an individual's goals in the current environment, or where group functions were fixed by group selection, if any exists (Boorse 1997: 10–11), but these will be a relatively minor matter. These alternatives – or variations on them that prove to be more satisfactory – all support a distinction between normal function and dysfunction or malfunction. All are also compatible with the idea that there is reasonable uniformity of functioning within an appropriate reference class of organisms. All are compatible with current views in population genetics about variation and polymorphism within species and can avoid the "essentialism" that may have marred earlier appeals to the notion of species-typical design (see Boorse 1997). Despite the disputes, I conclude, our intuitive notion of normal functioning is not without foundation, even if we still lack a consensus account of the best way to resolve problem cases.

such unwanted conditions for the abstraction to lead us to the category of dysfunctions (or harmful dysfunctions).[21]

Unlike Wakefield's approach, the normative approach I do consider a threat to public agreement is not constrained by an independent account of departures from normal functioning. Instead, it generalizes (incorrectly) from this picture of the reasons for seeking medical assistance. A disease is just an unwanted condition. At the social level, this might be the view that society may "construct" the notion of disease to reflect departures from any norms it holds.

Some argue for a version of this view by citing historical examples of cases where a departure from a norm clearly was classified as a disease, at least for a period of time. For example, Engelhardt (1974) argues that masturbation was so classified, and physicians of the period described its symptoms and effects. So was "drapetomania," the running-away disease of slaves. Similarly, whatever its biological basis, homosexuality was so classified until quite recently (Bayer 1981). Another recent example was the Soviet abuse of political prisoners by classifying them as mentally ill.

These historical examples, however, cannot prove the extreme normative view of how to understand disease. The same examples are fully compatible with the judgment that societies sometimes make grievous errors about diseases or egregiously abuse disease classifications. The fact that whales were classified as fishes for many centuries did not make them fishes, any more than masturbation or political opposition is a disease just because some past culture or social regime said so. In fact, the historical examples show that a normative approach to disease carries grave risks. It fails to let us say that these were errors that recognized methods of public reasoning, including the biomedical sciences, helped us expose.

If the extreme normative view were true, it would show up in our practice in a very different way. We would talk and behave differently than we do. Many people seek medical help for many unwanted conditions. They receive – and pay for – medical interventions that removes those conditions. If people generally counted as a disease any medically treatable unwanted condition, then consumers and providers of these services would commonly talk about them as diseases or pathology. But consumers and providers know that they are seeking or providing treatment for conditions that are not pathological. For example, when people want a nose, breast, or buttock reshaped by a plastic surgeon, they do not speak of the unwanted condition as a disease, however much they want the surgery. Nor do their surgeons. Of course, dysfunctional noses count as diseases or pathology, since noses have

---

[21] The biomedical sciences did not "abstract" the concept of disease from clinical practice in this way, however much that practice brought specific conditions to their attention. Our understanding of normal functioning and pathology emerged from a much more complex interaction of basic and applied scientific work, and now it informs medical practice itself.

normal species functions and normal functional organization (or simply normal anatomy). If the dysfunction or deformity is serious, it might warrant treatment as an illness.[22] But deviation of nasal anatomy from individual or social conceptions of beauty does not constitute disease. This distinction is well known to plastic surgeons.

Another example may be even more dramatic because the stakes are much higher. When women seek to terminate unwanted pregnancies, whether through a morning-after pill or an abortion, they do not speak of their pregnancy as a disease or a pathological condition. Like the medical professionals who treat them, they view unwanted pregnancies as the result of normal – perhaps all-too-normal – functioning.

It is interesting to note a contrast between American insurance practice regarding cosmetic surgery and that involving abortions. In the United States, most women who receive insurance through their employers or through individual private insurance plans have coverage for nontherapeutic abortions. Most private American insurance, then, recognizes an important difference between nontherapeutic abortions and cosmetic surgery. In contrast, poor women covered by Medicaid are barred by federal law from receiving federal money for abortions. The contrast is an obvious source of controversy for proposals to establish universal coverage in the United States.

In the Clinton administration's effort in 1993 to introduce universal insurance coverage, I served on the Ethics Working Group. At one point, David Eddy and I were asked to develop a definition of "medical necessity." Our definition omitted nontherapeutic abortion from the category of "medically necessary treatments of disease or dysfunction" since a normal pregnancy was not pathological in any way. Some task force members insisted that we redefine the concept of medical necessity to include (nontherapeutic) abortions automatically. When we asked how that could be done without also counting as medically necessary cosmetic surgery for noses deemed unattractive, we were told that the cases were different. On discussion, the differences had nothing to do with normal or abnormal functioning, but rather with other reasons for considering one intervention more important than the other. No one suggested that something became a disease by being an unwanted condition.[23]

---

[22] Anyone who doubts the appropriateness of treating some physiognomic deformities as serious diseases with strong claims on surgical resources should read Frances C. MacGreggor's (1979) classic study. Even where there is no disease or deformity, nothing in the analysis I offer precludes individuals or society from deciding to use health-care technology to make physiognomy conform to some standard of beauty. But such uses of medical technology will not be justifiable for meeting health-care needs, as defined earlier.

[23] An alternative proposal to ours included nontherapeutic abortions as mandated pregnancy-related services, attempting to dodge the question of whether they were really medically necessary. On the concept of medical necessity, see Sabin and Daniels (1994).

In our language and practice, as these examples suggest, we do not confuse unwanted conditions with pathology. We do not expand our category of diseases or pathology to include all the conditions we want to change medically. Were the extreme normative view correct, however, we would not draw the reasonably clear distinctions we do.

Though I oppose strongly normative views of disease, I do not oppose more modest appeals to norms in characterizing disease or disability, as in Wakefield (1992, 1997a,b). My purposes are satisfied when the line between the normal and the abnormal or pathological is, for most cases, uncontroversial and ascertainable by publicly acceptable methods, such as those of the biomedical sciences. It will not matter if what counts as a disease category is relative to some features of social roles in a given society, and thus to some normative judgments, provided that the basic notion of normal functioning is left intact. In any event, the importance of treating pathology depends on just such normative judgments. Any acceptable account would still, I presume, count infertility as a disease, even though certain individuals might prefer to be infertile and seek medical treatment to become so for all or part of their lives. Similarly, unwanted pregnancy is not a disease.

For our purposes in this account of just health, it is enough to know that the intuitive distinction underlying the biomedical view of health – that health is the absence of pathology – can be reformulated into a nonnormative (or naturalistic) distinction between normal functioning and pathology, even if this departs from some features of ordinary usage. Fortunately, there is much argument on how to draw this distinction, and disputes about it can generally be resolved by the publicly accessible methods of the biomedical sciences. This general argument holds even when we allow for heated disputes about the correct analysis of biological function, and even if we allow a modest form of normativism in describing what counts as a disease.

Health Needs, Normal Functioning, and Opportunity

We can combine our account of needs and of health into a characterization of health needs. Health needs are those things we need in order to maintain, restore, or provide functional equivalents (where possible) to normal species functioning (for the appropriate reference class by gender and age). Though our account of health was conceptually narrow, health needs are a broad, diverse set:

1. Adequate nutrition
2. Sanitary, safe, unpolluted living and working conditions
3. Exercise, rest, and such important lifestyle features as avoiding substance abuse and practicing safe sex
4. Preventive, curative, rehabilitative, and compensatory personal medical services (and devices)

5. Nonmedical personal and social support services
6. An appropriate distribution of other social determinants of health

The first five of these are what I characterized in *Just Health Care* as health-care needs. Adding the sixth set of socially controllable factors affecting health broadens this to an account of all health needs. The first three sets of items, and arguably the sixth, can be grouped under the heading of "intersectoral public health" (see Chapter 9). By adequate nutrition, I mean not only a sufficiently high caloric content, but also a balanced diet that conforms to recommendations based on good scientific evidence. Sanitary, safe, and unpolluted living and working conditions include clean water and air, housing appropriate for the environment, and measures to make travel reasonably safe. The promotion of healthy lifestyles requires appropriate and effective education, as well as the right incentives and disincentives. Measures to protect against domestic and other kinds of violence fall in to this category as well as into the broader category of the social determinants of health. The nonmedical personal and social support services can also comprise broad features of the legal structure that aim to include people with disabilities in the mainstream of productive, cooperative activity. The very broad set of needs included in the sixth item will be discussed more specifically in Chapter 3.

Obviously, we do not commonly think of all these things as health needs, partly because we tend to think narrowly about personal medical services when we think about health. But the list is not designed to conform to our ordinary notion of health care; it is intended to broaden our thinking. It points to a functional relationship between preserving health – maintaining normal functioning – and the many goods, services, and institutions that bear on health and its distribution.

Health needs, as characterized here, meet the requirement that they be *objectively ascribable*. More can be said about why there is such widespread agreement on the importance of meeting them. What is so important about normal species functioning? Why give such moral importance to health needs merely because they are necessary to preserve normal species functioning? To answer these questions, I shall develop my earlier remarks about the relationship between species-typical functioning and opportunity. The rest of this section presupposes that we have an interest in protecting the range of opportunities open to us. Later in this chapter, I consider the claim that we have an obligation to protect opportunity.

To begin with, we must defind a "normal opportunity range." The normal opportunity range for a given society is the array of life plans reasonable persons are likely to develop for themselves. The normal range thus depends on key features of the society – its historical development and its material wealth and technological development, as well as important cultural facts about it. In this sense, the notion of a normal opportunity range is socially relative. Facts about social organization, including the conception of justice regulating its basic institutions, will also determine how that normal range is distributed in the population. Nevertheless, the issue of a just distribution of fundamental goods aside, normal functioning offers us one clear parameter affecting the *share* of the normal range open to a given individual. It is this parameter that is affected by the distribution of health care and the meeting of other health needs affects. The special importance we attribute to meeting health needs, then, can be explained by the weight we attach to protecting our shares of the normal opportunity range against departures from normal functioning.

It is illuminating to contrast the way our existing social practice protects opportunity against ill health but not against variations in talents and skills. The share of the normal range is, after all, determined in a fundamental way by the individual's talents and skills. Some recent advocates of equality of opportunity have argued that justice requires redressing these inequalities as well (we return to this view later in the chapter). In contrast, the traditional weak view of equal opportunity – that careers should be open to talents – makes equality of opportunity relative to talents and skills. So, too, does Rawls's (1971) stronger conception: fair equality of opportunity (I discuss Rawls in more detail later in this chapter). On Rawls's view, however, since we know that skills and talents can be underdeveloped or mis-developed because of social conditions, such as family background or racist educational practices, equal opportunity should not accept the actual distribution of talents and skills as a given fact. If we believe that individuals should enjoy a *fair share* of the normal opportunity range, we will want to correct for special disadvantages that have led to the misdevelopment or underdevelopment of talents and skills, say through compensatory educational or job-training programs. Thus, even assuming that people are all healthy over a normal lifespan, individual shares of the normal opportunity range will not in general be equal, even when they are fair to the individual. Rawls's principle of fair equality of opportunity thus does not imply leveling individual differences that result from differences in talents and skills.[24]

The intuition behind fair equality of opportunity is to restore the fair opportunity range for individuals to what they would have if social arrangements were more just and less unequal. A similar intuition underlies our practice in protecting opportunity against ill health. The impairment of normal functioning by significant pathology, such as serious disease, injury, or disability, restricts individuals' opportunity relative to the portion of the normal range that their skills and talents would have made available to them

[24] In Rawls's (1971, 1993) theory, socioeconomic inequalities are allowed to work to the advantage of those with more marketable talents *only if the inequalities also maximally benefit the worst-off individuals,* who, we may suppose, have less marketable talents. Other theorists think redress should be more direct.

were they healthy. If individuals' fair shares of the normal range are the life plans they may reasonably choose, given their (corrected) talents and skills, then disease and disability shrink their shares from what is fair.[25]

Maintaining normal functioning by meeting health needs, including providing health care, has a particular and *limited* effect on individuals' shares of the normal range. It lets them enjoy that portion of the range to which their skills and talents would give them access, assuming that these too are not impaired by special social disadvantages. It does not presume that we should eliminate or level natural individual differences, which act as a baseline constraint on individuals' enjoyment of the normal range. Where, however, differences in talents and skills are the result of pathology, not merely normal variation, we should make, resources permitting, some effort to correct for the effects of the "natural lottery." (See Chapter 5 for further discussion of the distinction between treatment and enhancement.)

Two points about this conceptualization of the fair shares of the normal opportunity range need emphasis. First, some pathologies are more serious curtailments of opportunity than others relative to a given normal opportunity range. Within a society, this impairment gives a crude measure of the relative importance of meeting different health needs, but we must supplement this measure with fair procedures for resource allocation (see Chapter 4). Because normal opportunity ranges are defined by reference to particular societies, the same disease in two societies may impair opportunity differently, and so its importance may be assessed differently. For example, dyslexia may be less important to treat in an generally illiterate society than in a highly literate one. Thus, the social importance of particular diseases is a notion that we ought to view as socially relative.

Second, within a society, the normal opportunity range abstracts from important individual differences in what I will call "effective opportunity." For an individual who has a particular plan of life and who has developed certain skills accordingly, the effective opportunity range will be only a part of his fair share of the normal range. The impairment of the effective opportunity range for a skilled laborer who loses manual dexterity due to a disease may be greater than for a college teacher, but if both originally had comparable dexterity, their fair shares of the normal range would be equally diminished by the disease. Measuring the impact of disease on opportunity by reference to individuals' shares of the normal range, rather than by reference to its impairment of their effective ranges, abstracts from special

---

[25] Correcting for *socially* imposed deficits in talents and skills is one thing, but correcting for *naturally* imposed deficits in talents and skills or capabilities that result from pathology is another, or so some might argue (Nagel 1997). I claimed in the previous chapter that this contrast of natural and social is misleading because so much of the level of health and its distribution in a population is the result of socially controllable factors. Accordingly, I find this objection to my extension of the underlying intuition unjustified.

effects that derive from individuals' conceptions of the good or from their plans of life (Buchanan 1975). This way of proceeding seems plausible in light of judgments we are inclined to make about access to medical services. For example, we do not want to be in the business, I believe, of deciding who gets what medical services on the basis of occupation or other results of prior individual choices of a similar sort.[26]

My goal so far in this chapter has been to *explain* the special moral importance generally ascribed to meeting health needs, especially health-care needs. The explanation has two main features. First, health needs are paradigmatic among an important category of basic needs, things we need to maintain normal functioning. When we evaluate the well-being of others to assess what assistance we owe them, we give special weight to claims that involve such basic needs. We do not take into account all preferences that contribute to people's welfare or satisfaction; instead, we use a more selective scale of well-being. Second, protecting normal functioning helps to protect the range of opportunities. People share an interest in protecting the opportunities open to them; that shared interest, especially to the extent that people are aware of it, helps to explain the special weight people give to meeting health needs.

This explanation of features of our moral practice does not, however, constitute a justification for it. Rather, the explanation has the status of a finding in moral anthropology: Many people – perhaps all of us – use a selective scale for measuring the well-being of others when they consider what they owe others, and some features of that scale are further explained by reference to a shared belief they have in the importance of opportunity. Are these features of their moral beliefs and practice (or ours) justifiable? An account of just health should not simply describe and explain what we generally do; it should move us toward justification. That search for justification is the task of the rest of this chapter, first by extending Rawls's theory of justice as fairness to health, and then borrowing from its justification for a principle of assuring fair equality of opportunity; and then by arguing that some views critical of Rawls actually agree on the importance of protecting opportunity as well.

FAIR EQUALITY OF OPPORTUNITY AND HEALTH: EXTENDING RAWLS'S THEORY

Should we, as a matter of social justice, protect people's fair shares of the normal opportunity range? If justice requires protecting opportunity in this way, then it requires protecting health, according to our previous analysis. In fact, that analysis of health needs and their special importance shows us how

---

[26] Of course, the impact on the effective range is important when individuals decide whether they want to receive certain services.

to extend one prominent general theory of justice, Rawls's (1971) theory of justice as fairness (to be described in more detail shortly), so that it can address issues about health and health care. That extension will enable us to draw some justification from the arguments provided by Rawls for features his work shares with it, namely, the appeal to an objective, truncated scale of well-being and to the importance of protecting opportunity.

This extension of Rawls's theory is not trivial, since Rawls simplifies his theory by abstracting from the variations among people introduced by disease, disability, and premature death. His social contractors, as a first approximation, represent people who are fully functional over a normal lifespan. His account of justice applies to the simplified case involving idealized people who are never ill or disabled and who live full lives. By relaxing this simplification, the extension I propose greatly increases the power of Rawls's theory and arguably adds to its plausibility, for now it can respond to issues and to criticisms it could not before. I do not argue, however, for the overall acceptability of Rawls's theory. I make only a far more modest claim: If Rawls's general theory is correct, then, with my extension of it to health, it provides one plausible justificatory framework for relying on an objective scale of well-being that includes health needs and for our having an obligation of justice to protect opportunity (and therefore health). (Later in this chapter, I seek to borrow support from other views as well.)

Primary Social Goods and Needs

Key to my extension of Rawls's theory is showing how my nonwelfarist account of health needs and their relation to opportunity can be integrated into Rawls's index of primary social goods, his nonwelfarist method of assessing inequalities in well-being for the purposes of justice. (By contrast, a welfarist account of well-being is concerned with an experiential state, such as the satisfaction of preferences. Earlier, I argued that health needs are not reducible to the satisfaction of preferences.) The integration requires us to modify the concept of opportunity in an appropriate way.

A central feature of Rawls's theory of justice as fairness is the use of an index of primary social goods as his "objective" way of determining who is better off and who is worse off for purposes of justice. Since my strategy is to derive some justification for my analysis by showing how it allows us to extend Rawls's theory, I want to explain briefly how Rawls supports this feature. (What follows is not a defense of that theory but an explanation of how it can support my appeals to an objective account of needs and to a robust notion of equal opportunity.)

Rawls's justification for using the primary social goods has evolved along with other important changes in his theory. In his early work, Rawls justified the appeal to primary social goods as an implication of basic facts about human nature and a widely held account of rationality. In his later work, he realized that a full justification required appeal to a view of persons as free and equal citizens that is part of a shared democratic culture. Throughout his work, he remains committed to providing an objective basis on which to make uncontroversial judgments about who has better and worse lifetime prospects, which involves rejecting welfarist measures as irrelevant from the perspective of justice.[27]

For Rawls, justice requires giving some priority to improving the lifetime prospects of those who are worse off. This has two parts: (1) his rational social contractors selecting principles of justice have to think about which principles make their lifetime prospects acceptable, regardless of their social position, and (2) the principles they select require them to know who are worst off and how the basic structure of society can work to make them as well off as possible. Ideally, the same basis for judging inequalities can play a role in both kinds of decision.

In *A Theory of Justice* (1971: 78), Rawls points to standard problems with the measure of satisfaction or welfare that utilitarian theory employs for purposes of justice. Utilitarianism assumes very accurate measures of utility, which require a method of correlating scales of different persons (in order to know when the gains to some outweigh the losses to others). While we cannot expect too much precision, we cannot simply rely on estimates based on unguided intuition, which leave room for many forms of bias and resulting controversy. In works following *A Theory of Justice*, Rawls articulated other intuitive arguments against welfarist measures. These arguments are not themselves decisive, but they provide reasons for seeking an alternative.[28] I focus here on Rawls's defense of his objective scale rather than on his criticisms of a welfarist approach.

---

[27] There is controversy about whether the changes in his account deepen or weaken its justificatory force (Daniels 1996a: Ch. 8; Scanlon 2003 in Freeman 2003).

[28] One of Rawls's (1982b) intuitive objections to utility or welfare as a basis for interpersonal comparisons for purposes of justice is that the satisfaction scale forces us to view persons as mere "containers" for satisfaction. Accordingly, if A is better off than B because A contains more satisfaction, then we should want to be A and have A's preferences. To borrow a term from Bernard Williams (1973), the "satisfaction scale" undermines the integrity of persons. Thus, the satisfaction scale is incompatible with a view of the nature of persons that in turn underlies much of our moral practice. If we abandon this feature of our moral practice, with its truncated scale of well-being, in favor of a more complete one, we would have to give up much else, including our concern for the integrity of persons and our ability to offer prudential and moral advice. The implausibility of such radical changes counts as evidence for Rawls's view.

One further argument Rawls (1982b) offers for his nonwelfarist view is an argument against "social hijacking" by those who cultivate expensive tastes. This argument was the focus of my discussion in *Just Health Care*, but it is not decisive for reasons I note here. This intuitive argument points to the unacceptable risks of social hijacking when (A) we think that those who are worse off have some claim of justice for assistance from society and (B) we measure who is better and worse off for purposes of justice using a scale of welfare or satisfaction. Suppose further that moderate people adjust their tastes and preferences

In *A Theory of Justice* (1971), Rawls sought a basis for agreement in what he takes to be a shared conception of rationality, as well as some uncontroversial appeals to psychology and beliefs about human nature. Accordingly, the primary social goods are "things it is rational to want whatever else one wants. Thus, given human nature, wanting them is part of being rational" (223). That is, Rawls here asserted that a relatively uncontroversial account of rationality could help us work out the features of the index of these primary goods. The objectivity of the goods and the index connecting them derives in part from the agreement on that view of rational agents, and we could achieve this agreement without digging into the controversial preferences and values that shape different people's conceptions of happiness

so that they have a reasonable chance of being satisfied with their shares of social goods. Extravagant people, however, form exotic and expensive tastes, and they are desperately unhappy when their preferences are not satisfied. Since extravagant people are so unhappy compared to moderate ones, given equal or otherwise fair shares of resources, should we increase their shares?

If having less welfare than others is a reason to assist or compensate people, as (A) asserts, then unhappy people with extravagant tastes have a claim on us. But it seems unjust to deny more moderate people equal claims on further distributions simply because others have been extravagant. Rather, it seems reasonable and fair to hold people responsible for their unhappiness when it results from extravagant preferences, which could have been otherwise. This judgment about fairness leads to conclusion (C): Reject the claims of dissatisfied extravagant people.

The classic utilitarian, who seeks to maximize aggregate welfare rather than equalizing it, would reject (A) while retaining (B). It follows that we should not favor those with extravagant tastes. Indeed, since moderate people are more efficient at converting resources into welfare, we should steer new resources to them. The same reason may lead utilitarians to steer resources away from inefficient users such as people with serious, chronic illnesses or long-term disabilities. Dropping (A) thus seems especially problematic from the perspective of justice and health.

Two alternative responses preserve (A). Rawls rejects (B). Instead, for purposes of justice, we judge people to be worse off than others only if they are worse off according to an index of such primary social goods as liberty, power, opportunity, wealth and income, and the social bases of self-respect. For Rawls, society is responsible for distributing the primary social goods in a way that conforms to the fair terms of social cooperation, that is, to the principles of justice that would be accepted in the social contract he develops. Individuals are responsible for pursuing their conceptions of a good life – their goals, values, and preferences as they determine them – within the limits set by fair terms of social cooperation. People with extravagant tastes are responsible for addressing their own dissatisfaction with life and have no claims of justice on us.

A third response to the problem preserves (B) as well as (A). To save both conditions, however, proponents of this view must, like Rawls, qualify which people deserve our concern among those who are worse off than others. Specifically, people have a claim on us only if they have less *opportunity for welfare or advantage* than others through no fault or choice of their own. People who deliberately cultivate extravagant tastes do not have such a claim, but people who acquired such tastes through no fault of their own would. On this view, justice requires compensation for bad brute luck but not for bad option luck (the terminology derives from Dworkin [1981a,b] but plays this role in Arneson [1988] and G. A. Cohen [1989]). I discuss this view later in this chapter.

or the good life. We could remain neutral about those conceptions while claiming to provide goods all would want if they were rational.

In his later work, Rawls realized that the primary social goods should not be defended simply as an implication of a widely held account of human rationality; he also realized that their rationale does not rest "solely on psychological, social, or historical facts" (Rawls 2001: 58). To be sure, "various general facts about human needs and abilities, their normal phases and requirements of nurture, relations of social interdependence and much else" (58) help determine what count as primary goods. We also must have a "rough idea" about how the goods we consider primary play a role in rational plans of life. Still, the account of primary goods ultimately depends on a normative view of the nature of persons.

Persons, viewed as free and equal citizens, can be characterized as having two basic moral powers. All (nonpathological) citizens have a sense of justice: They seek terms of fair cooperation to resolve conflicting claims. All citizens have the power to form and revise their conceptions of a good life, determining for themselves their ends in life, including the religious or moral values they hold most dear. This political conception of free and equal citizens is a shared feature of democratic culture. It explains how reasonable people with different moral or religious views can all accept this characterization of persons.

This convergence on the notion of free and equal citizens provides the basis for working out their needs in terms of an objective list of primary social goods. The primary goods, Rawls says, are "given by reference to objective features of citizens' social circumstances, features open to public view: Their secured institutional rights and liberties, their available fair opportunities, their (reasonable) expectations of income and wealth seen from their social position" (Rawls 2001: 59). To emphasize this objective character, he points out that it is not "self-respect as an attitude toward oneself but the social bases of self-respect that count as a primary good. These social bases are things like the institutional fact that citizens have equal basic rights, and the public recognition of that fact and that everyone endorses the difference principle, itself a form of reciprocity" (60).

Primary goods "are what free and equal persons (as specified by the political conception) need as citizens" (Rawls 2001: 60; 1995: 187–90). These goods support their *capabilities* to function as free and equal citizens.[29] People who hold very different conceptions of the good life that derive from

---

[29] To Sen's suggestion that we should focus on capabilities instead of primary social goods, Rawls (2001: 169) replies, "... it should be stressed that the account of primary goods does take into account, and does not abstract from, basic capabilities: namely, the capabilities of citizens as free and equal persons in virtue of their two moral powers." Cf. Anderson (1999), who focuses Sen's discussion of capabilities on those of free and equal citizens, which brings the two accounts very close together (see Daniels in Freeman 2003).

different moral or religious worldviews still can agree on this political conception of the good, and this agreement forms a sufficient basis for comparing people for purposes of justice. (Our overlapping consensus on this political conception of the primary social goods, Rawls concludes, is compatible with the pluralism that is encouraged by conditions of social justice.)

Before integrating my account of health needs with Rawls's index of primary social goods, I need to say more about his concept of opportunity and his justification for a principle assuring fair equality of opportunity.

Fair Equality of Opportunity

Many people accept morally that there are winners and losers in competitions, whether in commerce, politics, or athletics, even where the prize is a share of important social goods. The competition, however, must be fair to all participants. Since major rewards in our society derive from jobs and offices, the competition for these positions must be fair. The concept of equal opportunity is meant to ensure that the terms of competition are fair, that overall we achieve procedural justice or fairness. Fair procedures will yield outcomes that are fair, even if unequal.

For Rawls, equality of opportunity acts as a constraint on procedural justice. If the basic structure of society works to the advantage of all and in a way that is open to all, then the distributions of goods and the resulting life prospects for individuals will be the outcome of a fair process. For Rawls, a key task is to explain the appropriate sense in which the basic structure of society must work to the advantage of all and be open to all. For the moment, it is important to see that Rawls invokes a specific view of equal opportunity as part of a procedural, not allocative, notion of justice.[30] Whatever allocation results from a system governed by his principles of justice is, on his view, fair or just.

The liberal political idea of equal opportunity emerged when capitalist democracies began to replace feudal monarchies. As capitalist democracies developed, the feudal idea that birth into a social class should determine opportunity in life became increasingly unacceptable. Perhaps this change occurred because capitalist markets could not function efficiently with a legacy of feudal constraints. A first approximation to a better principle governing opportunity calls for "careers open to talents" (Rawls 1971: 65ff.). When careers are open to talents, we judge applicants for jobs and offices by their actual talents and skills, not by irrelevant traits such as class background or family connections.

[30] Allocative principles, he suggests, match goods to individuals and their specific traits, including needs. The principles of justice as fairness, however, apply to the basic structure, constraining its design and how it works as a process that distributes goods independently of needs.

As social movements, especially in the twentieth century, protested other forms of exclusion from opportunities, the concept of equal opportunity evolved. The list of irrelevant traits expanded to include race, ethnicity, caste, gender, religion, and sexual orientation. In the United States, as well as in some other countries, these ideas were embodied in antidiscrimination legislation. Such laws prohibit using irrelevant traits as either legal or quasi-legal barriers to various kinds of opportunities – not only access to jobs and offices but also political participation and access to other public goods and services. We achieve *formal* equality of opportunity if, as this legislation requires, we select people for jobs and offices and give them access to other goods and services solely according to their talents, skills, and other resources, avoiding any bias in favor of irrelevant features.[31]

In U.S. society, with its long history of racism, just as in other societies with histories of race and caste discrimination, we know that social practices have led to the mis- and underdevelopment of the expectations, talents, and skills of excluded groups. The problem continues even after discrimination becomes illegal. The same is true of gender-biased attitudes, with their deep cultural and religious roots. If we judge people competing for jobs, educational slots, or offices solely on the basis of talent, remaining race or gender neutral, we may leave in place the strong effects of unfair practices and morally arbitrary social contingencies.

Even a just society that permits significant inequalities (supposing that justice permits inequalities) faces the danger that these inequalities, working in part through family structures, will lead to unequal development of expectations, talents, and skills. Consequently, the very concern that led emerging democratic societies to open careers to talents – to distribute opportunity more fairly – actually leads us to a stronger principle.

Rawls calls for *fair*, rather than merely formal, equality of opportunity because fair equality involves stronger measures to mitigate the effects of other inequalities on the development of talents and skills. For Rawls, public education offers one way to minimize the effects of race and class

---

[31] Racist or sexist attitudes of fellow workers or customers might have an effect on production costs, and this might make some officially irrelevant traits seem to be relevant to job performance. If our only concept of a relevant trait is based on notions of productivity, this might lead to views, like those of Milton Friedman (1962), that racist or sexist "tastes" are not in principle more objectionable or harmful in a market than tastes for a type of music. Rawls's account of relevance will in fact rest on the concept of free and equal citizens. It is by reference to our roles as free and equal citizens that we can clarify what traits are relevant or irrelevant (J. Cohen 2003). What counts as a relevant trait for a university might reasonably be thought to be broader than simple scholastic performance. Undergraduate life might be better for the diversity that is created by having musicians, artists, and athletes as well as good test takers. The concern about "relevance" is exactly what makes many think that "legacy" – having a parent who attended the college – is unfair, even though universities are legitimately concerned about sustaining a community of donors.

background. Of course, he intends a more uniform or equitable quality of public education than what we see in the United States, where de facto residential segregation and unequal political power lead to basic inequalities between the best suburban schools, serving rich white children, and the worst rural and urban schools, serving poor minority and white children. The effect is that American public schools end up replicating, not reducing, class and race inequalities.[32] In addition to more equitable public schools, fair equality of opportunity requires programs aimed at early educational intervention, like Head Start, or comprehensive day care programs of the sort that exist in some other countries. The day care programs might also provide fair equality of opportunity to women. The institutions needed to make opportunity fair would also have to work later in life as well, for example at the level of higher education, and possibly even in forms of adult education that permit people to improve their opportunities later in life.

Together, such educational structures moderate the influence of past unjust social practices, such as racism or gender bias, in partially just societies. Even in an ideally just society, they moderate the morally arbitrary effects of otherwise acceptable inequalities in the basic structure. They also temper the effects of families, where specific cultural or religious attitudes, permissible under conditions of justice, might work in part against fair equality of opportunity.

Rawls couples the fair equality of opportunity principle with the difference principle and calls the combination "democratic equality" (Daniels 2003). The difference principle says that inequalities in lifetime prospects (as measured by the index of primary social goods) are allowable if the inequalities work to make those who are worst off as well off as possible compared to alternative arrangements. In addition, inequalities allowed by the difference principle must not undercut fair equality of opportunity. As a result, equality of opportunity will not be undermined in the dramatic ways we now see in societies that tolerate whatever inequalities the market generates. Together these principles ensure that jobs and offices are open to all and that allowable inequalities among free and equal citizens work to everyone's advantage. Contractors would not accept principles that did not provide that kind of protection to all.

Fair equality of opportunity, Rawls argues, (partly) corrects for the moral arbitrariness of social contingencies, such as birth into one family and its social position rather than another. In addition to this social lottery, however, there is an equally arbitrary natural lottery for talents and skills, including motivational traits such as determination and diligence. This natural lattery shapes our prospects in life even assuming fair equality of opportunity. We

---

[32] The issue goes beyond the simple financing of schools, for neighborhood characteristics – housing, job prospects, de facto segregation, political power and participation – compound any simple differences in financing local education.

may deserve some credit for the way in which we develop and exercise our talents and skills, but we do not deserve (and are not responsible for) the results of the combined social and natural lotteries that contribute so much to our capabilities (Rawls 1971: 103–4; cf. Sher 1987).

The same intuition that judges fair equality of opportunity to be more acceptable than careers open to talents makes the difference principle intuitively more acceptable than the principle of efficiency. The principle of efficiency, prominent in welfare economics, says that an efficient arrangement is one in which no one's welfare can be improved without reducing the welfare of someone else.[33] This principle is weaker than the difference principle since an efficient arrangement offers no assurance that the worst off are as well off as possible. The stronger difference principle better *mitigates*, even if it does not eliminate, the arbitrary effects of the combined natural and social lotteries for talents and skills.[34] Rather than supporting a "trickle down" of gains from inequality, the difference principle softens the effects of the social and natural lotteries by requiring a maximal flow downward. In this sense, the principle ensures that the basic structure works to the advantage of all.

Rawls (1971: 101) remarks that the difference principle treats the *distribution* of talents and skills as a common asset. He does not mean that society "owns" these talents and skills; individuals own them in the sense that they are protected by basic liberties. He means only that the benefits people gain from exercising their talents are determined by rules that make that distribution of talents work to everyone's advantage, with priority to those who are worst off.

Despite mitigation, those with the most marketable talents and skills are likely to end up in the best-off groups, and losers in the lottery are likely to end up in the worst-off groups. The difference principle falls short of being a "principle of redress" that aims at compensating people for all social and natural contingencies that produce competitive disadvantage; it does not completely level the playing field (Rawls 1971: 100–1). (I return

---

[33] The principle of efficiency is another way of stating that an arrangement is *Pareto-optimal*. Situation A is Pareto-superior to B if A is produced by making someone in B better off without making anyone in B worse off. A situation is Pareto-optimal if there is no Pareto-superior position to it.

[34] A strong interpretation of the principle of efficiency would not let us move from an efficient arrangement (even to another efficient one) if doing so would make the rich worse off, whatever the gains to the poor. The difference principle, which requires that the worst off be made as well off as possible compared to alternative arrangements, better protects those who are likely to have the least marketable skills and talents than does this version of the efficiency principle. Even a weaker version of the efficiency principle that allowed choices among efficient arrangements would not require us to choose the one efficient alternative that makes the worst off as well off as possible.

to this issue later in the chapter.)[35] The same point about mitigation also holds for the fair equality of opportunity principle. As long we raise children in families, their opportunities in life will be affected by family background unless we interfere unduly with the basic liberties of parents (Rawls 1971: 74).

Even though the fair equality of opportunity and difference principles only mitigate the morally arbitrary influences of the natural and social lotteries on prospects in life, the combined force of Rawls's principles produces a very strong "tendency to equality" (Rawls 1971: Sect. 17). Protecting basic liberties as well as fair equality of opportunity involves significant limits on allowable inequalities. With fair equality of opportunity, and with a guarantee to all of effective political participation, the kinds of class privilege we witness, even in egalitarian welfare states, would be greatly reduced. The flood of talent that is produced by giving all groups a fair opportunity to develop their talents and skills would undercut the dominance the best-off groups have in perpetuating their control over economic and social institutions. Arguably, the incentives needed to encourage the development of socially valuable talents and skills would be reduced, so that the difference principle itself would authorize lesser inequalities. Thus, although there is no absolute limit on the amount of inequality allowed by the difference principle, its combination with the other principles and the priority that is given to them suggest that we would see much less inequality in a society governed by justice as fairness than the difference principle alone might allow. (I return to this point in Chapter 4 when I consider how Rawls's theory distributes the social determinants of health.)

Coupling the fair equality of opportunity principle with the difference principle is justified by several arguments that go beyond this intuitive consideration of the arbitrariness of social and natural contingencies. One argument is that principles acceptable to Rawlsian contractors form a stable conception of justice.[36] If one set of principles carries greater strain of commitment than another, they are less stable and that counts against them. The combination of fair equality and the difference principle involves less strain of commitment for those with less marketable talents and skills than a combination of less egalitarian principles, such as a principle of efficiency coupled with careers open to talents.

A further argument in favor of the fair equality of opportunity principle and the difference principle is that they provide a better social basis for

---

[35] The result is a "meritocratic" ordering despite the constraints on rewards imposed by the difference principle. See Daniels (1996a: Ch. 14); cf. Rawls (1971: 106–7).

[36] This argument, like the intuitive argument, is not made in the contract situation. Rather, this argument addresses the further requirement that principles chosen in the contract situation must form a stable conception of justice.

self-respect than the weaker principles of formal equality of opportunity or efficiency. Principles of justice involve recognition: They establish a public basis for viewing others as worthy of respect. This public recognition supports self-respect. The stronger principles say that society is committed to fair terms of cooperation that do not judge people's worth solely by the talents and skills they bring to the market; rather, they give people fair conditions under which to develop their capabilities.

Do these general reasons for protecting opportunity carry over to protecting normal functioning?

Extending Justice as Fairness to Health

To see who is better off and who is worse off for purposes of justice, Rawls appeals to an objective index of primary social goods rather than to a scale of satisfaction or welfare. Because he simplifies his task by assuming that all people are fully functional over a normal lifespan, his index does not have to address an important source of variation among persons. In the real world of variations in health status, as Arrow (1973) and later Sen (1980) point out, the index seems problematic. Who is worse off, Arrow asks, the rich sick person or the poor well one? Rawls's index of primary social goods seems to be too truncated once we drop the assumption that all people are normal. People with equal indices will not have equally good life prospects if they have different health-care needs. Moreover, we cannot simply dismiss these needs as irrelevant to questions of justice.

How can we integrate my emphasis on health and health-care needs with Rawls's index? A natural response is simply to add another entry to the index. For example, some propose adding health care to the list of primary goods (cf. Green 1976). If the index is incomplete, just expand it. In fact, Rawls is not averse in principle to making some additions, provided that "due precaution" is taken, and he mentions "leisure" and "freedom from physical pain" as possible candidates (Rawls 1995: 181).

One reason for due precaution is that we risk generating a long list of such goods, one to meet each need that some think is important. The added complexity of the longer list and the index formed from it makes less plausible Rawls's claim that the original primary social goods – basic liberties, opportunity, powers and prerogatives of office, income and wealth, and the social bases of self-respect – include only all-purpose means that reasonable people in democratic cultures agree comprise the needs of free and equal citizens. By adding items, especially specific ones, we are likely to lose our shared political conception of the needs of citizens.

Another reason for caution is that adding items makes it harder to establish an index. It becomes more difficult to avoid the complex problems of interpersonal comparison that face broader measures of satisfaction or welfare. Arrow (1973: 254) argued that adding health care to the index, and allowing its trade-off against income and wealth, would force Rawls into comparisons of well-being (or utility) he had hoped his index would avoid. Whether or not Arrow is right in this instance, he points to a more general problem that a more complex index must face.[37]

Broadening Fair Opportunity

Fortunately, a more plausible and simpler way to connect my account of health needs to Rawls's index of primary social goods is to broaden his notion of opportunity by including health-care institutions among the basic institutions involved in providing for fair equality of opportunity. Because meeting health-care needs has an important effect on the distribution of opportunity, the health-care institutions should be regulated by a fair equality of opportunity principle. Once we note the connection of normal functioning to the opportunity range, this strategy seems the natural way to extend Rawls's view.

With this proposal, the primary social goods themselves remain general and abstract properties of social arrangements – basic liberties, opportunities, and certain all-purpose, exchangeable means (income and wealth). Health care is not a primary social good, but neither are food, clothing, shelter, or other basic needs. We assume that the latter will be adequately supported by fair shares of income and wealth. The special importance and unequal distribution of health-care needs, like educational needs, are acknowledged by connecting the needs to institutions that provide for fair equality of opportunity. But opportunity, not health care or education, remains the primary social good.

Including health-care institutions among those that should protect fair equality of opportunity is compatible with the central intuitions behind wanting to guarantee such opportunity. Rawls is primarily concerned with the opportunity to pursue careers – jobs and offices – that come with various benefits. So, equality of opportunity is *strategically* important: A person's

---

[37] The problem of establishing the index is, I believe, difficult in any case and is present prior to the attempt to introduce health care as a distinct primary good. (I am indebted to Joshua Cohen for discussion of this point.) Rawls simplifies the problem of weighting items on the index by assuming that income and wealth correlate reasonably well with the overall value of the index. This simplification makes it easier to consider the effects of the difference principle. As a result, Rawls does not discuss in detail how to weight acknowledged primary goods, such as powers and prerogatives of position (including worker control over the workplace), against income. Nor does he tell us what to do when the simplifying assumption does not hold. This failure of the assumption might arise when, for example, income is not a proxy for the social bases of self-respect, say because such respect is undermined by hierarchical workplace arrangements that are more productive. Chapter 3 considers this issue in more detail, because cases may arise when income inequalities that would otherwise maximally help the worst off turn out to undermine their opportunity through negative effects on health status and thus opportunity.

well-being will be measured, for the most part, by the primary goods that accompany such jobs and offices. It is not enough simply to eliminate formal or legal barriers to persons seeking such jobs – for example, race, class, ethnic, or sex barriers. Rather, positive steps should be taken to enhance the opportunity of those disadvantaged by such social factors as family background. Any birth advantages from the natural and social lotteries are morally arbitrary, because they are not deserved, and to let them determine individual opportunity, and thus reward and success in life, is to make the outcomes arbitrary. So, positive steps – for example, better education – must be taken to provide fair equality of opportunity. (Fair equality of opportunity does not mean that individual differences no longer confer advantages; rather, the advantages are limited by the difference principle and work to the advantage of the worst off. See Daniels [1978].)

Just as we must use resources to counter the opportunity advantages that some get in the social lottery, we must also use resources to counter the disadvantages induced by pathology. We must meet health needs, including health-care needs. Social conditions – including class, gender, race, and ethnic inequalities in obtaining various goods – contribute significantly to the distribution of disease and disability. Much disease and disability is not simply a product of the natural lottery but is influenced by the social lottery as well. Because the social determinants of health have a clear effect on population health and its distribution, health is not so "natural" a good after all.[38]

This expansion of the scope of fair equality of opportunity does not mean that we are committed to the futile goal of eliminating or leveling all natural differences among persons. Meeting health needs has the goal of promoting normal functioning: It concentrates on a specific class of obvious disadvantages and tries to eliminate them. The fair equality of opportunity principle, as Rawls uses it, does not correct for all differences in talents and skills: It accepts their natural distribution as a baseline and leaves it to the difference principle to mitigate the effects on opportunity of being born with less marketable talents and skills. Similarly, the fair equality of opportunity principle applied to health needs does not rectify or level all inequalities in function among people. It aims only to keep people functioning normally and thus to assure them the range of opportunities they would have in the absence of disease or disability. (Other opportunity-based views, we shall soon see, challenge this Rawlsian view.)

Is the Broader Notion of Opportunity Problematic?

The notion Rawls uses is a narrow one focused on producing fairness in the competition for jobs and careers. We are using opportunity range in a

---

[38] Earlier I rejected the implications some might ascribe to Rawls's (1971: 62) distinction between health as a natural good and the primary social goods.

broader – and admittedly vaguer – sense when we think about the impact of health on individual shares of the normal opportunity range, that is, the array of life plans persons can reasonably choose in a given society. We have a good idea of what things interfere with the fair equality of opportunity to compete for jobs; we can estimate the costs of eliminating them and make social policy accordingly. The complaint is that determining what constitutes interference with a fair share of the normal opportunity range is much more complicated.

This complaint has some merit. Moreover, there is a clearer justification for the narrower concept. Access to jobs and careers is of great strategic importance because of the rewards attached to these positions. It is far less obvious that the broader principle can be justified solely by reference to the strategic importance of keeping shares of the normal opportunity range fair in all the dimensions the principle seems to require. For example, infertility is a departure from normal functioning that reduces an individual's fair share of the normal opportunity range and gives rise to claims for assistance on the fair equality of opportunity view (to be decided fairly under resource constraints; see Chapter 4). Infertility, however, does not interfere with access to jobs or offices and the rewards associated with them, even if it interferes with other basic functions of free and equal citizens, such as reproducing themselves biologically, an aspect of plans of life that reasonable people commonly pursue. Broadening Rawls's equal opportunity principle means that we must broaden the grounds on which we justify the importance of opportunity. The claim here is that we can modify the theory with few negative consequences.

The infertility example also suggests that the broader conception of opportunity is expansive in a way that the narrower one is not. Consider one way this expansiveness might seem to infect the principle. Suppose that supplying a computer to everyone who cannot afford one would do more to remove individual impairments of the normal opportunity range than supplying certain health-care services to those who need them. Does the fair equality of opportunity approach commit us to supply computers instead of or in addition to medical treatments?[39] The example is an instance of a far more general problem common to both conceptions of opportunity. Socioeconomic (and other) inequalities affect opportunity, broadly or narrowly construed, not just the health-care and educational needs that are important to protecting opportunity. Obviously, certain inequalities in wealth and income also conflict with fair equality of opportunity (on either construal). My approach rests on the specific calculation that institutions meeting health needs quite generally have a central impact on individual

---

[39] Using medical technology to enhance normal capacities or functions – say strength or vision – makes the problem easier: The burden of proof is on proposals that give priority to altering the normal opportunity range rather than to protecting individuals whose normal range is compromised.

shares of the normal opportunity range and should therefore be governed directly by the opportunity principle.[40]

A further worry about the broader notion of opportunity is that protecting fair shares of it would require eliminating individual differences among persons in a way that the narrower view does not demand. Actually, neither notion of opportunity requires such leveling. The main point was made earlier: The fair equality of opportunity account does not require us to level all differences among persons in their shares of the normal opportunity range. Rather, opportunity is *equal* for purposes of the account when certain impediments to opportunity are eliminated for all persons – most importantly, discrimination in job placement or impairments of normal functioning, where possible. But fair shares of the normal opportunity range will still not be equal shares: Individual variations in talents and skills determine those shares, assuming that these have already been corrected for the effects of social and natural advantages, where possible. This correction is what is implied by appealing to fair and not just formal equality of opportunity. Similarly, institutions meeting health needs have the limited function of maintaining normal functioning. They eliminate individual differences due only to (significant) pathology. Thus, the broad construal is no more committed to leveling or to a principle of redress against the inequalities of the natural lottery than is the narrow Rawlsian principle.

Using the broad account of opportunity in a theory of just health care offers important advantages in any case. Although meeting health needs would still be of special importance if we restricted opportunity to the narrow Rawlsian sense, the broader view captures the full importance we attribute to health as normal functioning. More compelling, the narrow view would yield what many would see as an age-biased and morally objectionable account of health care: Job and career opportunities are more important in early and middle stages of life than in later ones, but our health-care needs increase later in life. The broad view, as I show in Chapter 6, provides a way of avoiding age bias and plausible suggestions about just health care for the elderly.

Preserving Key Features of Justice as Fairness

Several important features of justice as fairness are preserved with this extension to health. First, the approach taken here allows us to draw some interesting parallels between education and health care. Both are strategically important contributors to fair equality of opportunity (in both the narrow and broad senses of opportunity). Both address needs that are not equally distributed. Various social factors, such as race, class, and family background,

---

[40] It should also be clear from the earlier discussion that coupling the difference principle with the fair equality of opportunity principle, as Rawls does in justice as fairness, means that many inequalities that we commonly observe interfering with opportunity will be significantly constrained in a just society, at least according to the extended theory we are discussing.

may produce special learning needs; so too may natural factors, such as learning disabilities.

To the extent that education aims at providing fair equality of opportunity, it must address these special needs. Thus, educational needs, like health-care needs, differ from other basic needs, such as food and clothing, which are more equally distributed. The combination of their unequal distribution and their great importance for opportunity distinguishes these needs from those basic needs we can expect people to purchase from their fair income shares, like food and shelter.

This comparison suggests that Rawls's argument about the importance of public education for fair equality of opportunity is readily broadened to include health care. Any justification for the one extends to the other. Making that extension helps preserve a central line of argument in justice as fairness.

A second point of fit between my analysis and Rawls's theory concerns the level of abstraction at which health needs are identified. In Rawls's contractarian theory, people must choose principles of justice for their society, but they make their choice in a rigidly defined hypothetical situation. One key feature of that situation is that contractors do not know their abilities, talents, place in society, or historical period. That is, they are behind a thick veil of ignorance that ensures that their choice is impartial in certain ways and reflects only their natures as free and equal moral agents. In selecting principles to govern health-care resource-allocation decisions, however, we need a thinner veil of ignorance, for we must know about some features of the society – for example, its resource limitations.

Using the normal opportunity range and not just the effective range as the baseline for measuring the importance of health-care needs has the effect of imposing a suitably thinned veil. Remember that the effective range of opportunity is the share of the normal range determined by an individual's actual choices about what life plans to pursue and what talents and skills to develop. In contrast, individuals' fair shares of the normal range are defined relative to the talents and skills they would have with normal functioning. Individuals' fair shares include the full range of life plans they might reasonably select, not just the ones they actually select. The normal range reflects basic facts about the society – since the normal range is socially relative – but it keeps facts about an individual's particular ends from unduly influencing social decisions. Ultimately, defense of a veil as a device depends on the theory of the person underlying the account, in particular on Rawls's view that moral agents are essentially free and equal. The intuition here is that persons are not defined by a particular set of interests but are free to revise their life plans (Buchanan 1975). Therefore, they have a fundamental interest in maintaining conditions under which they can revise their life plans as time goes on. This fundamental interest means that health care should aim at normal functioning and not select for those functions most important to individuals' past choices about plans of life. Protecting fair shares of the normal opportunity range is the reference point compatible with Rawls's view of persons as free and equal citizens.

Finally, placing health-care institutions under the opportunity principle can be viewed as a way of keeping the system as close as possible to the original idealization underlying Rawls's theory, namely, that we are concerned with normal, fully functioning persons with a complete lifespan (Rawls 1995: 184). Different features of health and broader social policy defend this idealization in different ways. Preventive health measures can be viewed as a first defense of the idealization: They act to minimize departures from the normality assumption. Included here are institutions that provide for public health, environmental cleanliness, preventive personal medical services, occupational health and safety, food and drug protection, nutrition education, and educational and other incentives to promote individual responsibility for healthy lifestyles. Proper distribution of other social determinants of health (see Chapter 3) also limits many pathologies. We might think of these policies and institutions as keeping us close to the less controversial, simplified core of Rawls's theory, for we have not yet had to correct for departures from normality.

Unfortunately, not all departures from normal functioning can be prevented, so we need institutions that correct for them. These institutions deliver personal medical, mental health, and rehabilitative services that restore normal functioning. Not all treatments are cures, so we need institutions and services to maintain people in a way that keeps them as close as possible to the idealization that all function normally. These institutions offer extended medical, mental health, and social support services for the (moderately) chronically ill and disabled and the frail elderly. Policies that include people with disabilities in working and social life also protect the idealization. Finally, we owe people health care and related social services even when they cannot be brought closer to the idealization. Terminal care and care for the seriously mentally and physically disabled are important examples. These services raise serious issues, for example about compassion and beneficence, that go beyond questions of justice.

Each element of health policy corrects in a particular way for a type of departure from the Rawlsian idealization that all people are functionally normal. It is better to prevent than to cure and better to cure than to compensate for lost functioning. But all these institutions and services are needed if fair equality of opportunity is to be guaranteed.

Rawls on Meeting Medical Needs

Although Rawls's early work abstracts from the problems of illness, disability, and premature death, his later work largely adopts the perspective proposed in this chapter (Rawls 1995: 184, n.14; 2001: 175, n.58). Providing medical care, say through some form of social insurance, should not be seen as a way "merely to supplement the income of the least advantaged when they cannot cover the costs of the medical care they may prefer. To the contrary: as already emphasized, provision for medical care, as with primary goods generally, is to meet the needs and requirements of citizens as free and equal. Such care *falls under the general means necessary to underwrite fair equality of opportunity and our capacity to take advantage of our basic rights and liberties*, and thus to be normal and fully cooperating members of society over a complete life" (Rawls 2001: 174, emphasis added).

One concern often raised about meeting health needs and treating them as especially important – say because of their connection to opportunity – is that we create a bottomless pit. We might have to pour all of our resources into meeting those needs, which are expensive and expansive, and have little left for anything else. Charles Fried (1978: Ch. 5), for example, argues that recognizing individual right claims to the satisfaction of health-care needs would force society to forego realizing other social goals. He cautions that we would end up worshipping the opportunity to pursue our goals but having to forego the pursuit. Here we have a different social hijacking argument, hijacking by needs rather than preferences. (See also Braybrook 1968.)

This objection is misdirected. Health care is not the only important social good. Despite the importance of opportunity, we must limit our spending on health care, and Chapter 4 will develop an account of fair process for setting limits to health services. Here I want to emphasize one point that follows from the claim that opportunity is only one of many important goods.

In his most recent work, Rawls notes that we might think about the limits to health care in the following way. Our design for a health system should not drain resources in such a way that the overall prospects of those who are worst off are worsened further. The thinking here is similar, he says, to that involved in trying to fix a decent social minimum (Rawls 2001: 173, citing Rawls 1971: S.44: 251f). The difference is that "the expectation of an assured provision of health care at a certain level (calculated by estimated cost) is included as part of that minimum" (Rawls 2001: 173). The calculation must take into account other requirements of a just system – sustaining an active and productive workforce, raising children and educating them, and providing for needs over the lifespan, including retirement. A just system must provide for more than health care. Justice stops us from falling into a bottomless pit of health needs.

We shall see in the next section that our extension of Rawls's theory to health allows him to respond to an important criticism, but I save my comments on the increased power of his theory for Chapter 3.

OTHER THEORIES OF JUSTICE, OPPORTUNITY, AND HEALTH

Rawls's theory of justice as fairness is the most fully developed general theory of justice that provides arguments for our obligation to protect fair equality of opportunity. The close fit between my account of health and health needs and Rawls's account of the needs of free and equal citizens enables me to borrow support from his view and simultaneously to extend its scope and power. Subsequent work by others, though critical of important aspects of Rawls's theory, also supports the idea that we have a social obligation to protect the range of opportunities open to us, though the form of such protection varies in significant ways. In this section, I argue that, despite these authors' differences from Rawls, the moral importance they ascribe to protecting opportunity strengthens – though with some qualifications – my account of the moral importance of health and of meeting health needs, and thus my answer to the first Focal Question.

I focus on two alternatives to Rawls: the capabilities approach developed by Sen (1980, 1990a, 1992, 1999), and later Nussbaum (2000), and the appeal to "equal opportunity for welfare or advantage" advocated by Arneson (1988) and G. A. Cohen (1989). Sen and Nussbaum argue that Rawls focuses on the wrong "space" when he takes the "target" of justice to be the distribution of primary social goods. The proper target of justice is the space of capabilities – the things we can do or be. I shall argue that the contrast is more apparent than real, at least when Rawls's theory is extended to health in the way I propose (Daniels 1990a). Meeting health needs is crucial to sustaining capabilities for the same reason that it is crucial to protecting a fair share of the opportunity range: Normal functioning is critical to both.

Arneson and Cohen argue that Rawls supports the wrong *principles* of justice – specifically, that his combination of fair equality of opportunity and the Difference Principle fails to protect people from unjust disadvantage. Justice requires that we compensate or assist people whenever they suffer a deficit in welfare or advantage through no fault or choice of their own. In the original formulation of their view, Arneson and Cohen argue that we must assure people of equal opportunity for welfare or advantage; in later versions, they give priority to improving the opportunity of those who have least opportunity for welfare or advantage through no fault of their own. Either version, despite important differences from Rawls, tells us that we have a social obligation to protect fair shares of the opportunity range. Some support for my account of the moral importance of health can be derived from this view as well. I take up each in turn.

Capabilities and the Proper Target of Justice

After the resurgence of work on justice prompted by Rawls's (1971) work, a debate emerged, beginning with Sen's Tanner Lecture (1980) about the proper goal or target of justice and especially of equality. If justice requires us to make people more equal in some regard, what should we equalize? Is it their happiness or welfare? The resources available to them? Rawls's primary social goods? Or something else?

Sen, like Rawls, rejects a welfarist view of the target of either equality or justice, but he also thinks that concerns about equality must focus on something other than the distribution of Rawls's primary social goods. Two people, he points out, will not be equally well off with the same index of primary social goods if, for example, one person has a significant disease or disability or distinctive nutritional needs and the other does not.[41] According to Sen, what matters from the point of view of equality or justice is different from either the primary social goods, which Sen identifies as resources distributed to people, or the welfarist happiness or desire satisfaction that might accompany the distribution of the resources.[42] Specifically, Sen (and later Nussbaum 2000) argue that the important thing is to give people an equal share of capabilities. These capabilities are the things that a person can effectively do or be. The distribution of these capabilities to function in various ways is what matters to justice. In later formulations, both Sen and Nussbaum focus on assuring people at least an adequate or sufficient set of capabilities rather than equality in capabilities, though they are not specific about what makes the set sufficient. To Sen's general characterization of the target of justice Nussbaum adds a specific list of basic human functionings or capabilities.

Sen assimilates the notion of capabilities to the neglected philosophical idea of positive freedom, which we may think of as the combined effects of having both liberty to do or be something and the means of exercising that liberty. As a result, people with certain disabilities or illnesses or nutritional needs will have less positive freedom, less of what matters to justice, than people with no disability or illness or nutritional needs, even if they enjoy the same index value of primary social goods. The index, Sen concludes, misses the point of seeking equality or justice.

Two issues arise. First, is our notion of the fair shares of the normal opportunity range really in a different space from the capabilities that concern Sen? If the conception of opportunity we have used is in the wrong space, it might not be able to explain the special importance of meeting health needs. Second, assume that we can address the first issue and that we are

---

[41] Sen inferred from Rawls's use of the index of primary social goods, plus his idealization that all people are fully functional over a normal lifespan, that Rawls's index could not measure what mattered and that an alternative view had to be developed. At essentially the same time, I was concerned with the same problem but focused on extending Rawls's theory to deal adequately with variations in health states. Sen introduced capabilities as the missing target, and I focused on protecting the range of opportunities by protecting normal functioning.

[42] G. A. Cohen (1993) argues that Sen's argument should lead him to the broader category of "midfare" that lies between resources, viewed as inputs, and any welfarist output or consequence of having the resources. Midfare is a heterogeneous set of consequences of having or using resources that may include capabilities but may involve other things as well. I focus on capabilities because I am less interested in the broader debate than in the connection of capabilities to normal functioning.

working in the appropriate space. Then, once Sen (or Nussbaum) weakens the goal to sufficient or adequate capabilities, what difference is there between the capabilities approach and the fair shares approach?

Fair Shares of the Normal Opportunity Range: A Capability Space
Normal functioning, we saw earlier, makes a significant but limited contribution to the range of plans of life people can reasonably adopt, given their talents and skills. People can reasonably adopt a plan of life if they have the capabilities to do and be what that plan calls for. I believe that this space, defined by what Rawls and I have called the opportunity range, is the capability space that Sen defines with a different terminology. To see the connection, think of a capability as an accessible or exercisable opportunity or option. Sen had conceptualized a "capability set" as an "n-tuple of doings or beings." That conceptualization seems to differ only in terminology from the more Rawlsian language we use when we talk about a fair share of the normal opportunity range and envision that idea as the set of life plans people can reasonably adopt, given their talents and skills.

I noted earlier that the conception of opportunity used in my extension of Rawls is broader than his, since he focused primarily on access to jobs and offices. Even if my modification avoids the charge that opportunity is but a resource, it might be claimed that Rawls's original conception of opportunity does not. Rawls thought differently. In reply to Sen's suggestion that we should focus on capabilities instead of primary social goods, Rawls says, " . . . it should be stressed that the account of primary goods does take into account, and does not abstract from, basic capabilities: namely, the capabilities of citizens as free and equal persons in virtue of their two moral powers" (Rawls 2001: 169). In effect, meeting the needs of free and equal citizens by distributing primary social goods in accordance with the principles of justice provides people with the capabilities required of free and equal citizens.[43]

Fair Shares of the Normal Opportunity Range and Adequate Capability Sets
Sen's capability view initially concerned the proper goal of equality. He offered it as an explication of the idea of "positive freedom"; for him, people have achieved equality when they have equality in positive freedom, that is, when their capability sets are equal. Conceptually, his notion is distinct from that of fair equality of opportunity, as found either in Rawls or in my extension of his view to health. Both views assure people fair equality of opportunity when we maintain their functioning as close to normal as possible while at the same time correcting for social inequalities in the development of talents and skills, and we then allow people to compete and

---

[43] Cf. Anderson (1999), who focuses Sen's discussion of capabilities on those of free and equal citizens, thus bringing the two accounts very close together (see Daniels in Freeman 2003).

cooperate based on the resulting distribution of talents and skills. There is no assumption that we seek equality in capabilities.[44]

If we could simply translate this claim about equality in positive freedom into an account of the goals of medicine – as I shall argue we cannot – then those goals would be dramatically expanded from the goal of protecting normal functioning. The goal of medicine would then be to reconstruct people in order to make their capabilities more equal. With this expansion, there would simply be no point in drawing a line between treatments and enhancements (see Chapter 5). We would be just as much obliged to enhance the capabilities of those who function normally, but with less than equal capabilities, as to keep people functioning as close to normally as possible. (One wrinkle in this approach is that we would not be obliged to correct for the effects of disease or capability where they work to increase equality in capabilities – for example, by reducing the capabilities of those with superior capabilities.)

To see why we cannot directly use the equal capabilities approach to expand the goals of medicine, we must examine Sen's account more carefully. One crucial point is that a theory of justice requires integrating concerns for equality with concerns for liberty and efficiency. Sen (1992) comments that we must reconcile our concerns about efficiency and equality in order to find out what justice requires. In other words, justice might not require us to pursue equality of capabilities directly after all. Instead, considerations of liberty or efficiency might require us to permit some inequalities and then mitigate their morally arbitrary effects. Sen does not discuss how this reconciliation would take place in a comprehensive theory of justice. Rawls, in contrast, does attempt a reconciliation: We should take *some* natural distribution of talents and skills as a baseline (usually the normal distribution). Although those with the least marketable capabilities will have lower prospects in life than those with more marketable capabilities, Rawls mitigates the effects of this basic inequality by requiring that inequalities in primary social goods like wealth and income be constrained so that they work to the advantage of those with the worst prospects in life. In this way, those with more marketable talents and skills must harness their advantages to maximize the prospects of those who have the least marketable talents and skills. In effect, Rawls divides responsibility for achieving our egalitarian goals between two different principles of justice. The principle

---

[44] One qualification is needed on both conceptions: We should understand that a capability set is the set of thing an individual can effectively do or be, allowing for the fact that the development of some capabilities may exclude the development of others, presumably as a result of individual (or family) choice. Sen does not want an individual's decision to develop some capabilities at the expense of others to give rise to a further claim on others for resources just because the choice has sacrificed some capabilities. I made a similar point earlier when I distinguished the effective opportunity range from an individual's fair share of the normal opportunity range.

governing equality of opportunity leaves the normal distribution of capabilities in place, but the principle governing overall inequality in life prospects
mitigates the effects of doing so.

If health care should come under a principle governing fair equality of
opportunity, then, for the general case, it too may leave the normal distribution of capabilities in place, focusing only on keeping people functioning
as normally as possible. We would have to rely on other principles of justice governing our inequalities in life prospects to mitigate the effects of this
pragmatic decision. Rawls's appeal to the "moral arbitrariness" of the natural
lottery for capabilities does not mean that the only reasonable way to address
this problem within a comprehensive theory is to devote extensive resources
to equalizing capabilities. We may be able to do better, even for those with
worse capabilities, by leaving the distribution of capabilities mostly in place
and mitigating its effects in other ways – at least that is his rationale. This dramatic restriction on the scope of what we can do in the name of equal opportunity – as compared to Sen's egalitarian account – may not be what Sen has
in mind, but then we need some clear idea of what restrictions are compatible with the overall demands of justice. (Rawls's rationale for the general
case does not preclude a more restrictive case-by-case assessment of claims
that eliminating some obviously disadvantaging [but normal] traits is justifiable on grounds that modestly extend the concept of equal opportunity.)

Even leaving aside the competing claims of liberty, efficiency, and equality,
the equal capabilities model does not, strictly speaking, involve a pursuit
of equal capability sets. This modification of what the view implies about
equality arises for a distinct but basic reason. We need a way to judge when
one set of capabilities is clearly worse than another, since sets may vary in
indeterminately many dimensions.

Sen offers an approach to ranking differences in capabilities. The importance of a particular capability will depend on the system of values – the
plan of life or conception of the good – adopted by an individual. John may
rank capability set A as better than capability set B, but Jane may make the
opposite judgment from her conception of the good. We may find some
cases in which all can agree that set C is worse than sets A and B, but we may
find a broad range of capability sets without consensus rankings. In fact, we
are most likely to find that the clear-cut cases in which a set (say C) is ranked
lower than others by all will be cases that include a significant departure from
normal functioning – a disease or disability that has a significant impact on
capabilities and thus on opportunities. In those cases, Sen's account agrees
with the one we have developed. But for a broad range of differences in
capability sets, there may be "incommensurability" in the sense that these
sets are ranked differently by people with different conceptions of what is
good in life. Because of this widespread incommensurability, our egalitarian
concerns do not commit us to pursuing equality of capabilities, but only to

assuring that individuals' capability sets are not distinctly worse than those of others.

This important qualification of the equal capability view brings it even closer to our focus on normal functioning. The two views will agree when pathology significantly undermines functioning. In theory, there may be cases where they agree that certain individuals have worse capabilities than others, even though no pathology underlies those deficits; in such cases, the equal positive liberty view will call for effective medical interventions, if they exist. When the fair equality of opportunity approach will allow other considerations, including opportunity calculations, to add such services remains to be seen on a case-by-case basis (as in the example of nontherapeutic abortion discussed earlier; see also Chapter 5).

We do not deny people equality of opportunity by failing to assist them in improving or developing every capability they want that some other people happen to have. If we thought that equality of opportunity demanded that we assist people in these ways, we would make the principle hostage to expensive and demanding preferences for certain capabilities. Just as we are not obliged to use our resources to make others happy when they are unhappy because of extravagant tastes, so too we are not obliged to improve any and every capability that they judge to be disadvantageous, given their plans of life (see n. 28).

This point has specific implications for those capabilities that affect access to jobs and offices, as Joshua Cohen (1995) has argued. Suppose that Jill succeeds in getting a job as office manager when Jack does not because Jill is better at motivating others to work and at resolving disputes. Does Jack now have a complaint against us: His access to a job he wants is diminished because he lacks the relevant interpersonal skills? Or can we reasonably reply to Jack that he is welcome to practice these skills and improve them – courses are offered at the local community college – but that the social and educational opportunities he has already enjoyed allow him to compete fairly for a wide variety of other jobs. We owe him nothing more in the name of equal opportunity, though he is free to invest further in himself.

At first sight, the egalitarian version of Sen's capabilities view seems to push us toward any intervention, including any use of health-care technology, that eliminates disadvantages in opportunity produced by inequalities in our capability sets. But, appropriately qualified, the view demands much less. In practice – if not conceptually – it comes quite close to the normal functioning view. Where there are significant deficits, of the sort caused by serious pathology, we get results similar to those given by the normal functioning view.

In Sen's more recent discussions and in Nussbaum's (2000) development of a similar view, the capabilities approach does not demand equality in capability sets but only adequacy or sufficiency.[45] My claim that this more modest capabilities view converges with my extension of Rawls to health is even easier to see. Indeed, since Sen offers no real account of the sufficiency or adequacy of capability sets, the goal of preserving normal functioning fairly under reasonable resource limits might provide what is missing.

In sum, the wrong-space objection is overstated, at least once my extension of Rawls's theory to health and health care is made. This extension eliminates the insensitivity to individual variation that motivated Sen's original critique of the index of primary goods. Despite the difference in terminology – capabilities versus opportunity – the two views largely converge. Sen and Nussbaum both acknowledge that the demand for equal or at least adequate capability sets requires integration with concerns about liberty and efficiency in a theory of justice, qualifying the degree to which claims of justice can be made about particular deficits in capabilities. Similarly, Sen's and Nussbaum's commitment to a public way of determining when one set of capabilities is worse than another means that many variations in capabilities are incommensurable and do not give rise to egalitarian claims. As a result, the key deficits in capabilities that are likely to produce agreement about claims on others will be those caused by significant disease or disability.

But Rawls's view also moves closer to that of Sen and Nussbaum. With the extension, Rawls is much more clearly concerned with meeting the needs of free and equal citizens so that they can carry out the functions and have the capabilities they require. Indeed, Rawls comes closer to Sen's concern about positive liberty in his remark that the "end of social justice" is to "maximize the worth to the least advantaged of the complete scheme of equal liberty shared by all" (Rawls 1971: 205; 1995: 326).[46] Indeed, Sen's own discussion of capabilities and positive freedom, as Anderson (1999) suggests, is most plausibly focused on those capabilities citizens must have

---

45 Nussbaum converts Sen's abstract conception of capabilities into a specific set of basic functionings. On her view, justice requires that people be assured the development of an adequate or sufficient set of these basic functions. Nussbaum notes that the conditions for assuring such development may well converge with some of Rawls's principles of justice. I believe that the convergence is extensive and that most of the functionings she calls basic can be mapped onto protections assured by the principles of justice. In any event, she has not explained how to resolve competing claims on resources needed to assure various claimants of adequacy of development of their basic functionings and when, if ever, trade-offs are allowed between improving the capabilities of those who have passed the threshold and of those who have not yet reached it. Here, again, a comprehensive theory of justice embodies a framework for integrating these various concerns of justice, and Rawls's theory, whatever its flaws, offers a comprehensiveness, with specific commitments, that is lacking in other approaches, including the Sen and Nussbaum elaboration of the importance of capabilities.

46 Rawls does not aim for positive freedom as directly as Sen (cf. Daniels 1975), but his concern for it is manifest in this passage.

to achieve democratic equality, a focus that emerges more clearly in Sen's more recent work.

Egalitarian (or Prioritarian) Opportunity for Welfare or Advantage

According to a second central strand of recent political philosophy, justice requires us to compensate or assist people whenever they suffer a deficit in welfare or advantage through no fault or responsibility of their own. Advocates of this view, originally called "equal opportunity for welfare" or "luck egalitarianism," trace its origins to Rawls's own defense of fair equality of opportunity and the Difference Principle (Rawls 1971: Sect 12; cf. Daniels 2003). Rawls claimed that his robust principles of justice as fairness capture the idea that the terms of fair cooperation must be "open to all" and "work to everyone's advantage." As we saw earlier, his intuitive defense of that interpretation turns on saying that the contingencies that result from the social or natural lottery are morally arbitrary and should not become the basis for allowable inequalities.

Nevertheless, Rawls's own principles do not correct fully for all such morally arbitrary contingencies. This shortfall leads to the charge I attribute to the opportunity for welfare view, namely, that Rawls supports the wrong principles of justice. For example, he allows the natural distribution of talents and skills to serve as a baseline against which we judge fair competition for jobs and offices. In such a meritocratic approach, people with few marketable talents and skills will end up among the worst-off groups, even if these groups are made as well off as possible (see Daniels 1978). In contrast, Rawls's critics advocate a stronger principle redressing all unchosen disadvantages in opportunity because it captures the concern about the moral arbitrariness of the natural and social lotteries and Rawls's own assertion that we should not let fundamental features of the basic structure of justice be determined by such arbitrary advantages.

In its early "egalitarian" manifestation, the opportunity for welfare or advantage view required equality of opportunity.[47] In its later "prioritarian" form, it focuses on giving priority to correcting deficits in opportunity for welfare or advantage among those who have the worst opportunities.[48] In either form, however, we owe such assistance or compensation only if the deficit in opportunity is the result of bad "brute" as opposed to "option"

---

[47] It emerged as a response to Ronald Dworkin's (1981a,b) and Rawls's (1982b) criticism that a welfarist approach opens the door to social hijacking by persons with expensive tastes. If we do not owe assistance to people who are worse off through their own choices or faults, then we owe nothing to those who cultivated expensive tastes. See footnote 28.

[48] Parfit (1995) argues that a commitment to egalitarianism requires us to level down if that is our only way to achieve equality. For example, we should blind all rather than leave some blind and others not. Since this is implausible, we should recast our egalitarian concern as the more modest concern to give priority to those who are worst off. (Arneson 1999a–c).

luck.[49] If we have made certain choices – undertaken certain options – that have risks we were or should have been aware of, then others do not owe us assistance. But if the deficit is something we are not responsible or at fault for, then it is the kind of bad brute or cosmic luck that is unfair to us.

Despite its important differences with Rawls, the opportunity for welfare or advantage view, in either its egalitarian or prioritarian form, discusses explicitly the centrality to justice of protecting people's opportunity. Moreover, it focuses on exercisable options or opportunities for welfare or advantage, not merely formal or theoretical ones. This feature is quite similar to the construction of fair shares of the normal opportunity range, at least if we assume that a reasonable plan of life is one to which people have access.[50] This point of convergence with the extension of Rawls to health is what I was seeking as a way to broaden support for the claim that we have obligations of justice to protect opportunity.

Despite its terminological overlap, however, the opportunity for welfare or advantage view diverges more significantly on some matters than does the capabilities view. I address two of these. The opportunity for welfare view is concerned about any deficit in welfare or advantage, even those that result from the distribution of talents and skills, so it is more *expansive* in its demands than a view that emphasizes normal functioning. Further, the opportunity for welfare view is more restrictive than a view focused on protecting normal functioning because it says that we have no obligation to assist people whose welfare or advantage deficits result from choices they have made, whereas my extension of Rawls says nothing about the corresponding issue of responsibility for health. Arguably, these points of divergence are more important than the point of convergence I want to emphasize.

Is the Opportunity for Welfare View Too Expansive?
A view focused on normal functioning will give priority to treating pathology over enhancing otherwise normal traits (see Chapter 5).[51] The opportunity for welfare or advantage view may seem to require use to eliminate disadvantage or loss of welfare regardless of whether pathology is involved. For example, a normal but very short child is no more responsible for his deficit in opportunity in a heightist world than is a child with growth hormone deficiency, a recognized pathology. If we should prevent or treat the latter, then arguably we should also do the same for the former if we are concerned about protecting opportunity. Someone who is too shy to be a good car salesman, but who is not suffering any psychological disorder, might

---

[49] Arneson (1999a, c) expresses worries about the distinction but still refers to his view as "responsibility regarding."

[50] G. A. Cohen (1993) refers to his view as one concerned about "access to advantage."

[51] Of course, not all pathology warrants assistance, and some uses of medical technology that do not involve prevention or treatment of pathology may also be justified.

demand assistance on the grounds that he is at a disadvantage through no fault of his own. Many other talent and skill variations would readily give rise to similar demands, and the approach seems to compel us to provide any medical technologies that would eliminate such deficits. Similarly, people with noses or faces not judged sufficiently beautiful or handsome are also excluded from an attractive range of career options – acting, modeling, news broadcasting. The egalitarian or prioritarian opportunity for welfare or advantage principle seems to expand the range of claims for assistance even into areas where most people feel they have little obligation to assist.

Arguably, the opportunity for welfare or advantage view does not expand in quite this way. To see why, consider the original intuitions behind it. Equal opportunity for welfare or advantage obtains when each person faces "an array of options that is equivalent to every other person's in terms of the prospects for preference satisfaction it offers" (Arneson 1988: 87; cf Arneson 1999c, 2002). We should picture this in the following way. Imagine that we view a person's life as a decision tree in which all possible life histories are represented. Equal opportunity for welfare obtains if each person's best path on the life tree ex ante has the same expected payoff in preference satisfaction (or advantage). Branches in the tree represent all possible choices, including choices about which preferences to act on or to develop.

Leaving aside the obvious information burden that such a conception involves,[52] to be able to claim that a specific deficit in a specific trait is the reason a person lacks equal opportunity for welfare, she must show that no such "best" path equivalent to other people's is open to her. She cannot simply say, "This is the path I prefer to follow, but doing so makes me worse off," for then her deficit in welfare is the result of her own choice and others need not assist her. If we let her choice determine whether others owe her assistance or compensation – say, by providing technology that can modify the offending trait – then the very reason for this approach, that it avoids the problem of social hijacking by expensive tastes, is undercut.

There is an important similarity here to what we saw in the case of incommensurable capabilities. When we examine a person's set of capabilities, we

---

[52] One form of the information burden is this: Can we really show that there is a best path of the sort required and that it is equal to that found in others' life trees? Another form of the burden is this: In a given case, we would find it very hard to tell whether a preference that makes a person miserable is one that he chose to develop at some earlier point in life. The information about an individual's history needed to answer this question may be hard to find and subject to considerable interpretation. The question may also point to a deeper incoherence in the account. An unchosen preference may reduce the happiness the person would have had on the "best path" because of some other irrelevant choice about something else she made earlier. Then this person is not owed assistance because, say, twenty years earlier, she could have gone left when she went right. Alternatively, it seems possible in almost all cases to construct a counterfactual scenario in which path chosen would have constituted a best path comparable to the best path others enjoy.

are likely to find disagreement about who is worse off because in a broad range of cases, the value of these capabilities depends on the individual's conception of what is good. Any convergence in judgment is likely to be in cases where people are significantly worse off, say because of serious pathology or poverty or loss of liberty. Since the capabilities view insists on an objective way of determining if someone has worse capabilities than others, we need to eliminate cases of incommensurability. In the equal opportunity for welfare case, a person's judgment that she is worse off than others rests on an overall satisfaction or welfare scale, but without an objective way to determine that a better path does or does not exist, there is no way to distinguish the view from an equal welfare principle. On a prioritarian version of the opportunity for welfare view, the same point can be made by an analogous argument: It is not enough to show that one is worse off than others; one has to show that one's best path still makes one worse off than others.

We must be careful, then, not to accept at face value the claim that any specific trait is the cause of a deficit in opportunity for welfare just because the person with the trait would do better if it were modified. Nevertheless, the scope of the opportunity for welfare view differs in principle from the scope of the normal functioning view. In both Rawls and my extension of Rawls, a baseline assigned by the natural lottery for talents and skills was taken as a given and equality of opportunity was defined relative to it. Its effects were only partly mitigated by Rawls's difference principle. The stronger equal opportunity for welfare or advantage principle rejects that appeal to a baseline and also rejects the more modest mitigation that the difference principle brings. In principle, compensation is owed for deficits in talents and skills, and, as Arneson (1999b) once put it, there is no "privileging" of disease and disability over talents and skills as sources of compensable deficits in opportunity. What the previous argument shows, then, is not that the two views agree on the importance of pathology but only that not every deficit in a trait is grounds for compensation.

It should be clear from this discussion that a view focused on normal functioning is likely to produce more agreement on the proper role of meeting health needs than one focused on directly protecting against deficits in opportunity for welfare or advantage.

Is the Opportunity for Welfare View Too Restrictive?
The opportunity for welfare or advantage view says that we do not owe assistance to people who are worse off than others as a result of choices they have made. Suppose that I enjoy and cultivate risk-taking through skiing, scuba diving, and hang gliding. Any medical problems that arise from these choices count as bad option luck and should not give rise to legitimate claims for medical assistance, say through public or private insurance plans where

all health-care costs and risks are shared.[53] Similarly, if, as an adult, I learn about the risks of a high-fat diet but continue to eat fatty food, then the medical problems I develop would seem to be the result of my own choices.

In contrast, the extension of Rawls that focuses on protecting normal functioning says nothing about personal responsibility for health. It says that we should protect normal functioning in order to meet the needs of free and equal citizens, but it does not require us to calculate responsibility for health needs. For the most part, this view is consistent with the broad range of our public health and medical practices in avoiding sanctions for responsibility. Because the opportunity for welfare principle "foregrounds" choice or responsibility (G. A. Cohen 1989), it offers weaker protection to health and is more restrictive than the Rawlsian view. At the same time, since many people support the idea of assigning some individual responsibility for health, the opportunity for welfare or advantage principle cannot be dismissed. We must consider the issue further.

The emphasis on choice or responsibility in the opportunity for welfare or advantage view was a response to the worry about social hijacking by person with expensive tastes (see footnote 28): If people choose to cultivate such preferences and are unhappy because they are not satisfied, we do not owe them assistance, as we would if their welfare deficit was not their own fault or choice. But people who make risky lifestyle choices and expect others to assist them when ill health results have some resemblance to those who cultivate expensive tastes: Owing them assistance for their irresponsible choices would hijack others. The opportunity for welfare or advantage view thus has consistency on its side, given its solution to the problem of expensive tastes. If, however, there are good reasons for not making people bear the cost of risky lifestyle choices, then consistency chains this view to an implausible policy.

Of course, that is not the only solution to the problem of expensive tastes. Rawls instead asks for a division of responsibility: Society is responsible for distributing the primary social goods in accordance with the principles of justice, and individuals must adjust their conceptions of the good accordingly. If they are disappointed but the terms of cooperation are fair, that is too bad for them. This proposal leaves unclear what we are to do about person who make risky lifestyle choices: Do their resulting health needs become a matter of individual responsibility? Or does the principle of fair equality of opportunity mean that society must absorb the cost of meeting health needs regardless of how they arise? The extension of Rawls to health thus

[53] A supporter of this view might say that the individual who skis and breaks a leg is only partly responsible, because she chose the higher risk but was nevertheless unlucky in having the accident (a change in temperature iced the trail). In reply, I think the view then becomes too complex to use in determining what we are obliged to do.

has some flexibility, but it comes at a cost. The failure to take a theoretical stand may seem unfortunately vague or, worse, a way to hide inconsistency about the meaning of individual responsibility.

Should we hold individuals responsible for their lifestyle choices, as the opportunity for welfare view seems to require? Some people accept the implications of this view. They conclude that we have claims on others for medical assistance only if we are sick through no fault or choice of our own. Others reject this conclusion. They find abandoning sick people to their chosen fate morally unacceptable, concluding that we have an obligation to fix the leg broken in a skiing accident simply because the skier cannot function normally if we do not. Perhaps they might say that we should share the burden of paying for voluntary risks, since we all take some such risks in order to make life worth living.[54] They may reject "responsibility" tests that would be needed to determine to whom we owe medical help: Such tests are intrusive and demeaning (like some welfare eligibility tests), violate standards of liberty and privacy, and are difficult and costly to administer. The net result is that, even if considering responsibility has intuitive appeal, it is not so central or important that it should override other considerations involved in justice.

Ascribing responsibility is difficult because of the strong association we find between risky behaviors and socioeconomic status, race, and ethnicity. These strong associations, though not strong enough to explain the effects of inequalities on health (see Chapter 3), make it hard to ascribe responsibility and make it look as if we are blaming the victims: Poorer and less educated people will be held more responsible when it is unclear whether the root causes are subtle effects of class or race position or choices that people make.

Some of these problems might be avoided if we clarify what counts as responsibility or fault and find a more publicly administrable way of addressing them. John Roemer (1995) argues that we should divide a population into "types" of people by reference to all their relevant biological and sociological traits and then see if a particular behavior is more or less typical of a person's type. If it is more typical, the person is less responsible for the behavior. If it is less typical, the person is more responsible. Thus, we might reduce the burden for bad health on those whose ethnic backgrounds led to a taste for fatty food; or we might find biopsychological markers for risk

---

[54] When we want people to internalize the costs of their own choices is a complex question. As Fried (1969) points out in a different context, we all impose risks on others (e.g., when we drive to the store for a newspaper) for which we do not expect to have to provide compensation. There is a reasonable reciprocity in risk imposition here. Perhaps we should accept some further reasonable reciprocity in expecting assistance for the risks we take in pursuing a reasonable range of human adventures, since everyone wants to pursue some pleasures (eating, drinking, hiking, running, bicycling, scuba diving) that involve taking risks. See Wikler (1978).

takers who thus form a type that should not be held as responsible for their high-risk behavior.

This approach does not capture the relevant notion of responsibility. Atypicality is a poor measure of effort or desert or responsibility. For example, it makes responsibility depend largely on what others do, not on what we do. In any case, we still face this outcome: If skiing is a common behavior of the rich but not of the poor, then the poor skier is more responsible for his broken leg in a skiing accident than the rich skier.

Whether or not this appeal to responsibility for bad health troubles us intuitively, putting too much emphasis on it ignores egalitarian considerations central to democratic equality. Our health needs, however they arise, interfere with our ability to function as free and equal citizens. Elizabeth Anderson (1999) generalizes the point. To keep people functioning as equal citizens, democratic egalitarians must meet their needs however they have arisen, since capabilities can be undermined by both bad brute and bad option luck. What is crucial is whether needs of the right *type* are met so that the necessary capabilities can he used. Consequently, income transfer schemes that conform with the difference principle should help those whose incomes are reduced by both bad option luck and bad brute luck. Basic institutions should not insist on knowing an individual's history to determine who is at fault.

Even if we do not emphasize responsibility in assigning of obligations of justice, we can still appeal to that concept through incentives and education. We do not tie our hands behind our backs in addressing the population and individual health issues raised by lifestyle patterns if we refuse to sanction bad choices and instead rely on improving health literacy and knowledge. We may also introduce incentives and even taxes to create some disincentives that are not primarily punitive or liberty-restricting. All things considered, then, the flexibility in the Rawlsian approach allows it to consider such reasons for not insisting on a strong assignment of individual responsibility for risky lifestyle choices. However, the opportunity for welfare/advantage view is able to compromise its strong stand about responsibility for various policy considerations, such as the difficulty of administering the strong responsibility view.

THE SPECIAL MORAL IMPORTANCE OF HEALTH: CONCLUSION

People attach special moral importance to health care and to meeting health needs more generally. Our first Focal Question asks how we can justify doing so. The first step in my answer is the observation that meeting these needs promotes normal functioning, and normal functioning, in turn, protects people's fair shares of the normal opportunity range. Meeting health needs allows people to choose among the life plans they can reasonably pursue, given their talents and skills. If people have a fundamental interest in protecting that opportunity range, then we may explain the protection of health we observe. To justify that special protection, we must show that justice gives us social obligations to protect that opportunity range. Several views of justice support a social obligation to protect the opportunity range. Rawls's theory of justice as fairness can be extended to address health needs through their connection to his principle of fair equality of opportunity. Other views, critical of Rawls in various ways, also support an obligation to protect this space of exercisable opportunities. The capabilities approach of Sen and Nussbaum differs from the opportunity-based view more in terminology than in concept. The opportunity for welfare or advantage principle also requires us to protect an opportunity space, despite its disagreements with Rawls about what must be protected within that space. My answer to the first Focal Question thus goes beyond the answer I gave in *Just Health Care* in two ways: It generalizes the answer to all health needs, not just health care, and it draws support for an obligation to protect opportunity from views critical of Rawls as well as from Rawls.

Our next tasks are to address the other two Focal Questions and draw out the implications of the integrated theory that results.

3

When Are Health Inequalities Unjust?

The Social Determinants of Health

When is an inequality in health status between different socioeconomic groups unjust? More generally, when is an inequality in health status between different demographic groups unjust? An account of just health should help us determine which health inequalities are unjust and which are acceptable. Recognizing these distinctions will help us to remedy injustice and establish just institutions.

These versions of the second Focal Question (see Chapter 1) involve issues that move beyond simply knowing why health is of special moral importance and how that importance can guide us in extending general theories of justice to matters of health and its distribution. Knowing that protecting health protects opportunity does not, by itelf, tell us when inequalities in health, like inequalities in opportunity more generally, are unjust. Health is produced not just by having access to medical prevention and treatment but also, to a measurably great extent, by the cumulative experience of social conditions across the lifecourse. When a sixty-year old patient presents to the emergency room with a heart attack to receive medical treatment, that encounter represents the results of bodily insults that accumulated over a lifetime. Medical care is, figuratively speaking, "the ambulance waiting at the bottom of the cliff."

We have known for over 150 years that an individual's chances of life and death are patterned by social class: The more affluent and better educated people are, the longer and healthier their lives (Villerme 1840, cited in Lynch et al. 1998). When these inequalities are present in poor, developing countries, it is tempting to think that poverty and deprivation adequately explain them. We should avoid the temptation. Some rather poor countries pursue policies that produce excellent aggregate health outcomes while

In this chapter I draw heavily on Daniels, Kennedy, and Kawachi (1999, 2000). I appreciate the willingness of my coauthors to let me use that material in this chapter, and I also thank Ichiro Kawachi for the discussion of new material in it.

moderating significantly the degree of health inequality. In addition, these effects of socioeconomic status (SES) are present as well in rich, developed countries, where the sources of inequality are not deprivation and deep poverty. More striking, these patterns persist when there is universal access to health care – a fact quite surprising to those who think that financial access to medical services is the primary determinant of health status.

In addition to socioeconomic inequalities[1] that are correlated with health inequalities, we have extensive evidence about patterns of racial and ethnic disparities in many countries. Many of these inequalities are due to the way in which social exclusion and patterns of discrimination push ethnic minorities (or majorities, as in some former colonies, like South Africa) into the lowest socioeconomic groups. Still, there is often a significant residual effect of race, as in the United States, even when correlations are controlled for income, education, and insurance levels. There are also striking patterns of gender inequality in health in some countries – leading Sen (1990) to ask where the millions of "missing" women are in some Asian countries, as compared to gender ratios in developed countries. These forms of health inequalities are the focus of the broader version of my second Focal Question: When are inequalities in health status between different groups unjust?

Of course, we cannot infer *causation* from *correlation*, and correlations alone will not support judgments about injustice. To know whether one inequality is a cause or determinant of another, and then to ascribe some judgment about inequity to it, we have to know something about the mechanisms at work. We need to know, for example, that although poor health or disability can lead to lower income, which can be a significant consequence in many settings, such "health selection," as it is called, explains only part of the correlation between low income and poor health in general,[2] and we have good reason to suppose the existence of mechanisms that work in the other direction, from socioeconomic inequality to health differences. Being less well educated, for example, can lead to engaging in some risky patterns of behavior, and these risks increase health inequalities.[3] But even

[1] Deaton (personal communication, July 13, 2006) cautions against thinking that the various components of SES (income, education, social class) all work the same way and that the convenience of combining them may be outweighed by the inaccuracy that can result. See also Deaton (2002a,b).

[2] Deaton (personal communication, July 13, 2006) and Case and Deaton (2003) point to the impact of ill health on early retirement and thus on income reduction; Case and Deaton argue that the significantly worse self-reported health of those in the lowest income quartile compared to those in the highest is primarily driven by the ill health of those out of work, presumably because they are ill. Health selection may have a greater effect on income than class. Cf. Marmot (1994).

[3] Behavior risk factors nevertheless contribute significantly to inequality: Jha et al. (2006) show that smoking contributes nearly half of the male mortality in the lowest social class in four countries.

this mechanism fails to explain the general effect of socioeconomic inequality on health (Marmot 2004), and researchers are exploring more promising mechanisms. But even if more work is needed to clarify the exact mechanisms, it is not unreasonable to talk here about the social "determinants" of health (Marmot 1999). To the extent that these social determinants are socially controllable, we clearly face questions of distributive justice.

In some ways, gender and race or ethnic inequalities are easier to address than class inequalities. Since these kinds of inequalities are the result of social exclusion and other unjust practices aimed at vulnerable groups, we are generally and justifiably inclined to view them as inequities. Identifying them, however, does not make them easy to remedy.

Socioeconomic inequalities pose harder questions since few people are radical egalitarians opposing all forms of such inequalitiy. Many who are not at all troubled by significant inequalities in income, wealth, or opportunites for a higher quality of life are particularly troubled by health inequalities. They believe that a socioeconomic inequality that otherwise seems just becomes unjust if it contributes to health inequalities. Is every health inequality that results from unequally distributed social goods unjust? If there is an irreducible health gradient across socioeconomic groups, does that make the very existence of those inequalities unjust? Does a concern about health inequalities drive us to even more radical forms of social and economic egalitarianism than we had imagined we were committed to?

Alternatively, are some health inequalities the result of acceptable trade-offs? Perhaps they are simply unfortunate by-products of inequalities that work in other ways to help worse-off groups. For example, it is often claimed that permitting inequality provides incentives to work harder, thereby stimulating growth that will ultimately benefit the poorest groups. To whom must these trade-offs be acceptable if we are to consider them just? Are they acceptable only if they are part of a strategy aimed at making the situation more just? In our judgments about justice, does it matter exactly how social determinants produce inequalities in health status?

Unfortunately, these questions have been almost totally ignored within the field of bioethics, as well as within ethics and political philosophy more generally.[4] With some significant exceptions, bioethics has not looked "upstream" from the point of delivery of medical services to the role of the health-care system in improving population health. Bioethics has even more rarely looked further upstream to the distribution of social goods that determine the health of societies (cf. Marchand et al. 1998).

This omission is quite striking, for bioethics here lags behind both social science and policy concerns. The social science literature on social determinants of health has grown impressively for a quarter of a century. More

---

[4] Sen (2004) is an important exception.

important, a concern about health equity and its social determinants has emerged as an important consideration in the policies of several European countries over the past two decades (Benzeval et al. 1995; Ostlin and Diderichsen 2001). WHO has devoted growing attention to inequalities in health status and the policies that cause or mitigate them. So have research initiatives, such as the Global Health Equity Initiative, funded by the Swedish International Development Agency and the Rockefeller Foundation (cf. Evans et al. 2001). In the past decade, there has emerged a growing social science and policy concern about health disparities in the United States, although its focus has largely been on issues of race, not class, with a few important exceptions.

To fill this bioethical gap, I shall argue that we must supplement a widely cited intuitive analysis of what health inequalities are unjust – those that are avoidable, unnecessary, and unfair (Dahlgren and Whitehead 1991; Whitehead 1992) – with a more systematic account. In the previous chapter, I turned to Rawls's theory of justice as fairness, as well as to other recent work in distributive justice, to show that there is broad support for obligations to protect opportunity. I drew on that support to back my claim that there is a special moral importance to meeting health needs. Here I turn again to Rawls's theory to illustrate what an account of the just distribution of the determinants of health might look like. My contention is that – quite unintentionally – Rawls's theory provides a defensible account of how to distribute the social determinants of health fairly and thus tells us something useful about when health inequalities are unjust. Specifically, each of his principles of justice as fairness governs a cluster of key social determinants of health. General conformance with these principles will consequently flatten the socioeconomic gradient of health as much as we can reasonably demand (and, arguably, considerably more than we observe even in wealthy nations with developed social welfare protections). *In effect, social justice in general is good for population health and its fair distribution.* There will remain a problem of residual health inequalities produced by otherwise justifiable inequalities, and we shall consider the extent to which justice as fairness gives any guidance about them.

In turning to Rawls to illustrate what an account of the distribution of the determinants of health might look like, my intention, as in the previous chapter, is neither to argue in favor of Rawls's theory nor to presuppose its truth.[5] Nevertheless, the extension of the power and scope of his theory that results from the argument in both chapters is of some methodological interest, a point I return to later. First, however, I shall describe some of

---

[5] Sen (2004) provides another illustration, arguing that health inequity is clearly connected with social injustice more broadly and is not to be confused with health inequality.

the findings from recent social epidemiological work and point to their serendipitous connection to Rawls's principles of justice.

SOCIAL DETERMINANTS OF HEALTH: SOME BASIC FINDINGS

Four central findings in the literature on the social determinants of health have implications for an account of justice and health inequalities. First, if we look across nations, the national income/health gradients we observe are not the result of some fixed or determinate laws of economic development but are influenced by social policy choices. The wealth of nations matters up to a relatively modest point, but policies always matter, and arguably they matter more in poor countries. Second, if we look within societies, the individual SES/health gradients we observe are not just the result of the deprivation of the poorest groups. Rather, a gradient in health operates across the whole socioeconomic spectrum within societies even where universal medical coverage and other welfare programs are in place. Third, although there is broad agreement that the degree of social inequality contributes to the steepness of a society's health gradient, there is conflicting evidence and a complex debate about whether the steepness of the gradient is affected by the degree of income inequality in a society. Fourth, there are reasonable hypotheses identifying some social and psychosocial pathways through which inequality affects health. These causal pathways can be molded or changed by specific policy choices that should be guided by considerations of justice, and they point to institutions that are appropriately governed by Rawls's principle of justice as fairness.

Cross-National Evidence on Health Inequalities

The finding that prosperity is related to health, whether measured at the level of nations or individuals, might lead one to the conclusion that these income/health gradients are inevitable. But evidence suggests otherwise. Figure 3.1 shows the relationship between the wealth and health of nations as measured by per capita gross domestic product (GDPpc) and life expectancy. There is a clear association between GDPpc and life expectancy, but only up to a point. The relationship levels off beyond about $8,000 GDPpc, with virtually no further gains in life expectancy. This leveling effect is most apparent among the advanced industrial economies that largely account for the upper tail of the curve in Figure 3.1.

Closer inspection of this figure points out some startling discrepancies. Though Cuba and Iraq (before the second Iraq war) are equally poor (GDPpcs about $3,100), life expectancy in Cuba exceeds that in Iraq by 17.2 years in 1995 (and no doubt by more now). And while the difference between the GDPpc for Costa Rica and the United States is enormous

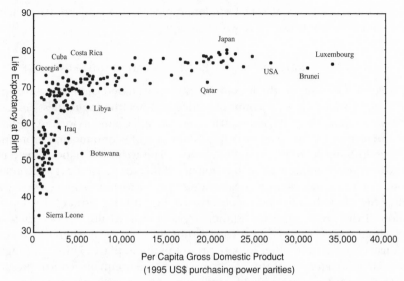

FIGURE 3.1. Relationship between Country Wealth and Life Expectancy. *Source:* United Nations Human Development Report Statistics 1998.

(about $21,000), Costa Rica's life expectancy is nearly the same as that of the United States. In fact, despite being the richest nation on earth, the United States performs rather poorly on health indicators (i.e., forty-fourth in life expectancy at birth)[6].

Taken together, these observations support the notions that the relationship between economic development and health is not fixed and that national health achievement is mediated by factors other than aggregate wealth. Culture, social organization and government policies, among others, are important in determining population health and thus in explaining the differences in health outcomes among nations. Variations in these socially controllable factors are thus important from the perspective of social justice.

Individual SES and Health

At the individual level, numerous studies have documented the "socioeconomic gradient." On this gradient, each increment up the socioeconomic hierarchy is associated with improved health outcomes over the rung below (Black et al. 1988; Davey-Smith et al. 1990; Pappas et al. 1993; Adler et al. 1994). Note that this relationship is not simply a contrast between the health

[6] CIA Factbook, https://www.cia.gov/cia/publications/factbook/rankorder/2102rank.html, accessed July 18, 2006.

of the rich and the poor, but is observed across all levels of SES (remember that not all the components of SES – income, education, social class – behave identically; see footnote 2). Though the effects of income or wealth work across the SES spectrum, the gradient is steeper at lower income levels, with considerable flattening out at the highest income levels. This "concavity" of the gradient means that transfers of resources from the best-off to the worst-off SES groups would improve aggregate health and would have little negative effect, if any, on the best-off groups. (I return to this point in my later discussion of Rawls's difference principle.)

What is particularly notable about the SES gradient is that it does not appear to be explained by differences in access to health care. Steep gradients have been observed even among groups of individuals, such as British civil servants, with adequate access to health care, housing, and transport (Davey-Smith et al. 1990; Marmot et al. 1998). The Whitehall studies of British civil servants provide strong support for such a gradient, not only for mortality rates and life expectancy, but also for morbidity rates across a range of diseases. Strikingly, some of these studies show that civil service rank explains more of the risk of premature heart disease among ranks than such standard risk factors as smoking, serum cholesterol level, or blood pressure (Marmot et al. 1984).

Importantly, the steepness of the gradient varies substantially across societies. Some societies show a relatively shallow gradient in mortality across SES groups. Others, with comparable or even higher levels of economic development, show steeper gradients in mortality rates across the socioeconomic hierarchy.

Relative Income and Health

A lively debate exists in the empirical literature about whether income inequality, as opposed to absolute levels of income, helps to determine the steepness of the gradient. Were this true, we might find that middle income groups in a country with high income inequality have lower health status than comparable or even poorer groups in a country with low income inequality. There is some evidence for this pattern in the United States if variations among states in inequality are examined (Kennedy et al. 1998; Lynch et al. 1998; Subramanian and Kawachi 2006), but there are conflicting study results as well (Mellor and Milyo 2002; Deaton and Lubotsky 2003). This effect, if it can be established, is apparent in Figure 3.2, where the prevalence of self-reported fair/poor health is higher for almost every income group (and the gradient is steeper) for those living in states with the highest income inequality (Kennedy et al. 1998). This effect of shifting the curve, if it is supported by the empirical findings, would suggest that income inequality has an effect over and above what is implied by the concavity of the SES gradient itself.

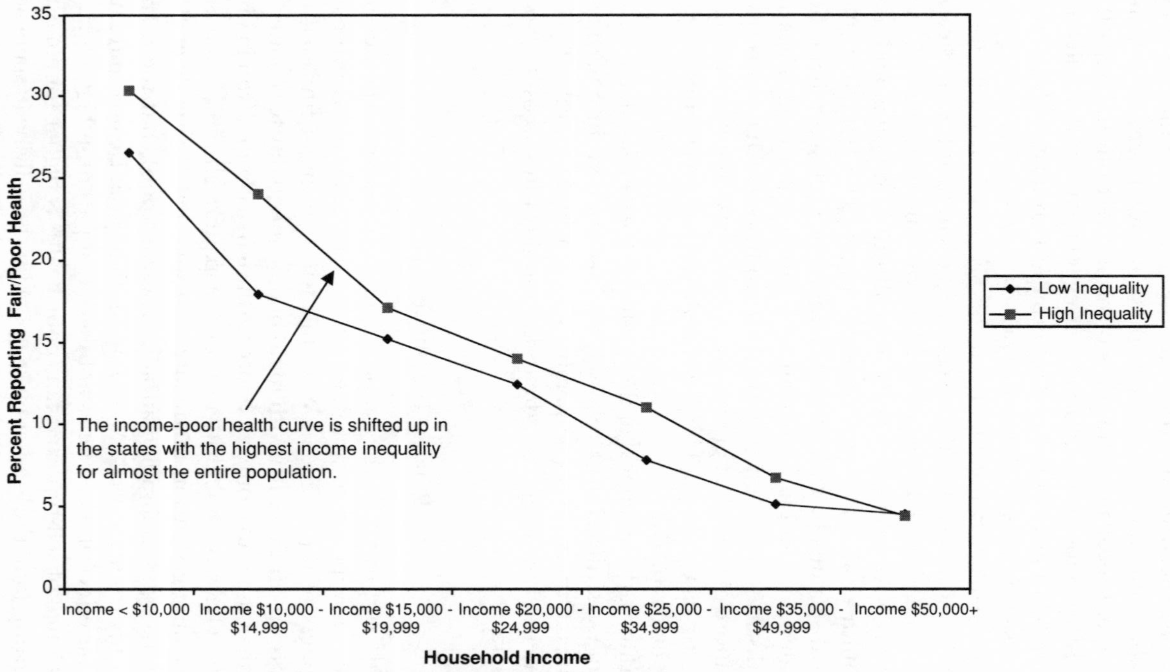
Percent Reporting Fair/Poor Health
35
30
25
20
15
10
5
0
The income-poor health curve is shifted up in the states with the highest income inequality for almost the entire population.
Low Inequality
High Inequality
Income < $10,000
Income $10,000 - $14,999
Income $15,000 - $19,999
Income $20,000 - $24,999
Income $25,000 - $34,999
Income $35,000 - $49,999
Income $50,000+
Household Income

FIGURE 3.2. Self-Rated Health and Individual Household Income.

Leaving aside the contentious results of these studies,[7] it is worth noting why the income relativity thesis has attracted such interest. If it is true, it is not just the size of the economic pie but how the pie is shared that matters for population health. It is not the absolute deprivation associated with low economic development (lack of the basic conditions necessary for health, such as clean water, adequate nutrition and housing, and general sanitary living conditions) that explains health differences among developed nations but the degree of *relative deprivation* within them. Relative deprivation refers not to a lack of the goods that are basic to survival, but rather to a lack of sources of self-respect that are deemed essential for full participation in society. (These "recognitional" features of just arrangements are emphasized in Rawls's account, as we shall see.) If the income relativity thesis can be established, it would then require elaboration of the causal mechanisms that underlie it.[8]

The income relativity thesis is interesting and worth further investigation, but it has only a modest bearing on the claims I pursue in this chapter. As we shall see, there is strong evidence that health inequalities are reduced if we concentrate first on making the worst-off groups socially and economically as well off as possible, paying special attention to improvements in human capital and investments in public health. If true, the income relativity thesis

---

[7] Sparked by Wilkinson's (1992) paper showing a correlation between national measures of income inequality and the gradient of health inequality among a select groups of Organization of Economic Cooperation and Development (OECD) countries, researchers in the United States and elsewhere found conflicting results during the subsequent decade. The initial positive results from the OECD countries disappear when a full rather than a selected set of them is studied. Negative results are also found primarily in countries more egalitarian than the United States (Sweden, Japan, Canada, Denmark, New Zealand), as noted by Subramanian et al. (2003) and Subramanian and Kawachi (2004). Some negative results are also found in the United States, especially if units of aggregation are smaller, such as municipalities rather than states. A significant number of U.S. studies support the claim, especially at the state level. Positive results are also found in a recent study in Chile, a country with more income inequality than exists in the United States (Subranamian et al. 2003).

This pattern of seemingly conflicting results might be explained if income inequality affects health inequalities only above some threshold level of inequality, a threshold crossed in the United States and more unequal countries but not in more egalitarian countries (Subramanian and Kawachi 2004). Alternatively, the effect of income inequality might be countered by more egalitarian social policies, such as the more redistributive health and welfare policies in other OECD countries. This latter alternative highlights an important point about the claim generally made by supporters of the income relativity thesis: Income inequality is a causal factor that works through various mechanisms, political, social, and possibly individual (e.g., stress), and is not claimed to be "by itself" or "per se" a cause of health inequalities.

[8] In the United States, in those studies that support the thesis, the strength of this relationship between social inequality and health inequality is not trivial. One study of U.S. metropolitan areas, rather than states, found that areas with high income inequality had an excess of death compared to areas of low inequality that was equivalent in magnitude to all deaths due to heart disease (Lynch et al. 1998).

would strengthen support for giving priority to making the worst off as well off as possible, for it would make an even stronger claim that it works to the advantage of all. In addition, it might point us to other mechanisms that we may have to address.

Pathways Linking Social Inequalities to Health Inequalities

To address key issues about social policy and distributive justice, we must better understand the mechanisms underlying the correlations between health outcomes and social inequalities in income, education, and other factors. Unless we know something about these underlying causal mechanisms, we cannot focus properly on the socially controllable factors that a just policy must regulate. Fortunately, there are plausible and researchable pathways through which social inequalities produce inequalities in health.

The first empirical result I highlighted earlier was the claim that social policy, more than the wealth of nations, explains variations in health outcomes across countries. Developing countries that invest heavily in human capital, for example in education, have better health outcomes. Indeed, one of the strongest predictors of life expectancy among developing countries is adult literacy, particularly the disparity between male and female adult literacy, which explains much of the variation in health achievement among these countries after accounting for GDPpc. Similarly, in the United States, differences between the states in women's status – measured in terms of their economic autonomy and political participation – are strongly correlated with with female mortality rates (Kawachi and Kennedy 1997; Kawachi et al. 1999). Even if we do not know all the underlying mechanisms through which improved education, including female literacy, improves health outcomes, we have good evidence that investment in this socially controllable factor has measurable health effects.

The second empirical thesis I highlighted concerned the strong effect of a socioeconomic gradient of health. This gradient is demonstrated even where socioeconomic inequality does not mean absolute deprivation in material goods or access to health care – as in the Whitehall studies. Indeed, if we focus on the British civil servants, one important variable in their job situations concerns their degree of control over work (Marmot 2004). Such control may affect the kinds of stress people are exposed to, and this in turn may affect basic immune mechanisms or may directly impact the course of certain diseases. Uncovering mechanisms here is a complex research program that may require work on both animals and humans, including some carefully selected natural experiments. How readily we can convert this understanding of mechanisms into modifications of social policy, including, for example, the organization of the workplace, remains to be seen.

Our third thesis concerned the controversial evidence about the degree of income inequality and its effects on health. It may be premature to look for mechanisms since the basic association is controversial. Still, we may better understand some of the mechanisms through which income inequality might work if we note some of the related studies.

In the United States, the states with the most unequal income distribution invest less in public education, have more uninsured persons, and spend less on social safety nets (Kaplan et al. 1996; Kawachi and Kennedy 1997). Differences in human capital investment are particularly striking. These are demonstrated for educational spending and, more importantly, for outcomes; even when controlling for median income, income inequality explains about 40 percent of the between-state variation in the percentage of fourth-grade children who are below the basic reading level. Similarly strong associations are seen for high school dropout rates. These data clearly show that educational opportunities for children in states with high income inequality are quite different from those in more egalitarian states. Furthermore, these early effects not only have an immediate impact on health, increasing the likelihood of premature death during childhood and adolescence (as evidenced by the much higher death rates for infants and children in the high-inequality states), but also have lasting effects showing up later in life as part of the SES gradient in health (Bartley et al. 1997; Davey-Smith et al. 1990).

These societal mechanisms are tightly linked to the political processes that influence government policy. For one thing, income inequality appears to affect health by undermining civil society. Income inequality erodes social cohesion, increasing social mistrust and reducing participation in civic organizations – two features of civil society (Kawachi and Kennedy 1997; Kawachi et al. 1997). Lack of social cohesion, in turn, is reflected in significantly less political activity (e.g., voting, serving in local government, volunteering for political campaigns), thus undermining the responsiveness of government institutions in addressing the needs of the worst-off groups. This is demonstrated not only by the human capital investment data presented earlier but also by the lack of investment in human security. States with the highest income inequality, and thus the lowest levels of social capital and political participation, provide far less generous social safety nets.

AN INTUITIVE ANALYSIS OF HEALTH INEQUITIES

In the public health literature (Braveman 1999), there is an influential intuitive answer to our second Focal Question, namely, Whitehead's (1992) and Dahlgren and Whitehead's (1991) claim that health inequalities count as inequities when they are *avoidable, unnecessary,* and *unfair.* How do these conditions fit together?

Presumably, inequalities that are avoidable and unnecessary but not unfair do not count as inequitable. For example, if lung cancer rates differed between smokers and nonsmokers, and if smoking rates were not themselves strongly influenced by SES, ethnicity, or gender but seemed completely a matter of individual, voluntary, informed choice, then we might not think the cancer rate inequality unfair and thus not inequitable. Similarly, an inequality may be unfair but also unavoidable or even necessary, given our inability to change certain conditions. For example, suppose we learned that the mortality rate of certain workers, say truck drivers, means that their life expectancy is lower than that of other workers, and many believe (intuitively) that this is unfair. We may be able to reduce that higher mortality rate through road and equipment improvements and through better training of drivers and enforcement of traffic laws, but suppose there remains an elevated mortality rate that seems unavoidable, or perhaps necessary given the importance of trucking. Some may insist that the inequality is still unfair, if unavoidable, even though they would conclude that the inequality is not an inequity. If we can agree on what is avoidable, unnecessary, and unfair, and if this analysis is correct, then we can agree on which inequalities are inequitable.

The Whitehead–Dahlgren analysis is deliberately broad. It not only includes socioeconomic differences but others as well. Age, gender, race, and ethnic differences in health status exist that are independent of socioeconomic differences, and they raise distinct questions about equity or justice. For example, should we view the lower life expectancy of men compared to women in developed countries – as much as six years' difference in some observations – as an inequity?[9] If it is rooted in biological differences that we do not know how to overcome, then, according to this analysis, it is not avoidable and therefore not an inequity. Perhaps not all of it is unavoidable – higher smoking rates for men or higher workplace risks may explain some of the difference. But how much? This is not an idle controversy: Taking average rather than gender-differentiated life expectancy in developed countries as a benchmark or goal will yield different estimates of the inequity women face in some developing countries.[10] In any case, the analysis of inequity here is only as good as our understanding of what is avoidable or unnecessary.

The same point applies to judgments about fairness. Is the poorer health status of a social class or ethnic group that engages in heavy drug and alcohol use unfair? We may be inclined to say it is not unfair, provided that the use or avoidance of drugs and alcohol is truly voluntary. But if many people

---

[9] Sen (2004) points to the gender inequality and denies that it is an inequity, not because we could not do something about it but because what we could do, e.g., give men more health care than women, would be discriminatory, violating "process" constraints on fair treatment.

[10] Murray's reduction of the male–female gender gap to 2.5 years from an observed 6 years, based on extrapolation from some cases and assumptions about greater exposure to risk, was criticized as possible gender bias in the construction of DALYs. See Anand and Hanson (1998).

in an ethnic group or class behave similarly, there may also be factors at work that reduce the autonomous nature of their behavior and how much responsibility they should bear (Wikler 1978; Roemer 1995). The analysis thus leaves us with judgments about responsibility that are complex and unresolved; as a result, we have continuing disagreements about fairness (or avoidability).

The poor in many countries have no clean water, sanitation, adequate shelter, basic education, vaccinations, and prenatal and maternal care. As a result of some or all of these factors, there are infant mortality differences between them and richer groups. Since social policies could supply the missing determinants of infant health, the inequalities are avoidable.

Are these inequalities also unfair? Most of us would immediately think that they are, perhaps because we believe that international (Pogge 2002) or domestic policies that create and sustain poverty are unjust. We also believe that social policies that compound poverty with lack of access to the determinants of health are doubly unfair. Of course, libertarians would disagree. They would insist that what is merely unfortunate is not unfair; on their view, we have no obligation of justice, as opposed to charity, to provide the poor with what they are missing. Many of us might reject the libertarian view as itself unjust because of this dramatic conflict with our beliefs about poverty and our social obligations to meet people's basic needs.

The problem becomes more complicated, however, when we remember one of the basic findings from the literature on social determinants: We cannot eliminate health inequalities simply by eliminating poverty. Health inequalities persist even in societies where poor people have access to all the determinants of health noted previously. Furthermore, these health inequities persist as a gradient of health throughout all SES classes, not just between the very poorest groups and those immediately above them. Some of the mechanisms may be difficult to avoid and may depend on deep structural features of an economy. Thus, educational and skill differences that steer people into hard manual labor rather than nonmanual labor significantly affect the rate at which poor health is self-reported (Case and Deaton 2003). Whether we consider these mechanisms and their effects unfair may depend in part on our views about the fairness of overall social inequality.

At this point, many of us are forced to reexamine what we believe about the justice of the remaining socioeconomic inequalities. Unless we believe that *all* socioeconomic inequalities (or at least all inequalities we did not choose) are unjust – and very few do so – we must consider more carefully the problem created by the health gradient and the fact that it becomes steeper as inequality increases. Our judgments about the intuitive notion of fairness in the Dahlgren–Whitehead account provide less guidance in thinking about the broader issue of the social determinants of health inequalities even if we, rightly or wrongly, felt confident in appealing to them when rejecting the libertarian position. Indeed, we may even believe that some socioeconomic inequality is unavoidable or even necessary and therefore is not unjust.

A RAWLSIAN ANALYSIS OF HEALTH INEQUITIES

One reason we develop general ethical theories, including theories of justice, is to provide a framework for settling important disputes about conflicting moral beliefs or intuitions of the sort facing the Whitehead–Dahlgren analysis. For example, in *A Theory of Justice*, Rawls sought to leverage our relatively broad liberal agreement on principles guaranteeing certain equal basic liberties into an agreement on a principle limiting socioeconomic inequalities, a matter on which liberals considerably disagree (J. Cohen 1989). His strategy was to show that a social contract designed to be fair to free and equal people ("justice as [procedural] fairness") would not only justify the choice of those equal basic liberties but would also justify the choice of principles guaranteeing equal opportunity and limiting inequalities to those that work to make the worst-off groups fare as well as possible.

Rawls's account, though developed to answer this general question about social justice, also provides principles for the just distribution of the social determinants of health, unexpectedly adding to its scope and power as a theory. The extra power of the theory is a surprise, since, as I emphasized earlier, Rawls deliberately simplified the construction of his theory by assuming that his contractors are fully functional over a normal life span. Examining the social determinants of health inequalities from the perspective of Rawls's theory is particularly appealing because justice as fairness is egalitarian in orientation (Daniels 2003) and yet justifies certain inequalities, such as those in income and wealth, that contribute to health inequalities. In addition, my extension of Rawls links the protection of health to the protection of equality of opportunity, again setting up the potential for internal conflict. To see whether this combination of features leads to contradictions in the theory or to insight into the problem, we must examine the issue in more detail.

Rawls on Allowable Inequalities

How does Rawls justify socioeconomic inequalities? Why wouldn't free and equal contractors simply insist on strictly egalitarian distributions of all social goods, just as they insist on equal basic liberties and equal opportunity?

Rawls's answer is that it is *irrational* for contractors to insist on equality if doing so would worsen their lifetime prospects.[11] If incentives to develop

---

[11] This reasoning from the perspective of Rawlsian contractors is the central argument in Rawls and is to be contrasted with the "intuitive" argument discussed in Chapter 2 that turned on the moral arbitrariness of the natural distribution of talents and skills.

skills and take risks increase social productivity, then the social pie that gets divided may be increased so much that less than equal shares for those who are worst off are still absolutely larger than equal shares of a smaller social pie. Specifically, Rawls argues that contractors would choose the difference principle, which, as we noted in Chapter 2, permits inequalities provided that they make the worst-off groups in society as well off as possible.[12] The argument for the difference principle appears to suggest that relative inequality is less important than absolute well-being, a suggestion that is in tension with other aspects of Rawls's view. The tension is illustrated by Rawls's insistence that inequalities allowed by the difference principle should not undermine the value of political liberty or the requirements of fair equality of opportunity. The priority given these other principles over the difference principle thus limits the inference that Rawls has no concern about relative inequality. Specifically, as we shall see, these principles work together to constrain inequality and to preserve the social bases of self-respect for all.

Two points will help avoid misunderstanding of the difference principle and its justification. First, as we saw in Chapter 2, it is not a mere trickle-down principle, but one that requires maximal flow to help the worst-off groups. The worst off, and then the next worst off, and so on (Rawls [1971] calls this "chain connectedness") must be made as well off as possible, not merely somewhat better off, as a trickle-down principle implies. The difference principle is thus much more demanding than a principle that would permit any degree of inequality provided that there was some trickle of benefits to the worst off.[13] Indeed, it is more egalitarian than alternative principles that merely assure the worst off a "decent" or "adequate" minimum. Part of the rationale for the more demanding principle is that it would produce less strain of commitment, less sense of being unfairly left out, at least for those who are worst off, than principles that allow more inequality (J. Cohen 1989). Indeed, from what we have learned about the social determinants of health, the more demanding difference principle would also produce less

---

[12] A careful discussion of Rawls's argument for the difference principle and the extensive critical literature it has generated is beyond the scope of this chapter. It is important, however, to distinguish Rawls's own social contract argument from the many informal and intuitive reformulations of it. See Barry (1989) and G. A. Cohen (1992, 1995). Some controversy is fed by Rawls's (1971: Sect. 13) different formulations of the difference principle; some comes from the complexity of other assumptions involved in his argument, such as "chain connection" and "close-knittedness"; some follows from disagreement with giving such strong priority to the worst off, regardless of the benefits lost to others and regardless of how well off the worst off are. For a useful discussion, see Williams (1995).

[13] What was said previously applies to the ideal case, where a society is in general conformance with the principles of justice. In a nonideal setting, where we may be making a system more just, Rawls is willing to say that an improvement is not unjust as long as it moves the worse-off groups closer – even if not maximally closer – to being as well off as possible.

health inequality than any other principles that allow inequalities. By flattening the health gradient, it also benefits middle-income groups, not simply the poorest. In this regard, its benefits are important beyond the level where we have helped the worst off to achieve "sufficiency." This point provides a reply to those who suggest that the difference principle has no appeal once the worst off are sufficiently provided for (Gutmann and Thompson 1996).

Second, when Rawlsian contractors evaluate how well off the principles they choose will make them, they are to judge their well-being by an index of "primary social goods" (see Chapter 2; also see Rawls 1971: 62; 1993: Ch. 5). The primary social goods, which Rawls thinks of as the "needs of citizens," include liberty, powers, opportunities, income and wealth, and the social bases of self-respect. (These objective measures of well-being should be contrasted with measures of happiness or desire satisfaction that are familiar from utilitarian and welfare economic perspectives.) In his exposition of the difference principle, Rawls illustrates how it will work by asking us to consider only the simpler case of income inequality. In doing so, he *assumes* that the level of income will correlate with the level of other social goods on the index.

This simplification can be misleading. In crucial cases – including those involving health – the correlation may not occur and it will be essential to use the whole index, rather than just the income component, to measure how well off people are.[14] For example, let us suppose that having "democratic" control over one's workplace is crucial to self-realization and the promotion of self-esteem (J. Cohen 2001). Marmot (2004) documents how hierarchical workplaces may create health inequalities through the effect of status on stress. Suppose further that hierarchical workplaces are more efficient than democratic ones, providing higher incomes for the worst-off workers than democratic workplaces. Then the difference principle does not clearly tell us whether the hierarchical workplace contains allowable inequalities since the worst off are better off in some ways (economic) but worse off in others (health and thus opportunity and self-respect). Without knowing the weighting of items in the index, we cannot use it to say clearly what inequalities are permitted. When we evaluate which income inequalities are allowable, by asking which ones work to make the worst-off groups as well off as possible, we must judge how well off groups are by reference to the *whole* index of primary goods and not simply the resulting income.

This point is of particular importance in the current discussion. My extension of Rawls in Chapter 2 treats health status as a determinant of the opportunity range. Since opportunity is included in the index of primary social goods, the effects of health inequalities are thereby included as well. I also

---

[14] In thinking about the impact of income inequality on health, Deaton (personal communication, July 2006) makes a related point when he cautions that we should think more broadly about social inequality and not income alone.

noted earlier that the social bases of self-respect are among the primary social goods on the index. From Marmot's (2004) work, we may infer that hierarchical workplaces not only undermine health, and thus opportunity, but do so because there is inadequate protection of self-respect. Clearly, we must use the whole index, not the simplifying assumption that income correlates with all other items on it.

Unfortunately, Rawls says very little about how items in the index are to be weighted. This is one of the crucial points on which the theory says less than we might have wished. Therefore, we have little guidance about how these primary goods are to be traded off against each other in constructing the index. This silence pertains not only to the use of the index in the contract situation, but also to its use by a legislature trying to apply the principles of justice in a context where many features of a society are known.

Flattening the SES Gradient of Health

Now that we have seen why Rawls believes that inequalities are allowable under some conditions, we can consider how those general inequalities affect the distribution of health and contribute to health inequalities. If allowable general inequalities magnify health inequalities, we might conclude that justice, as Rawls conceives it, is not good for our health. Instead, we shall see why social justice, as described by Rawls's principles, is good for our health and promotes its fair distribution.[15] This will permit us to give a more satisfying answer to the second Focal Question.

To understand this claim, let us start with the ideal case, a society governed by Rawls's principles of justice as fairness that seeks to achieve what Rawls calls "democratic equality" (Rawls 1971; Daniels 2003). Consider what the society requires in distributing the social determinants of health. In such a society, all are guaranteed equal basic liberties (Rawls 1982a), including effective exercise of (or worth of) political participation (Daniels 1975; cf. Rawls 1995). In addition, there are institutional safeguards aimed at assuring all, richer and poorer alike, the value of effectively exercisable political participation rights. Without such protection, basic capabilities of citizens cannot develop. Recognizing that all citizens have these capabilities protected is critical to preserving self-esteem, on Rawls's view. In requiring institutional support for political participation rights, Rawls (1995) rejects the claim that freedom of speech of the rich is unfairly restricted by limiting their personal expenditures on their own political campaigns, a limitation the Supreme Court ruled unconstitutional in *Buckley* v. *Valeo*. After all, the limitation does not unduly burden the rich compared to others. There is evidence that political participation is itself a social determinant of health.

---

[15] Sen (2004) too makes the point that social justice broadly understood is crucial to identifying and addressing health inequity.

Therefore, the Rawlsian ideal assures institutional protections that counter the usual effects of socioeconomic inequalities on participation and thus on health.

The Rawlsian ideal of democratic equality also involves conformity with a principle guaranteeing fair equality of opportunity (see Chapter 2 for a discussion of this principle). Not only is discrimination prohibited by the principle, but it requires strong measures to mitigate the effects of socioeconomic inequalities and other social contingencies on opportunity. In addition to equitable public education, such measures would include developmentally appropriate day care and early childhood interventions to promote the development of capabilities independently of the advantages of family background. Such measures match or go beyond the best models of such interventions we see in European efforts to provide day care and early childhood education. We also note that the strategic importance of education for protecting equal opportunity has implications for all levels of education, including access to graduate and professional education and continuing adult education in a world where work skills must be continuously upgraded.

The equal opportunity principle also requires extensive public health, medical, and social support services aimed at promoting normal functioning for all, as we saw in Chapter 2. It even provides a rationale for the social costs of reasonable accommodation of persons with incurable disabilities, as required by the Americans with Disabilities Act (see Chapter 5). Because the principle aims at promoting normal functioning for *all* as a way of protecting opportunity for all, it aims at both improving population health and reducing health inequalities. Obviously, this requires universal comprehensive health care, including public health, primary health care, and medical and social support services.

To act justly in health policy, we must understand how socioeconomic (and other) inequalities work to produce differential health outcomes. Suppose that, as Marmot (2004) argues, structural and organizational features of the workplace that induce stress and loss of control tend to promote health inequalities. If this is true, then those features should be modified to reduce their negative effects on health as a public health requirement of the equal opportunity approach; this is on a par with the requirement to reduce exposure to toxins in the workplace (see Chapter 7). Moreover, modifying such features would be favored by Rawls's emphasis on securing the social bases of self-respect.

Finally, in the ideal Rawlsian society, the Difference Principle significantly reduces allowable inequalities in income and wealth and, more generally, in the index of primary social goods.[16] The inequalities allowed by this

---

[16] G. A. Cohen (1992) has argued that a *strict* interpretation of the difference principle would allow few incentive-based inequalities; for a more permissive view, see Daniels (2003).

principle (together with the principles assuring equal opportunity and the value of political participation) are probably more constrained than those found in even the most industrialized societies. If so, then the inequalities that conform to the difference principle would produce a flatter gradient of health inequality than we currently observe in even the more extensive welfare systems of Northern Europe.

Earlier, I noted the lively ongoing debate about the effects of income inequality on health inequalities. I believe my claim that the difference principle would flatten gradients more than principles calling for weaker constraints on inequality is true even if the income relativity thesis turns out not to be supported by the evidence. The difference principle is about how well off the worst off are in absolute terms, and though applying it may reduce relative inequality, it would affect mainly health inequalities even if the income relativity thesis does not hold. Those who oppose the income relativity thesis in any event endorse the basic facts about a socioeconomic gradient of health. Pulling the bottom up in absolute terms – coupled with other social policies of the sort assured by the other principles of justice as fairness – would therefore flatten the gradients. If income relativity does have a further effect on health inequalities, then my claim is strengthened further.

In short, Rawls's principles of justice as fairness regulate the distribution of the key social determinants of health, including the social bases of self respect. Nothing about the theory, or my extension of it in Chapter 2, should make us focus narrowly on medical services. Properly understood, justice as fairness tells us what justice requires in distributing all social determinants of health. Nor, I should add, does the fact that we should focus on the distribution of goods in addition to health care mean that health care is no longer of special moral importance. Not only does health care make its own significant contribution to population health, but even if all the other socially controllable factors were properly distributed, some pathology would remain and we would have to respond to its impact on opportunity. Health care may not be the only good of special moral importance, given the moral importance of health, but it remains a good of special moral importance.

Residual Inequalities: Unjust or Not?

We still face an interesting theoretical issue, as well as many practical issues in our nonideal or partially just world. First, the theoretical issue. Even if the Rawlsian distribution of the determinants of health flattens health gradients further than those observed in the most egalitarian developed countries, we must still expect some health inequalities. In part, this may happen because we may not understand all the relevant causes or the interventions for modifying them. The theoretical issue is whether the theory requires us to reduce *further* those otherwise justifiable inequalities because of the inequalities in health status they create.

We should not further reduce those inequalities if doing so reduces productivity so much that we can no longer support the institutional measures we already employ to promote health and reduce health inequality. Our commitment to reducing health inequality should not require steps that threaten to make health worse off for those with less-than-equal health status. So, the theoretical issue reduces to this: Would it ever be reasonable and rational for contractors to accept a trade-off in which some health inequality is allowed in order to produce some nonhealth benefits for those with the worst health prospects?

We know that in real life people routinely trade health risks for other benefits. They do so when they commute longer distances for a better job or take a ski vacation. Some such trades raise questions of fairness. For example, when is hazard pay a benefit workers gain only because their opportunities are unfairly restricted, and when is it an appropriate exercise of their autonomy (see Chapter 7)? Many such trades are ones we think it unjustifiably paternalistic to restrict; others we see as unfair.

Rawlsian contractors, however, cannot base such trades on specific knowledge of their own values. They cannot decide that their enjoyment of skiing makes it worth the risks to their knees or necks. To make the contract fair to all participants, and to achieve impartiality, Rawls imposes a thick "veil of ignorance" that blinds them to all knowledge about themselves, including their views of the good life. Instead, they must judge their well-being by reference to the index of primary social goods (noted earlier) that includes a weighted measure of rights, opportunities, powers, income and wealth, and the social bases of self-respect. But our theoretical question about residual health inequalities reminds us that the theory says too little about the construction of the index to provide us with a clear answer.

One of Rawls's (1971) central arguments for singling out a principle protecting equal basic liberties and giving it (lexical) priority over his other principles of justice is his claim that once people achieve some threshold level of material well-being, they will not trade away the fundamental importance of liberty for other goods. Making such a trade might deny them the liberty to pursue their most cherished ideals, including their religious beliefs, whatever they turn out to be. Can we make the same argument about trading health for other goods?

There is some plausibility to the claim that rational people should not trade health for other goods. Loss of health may prevent us from pursuing what we most value in life. We do, after all, see people willing to trade almost anything to regain health once they lose it.

If we take this argument seriously, we might conclude that Rawls should give opportunity, including the effects of health status, a heavier weighting in the construction of the index than income alone.[17] Such a weighting would mean that absolute increases in income for the worst off that might otherwise have justified increasing relative income inequality, according to the difference principle, now fail to justify those inequalities because of the negative effects on opportunity. Although the income of the worst off would increase, they are not better off according to the whole (weighted) index of primary social goods, and so the greater inequality is not permitted. Rawls's simplifying assumption that income correlates with other goods fails in this case (as it did in the hypothetical example of workplace democracy cited earlier).

Nevertheless, there is also strong reason to think that the priority given to health, and thus opportunity, is not as clear-cut as the previous argument implies, especially where the trade is between a *risk* to health and other goods that people highly value. Refusing to allow any (ex ante) trades of health risks for other goods, even when the background conditions are otherwise fair, may seem unjustifiably paternalistic, perhaps in a way that refusal to allow trades of basic liberties is not.

I propose a pragmatic route around this problem, one that has a precedent elsewhere in Rawls. Fair equality of opportunity, Rawls admits, is only approximated even in an ideally just system, because we can only mitigate, not eliminate, the effects of family and other social contingencies (Fishkin 1983). For example, only if we were willing to violate widely respected parental liberties could we intrude in family life and "rescue" children from parental values that arguably interfere with equal opportunity. Similarly, though we give general priority to equal opportunity over the difference principle, we cannot achieve complete equality in health any more than we can achieve completely equal opportunity. Even ideal theory does not produce perfect justice. Justice is always rough around the edges. Specifically, if we had good reason to think that "democratic equality" had flattened inequalities in accord with the principles of justice, then we might think we had done as much as was reasonable to make health inequalities fair to all. The residual inequalities that emerge with conformance to the principles are not a compromise with what justice ideally requires; they are acceptable as just.

So far, we have been considering whether the decision about such a tradeoff can be resolved from the perspective of individual contractors. Instead, suppose that the decision is to be made by the legislature in a society that conforms to Rawls's principles. Because those principles require effective political participation by all socioeconomic groups, we can suppose that

---

[17] Rawls (1971: 93) does suggest that since fair equality of opportunity is given priority over the difference principle, within the index we can assume that opportunity has a heavier weighting.

the groups most directly affected by any trade-off decision have a voice in the decision. Since there is a residual health *gradient*, groups affected by the trade-off include not only the worst off, but those in the middle as well. Developing a democratic process that involved deliberation about the trade-off and its effects might be the best we could do to answer the theoretical question (see Chapter 4).

In contrast, where the fair value of political participation is not adequately assured – and we doubt that it is so assured in even the most democratic societies – we have much less confidence in the fairness of a democratic decision about how to trade health against other goods. It is much more likely that those who benefit most from the inequalities, that is, those who are better off, also wield disproportionate political power and will influence decisions about trade-offs to serve their interests. It may be that the use of a democratic process in nonideal conditions is the fairest resolution we can practically achieve, but it still falls well short of what an ideally just democratic process would involve.

A BRIEF REMARK ON METHOD

The examination of practical questions in ethics has implications for ethical theory, since influence is not just unidirectional. Rawls's "ideal" theory was formulated in a way that assumed away problems of health. By examining what justice requires in health care, it was possible to revise the theory so that the idealizing assumption could be dropped, thus extending its power. In turn, the extended theory informs practical deliberation about institutional design (see Chapter 9). By connecting recent empirical work on social determinants with the normative theory, we further extend its power.

There may be more here than an extension of scope. When an empirical theory turns out to explain new phenomena that were not part of the evidentiary base for its laws, we tend to conclude that the concepts incorporated in it are "projectible" in a desired way. We may think of them as better confirmed as a way of dividing up or describing the world. Rawls began with certain political concepts thought crucial to our well-being – to meeting our needs as free and equal citizens of a democracy. Using these ideas, the goal was to select terms of cooperation that all free and equal citizens could agree are fair and reasonable. It then turns out, in light of the social science literature, that the aspects of well-being captured by these ideas expand to include the health of the population as well. Whatever controversy may surround some of these political components of well-being, they do connect – albeit empirically – to an incontrovertibly objective component of our social well-being, namely, the health of the population. If this were an empirical rather than a normative theory, we would think that the evidence of projectibility counted in its favor and constituted support for the theory. Is there additional support for Rawls's theory?

One view is that there is not. If the facts about population health turned out to be different, so that socioeconomic inequality did not produce the health gradients we observe, then we would not be inclined to say that there was less support for Rawls's political theory. Instead, we would say that these kinds of facts should not matter to the support of the theory. The proponent of this view might still say that the theory has the resources to respond to the actual facts, and that it can answer questions it was not originally designed to answer. But there is no extra support here because, if the facts were different, we would not have subtracted support from the theory.

There is another way to view the situation. True, we might not reduce the support we now give the theory if the facts were different about the relationship between socioeconomic inequality and health. This does not, however, mean that we should not increase the support we think the theory has if it turns out to have the projectibility described earlier. Lack of evidence of greater projectibility is not evidence against a theory; it is and should be a neutral finding. If, however, we found that population health was undermined by greater political well-being of the sort the original theory talked about (before its extension), then we would have a puzzle to address. Why is one aspect of our well-being working in opposition to other elements of it?[18]

This discussion is admittedly too brief to establish a firm conclusion, but I am inclined to think that there is some support for Rawls's theory from the fact that it generalizes to population health in this way. It is the coherence among these different areas of evidence and principle that gives us grounds for thinking that the theory has additional justification (Daniels 1996a). This does not mean, of course, that objections to the theory, which I have deliberately not addressed, should be ignored. Despite this view about increased support, my appeal to Rawls is intended primarily to provide an illustration, not an endorsement.

Why Has Bioethics Ignored the Social Determinants of Health?

The general answer that emerges to the second Focal Question is that a health inequality is an inequity if it is the result of an unjust distribution of the socially controllable factors affecting population health and its distribution.

---

[18] This point provides an answer to an objection Sudhir Anand and Fabienne Peter (personal communication, 2001) raise: Since my extension of Rawls's equal opportunity principle to cover health care implies that we should view as health-care needs whatever is involved in the promotion of normal functioning, as in Chapter 2, why invoke the rest of Rawls's principles? Are they needed? If conformance with the principles of justice made our health worse, strong tension would emerge between the fair equality of opportunity principle account of the importance of health and health care and the way in which Rawls's principles distribute the social determinants of (poor) health. Two aspects of well-being would be pulled in opposite directions. That they pull together in this world makes the appeal to the full range of Rawls's principles interesting and not a mere redundancy.

A good illustration of a just distribution of those factors is offered by Rawls's principles of justice as fairness. My use of a Rawlsian illustration is not intended to be exclusive, and I noted earlier that Sen (2004) similarly suggests that we need to appeal to a view about social justice to say when a health inequality is an inequity. I conclude this discussion by returning to an issue raised earlier: the failure of bioethics to look upstream from medicine to the social determinants of health and health inequalities and to matters of social justice more generally.

The failure of bioethics to look at the social determinants of population health is not primarily a philosophical failing, nor is it simply disciplinary blindness to the social science or public health literature. Rather, people in bioethics, like the public more generally, concentrate on medical care rather than social determinants for complex sociological, political, and ideological reasons that we can only mention here. The public, encouraged by scientists and the media, is fascinated by every new biomedical discovery and has come to believe that our "success" in improving population health is entirely or largely the result of exotic science. Vast economic interests benefit from keeping the public and the field of bioethics focused on this scenario. The economic incentives to people in bioethics come largely from medicine and the scientific and policy institutions that interact with medical delivery. The idea that scientific medicine is responsible for our health blinds us to socioeconomic inequality as a source of worse population health. Science, we are told, can rescue us all from our shared biological fate. Therefore, we should all unite in supporting a focus on medicine and, if we care about justice, on the equitable access of all to its benefits. Challenging deeper inequalities in society, however, is divisive, not unifying, and it threatens those with the greatest power and the most to lose. In the absence of well-organized social movements capable of challenging that inequality, the complaints of public health advocates pointing out the need for more basic change, rather than simply joining existing forces asking for more and better medical care, may seem utopian. However, it remains important to point to the broader ways in which social justice underlies public health (Daniels 2007a).

4

How Can We Meet Health Needs Fairly When We Can't Meet Them All?

Accountability for Reasonable Resource Allocation

Knowing that health is of special moral importance because of its impact on opportunity gives us general guidance in the design of systems that meet health needs. Similarly, knowing that achieving equity in health requires broader social justice gives us general guidance about social policy that impacts health. Unfortunately, this general guidance does not tell us how to meet health needs fairly when we cannot meet them all, our third Focal Question. The general principles of justice for health that we have been discussing are simply too general and too indeterminate to resolve many reasonable disputes about how to allocate resources fairly to meet health needs, and we lack a consensus on more fine-grained principles. Moreover, we cannot avoid this problem. It arises in all health systems whether or not they meet other basic requirements of justice – for example, whether or not they provide universal access to preventive and curative public health and medical services.

The moral controversy that surrounds the creation of winners and losers in resource allocation decisions results in a *legitimacy problem:* Under what conditions do decision makers have the *moral authority* to set the limits they impose? To solve this legitimacy problem and to answer the third Focal Question, we must supplement general *principles* of justice with a fair *process* for setting limits.[1] Such a process holds decision makers accountable for the reasonableness of the limits they set. Our characterization of a fair process

---

[1] Were this book about the theory of justice in general, I would have to explain why I am opposed to using a democratic deliberative process to derive all aspects of justice (Daniels 1999); instead, in this account of justice and health, I am simply invoking it to supplement the problems left unaddressed by the principled account developed thus far in Part I.

Material for this chapter draws on several earlier publications coauthored with James Sabin (1997, 2002), and on Daniels (1993). I greatly appreciate that multiyear collaboration and the chance to incorporate that material here.

must be general enough to apply in both developed and developing countries and in health systems with public, private, and mixed organizational forms, though, of course, details will have to fit the institutional context. I return to some of these applications in later chapters.

THE NEED FOR LIMIT SETTING

First, I must show that setting limits is a general requirement of justice, not something we must regrettably do only in countries with few resources and should resist doing in wealthier ones. It may seem paradoxical that an account focused on the claim that meeting health needs is of special moral importance because of their impact on opportunity implies that we must nevertheless set limits to meeting these needs. However, although health is important to the protection of opportunity, it is not the only good that is important in this way. Many things affect and protect our exercisable opportunities – education, job training, job creation – even law and order. We must make reasonable decisions about how to support all these and other opportunity-promoting measures with the resources we have.

Opportunity is also not the only important social good. Basic liberties must also be protected, including institutions that assure people that they can effectively exercise them, especially their right of political participation. Further, opportunity is expanded as we increase societal wealth and knowledge. As a result, decisions about economic growth rates and social policies that affect them are tightly linked to decisions that affect the levels of health needs and the resources available to meet them. However important health care is, we must weigh it against other goods and other ways of promoting opportunity. Investing in health care has opportunity costs even though it helps to promote opportunity.

Even if setting limits is in general necessary, isn't it unfair to limit meeting health needs as a result of avoidable waste or inefficiency or even profits? Creating losers unnecessarily surely seems unfair. For example, some point to the fact of profit taking, and of marketing and other overhead costs in the United States, as sources of unfair or unjustifiable limits on resources.[2] Some health plans in the United States, especially for-profit plans, spend as much as 25 to 30 percent of every premium dollar on nonmedical benefits. These dollars go to marketing, administrative costs, and returns to investors. If so much of their premium revenue is drained into costs that deliver no direct benefit to patients, then how can we tolerate the limits these plans set on beneficial services? This complaint has great power and resonates with many practitioners, who believe it gives them an excuse to "game the system"

---

[2] In the American system, it is especially hard to "say no" (or set limits) because "savings" are not part of a closed system of resource allocation in which physicians can be confident that they will do more good elsewhere (Daniels 1986).

and find ways to benefit patients by breaking or avoiding rules intended to contain costs.

To this critique of profit-driven cost containment I reply that one injustice does not justify another. While making systems more efficient will contribute to their fairness overall (Daniels et al. 1996, Daniels, Bryant, Castano, Dantes, Khan, and Pannarunothai, 2000; Daniels et al. 2005, and Chapter 9), this does not mean that we should avoid allocating available resources in a fair, publicly accountable way. Avoiding discussion of how to set limits fairly thus risks adding unfair limit setting to a system that is already unfair in other ways. The fact of nonideal conditions in any system – inefficiency, profit taking at the expense of meeting needs, lack of universal coverage – does not exempt us from the task of learning how to set limits fairly.

Limit Setting and Moral Controversy

Decisions to limit meeting health needs are made by many different people at different levels within the health-care system and society more generally – from insurance plans that require patients to try less expensive remedies before covering an expensive new treatment, to provincial health directors who use funds to upgrade surgical facilities at the provincial hospital rather than to provide adequate physicians for rural health centers, to highway planners who trade safety for cost in a highway curve. These decisions have a broad range of consequences, some significant, some barely noticeable, for patients and the public. Despite the range of effects that setting limits can have, they share two critical features. First, though all of them may be considered medical, technical, or contractual, they all rest on value judgments *about which reasonable people may disagree*. Second, general principles of justice do not resolve many of these controversies. The opportunity principle defended in Chapter 2 simply cannot answer a central resource allocation question such as "How much priority should we give to treating the sickest or most disabled patients?" Exploring this question in some depth will illustrate my point.

To start with, imagine two extreme positions. At one extreme is the view that we should give priority to treating the worst-off patients. One might think that the fair equality of opportunity principle, or other views that give priority to those with the worst opportunity, would lead us to this extreme position. At the other extreme is the view that we should give priority to whatever treatment produces the greatest net health benefit (or greatest net health benefit per dollar spent), regardless of which patients we treat. Some utilitarian views are committed to this principle, and it is embedded in standard methods for calculating the cost-effectiveness of alternative treatments.

These extreme positions have different implications for specific resource allocation decisions. Suppose that a health plan or a public agency operated under a fixed budget and could invest $1 million in providing treatment A to one group of patients or treatment B to another group of patients, and suppose that the investment in equipment and personnel requires that we devote the $1 million to either A or B, not to some of each. The extreme view that says we should give complete priority to the worst off settles the matter by determining whether patients needing A are worse off than patients needing B. No attention is then paid to the outcomes for either group of patients. The other extreme view settles the matter by asking only what the outcomes are: We should invest in whichever technology produces the net maximum benefit, regardless of how badly off people are before they are treated.

In practice, most people reject both extreme positions. This fact emerges in both moral and empirical examinations of these kinds of cases (Nord 1999; Dolan et al. 2005). Though many people end up agreeing that some, but not complete, priority should be given to those who are sickest, there is also considerable disagreement. A distinct but small minority adheres to one or the other extreme position. Those in the middle differ in their degree of commitment to helping those who are worst off. They may want to help the worst off provided that the benefits others must then sacrifice are not too great, but there is a range of beliefs, backed by reasons, about what level of sacrifice is too great. Once we abandon either extreme position, we are in an area where general principles give no guidance. Because they give no guidance, we need a fair process to resolve disputes among the various views for which people will argue.

Similar points emerge if we consider this problem: When should we allow an *aggregation* of modest benefits to larger numbers of people to outweigh more significant benefits to fewer people (Kamm 1987, 1993; Daniels 1993) For example, when – if ever – should curing a large number of minor headaches outweigh adding thirty healthy years to a small number of lives? One extreme position is that we should maximize aggregate health bene-fits, allowing all possible ways of doing so. The utilitarian underpinnings of standard cost-effectiveness analysis may drive us to this extreme position. The opposite extreme position is that we should never allow the aggrega-tion of benefits, even when we are considering benefits of the same type: We should not, for example, save five lives in preference to saving three except by lottery.

In the United States, we have an actual example of the public rejection of the extreme view that any aggregation is permissible in the pursuit of maximum benefits. In June 1990, the Oregon Health Services Commission released a list of treatment/condition pairs ranked by a cost–benefit calcu-lation as part of an effort to rationalize Medicaid benefits. Critics were quick to seize on rankings that seemed completely counterintuitive. For example, capping teeth was ranked higher than – more important than – appendec-tomy (Hadorn 1991). The reason was simple: An appendectomy then cost many times the price of capping a tooth. Simply aggregating the net medical benefit of many capped teeth yielded a net benefit greater than that produced by one appendectomy. Ultimately, the Oregon Health Services Commission revised its methodology, placing whole categories of services that delivered major benefits to seriously ill patients out of reach of this form of universal aggregating.

The aggregation problem is a case in which the equal opportunity account, like the broader family of views we noted earlier, ends up giving answers that are indeterminate. Our account focuses on using resources to promote normal functioning as a specific, limited way of protecting the opportunity range (or capability sets) of individuals. Accordingly, we will have to pay attention to the significant gains in opportunity that come from concentrating resources on those with significant deficits, and this account may plausibly refuse to allow those gains to be outweighed by many trivial gains to others. It must also not ignore the loss of opportunity of those with moderate conditions, and therefore it must permit some kinds of aggregation. [3] Unfortunately, our account remains too indeterminate to be of help in resolving disputes about which aggregations can best protect fair equality of opportunity under resource constraints.

One further type of problem illustrates the same point: How much should we favor producing the *best outcome* with our limited resources as opposed to giving people a *fair chance* of deriving some benefit from them? A utilitarian account might opt directly for maximizing the expected payoff, directing resources to the patient group with the greatest expected benefit. A more egalitarian approach, or one that gave more weight to the subjective value that each person would place on the level of benefit that might be possible for her, might favor a lottery giving equal chances to all who might in any way benefit. In the philosophical literature on this topic, a number of middle positions have been defended, including calls for proportional or weighted lotteries. In such a lottery, people with greater expected benefits are given more chances to get the treatment than those with lesser expected benefits (Brock 1988; Kamm 1993).[4]

Perhaps we are looking in the wrong place when we look to general accounts of distributive justice for principles that would allow us to solve these three "unsolved" rationing problems or other morally controversial

---

[3] Some philosophers reject aggregation even in these cases, insisting that we rely solely on pairwise comparisons among competitors, ignoring the relative number of people in each category (Scanlon 1998). For my argument here, it suffices that such views remain deeply controversial.

[4] There is some arbitrariness to the precision that results from such weighted lotteries, since there is no plausible theory telling us just how much weight to give to providing equal or fair chances versus favoring outcomes. This arbitrariness would seem less troublesome if the weightings were determined by a fair, deliberative process of the sort argued for in this chapter.

problems about limits. If we need more fine-grained principles to apply to cases like these, perhaps we should start with the cases. Later, we can try to find acceptable principles for them.

Pursuing such a strategy, Kamm (1993) proposes that we examine carefully selected hypothetical cases that sound quite fantastical to nonphilosophers rather than examining real cases with all their complexity. By varying these simplified cases, which function as thought experiments, she hopes to uncover the underlying moral structure or "inner program," as she puts it, of our beliefs (cf. Daniels 1998c). For example, we definitely view some utilities or benefits we might gain as trivial and incomparable to those involved in saving lives. Thus, we would not decide which of two people to save because, by saving one rather than the other, we can additionally cure a sore throat. Curing the sore throat is an "irrelevant utility." Losing a leg or an arm, however, is a significant loss, and Kamm's examination of hypothetical cases yields the judgment that we rightly give higher proportional chances to saving a life and a leg than to just saving a life. Even though we would prefer to save a single life rather than a single leg, Kamm concludes that we should agree to give some proportional chance to saving many legs rather than one life. At the macro level of resource allocation, Kamm continues, we should be willing to forego helping a few people who might die if we did not cure their diseases in order to help a much larger number of people who would lose legs.

Whether fine-grained principles such as those Kamm argues for ultimately provide the basis for a consensus on fair distribution, they are not likely to do so in the short or middle term. Since we have no prior consensus on fine-grained principles that solve these rationing problems, they cannot substitute for a fair process for resolving disputes in the real time of decision makers. This kind of inquiry, however, provides excellent input into a fair, deliberative process. Encouraging this kind of investigation and the dissemination of its results will enhance the quality of deliberation about limits in whatever fair process is constructed.

Moral Legitimacy and Fair Process

Since questions about the fairness and legitimacy of limit setting are appropriately posed from the perspective of those whose health needs are not met because others' needs are met instead, we should ask: Why or when – under what conditions – should patients or clinicians or members (or drivers, as in the earlier highway planning example) who think an uncovered service (or unprotected risk) is appropriate or even medically necessary accept as legitimate the limit-setting decision of a health plan or district authority (or highway planner)? The legitimacy problem asks, "Under what conditions should moral authority over these matters be placed in the hands of private organizations, such as health plans, or in the hands of the administrators who make such decisions in public agencies?" This is not just a question about *who* makes the decisions, for example, about whether they have conflicts of interest when they make them. It is about *how* the decisions are made. Must legitimate authorities, for example, openly share the reasons for their decisions, or is it enough for them to publicly announce the results of their deliberations?

The legitimacy and fairness problems are distinct issues of justice. A legitimate authority can act unfairly, and an illegitimate one can deliver fair decisions. Still, they are related. We may reasonably accept an authority as legitimate only if it abides by a procedure or process or even substantive constraints (e.g., constitutional protections) that we consider generally fair. If it abandons the fair procedure, it may lose its legitimacy. Similarly, if an authority that claims no legitimacy employs a fair procedure, especially where there may be prior disagreement about what counts as a fair outcome, we may not only accept the outcome as fair but even ascribe it legitimacy if the authority acts consistently.

If we have no consensus on principles capable of resolving disputes about resource allocation for health and health care, then we must find a fair process whose outcomes we can accept as just or fair. The fair process addresses the legitimacy problem as well. This is a classic appeal to procedural justice, but it is important to see the specific role assigned to it.

In Rawls's theory of justice as fairness, he views the whole social contract construction that leads to the selection of the principles as an example of procedural justice (see Chapter 2).[5] In that case, we have no consensus on how to resolve classic conflicts in liberal political philosophy between claims of liberty and claims of equality. Finding a process for selecting principles that is fair to all parties making choices – to all of us, regardless of who we are or what we bring to the table – is the task of properly designing the social contract situation. One result of Rawls's strategy is a defense of the general principle of fair equality of opportunity that I

---

[5] Rawls distinguishes *pure* procedural justice from both *perfect* and *imperfect* procedural justice. In both perfect and imperfect procedural justice, a prior criterion exists for what counts as a desired outcome. Suppose that a fair outcome for dividing a birthday cake is to give equal pieces to all children. If we assume that the birthday child can cut the cake into equal parts and desires as big a piece as possible, then if this child is required to take the last piece, we have a case of perfect procedural justice. A criminal trial is an example of imperfect procedural justice. There is a prior criterion: All and only those who committed crimes in the right state of mind are convicted. But trials are only generally successful at determining who fits that description. In contrast, in pure procedural justice, we have no prior criterion for what counts as a just outcome. Rawls's social contract is intended to be an example of pure procedural justice. The fair process I seek will turn out to be pure as long as we have no consensus on fine-grained distributive principles; it will be imperfect at best for anyone who insists that some particular principle tells us what the just outcome should be.

drew on to provide support for the analysis of health and opportunity I propose.

My appeal to procedural justice to supplement that opportunity principle is not an abandonment of the principle, which serves well enough to guide thinking about more basic design features of the health-care systems. Rather, fair process is needed to resolve disputes about allocation that are not addressed by the more general principle. Such disputes are still matters of distributive justice.

THREE INADEQUATE APPROACHES TO FAIR PROCESS

Three familiar ways of trying to address the legitimacy and fairness problems prove inadequate, though each provides some insight into elements of a proper account.

Market Accountability

One idea prominent in the United States and some other countries with large private health-care sectors is that there is nothing unfair or illegitimate about the limits we encounter when we make informed purchases of health insurance. Indeed, in this view, we each legitimize these limits with our purchase of an insurance plan just as we do when we buy a car. As long as there is clear coverage language in subscriber contracts, there is no special problem of legitimacy facing health plans that make limit-setting decisions any more than there is a problem of legitimacy facing automobile manufacturers when they make decisions regarding product features and design. If a car manufacturer makes cost-cutting decisions that affect the quality of a product, the market provides a mechanism for putting a price on that decision and allowing consumers to match their preferences with the price of products. Although some safety features of automobiles are mandated by law, and although consumer protection legislation provides some further defense against duplicitous practices by car manufacturers, we already have similar protections in the case of health care through insurance law and tort litigation. Beyond that, the market – for cars or health insurance – provides an efficient mechanism for matching consumer preferences to market share. Accordingly, if consumers do not like the limit-setting decisions of a medical insurer, they are free to purchase other medical insurance that better meets their preferences. The obligation of the insurer, like that of the auto manufacturer, is to be honest and forthright about the features of the product, eschewing deception. There is no further obligation to provide access to a process of decision making to make sure that it meets some standard of fairness that plays no role in a market economy.

The analogy to purchasing a car fails for several reasons. First, uncertainty is a much greater factor in markets for medical insurance than it is in markets for autos (Arrow 1963). With cars, we have a good idea of what our needs are (how many passengers, driving style, etc.) and reasonably good information about outcomes (gas mileage, service record, etc.). We have much greater trouble anticipating our needs for health care, and we have not yet developed an adequate technology for reporting on the quality of health plans. Second, most Americans receive their health insurance through their employers, who select the health plans for their employees. The market ideology that says that people consent with their purchases to the limits that insurers impose on them does not reflect the actual situation of most insured Americans, who cannot practically "vote with their dollars" even if (in theory) that would constitute consent. If they are lucky enough to have insurance at all, it comes with the job, and the only choice they have is to change jobs, if they can. Nor should we say that we consent to the terms of the medical insurance policy because we consent to having our employer select our insurance coverage for us. Although some employers may seek a plan that produces good value for money, it would be naive to think that an employer's interest in containing costs can always be translated without controversy into an employee's interest in accepting compromises in coverage. The employer is not the employee's fiduciary agent (cf. Fuchs and Emanuel 2005). Third, we have a widely recognized moral obligation to meet people's medical needs, within reasonable resource constraints, but we do not have a social obligation to meet people's preferences or needs for autos.

Nevertheless, there is something useful in the idea of market accountability, namely, its requirement that people be adequately informed about the choices they face – or the limited options they have. The fair process I describe shortly builds on this goal of providing adequate information and carries it an important step further. It will turn out that it is crucial to understand the rationales for limit-setting decisions, not simply the options that limits give us.

"Majority Rule" and Fair Process

If we must rely on a fair process, some may ask, what is the mystery? Citizens use democratic procedures and majority rule – directly or indirectly – to resolve other policy disputes. Why not adopt the same solution to limit setting for health care?

The democratic process should be the ultimate authority for settling disputes about limit setting in health care, but we should understand that process in a particular way if it is to have legitimacy as a way of resolving moral disputes about the distribution of health care. Some of the conditions I describe shortly as necessary elements of a fair process draw heavily on a particular conception of democratic legitimacy. It emphasizes the *deliberative* component of the democratic process, not merely a procedural appeal to majority rule (Sunstein 1993; J. Cohen 1994, 1996a,b; Rawls 1995; Gutmann and Thompson 1996; Estlund 1997).

What gives majority (or plurality) rule its legitimacy as a procedure for resolving moral disputes about public policy and the design of institutions? One prominent answer, sometimes referred to as the "aggregative" conception of democracy (J. Cohen 1996a: 14), holds that the procedure is fair and acquires legitimacy simply because it counts everyone's interests equally in the voting process. Adults are presumed to be the best judges of their own interests, and can present and advance them in the political process.

Something important is left out of this proceduralist view of the virtues of aggregation through voting. It allows us to compel people to abide by a majority rule, even where there are matters of fundamental moral disagreement, simply by aggregating the *preferences* of the voters, whatever they happen to be.[6] In a large group with the option of buying only one flavor of ice cream, vanilla or chocolate, we might settle the dispute by voting. Everyone's interests are counted, since the frustration of, say, vanilla lovers is offset by the greater aggregate pleasure of chocolate lovers.

A majority decision that compels people to act in ways counter to their fundamental beliefs about what is morally right is not like frustrating a taste for vanilla ice cream, however. Settling moral disputes simply by aggregating preferences ignores some fundamental differences between values and preferences, since ideally we would like to resolve moral disputes through argument and deliberation about reasons that we consider convincing. When a good moral argument persuades us that our original belief about what is right is incorrect, we may be chagrined, but we should be grateful as well for being spared doing what is wrong. It is more important to end up knowing what is right and doing it, given our motivation to act in ways that we can justify morally, than it is to get our way. This observation helps to explain why, in cases of moral disagreement, we are not satisfied simply to be told that "a majority of people think otherwise." Majorities can be morally wrong and may make us do the wrong thing. In addition, they may be moved by reasons that minorities cannot even accept as relevant to resolving the dispute. The aggregative account fails as an account of the legitimacy of a democratic procedure because it ignores the way reasons play a role in our deliberations about what is right.

A deliberative view of democratic legitimacy imposes some constraints on the kinds of reasons that can play a role in deliberation. Reasons must

---

[6] Joshua Cohen notes that an aggregative view might arguably be extended to give some protection against outcomes that involved discrimination against targets of stereotyping or hostility, e.g., against people with disabilities or racial minorities. A process that allowed simple aggregation of those preferences arguably does not give people equal consideration and so violates its own rationale (J. Cohen 1996b: 15).

reflect the fact that all parties to a decision are viewed as seeking terms of fair cooperation that all can accept as reasonable. Where their well-being or fundamental liberties or other matters of fundamental value are involved and at risk, people should not be expected to accept binding terms of cooperation that rest on types of reasons they find unacceptable. For example, reasons that rest on matters of religious faith will not meet this condition. Reasonable people differ in their religious, philosophical, and moral views, and yet we must seek terms of fair cooperation that rest on justifications acceptable to all.

A deliberation that appeals only to the kinds of reasons that all can recognize as acceptable or relevant may still not arrive at a consensus. To settle the practical matter, we must still rely on a majority (or perhaps a supermajority) vote. Relying on a majority vote to settle the matter nevertheless has an important advantage over the purely proceduralist (or aggregative) account. The minority is not being compelled to do something for reasons it thinks irrelevant or inappropriate – even if it does not accept the weight or balance given to various considerations by the majority. On the aggregative view, the minority has to accept that it loses only because more people prefer an alternative, for whatever reasons. On the deliberative democracy view, the minority can at least assure itself that *the preference of the majority rests on the kind of reason that even the minority must acknowledge appropriately plays a role in the deliberation.* The majority does not exercise brute power of preference, but is constrained by having to seek reasons for its view that are justifiable to all who seek mutually justifiable terms of cooperation.

The constraints on reasons that are involved in accountability for reasonableness have a similar effect. This is true even though the decision-making procedure is often itself not a democratic one, especially when it takes place in a privately controlled health plan. Still, if the private health plan publicly reveals the grounds for its decisions, and these reasons are relevant to deciding how to meet varied patient needs under resource constraints, then even those who disagree with specific decisions should acknowledge that they are reasonable decisions aimed at producing fair outcomes. If everyone affected by these decisions should acknowledge this, then decision makers are well on their way to earning or achieving legitimacy for their process. We are getting ahead of our story, however, and should return to consider one further alternative.

Empirical Ethics and a Cost-Value Methodology

The third alternative to constructing a fair process is to develop an ethically sensitive, empirically based methodology for making resource allocation decisions. If the methodology incorporates social values, as measured by social scientists, then decision makers using it can be confident that the results reflect what the public considers acceptable. Such a methodology would be usable at many levels in a system and would yield results that are publicly accountable.

A starting point for such an approach might be traditional cost-effectiveness (or "cost-utility") analysis (CEA). The technique requires converting all effects of an intervention on both mortality and morbidity into one outcome measure (such as the QALY or the DALY). Then all costs are calculated and a ratio of costs to effects is determined. With proper standardization, the ratios can then be used to compare a broad range of interventions on different categories of patients. If we select the best cost-effectiveness ratio, we are maximizing the health benefits we gain by spending additional dollars.

Unfortunately, that methodology carries with it some morally controversial – and, many insist, unacceptable – assumptions (Brock 1998; Nord 1999; Hausman 2006; IOM 2006). One key assumption with troubling consequences is that a unit of benefit, such as a QALY or DALY, has the same worth regardless of who gets it. Yet, it may well matter morally to us that someone who is much more ill gets the extra benefit rather than someone less ill. We may also be unwilling to aggregate minor benefits across large populations in order to outweigh major benefits, such as saving lives, for a few. As we noted earlier, (admittedly crude) cost-effectiveness rankings of medical treatments led to publicly unacceptable results in the Oregon effort at establishing funding priorities for Medicaid.

When we select an intervention – be it a screening protocol or a drug regimen or a rule regulating air pollution – because it has the best cost-effectiveness ratio among the alternatives, we are maximizing health benefits at the margin per dollar spent, regardless of how the benefits are distributed. To summarize some earlier points, consider three ways this maximizing strategy conflicts with concerns about equity. First, it gives no priority to those who are worse off or in greater need. Most people want to give some priority to those who are worse off even if they do not want to give them complete priority. Second, CEA allows us to aggregate minor benefits to larger numbers of people so that they outweigh significant benefits to fewer people. Yet, even though most people accept some forms of aggregation, they reject unrestricted aggregation, refusing to allow, for example, lifesaving treatments to a few to be outweighed by very minor benefits to the many. Third, CEA doggedly pursues "best outcomes" while denying fair chances for some benefit to those with worse outcomes. Yet, most people reject a strict maximizing strategy, preferring to give people a fair chance of receiving some benefit. We have considerable trouble agreeing on what the appropriate middle ground is in each of these priorities, aggregation, and best outcomes/fair chances problems, and we have no prior consensus on principles that can resolve these problems. Because of the way in which CEA ignores distributive and other value issues, CEA by itself cannot serve as a decision procedure, even if it can be a useful input into one.

Some propose that we should modify a cost-effectiveness analysis so that it avoids this kind of moral objection. We might, through empirical study, provide "ethical weights" for outcomes so that they reflect public values about the kinds of trade-offs involved in medical resource allocation (Williams 1997; Menzel et al.1999; cf. Haninger 2006). Alternatively, we might abandon traditional cost-effectiveness methodology and substitute for it an empirically based "cost-value" approach (Nord 1999).

How might we measure people's values so that we can tell what kinds of trade-offs they would approve in resource allocation decisions? One proposal is to survey people by asking them about the "person trade-offs" they are willing to make when they face hypothetical forced choices as medical resource allocators (Nord 1999).[7] Suppose we know that we can fund only one kind of medical service, A or B. Treatment A affects people with a more serious prior condition than the people treated by B. We can ask people when they would trade treating X number of people by A for treating Y number of people by B. The claim is that these person-trade-off questions uncover directly the value to people of one service as opposed to the other, given the information people have about initial health states and health outcomes. With improvements in the survey methods, we could gather information about a broad range of trade-offs that people are willing to make.

There are important concerns about this methodology and the values we can extract from it. Its proponents are aware, for example, that the values people assign are very much affected by the way questions are framed, giving rise to "starting point biases." If the same surveys are repeated, there is variation in the answers, meaning that "test-retest validity" is problematic. There is also considerable variation in the responses people give within a population, and there is evidence that these variations correlate with attitudes – for example, with political affiliation (Nord 1999: 130). Ignoring this variation, say by using a median within the range of answers people give, risks ignoring the moral disagreement underlying it. This problem raises a serious worry about the degree to which the empirical results could be used to substitute for actual deliberation by decision makers.

Suppose, however, that we find considerable convergence in a population (or subgroup) on the magnitudes involved in trade-offs. What should we make of it? Is this prevalent preference the equivalent to a predominant taste for chocolate over vanilla ice cream? Or is it a considered value of the sort that emerges in moral deliberation? In large-scale surveys, it is less likely that we can capture reflective values. On the other hand, developing and deploying more complex methods involving a series of questions may uncover evidence about what *reasons* people give weight to, and not simply their unconsidered *preferences*, but it does so at the risk of sampling far fewer

---

[7] The approach is a variation on a standard economic approach seeking "indifference" points or curves indicating when an individual finds two benefits or outcomes equivalent.

people. Current methodologies fall short of what would be needed by sampling too few of by inadequately eliciting new values from larger numbers.

Setting aside these methodological worries, there remains a normative objection to this empirical approach. This Anthropological Objection asks: "*So what* if we happen to have these preferences (that empirical researchers call values)? *Should* we hold them? We could, after all, have had others. No doubt other cultures, or subgroups within our own, have different preferences. Can we defend them morally, or can we only say that this is what *we* happen to prefer?" The objection invites us to place the information the empirical investigation gives us in a more deliberative context, which is exactly what we are proposing.

We might attempt a Democratic Reply to the Anthropological Objection. If we had good evidence about what the public believed about these matters, then we might be able to construct a socially acceptable table giving weights to types of outcomes and use this table as a *proxy* for more direct democratic decision making. Policy makers responsible for resource allocation decisions could try to establish legitimacy for their decisions by saying that they reflect what the public believes should be done.

The Democratic Reply must be rejected if it is taken literally. Simple democratic voting, or the proxy for voting embodied in the person trade-off or some other survey method, faces the objections that we raised earlier, at least when we are concerned with moral disagreements. Merely aggregating preferences through voting or surveying ends up making majority might determine what is right, with no real constraints on the kinds of reasons that play a role in the decision. In moral disagreements, we want people to bring reasons to bear in an effort to persuade each other.

We want instead a deliberative process that takes seriously the considerations people bring to a dispute. A dispute that is resolved by democratic procedures after careful deliberation about the various reasons put forward on both sides has in its favor the fact that *even losers will know that their beliefs about what is right were taken seriously by others*. This deliberative component of fair democratic process is missing if we simply think of the weightings generated by person trade-offs as a proxy for voting.

Nevertheless, if people responsible for decision making at various levels within a health-care system view the results of a refined person trade-off study as an input to their deliberation, then we can retain the deliberative component of fair democratic process. This is the more plausible scenario for using this information.[8] Including the results of unmodified cost-effectiveness analyses in a deliberative process could also be of some use. In a fully deliberative context, the disturbing – and many would say unfair – implications of cost-effectiveness analysis could at least be introduced

---

[8] Eric Nord (personal communication) suggests that this is how he believes this kind of information should be used, as an input to a fair, deliberative process.

and the value of the analysis assessed in light of those concerns. In the absence of an open deliberative process, however, cost-effectiveness analysis carries the risk that important distributive concerns will be ignored. Without corrective deliberation, cost-effectiveness analysis is an inadequate framework for decision making.[9]

ACCOUNTABILITY FOR REASONABLENESS

Several ways of addressing or avoiding the legitimacy and fairness problems – the philosophical search for fine-grained distributive principles, market accountability, the majority rule approach, or the survey of public attitudes – give us important clues to the components of a fair process for setting priorities among health needs, but they do not substitute for it. In the rest of this chapter, I shall try to characterize the general conditions such a process must meet if it is to yield outcomes that are perceived as fair and legitimate. My account should be general in two ways. It should be appropriate for publicly administered systems or agencies as well as for private health plans within a mixed system. It should also work for limits to medical services as well as for broader issues of health needs, such as those that arise in public health and regulatory settings where population health is the explicit goal, as well as in non-health-sector decisions where there is a significant impact on health.

The fair process I propose aims for a robust form of public accountability. Specifically, "accountability for reasonableness" is the idea that the reasons or rationales for important limit-setting decisions should be publicly available. In addition, these reasons must be ones that fair-minded people can agree are relevant for appropriate patient care under resource constraints (Daniels and Sabin 1998a). This central thesis needs some explanation, for it is quite different from the more familiar and less demanding idea of market accountability discussed earlier.

By "fair-minded" people, I do not simply mean my friends or people who happen to agree with me. I mean people who seek to cooperate with others on terms they can justify to each other. Indeed, fair-minded people accept rules of the game – or sometimes seek rule changes – that promote the game's essential skills and the excitement their use produces. For example, they want rules that permit blocking in football, but not clipping or grabbing face masks, because they want to encourage teamwork and skill, not the mere advantage that comes from imposing injuries. Of course, having rules of a game that fair-minded people accept does not eliminate all controversy about their application. It does, however, narrow the scope of controversy and the methods for adjudicating it.

9 The position taken here is very briefly discussed in Gold et al. (1996) and is developed further in IOM (2006: Ch. 4).

In the "game" of delivering health care or meeting a broader set of health needs, fair-minded people will seek reasons ("rules") they can accept as relevant to meeting health needs fairly under resource constraints. As in football, the rules shape a conception of the common good that is the goal of cooperation within plans, even when plans compete. In the allocation of health resources, as in football, some will seek "mere advantage" by ignoring the rules, or by seeking rules that advantage only them, and there will be disagreement about how to apply the rules. Still, the fair-minded search for mutually acceptable rules narrows the scope of disagreement and provides the grounds on which disputes can be adjudicated.

Accountability for reasonableness obviously goes beyond what is required by market accountability alone. Market accountability requires only that we be informed about the options insurers give us and about their record of performance. Accountability for reasonableness requires that we also know the reasons for the insurer's (or government agency's) policies and decisions, and that these policies and decisions be based on the kinds of reasons fair-minded people consider relevant in providing high-quality care to all with limited resources. Market accountability leaves it to the consumer to infer from the choices available what commitments a health plan has to responsible patient-centered care. Accountability for reasonableness requires that there be a way to reconsider decisions when their application in specific cases is problematic. It also requires a mechanism to revise and improve decisions over time as we learn from experience. In these ways, accountability for reasonableness requires the health plan or public agency to be explicit about its value commitments. Such accountability also allows all of us to learn what those commitments imply and to challenge them in a thoughtful way.

Elsewhere I have argued that four conditions make more precise the notion of accountability for reasonableness (Daniels and Sabin 1997, 1998a):

1. *Publicity Condition:* Decisions regarding both direct and indirect limits to meeting health needs and their rationales must be publicly accessible.
2. *Relevance Condition:* The rationales for limit-setting decisions should aim to provide a *reasonable* explanation of how the organization seeks to provide "value for money" in meeting the varied health needs of a defined population under reasonable resource constraints. Specifically, a rationale will be "reasonable" if it appeals to evidence, reasons and principles that are accepted as relevant by ("fair minded") people who are disposed to finding mutually justifiable terms of cooperation. Where possible, the relevance of reasons should be vetted by stakeholders in these decisions – a constraint easier to implement in public than in private institutions (more on this point shortly).

3. *Revision and Appeals Condition:* There must be mechanisms for challenge and dispute resolution regarding limit-setting decisions, and, more broadly, opportunities for revision and improvement of policies in the light of new evidence or arguments.

4. *Regulative Condition:* There is either voluntary or public regulation of the process to ensure that conditions 1–3 are met.

Taken together, the four conditions bring decision making about meeting health needs out of a mysterious black box – whether the box is a private health plan, as in the United States or Colombia, or a publicly administered health care or other regulatory agency – and make it possible to assess health plan and public agency decisions in the light of wider societal views about fairness. The four conditions connect decisions at any institutional level to a broader educative and deliberative democratic process.[10]

For private health plans and public agencies to acquire and sustain legitimacy for their limit-setting decisions, they must see themselves, and be seen by others, as contributors to a broader deliberative process that they embrace. The four conditions help solve the legitimacy and fairness problems by placing public agencies and even private health plans – arguably a harder case than public agencies – visibly in that role. Embracing these conditions and the way in which they connect internal decisions to broader public deliberation clearly carries many of these organizations beyond the dominant perceptions they currently have of their organizational and (in many cases) "corporate" culture. It makes them accountable to more than their own boards of directors and – if they have them – to stockholders. In an intensely competitive environment, embracing these conditions may be easier for associations of organizations than for individual health plans, though it may also be possible to show that there is some market value to having a visible record of commitment to patient-oriented decision making.

The Publicity Condition

The publicity condition requires that rationales for decisions such as coverage for new technologies or the contents of a drug formulary be accessible to clinicians and patients, whether subscribers in a private health plan or citizens in a publicly administered system. To see what this condition means in practice, consider how one leading American health plan disseminated its coverage decision for biosynthetic growth hormone (in 1993). (Though the example is American, the point is quite general.) In a Medical Director's

---

[10] These conditions were developed independently but fit reasonably well with the principles of publicity, reciprocity, and accountability governing democratic deliberation cited by Gutmann and Thompson (1996). For reservations about their account, see Daniels (1999).

Letter distributed to all clinicians, the policy stated that growth hormone treatment would be covered (for those with a contractual drug benefit) only for children with growth hormone deficiency or Turner's syndrome. No explanation was offered for these restrictions in coverage. Other plans placed similar coverage restrictions on growth hormone treatment and also failed to say why.[11]

The point of offering the rationale is made clearer when we imagine parents who want the treatment for a child who will be short but who does not fit the patient selection criteria. What can be said to them that would make the limitation seem reasonable and based on considerations that include the welfare of patients?

When the committee of the health plan charged with making a coverage decision for growth hormone originally made its decision, it deliberated carefully about two reasons for the restrictions, drawing on literature reviews and expert opinions. First, growth hormone therapy had not been shown to increase the ultimate adult height in short children who were not deficient in growth hormone. Second, independent of the question of effectiveness, the committee considered that while extremely short stature may be disadvantageous, in the absence of growth hormone deficiency it should not be considered an illness and therefore should not be eligible for treatment.

Failure to be clear about these reasons in either coverage committee minutes or the disseminated coverage decision has important consequences. The first reason has obvious relevance to anxious parents who must take it into account. However, if efficacy and safety were later demonstrated, and if the second reason had not been publicly stated and explicitly defended, then it might seem that coverage would have to be provided. The distinction between treatments for disease or disability and therapies that enhance otherwise normal traits is crucial in other coverage decisions; therefore, when such a distinction is used, it ought to be stated clearly and defended explicitly (see Chapter 5). Consequently, being explicit about the underlying reasoning demonstrates the coherence and consistency of an overall policy about coverage, even to the parents of the short child. It demonstrates commitment to an even-handed appeal to reasons and principles, so that relevant similarities and differences in particular cases are recognized and attended to. It is noteworthy that the National Institute for Clinical Excellence (NICE) in the United Kingdom has made explicitness about the rationales for its decisions about coverage for new technologies within the National Health Service (NHS) part of its method of operation.[12]

---

[11] Two broader studies showed some variation in insurance practices, however (Finklestein et al. 1998; Daniels and Sabin 1998b).

[12] NICE no doubt learned the importance of open communication from cases of inadequate transparency, as the Child B case (Ham and Pickard 1998), but Michael Rawlins, the director

One important effect of making public the reasons for coverage decisions – or other resource allocation decisions impacting population health – is that, over time, the pattern of such decisions will resemble a type of "case law." The case law model will help us see that the benefits of the publicity requirements of Condition 1 are internal to the health plans or public agencies committed to it, leading to more efficient, coherent, and fairer decisions over time. The benefits of publicity requirements are also external, since the emerging case law can strengthen broader public deliberation and contribute to the perceived legitimacy of the decision makers.

One important requirement of fairness is that similar cases be dealt with similarly and that differential treatment be justified by relevant reasons. A body of case law establishes the presumption that if some individuals have been treated one way because they fall under a reasonable interpretation of the relevant policies or rationales, then similar individuals should be treated the same way in subsequent cases. The earlier decision reflects a *commitment* to continue to act on the cited reasons and rationales in future similar cases. There is a presumption that the earlier reason-based deliberation about a case will be applied to similar cases in the present.

There are two ways to rebut this presumption that a subsequent case should be treated similarly to an earlier one. The least disruptive rebuttal involves showing that the new case differs in relevant and important ways from the earlier one, justifying different treatment. A much more disruptive rebuttal involves rejecting the reasons or principles embodied in the earlier case. Sometimes such a revision of past policy is justifiable and required. The respect for past commitments embodied in case law does not mean that past errors of judgment cannot be corrected by new deliberation.[13]

A commitment to the transparency that case law requires improves the quality of decision making. An organization that articulates explicit reasons for its decisions becomes more focused in its decision-making deliberations. It might, for example, develop a checklist of key features of coverage decisions, such as the specification of patient selection criteria, and relevant reasons for those criteria, such as the limits of evidence from clinical trials or the range of patients for whom risk-benefit ratios are acceptable. This explicitness makes it easier for a committee deliberating about coverage to identify the relationship between one decision and others it has made or will have to make. It may become more sensitive to the ways in which the

---

of NICE, explicitly cites accountability for reasonableness as a source of NICE's emphasis on both publicity and the involvement of citizens in deliberation about value issues (Rawlins 2005).

[13] Case law involves a kind of institutional equilibrium – movement between deliberation and practice – checking one against the other (Rawls 1971; Daniels 1996a). The considered judgments in past decisions constitute relatively fixed points that can be revised only with careful deliberation and good reasons.

reasons or principles it invokes sometimes conflict. Then it must engage in a difficult deliberation about how to resolve the conflict and articulate the reasons for the particular resolution.[14]

The disciplined search for coherent reasons embodied in such a case law approach leads to fairer decisions over time for two reasons. First, formal requirements of fairness are better met since public clarity about rationales will promote consistent treatment of similar cases. Second, the discipline involved in specifying the appropriate reasons and making sure that they really bear on the case promotes thoughtful evaluation of these reasons and their foundations. To the extent that we are then better able to discover flaws in our moral reasoning, we are more likely to arrive at fair decisions. None of this is as likely to happen without a commitment to going public with the rationales for decisions and policies.

If the process improves the fairness of decisions formally and substantively, then over time people will understand better the moral commitments of the institutions making these decisions. If an institution is committed to arriving at fair decisions in a publicly accountable way, we can expect that over time people will recognize this commitment and will come to see the institution as acting (more) fairly. Only by being explicit about reasons can health plans or public agencies demonstrate that the solutions they adopt for coverage under resource constraints reflect reasons and principles that everyone affected by those decisions should take seriously.

Fear of litigation and of exposure in the media are the most commonly expressed objections to our proposal that organizations be more explicit and accountable about the reasons underlying their limit-setting decisions regarding new technologies. Specifically, organizations are concerned that being explicit about reasons would "open the door to attack" from dissatisfied patients and their lawyers or reporters. This concern is apparent in private health plans in the United States, but it is also a real concern in publicly administered health systems elsewhere (cf. Ham and Pickard 1998). In part, the fear is that the organization would be exposing the jugular vein of its policies by laying out the grounds for its defense, thereby making itself vulnerable to rebuttal by expert witnesses or to "gaming" regarding insurance coverage.

The objection and any reply to it both suffer from being speculative. There is simply no evidence that failing to provide reasons protects an organization against litigation or that giving them opens it up to more litigation or more successful litigation. Nor is there evidence that providing sound

---

[14] Schauer (1995: 657) notes that "decision makers themselves are unlikely to fully apprehend and appreciate this function [that reason giving increases discipline], for most decision makers underestimate the need for external quality control of their own decisions. But when institutional designers have grounds for believing that decisions will systematically be the product of bias, self-interest, insufficient reflection, or simply excess haste, requiring decision makers to give reasons may counteract some of these tendencies."

reasons for decisions makes an organization more vulnerable to bad press. Indeed, if earlier American experience with termination-of-treatment decisions is any guide, courts will be less likely to substitute their own decisions about provision of new technologies if they see health plans or public agencies use robust, careful, deliberative procedures and base their conclusions on reasonable arguments that appeal to the evidence produced in the evaluation. The best defense against the charge that an organization is negligent in providing care promised by contract or by legislation is to show that the reasons for limiting access to that care are weighty and justifiable and that decisions were actually based on them. Since courts are notoriously bad places for the technical assessment of evidence, the courts themselves have good reason not to intrude in decisions about which technologies and treatments have met some reasonable standard of evidence regarding their safety, efficacy, and medical appropriateness.

Another reason to fear openness is the belief that increased openness about limit-setting decisions and policies will increase distrust of doctors and the health care system itself. This is an empirical claim; lacking real evidence, it is speculation. An alternative view is that as health plans and public agencies begin to address the legitimacy and fairness problems by demonstrating that they base limit-setting decisions on a concern for meeting the needs of patients in a covered population under reasonable resource constraints (our Publicity and Relevance Conditions), trust will increase. This empirical claim is also speculative, but since the current approach does not satisfy anyone, greater openness is the better strategy.

There is an even stronger reason for endorsing accountability for reasonableness: Not allowing health plan members or citizens to understand how and why limits are being set deprives them of an opportunity to participate in a fundamental form of social governance – the allocation and rationing of services so important for a fundamental human good. Transparency has the potential for enhancing the democratic process by helping our society learn how to allocate health care resources thoughtfully and fairly.

The Relevance Condition

The second condition imposes two important constraints on the rationales that can be used to argue for the reasonableness of a limit-setting decision. Specifically, the rationales for coverage decisions should aim to provide (1) a *reasonable* construal of (2) how the organization or public agency seeks to provide "value for money" in meeting the varied health needs of a defined population under reasonable resource constraints. The constraints are similar in private or public coverage decisions for medical services and for public regulatory decisions that bear on health risks faced by populations (IOM 2006). Both constraints need explanation.

What Reasons Are Relevant?

We may think of the goal of meeting the varied needs of patients or citizens under reasonable resource constraints as a characterization of the *common or public good* pursued by everyone engaged in delivering and receiving this care or risk protection. This goal is avowed in mission statements and medical management philosophies by many private health plans, whether they are for-profit or not, and it is part of the public understanding of the mission of public health care and regulatory agencies. It is avowed by the clinicians engaged in treatment, who have professional obligations to pursue their patients' best interests. Finally, it is avowed by patients seeking care, who – as long as they are confident that their own needs will be addressed – also want a cooperative scheme that provides affordable, nonwasteful care.

It is not enough simply to specify the goal of the cooperative enterprise. Reasoning about that goal must also meet certain conditions. Specifically, a construal of the goal will be reasonable only if it appeals to reasons, including values and principles that *are accepted as relevant* by people who are trying to find ways of cooperating with each other on mutually acceptable terms. We need to see why this further constraint on reasoning is necessary to be more specific about what it means.

We can begin by asking why giving reasons is appropriate or even demanded in some legal contexts but not others. For example, in the United States, no reasons are given when juries give verdicts, when state supreme courts refuse review, when trial judges rule on objections, or when zoning authorities refuse to grant variances. In his discussion of this question (the examples are his), Frederick Schauer (1995: 658) notes that giving reasons (viewed as general rules under which cases are subsumed) is a way to show respect for persons and to "open a conversation" rather than to forestall one:

Announcing an outcome without giving a reason is consistent with the exercise of authority, for such an announcement effectively indicates that neither discussion nor objection will be tolerated. When the source of a decision rather than the reason behind it compels obedience, there is less warrant for explaining the basis for the decision to those who are subject to it. But when decision makers expect voluntary compliance, or *when they expect respect for decisions because the decisions are right rather than because they emanate from an authoritative source, then giving reasons become a way to bring the subject of the decision into the enterprise.* (Emphasis added)

Private health plans and public agencies cannot claim to be authoritative sources since their decisions will be respected only if they are seen as right – that is, as fair and legitimate. To achieve acceptance and compliance, they "must bring the subject of the decision into the enterprise." The "conversation" the health plan has must be with stakeholders who have diverse moral perspectives on the issues under discussion. Consequently, the giving of reasons must itself respect the moral diversity of those affected by the decisions.

Not just any kind of moral reason, compelling as it might be to the decision maker (or the patient), will seem appropriate or relevant to those affected by the decision. The reasons offered by decision makers must be the types of reasons that patients can recognize as relevant and appropriate for the purpose of justifying decisions.

To illustrate the point, consider the criteria for technology assessment used by a private association of health plans in the United States, the Blue Cross/Blue Shield Medical Advisory Panel (MAP). MAP requires that (1) the technology must have final approval from the appropriate government regulatory body; (2) the scientific evidence must permit conclusions concerning the effect of the technology on health outcomes; (3) the technology must improve net health outcomes; (4) the technology must be as beneficial as any established alternative; and (5) the improvement must be attainable outside investigational settings. (I return to more controversial criteria, such as cost-effectiveness, shortly.)

Each of the criteria involves a publicly accessible method of reasoning. Thus, it is easy to establish that a technology has final approval from appropriate regulatory bodies or to establish that controlled clinical trials have been run and show some net health benefit. Adequately trained reviewers can usually agree on the quality of the evidence produced by the studies or expert panels.[15] Showing that the treatment involves a net benefit to patients, and that there is at least as much net benefit as provided by an alternative therapy, also involves publicly accessible methods of reasoning, though some further elements of judgment that include evaluation are also involved. There might be some disagreement, for example, about the relative importance of the benefits and risks of the treatment, but the issues will then be clear. Nevertheless, these criteria are ones that all stakeholders should accept as relevant and appropriate – if not sufficient – for making decisions about including new technologies in benefit packages. (These criteria may not be sufficient since they do not consider costs or cost-effectiveness, which are crucial when decisions are made under strict budget constraints.) We can contrast publicly accessible criteria like these with ones that derive from specific religious views not accessible to nonbelievers, such as the belief that an unproven remedy ought to be available because it might be the occasion for a miracle.

This appeal to the miraculous should be distinguished from disagreements about how to address uncertainty, as in the moral controversy regarding last-chance therapies. There is more than one reasonable way to weigh the importance of the stewardship of scarce resources, the generation of new knowledge through research, and the meeting of urgent patient needs.

---

[15] This is not always the case. See Daniels and Sabin (2002: Ch. 5), for a discussion of how evidence was judged regarding the effectiveness of bone marrow transplants for breast cancer. See Aubrey et al. (2006).

Consequently, health plans or even public agencies might decide these matters differently, and yet their conclusions may each be fair (Daniels and Sabin 1998b).

Earlier I argued that a health plan or public agency deciding to cover growth hormone treatment only for patients with growth hormone deficiency should provide an explicit rationale for that decision. In that case, the rationale restricts the goal of meeting patients' needs to the treatment of disease and disability and excludes the enhancement of otherwise normal conditions. This reason for excluding some therapies and limiting the use of others is controversial (an issue I return to in Chapter 5; see also Buchanan et al. 2000: Ch. 4). Many may accept it as a reasonable limit on the goals of medical coverage, but others (as I suggested in Chapter 2) may argue that the goals of medical treatment should be broader. For example, they might think that normal conditions still impose some competitive disadvantage, and if we have medical interventions that could ameliorate these disadvantages, we should use them. They might argue that if treatment of disease and disability is justified on the basis of protecting opportunity, we should cover the use of growth hormone for a disadvantageous condition like extreme shortness, even if it appears to be a normal variation.

Still, proponents on both sides of this dispute can recognize that reasonable people might disagree about the specific requirements of a principle protecting opportunity. Both sides of the dispute about the scope of the goals of medicine nevertheless should recognize the relevance and appropriateness of the kind of reason offered by the other, even if they disagree with the interpretation or application of the principle.

Unlike some public agencies elsewhere, private health plans in the United States do not make *comparative* decisions about technologies and treatments under global budgets (Daniels and Sabin 1999). Where comparative decisions are made, the perception that the decision-making process produces winners and losers is very clear. (In comparative decisions, such as those made under budget constraints, meeting the needs of one set of patients is deemed more important than meeting the needs of others.) Patients denied coverage for treatments will legitimately complain that they are made worse off than others whose treatments were covered. What weight should we give to patients' complaints that they are made worse off than other patients by an unfavorable decision?

Clearly, any decision to cover a treatment benefits some people, just as any decision to exclude a treatment from coverage disadvantages other people (unless the treatment would have been harmful). The same can be said about a decision to protect a population against one health risk as opposed to another. Every (comparative) decision will make some people better off and some worse off than they would be as a result of some other coverage decision. Because comparative coverage decisions always advantage some and disadvantage others, mere advantage or disadvantage is not a relevant reason in debates about coverage.

There are, however, two sorts of reasons concerning relative advantage or disadvantage that all should consider relevant. First, if a coverage or risk protection decision disadvantages one group of people more than others who are similar in all relevant ways, the decision violates the formal requirement of justice that similar cases be treated similarly. Here the reasoning points to morally objectionable arbitrariness in the outcome. In contrast, if the decision involves an appeal to (say) a lottery for purposes of patient selection, then there is a relevant difference in the winners and losers, namely, that they won or lost the lottery.

Second, if a decision disadvantages someone (and others like him) more than anyone need be disadvantaged under available alternatives, then this too is a reason that all should consider relevant. The mere fact of being disadvantaged relative to others is a necessary feature of these situations, but being disadvantaged more than anyone need be is not a necessary feature. It is the basis for a complaint that each person would want to be able to make if he of she was the person so severely disadvantaged. Therefore, it is a reason that meets the constraints of the Relevance Condition.

Cost Effectiveness

How should we view the claim that a treatment or regulation providing protection against health risks will not be provided because it costs too much? The British agency NICE, we saw, must include cost-effectiveness when making coverage decisions within the NHS, and the Office of Management and Budget wants to add CEA to the arsenal of methodologies for evaluating risk regulation in the United States.

Some cases of cost-worthiness or cost-effectiveness are easier than others. For example, when one treatment or regulation to protect against risks provides comparable benefits at lower cost, cost-effectiveness is widely seen as a relevant and acceptable reason. Outside that simple case – the same outcomes at lower cost – the claim that some technology is too expensive or not cost-effective becomes controversial. For example, if slightly greater net benefits are possible, especially the decreased risk of death, but only at a much greater cost, there is a strong risk of being criticized for putting so direct a price on the value of life. NICE, for example, faced considerable criticism when it decided not to cover an expensive drug that produced only modest benefits for patients with Alzheimer's disease. Similarly, in the early 1990s, it was demonstrated that tissue-type plasminogen activator (TPA) was more widely used in the United States than in Canada, where it was deemed less cost-effective than a cheaper but less effective drug, streptokinase. In cases such as these, reasonable people will disagree about how to weigh costs and effectiveness for different patient populations.

However, reasonable disagreement about specific applications does not mean that cost-effectiveness is an irrelevant reason. Rather, the disagreement concerns what a fair process must manage and incorporate within deliberation. As the example of NICE shows, some public systems consider

cost-effectiveness a relevant reason and then try to manage the moral disagreement that results through transparency and public input into its process. In private U.S. health plans, there is great reluctance to publicly
embrace cost-effectiveness, in part because managers see this as a "social"
decision and in part because each plan is afraid to be labeled as the first
explicit "rationer" in its market area (cf. Daniels and Sabin 2002; Neumann
2004). Indeed, in the United States, even a public agency such as the Centers
for Medicare and Medicaid Services (CMS), which manages Medicare and
Medicaid, fears embracing cost-effectiveness because it fears being labeled
as a rationer in a society of plenty (Tunis 2004).

Even through some public and most private health providers in the
United States do not emphasize cost-effectiveness or opportunity costs, such
reasons, appropriately supported, would meet the Relevance Condition. If
people share the goal of meeting the varied medical needs of a population
covered by limited resources, and if they share a commitment to justifying
limitations by using reasons all can consider appropriate and relevant, then
they would be interested in a reason that said that a particular intervention fell below some defensible threshold of cost-effectiveness or relative
cost-worthiness. Not providing a treatment that is marginally effective but
quite costly – the only treatment available – would not make the affected
patient population worse off than anyone need be, for under reasonable
resource constraints, there will always be patients whose conditions have no
cost-worthy treatment. In these cases, it is necessary to establish the factual
presuppositions that underlie the reason. A health plan or public agency
has to show that its resources are limited in a reasonable way, that the costs
and effects are as claimed, that the competing interventions that it would
approve are superior in the ways claimed, and that there are no special
reasons of distributive fairness that override these considerations.

Vetting the Relevance of Reasons
How should the relevance of reasons be determined? Where possible, stakeholders affected by decisions should have input in determining which reasons count as relevant. In the case of many decisions made by public agencies, this feature of fair process is not only feasible but is required as part of
the administrative process. For example, American regulatory agencies must
subject proposed rules to public comment and hearings. In my earlier characterization of the legitimacy problem, I urged that we take the perspective
of those affected by a decision, including those whose health needs are not
met when priority is given to the needs of others. Stakeholder involvement
would thus be one clear way of introducing that perspective. Citizen's Coun-
cils provide input into decision making by NICE in the United Kingdom, a
recognition of the importance of such input to public agencies.

However, where, private organizations, such as American health plans
or nongovernmental organizations (NGOs) in developing countries, make

limit-setting decisions, it may not be possible to expect or require stakeholder participation in the vetting of reasons, although "consumer participation" has been strongly advocated by some commentators (Emanuel 1992, 2002; Rodwin 1997) and is sometimes part of the "community outreach" effort of NGOs. Since we are seeking an account of fair process that can be used by all institutions where limit setting is carried out, it may be necessary to compromise on the issue of stakeholder involvement in some contexts, even if such involvement would clearly improve accountability for reasonableness. A key issue is whether this is a compromise of principle or not. The answer turns on the role of stakeholder involvement in establishing legitimacy.

Some people intuitively think that consumer or stakeholder participation would contribute to legitimacy directly and that it is necessary for legitimacy to be achieved. There are two central rationales for this view. On one, consumer participation is necessary for legitimacy because participating consumers *represent* other consumers or the public as a whole. Through their representation, the decision-making process is made more democratic. On this rationale, consumer participation promotes legitimacy through this democratization of the process. On the second rationale, consumer participation is seen as a form of *proxy consent*. The participants consent on behalf of all others, and their full involvement in the informed decision acts as a substitute for actual consent by others.

Both of these rationales suffer from the same fatal flaw. In the vast majority of situations, there is no plausible sense in which the consumers selected to participate actually represent other consumers in the sense that elected officials or those to whom they delegate authority represent the public. We have no publicly endorsed mechanisms that establish a selection process as a form of democratic representation, and there is no recall authority over the alleged representatives. The closest we come to such representation is when publicly authorized officials, over whom we do exercise democratic control, designate particular consumers to participate on an advisory body or commission or even in a decision-making process. The delegated authority granted to these consumer participants, however, does not exist for consumers in the many limit-setting decisions made by private organizations, with the very rare exception of organizations with a consumer governance structure like the Group Health Cooperative in Washington State.

The complete absence of any democratic representational procedure or proxy selection process constitutes a decisive objection to these claims that consumer participation contributes to legitimacy. This means that consumer participation is not generally either a necessary or a sufficient condition for establishing legitimacy. Even without consumer participation, it is possible to achieve accountability for reasonableness and thus legitimacy, and even with consumer participation, a process not aimed at accountability for reasonableness will not achieve legitimacy.

Nevertheless, stakeholder participation can increase the legitimacy of limit-setting decisions in both private and public organizations by increasing accountability for reasonableness. What is crucial here, however, is the way such accountability contributes to legitimacy. How would stakeholder participation enhance accountability for reasonableness? It would increase the likelihood that a broader range of relevant reasons and rationales will be aired in the decision-making process. One study of consumer voice in a public sector mental health managed care program showed, for example, that consumer participation highlighted issues like the need for better hospital discharge planning with families or more Spanish language services (Sabin and Daniels 1999). Similarly, a study of limit setting in Canada showed that consumers can make a strong contribution to cancer policy, provided that there is a critical mass of consumers and provided that they have time to build trust with other members of the decision-making group (Singer et al. 2000).

A second way in which consumer participation can enhance accountability for reasonableness is by providing a clear mechanism to achieve transparency. Consumer participants are not sworn to secrecy about their deliberations because accountability for reasonableness requires publicity about rationales. Participants become potentially important for achieving that publicity. When publicity is not expected, however, consumer participants might be required to treat the process as secret, which would coopt them away from the role that accountability for reasonableness asks them to play.

The key idea behind accountability for reasonableness is that fair-minded people will agree that the reasons underlying a decision are relevant to meeting health care needs fairly under reasonable resource constraints. Having a properly broad range of stakeholders – especially consumers affected by the decisions – play the role of fair-minded individuals gives more credibility to the goal of having all relevant reasons considered. By breaking the direct connection to representation, this approach avoids the trap of thinking that every idea held in a diverse society must have its direct representative present in the deliberation. The approach does not pretend, however, that organizationally based deliberation can substitute for broader democratic processes. It can facilitate those processes, by modeling wider deliberation and educating the public by making its work transparent, but it is not a substitute for full democratic procedures.

Stakeholder participation is given meaning and direction and a connection to the problem of legitimacy if its goal is to improve accountability for reasonableness. It can do this by enhancing the deliberative process at the point of decision making, broadening perspectives, testing rationales for acceptability by fair-minded people, and helping to convey the transparency the process requires. To the extent that accountability for reasonableness is thus improved by consumer participation, the legitimacy of decisions is enhanced.

In short, my suggestion is that accountability for reasonableness is the guiding aim of stakeholder participation – whether in public or private institutions – and participation increases legitimacy only to the extent that it improves such accountability. Considering stakeholder participation, as instrumental, rather than as a role of intrinsic importance, may seem inadequate to some, but this instrumental role gives us a more defensible account of how legitimacy is achieved. As we shall see in Chapters 10 and 12, stakeholder participation is an important feature of accountability for reasonableness in public limit-setting decisions in developing countries.

The Revisability and Appeals Condition

How may a decision concerning coverage of an intervention be challenged by those affected by it? How can a faulty policy be improved? I begin with the more familiar case of limits to health care and generalize briefly to other decisions limiting the meeting of health needs at the end of this section.

Dispute resolution procedures, whether in private health plans or publicly administered health systems play three distinctive roles. Internally, within private or public plans, these procedures give members or citizens – and their physician advocates – a form of due process through which to attempt to reverse adverse decisions. Often a coverage rule, perhaps a restriction in a drug formulary, applies without harm to a group of patients but not to all individuals. We must not unduly burden or harm some in order to gain a collective advantage through limit setting (Daniels et al. 2003). Also internally within public or private health schemes, dispute resolution procedures give participants an opportunity to present their point of view. The procedures create the potential for altered and improved decisions. Externally, these procedures also educate society about the need for limits and the ways in which limits can be set fairly.

Internally, the Revisability and Appeals Condition closes the gap between decision makers and those who are affected by their policies. If done well, it engages a broader segment of stakeholders in the process of deliberation. Through these mechanisms, parties that may not have participated in the original decision-making process and whose views may not have been clearly heard or understood find a voice, even if after the original fact.

Because the reasons involved in the original decision are publicly accessible (the Publicity Condition), and because decisions focus on meeting the health needs of the insured population under resource constraints (the Relevance Condition), people using the Revisability and Appeals Condition to challenge a decision are able to understand the basis on which the decision was made. Even if they did not participate in the original deliberation, the Publicity and Relevance Conditions empower them to reopen the process in the most effective manner.

Of course, this does not mean that every challenge leads to a reconsideration of the decision by the original group responsible for it. It does, however, mean that good arguments that plausibly challenge the original decision gain a visible and public route back into the policy making process. The health plan's (or public agency's) decision-making process is thus enriched by the new resources for argument of the grievance process since those affected adversely by the original decision must give reasons for modifying the original decision. Whether specific decisions are actually changed or not, if the arguments raised by these appeals lead to honest reconsideration of the original decision on its merits, they enhance the legitimacy of the decision-making process and its likelihood of achieving fair outcomes. This task educates everyone involved. That is, the appeals and reconsiderations become part of the broader social deliberation about the problem of limits. They enable and enhances that broader social process and helps to improve its quality.

With a well-developed internal dispute resolution process, patients or clinicians adversely affected by decisions may be less inclined to seek the help of authorities or institutions. Even if litigation and legislation are pursued, however, the presence of a strong internal dispute resolution mechanism can lead to improved external deliberation. This is especially true if the courts come to expect a robust internal mechanism and take up issues only when there is reason to think that internal mechanisms have failed.

Externally, the Revisability and Appeals Condition contributes to broader social deliberation about the problem of limits and ultimately to democratic governance of health care itself. Even if enrollees and clinicians do not participate in the original decision making about limits, the Revisability and Appeals Condition empowers them to play a more effective role in the larger societal deliberation about the issues and to provide wider social oversight of the limit-setting process.

The Revisability and Appeals Condition can also be used outside the health-care sector, for limits on meeting health needs are set through broader resource allocation decisions regarding various goods. In these broader settings, however, we are primarily concerned with the availability of legal and political institutions and procedures capable of reopening and revisiting decisions that should be reconsidered. Their specific form and their effectiveness obviously depend on many aspects of the legal and political culture in a country, an issue I cannot explore even in general terms here. Functionally, however, the Revisability and Appeals Condition says that there must be effective mechanisms for revisiting these decisions. These mechanisms – whatever their specific forms – must function in a timely way so that errors can be corrected and specific harms to individuals or groups remedied or avoided. Further, as in the health sector, how effectively parties can use these mechanisms and how effectively they can improve the quality of limit-setting decisions depends on the publicity of the rationales for those decisions and on the system's commitment to confine itself to relevant reasons.

The Regulative Condition

The purpose of the Regulative Condition is to ensure that the conditions of Publicity, Relevance, and Revisability are met. The most likely way these conditions can be met for either public agencies or private institutions is through some form of public regulation. In the United States, an example of such regulation is state laws requiring insurers to submit to an independent review of denials of care if internal appeals were exhausted. Obviously in publicly administered systems and in public agencies within mixed systems, only some form of public regulation could ensure that the other conditions are met.

We might hope that in a mixed system such as the United States, private regulatory mechanisms will emerge to ensure that the health plans abide by the constraints involved in the Publicity, Relevance, and Revisability Conditions. For example, a private system of accreditation standards might require health plans to carry out a technology assessment that complies with these conditions, for example by modifying the existing National Committee for Quality Assurance standards (Daniels and Sabin 2002). Employers and others seeking to do business only with accredited health plans would then be assured that these organizations had taken steps to address fairness and legitimacy problems.

Ultimately, however, there is a coordination problem facing the private implementation of the four conditions. If all organizations agreed, either through voluntary self-regulation or publicly imposed regulation, to give explicit leasons for their decisions, the risk to any one organization from the change would be reduced. Otherwise, each might reasonably fear being the first to give reasons in an already litigious climate. The effect of such universal reluctance may be that all organizations are worse off because all then face less trust and more litigation. If coordinated reason giving led to less litigation and more trust, then all would benefit from cooperation with the conditions we propose.[16]

OBJECTIONS AND REPLIES

I conclude this chapter by addressing briefly three objections to the approach I have just described. The first challenges the demand for publicity as part of accountability by claiming that better results will happen if we allow experts to work quietly behind the scenes. My reply is that accountability for reasonableness is an appropriate middle ground between explicit

---

[16] If organizations that give reasons (call them "ice breakers") actually benefited, then the coordination problem we describe comes from a misestimate of what self-interested action calls for. It is the misestimate that sets up the public goods problem (the many-person prisoner's dilemma) informally described in the text. If organizations that act as ice breakers when others fail to do so actually do worse, then we have a true many-persons prisoner's dilemma.

and implicit rationing. The second objection is that the approach tolerates different fair decisions about otherwise similar cases, provided that the procedure was followed, violating a formal principle of justice that like cases be treated similarly. My reply is that we may have to live with conflicting decisions, but there need be no violation of a formal principle. The final objection is that we have no assurance that a process that enhances democracy actually leads to better decisions.

Critics of Publicity

In the policy literature on rationing and resource allocation in health care, two polar positions have been staked out. Some advocate "explicit" rationing in which principles by which decisions will be made are publicly announced. The opposing pole calls for avoiding the divisiveness that might accompany making hard choices and putting decisions into the hands of experts who know the situation best.

Consider first the view that explicit limit setting is impractical and too socially divisive. Open, public, limit-setting decisions have costs. They involve openly favoring some claims against others, possibly in life-or-death situations. We can expect the losers – whoever they turn out to be – to fight the decision, and when limits cause suffering to identifiable individuals and groups, the public may also protest against the decisions. The costs of publicity may also include threats to important public values. In a celebrated book, Calabresi and Bobbit (1978) argue that the costs may include eroding such values as the sanctity of life, and that more indirect decision-making methods might accomplish the same distribution but without the public costs. Some then conclude that public decision making will be infeasible.

The argument against public accountability combines sociological description and ethical analysis. At the level of description, proponents of the argument cite the practical burdens and social conflict that explicit rationing may cause. Ethically, the claim is that nonpublic rationing methods are sometimes morally superior to public ones once we weigh all costs and benefits (Klein 1995; Mechanic 1997; but cf. Mechanic 2000).

To the charge that publicity is infeasible I reply that nonpublicity is also infeasible for a very basic reason – it does not work. The public is too suspicious, especially of private organizations and especially for-profit ones, but even of bureaucrats in publicly administered systems, to accept implicit limit setting. To the claim that nonpublicity is preferable to publicity because it better preserves important public values, I reply that nonpublicity risks undercutting the public sense that the system is fair. People increasingly accustomed to using the Internet to bypass experts and seek their own information are not willing to accept decisions on the basis of authority. In this climate publicity may be necessary for public acceptance of limit setting, provided it is done fairly and legitimately. Whereas nonpublicity has been tried and failed, publicity has not yet been seriously attempted.

In reply to advocates of explicitness, I note that we cannot always be explicit about the principles or reasons that we find persuasive when all the arguments are made. The problem comes from demanding that the explicitness be ex ante. Instead, the Publicity Condition in accountability for reasonableness calls for making the grounds for decisions public once they have been deliberated about, so that they can be evaluated by a broader democratic deliberative process over time.

The middle ground, then is this: Accountability for reasonableness insists on being explicit about the grounds for decisions once those grounds have been deliberated about in the context of a specific case.

Fair Process and Conflicting Decisions

Is there more than one just or fair way of deciding an issue? If we are governed by clear principles this might seem implausible. Fine-grained principles should lead to a specific answer when they are reconciled with each other and with all the facts of a case. But in a fair process, different decisions about similar cases may arise. Imagine two U.S. states deciding differently about pollution standards for automobiles after each has gone through a careful deliberation and weighed the benefits and costs differently. They might have drawn on the same evidence and quantified the outcomes similarly, but across state lines there may be reasonable moral disagreements about how to weigh different considerations.

A more familiar example might arise in a medical context where either a local public health authority, as in the United Kingdom, or a private health plan, as in the United States, arrives at different coverage decisions for specific patients under identical conditions. Both Jack and Jill (and, we may suppose, their physicians as well) claim that they need a particular high-dose chemotherapy with stem cell support for their advanced cancers. Let us suppose that this treatment has not yet been shown to provide a net benefit for the condition, which is in any case fatal on standard treatments. After careful deliberation, weighing such relevant reasons as the importance of conserving resources against compassionate use of unproven therapies, one health authority (or health plan) approves the regimen for Jack and the other denies it to Jill. Should we agree if Jill complains that she has been treated unfairly?

Jill might insist that a fundamental principle of justice has been violated, the *formal* principle that like cases be treated similarly. If her case is just like Jack's in all relevant ways, then either both or neither should get the treatment. The formal principle does not tell us how both should be treated, only that they should be treated similarly. Specifically, if there are *reasons* why Jack should get the treatment, Jill insists, then they apply equally to her, and she should receive it as well.

Jill's complaint that a formal principle of justice is violated actually turns on the existence of a substantive reason or principle behind the decision to treat Jack. To see this point, consider this variation on the case: In both health authorities (or health plans), a coin is flipped about whether to give the treatment. Jill loses and Jack wins. When Jill complains that like cases are being treated dissimilarly, we can now say, "The cases are unlike: There was a coin toss, and you lost and he won." There is no violation of the formal principle if a non-reason-based procedure is used to distinguish the cases, as there is in a coin toss. Alternatively, we can construe this as a case in which a principle is appealed to and uniformly applied, namely, the principle that winners but not losers of coin tosses (or other random processes) will get the treatment.

Neither Jack's nor Jill's health authority (or health plan) flips coins, however. Using their different procedures, each encourages reason giving and deliberation about cases in light of those reasons. We presuppose that the difference in their procedures for managing these cases rests on a difference in the weights the two organizations give to certain values: the values of urgency, stewardship, and shared decision making with patients. Suppose further that we rightly claim that there is no argument we all can accept that shows that one weighting of these values is clearly morally more justifiable than the other. That weighting is itself the focus of reasonable disagreement. No principle enjoys our endorsement independently of the fair procedure we are employing. A reason that may seem compelling or decisive in one process may not be in another. To be sure, we are not flipping coins in either case. We are deliberating carefully in a reason-driven and reason-giving way. But the weight given reasons in each setting is a reasonable reflection of other moral disagreements and moral uncertainty – the very uncertainty about what counts as a just outcome that compels us to adopt a procedural approach to fair outcomes. Jill can be told this: Jack was given the treatment because his plan reasoned about his case differently than your plan, and both ways of reasoning are relevant and arguably fair.

How tolerable would a system be if it produced situations in which Jack and Jill were treated differently? It may well make a difference how centralized or decentralized a system is. In a decentralized system such as the United States, for example, it may be difficult to require insurance schemes to use one rather than another procedurally fair way of deliberating about cases. On what basis should the choice between procedures and weightings be made? Can we show a superior outcome to insisting on one such process rather than another? Without such a compelling regulatory reason, we might have trouble justifying public regulation requiring just one form of managing last-chance cases.

Despite the decentralization of the U.S. health-care system, however, the courts arguably can impose a unifying framework. Jill might sue her health plan and point to Jack's plan as evidence that she is not being treated fairly. In practice, the courts could make unworkable an effort to experiment with different fair procedures to determine their advantages and disadvantages.

On the other hand, what has often carried the day in actual suits on these matters is the demonstration that a health-care organization was arbitrary and lacked a fair process. If each of the fair procedures constitutes a reasonable defense against that sort of claim, then the courts might welcome an effort to rely more directly on the use of fair procedures. An analogy here would be the way in which the courts have welcomed decision making by hospital ethics committees in place of frequent lawsuits.

Would a compelling regulatory reason be that we find differential treatments unacceptable and have to avoid them, if only by insisting on a uniform process by convention? That might be true in a decentralized system, but it seems even more likely to be true in a national health care system. In the United Kingdom for example, it might seem more troubling that Jill did not get her transplant in Oxford but Jack got his in Cambridge. Here too, however, there might be disagreements among *meaningful political units*, the districts, about which decision-making procedure was best. If that is true, then there might be even more reason to tolerate variation than there is in the United States, where people are grouped into insurance schemes, not meaningful political units that have democratic ways of selecting their procedures. Nevertheless, in England and Wales, NICE was charged with proposing uniform coverage decisions for the NHS to avoid variation across health authorities.

How acceptable differential treatment would be seems to depend, then, on whether a persuasive political rationale for uniformity can be developed. In a mixed, decentralized system, the political rationale would have to be sufficient to override the presumption that private insurers or different states have the authority to select from among a set of comparably fair procedures. Of course, the political rationale might simply be that the legal system would not allow differential treatment; but that too remains to be seen. In a national health care system, the political rationale for uniformity would have to show that differential treatment among districts is less acceptable than allowing them to select their own procedures. If meaningful political units, like districts, felt strongly enough about their choices of procedures, the costs of uniformity might be too high. For the problem we are facing, then, it remains unclear how unacceptable it would be for Jack to get a last chance when Jill does not.

Democracy and Moral Authority

Deliberation by health plans or public agencies that meets the four conditions does not *substitute for* any democratic process. Rather, it *facilitates* that process. The four conditions compel decision makers in health plans or public agencies to contribute their deliberative capacities to whatever broader public deliberation is conducted through democratic institutions, formally or informally. The arrangements required by the four conditions provide grist for the deliberative mill, not a replacement for broader democratic processes. Ultimately, these broader democratic processes have authority and responsibility for guaranteeing the fairness of limit-setting decisions.

These four conditions have a small bearing on a deep question about the legitimacy of democratic authority. Compliance with them will lead to *better* decisions by limit-setting organizations. They are better in at least this sense: They will rest on a more coherent set of reasons and arguments that fair-minded persons consider relevant. But are they better in the sense that they are more likely to be just or fair decisions, as judged by some view of justice *independent* of the process of decision-making itself?

This deeper and more difficult question goes to the heart of democratic theory. Some theorists (including Plato) suggest that moral authority requires having the moral expertise to make morally correct decisions. Authority comes from getting moral questions right. According to these theorists, a process that does not improve our chances of getting the right answers about laws and policies cannot claim legitimacy.

The problem with this elitist approach, according to its critics, is that we should not expect people to surrender moral authority to experts. But if we reject the idea of experts, are we reduced to accepting as morally legitimate whatever results from the democratic process? We might be happier about the democratic process if we had some assurance that exercising it properly, including deliberatively, increased our chances of getting better laws and policies – "better" from a perspective independent of the democratic process itself. This problem about whether there is any epistemic authority to democracy – whether it helps us get things right – lies at the core of much current debate about democratic authority.

I cannot hope to resolve this question, especially given the limited context of decision making about health that I focus on. However, as I have argued in this chapter, accountability for reasonableness improves the quality and coherence of the decision-making process. And, on at least some views of how we might arrive at an independent account of what is just, this kind of improvement makes it more likely that deliberation will lead to correct answers (Estlund, 1997).

In this chapter, I have offered a description and a theoretical defense of four conditions that establish accountability for reasonableness. I take this account to be an answer to our third Focal Question. This proposal, however, is not just a pie-in-the-sky theory. The conditions proposed are connected to existing best practices in health plans and public agencies in the United States and abroad (Coulter and Ham 2000; Daniels and Sabin 2002; Edgar 2000; Ham and Robert 2003; Martin, Bernstein, and Singer 2003; Martin et al. 2001; Martin, Hollenberg, et al. 2003; Martin, Shulman, et al. 2003). I offer a theoretical rationale for unifying a strategy to build on these best practices. As organizations, agencies, and the public gain experience with setting limits fairly, each new question will not require the equivalent of lifting ourselves by our bootstraps. Even in the absence of any widely acceptable principles that would deductively yield one and only one answer to questions about limits, accountability for reasonableness allows organizations and society itself to increase their skill at reaching justifiable conclusions. In Chapters 10–12, I examine several contexts in which accountability for reasonableness can be put to practical use in meeting health needs fairly.

Our next task, however, is to show that the answers provided to the three Focal Questions form an integrated theory with specific implications for health and health care. That task is taken up in Chapter 5.

5

What Do We Owe Each Other?

Implications of an Integrated Theory of Justice and Health

In the previous three chapters, I have answered the three Focal Questions
that a theory of justice for health must answer. First, health is of special
moral importance because protecting normal functioning helps to protect
the range of exercisable opportunities open to people and because various
theories of justice support the idea that we have an obligation to protect
opportunity and thus health. Second, a health inequality is unjust when it
results from an unjust distribution of the socially controllable determinants
of population health, as illustrated by Rawls's (1971) principles of justice
as fairness. In effect, we cannot have health equity without broader social
justice. Finally, to meet health needs fairly, we must supplement the principles of justice that emerge in answering the first two questions with a fair,
deliberative process.

Do these answers work together to address the Fundamental Question
with which we began? Do they tell us what we owe each other to promote
and protect health in a population and to assist people when they are ill
or disabled? To see whether or not they do, we must now examine the general implications of our answers for some of the major policy problems that
bear on the just distribution of health. Do we owe each other universal
promotion and protection of health – not only in universal coverage for
medical services but in equitable protection against health risks through
both public health and non-health-sector measures that affect health? Do
these obligations mean that there is a right to health, and what entitlements
follow from such a claim? What are the limits to such obligations? What
do we owe people when we cannot protect their health by restoring normal functioning – for example, people with certain disabilities? Do we owe
people measures that do more than protect normal functioning if we have
medical technologies that can enhance otherwise normal capabilities? And
does assigning society the obligation or responsibility for promoting health
mean that individuals have no responsibility for their health? In this chapter, we examine whether the broadest implications of our earlier answers

work together to give coherent guidance about what we owe each other. In Part III, we continue to explore their implications in more specific applications after responding to challenges to the theory in Part II.

SOCIAL OBLIGATIONS TO PROTECT AND PROMOTE HEALTH FOR ALL

Our answers to the three Focal Questions have a direct bearing on how we should think about health for all. First, meeting the health needs of all persons, viewed as free and equal citizens, is of comparable and special moral importance. Specifically, since meeting health needs protects the range of opportunities people can exercise, then any social obligations we have to protect opportunity imply obligations to protect and promote health for all people. Various recent theories of justice, despite their differences, affirm that we have such social obligations to protect opportunity, and so they converge on the importance of protecting health.

Second, just health requires that we protect people's shares of the normal opportunity range by treating illness when it occurs, by reducing the risks of disease and disability before they occur, and by distributing those risks equitably. Within the medical system, this means that we must give all people access to services that promote and restore normal functioning, and we must not neglect preventive measures in favor of curative ones. It means that we must look beyond the medical system to traditional public health measures that profoundly affect risk levels and their distribution. We must also look beyond the health sector to the broader social determinants of health and their distribution. Since we cannot meet all the health needs that arise inside or outside the health sector, we must be accountable for the reasonableness of the resource allocation decisions we make.

Justice and Preventive Health

Justice in preventive health thus requires (1) reducing the risks of disease and disability and (2) seeking an equitable distribution of those risks. The first requirement is obvious. It is often more effective to prevent disease and disability than it is to cure them (or to compensate individuals for loss of function when cure is not possible). Cost-effectiveness arguments will have some bearing on claims about the appropriate distribution of acute versus preventive measures (Russell 1986). Since it is better in general to avoid the burdens of disease than to reduce them once they occur, many types of preventive measures will be emphasized in a system governed by my account of just health.

The second requirement should also seem obvious, given our earlier discussion of the social determinants of health. We saw that our ability to determine when a health inequality between different groups was unjust depended on knowing something about the fair distribution of the determinants of health. Consider the point from the perspective of occupational health. Suppose that a health-care system is heavily weighted toward acute care and provides equal access to its services. Thus, anyone with severe respiratory ailments – black lung, brown lung, asbestosis, emphysema, and so on – is given adequate, comprehensive medical services as needed, but little is done to reduce exposures to these risks in the workplace. Does the system meet the demands of justice?

My account of just health says that such a system is incomplete and unjust. If some groups in the population have different risks of getting ill, it is not sufficient merely to attend to their illnesses. Where risk of illness differs systematically in ways that are avoidable, guaranteeing equal opportunity requires that we try to eliminate the differential risks and to prevent the excess illness of those at avoidable greater risk (of course, subject to resource limits and fair process in setting limits). Otherwise, the burdens and risks of illness will fall differently on different groups and the risk of impaired opportunity for those groups will remain, despite the efforts to provide acute care. Care is not equivalent to prevention. Some diseases will not be detected in time to be cured. Some are not curable, even if they are preventable, and treatments will vary in efficacy. We protect equal opportunity best by reducing and equalizing the risk of these conditions arising. The fact that we get an equal chance of being cured once ill because of equitable access to care does not compensate us for our unequal chances of becoming ill.

For these reasons, the fair equality of opportunity account places special importance on measures aimed at the equitable distribution of the risks of disease. Some public-health measures, such as water and waste treatment, have the general effect of reducing risk. But historically, they have also had the effect of equalizing risk among socioeconomic classes and among groups living in different geographical areas. Many other environmental measures, such as recent clean air laws and pesticide regulations, have both general effects on risk reduction and specific effects on risk distribution. For example, pollutants emitted from smokestacks have a different effect on people who live downwind from those who live upwind. Gasoline lead emissions have a greater effect on urban than rural populations. But other health-protection measures primarily affect the distribution of risks: The regulation of workplace health hazards is perhaps the clearest example. Only some groups of workers are at risk from workplace hazards, though many workers face some risk or other, especially in manufacturing settings. In just health, stringent regulation in all of these ways must be part of the health-care system.

What other sorts of social policies should governments pursue to reduce inequalities in health risks, especially in light of what we now know about the social determinants of health? The options should include policies aimed at equalizing individual life opportunities, such as investment in basic education and other early childhood interventions, affordable housing, income security, and other antipoverty policies. We know, for example, that early childhood interventions, like the Perry High/Scope Project (Schweinhart et al. 1993), have lasting effects on educational achievement, employment, marriage, and the reduction of mental illness. The War on Poverty's Head Start program produced lasting effects on educational achievement; educational achievement, in turn, has a direct influence on health behavior in adulthood, including diet, smoking, and physical activity (Acheson 1998). Other policies that might reduce differential risks could explore changes in worker control and authority in the workplace (Marmot et al. 1997). Though the connection between these broad intersectoral social policies and health may seem somewhat remote, and though they are rarely linked to health issues in our public policy discussions, growing evidence suggests that they should be so linked.

One central implication of this view about health for all is that there should be universal access, based on health needs, to whatever public health and personal medical services support fair equality of opportunity under reasonable resource constraints. This implication must be unpacked since health needs are met in various ways, through public health as well as personal medical services.

Public health services promote the conditions that reduce certain risks of disease or disability. They reduce risks by assuring clean, safe living and working environments and by protecting against infectious diseases. These services should attend to the risks faced by the entire population and aim to reduce these risks in an equitable fashion.

However much we can reduce risks to population health, in an equitable fashion, some people will still become ill or disabled and require personal medical services or other forms of social support. Even if the proper arrangement of the social determinants of health and adequate attention to public health greatly reduce the disease and disability in a society, most people will still need medical care at various points in their lives, especially as they age. To protect the range of opportunities for those whose loss of normal functioning we cannot prevent, we will have to devote significant resources to such medical and social support services (Daniels 2007b; cf. Sreenivasan 2007). Obviously, careful deliberation by a fair process will be needed to determine the proper allocation of resources to prevention versus cure and social support.

Personal medical services considered essential to promoting fair opportunity for all must be accessible to all. This will generally mean universal coverage through public or private insurance for an array of "decent" or "adequate" services in order to protect fair equality of opportunity. There should be no obstacles – financial, racial, geographical, and so on – to access to the basic tier of the system. Determining what is in that basic tier must be clarified in light of arguments about how to protect fair equality of opportunity under reasonable resource constraints; these arguments require a fair process (accountability for reasonableness) for appropriate democratic deliberation (see Chapter 4). The theory rules out arbitrary exclusion of whole categories of services that meet the kinds of needs found in the basic tier. Historically, for example, preventive services, mental health care, rehabilitative, and long-term care services have been excluded from both public and private insurance schemes for various cultural and economic reasons. Most of these categorical exclusions are unjustifiable from the perspective of protecting normal functioning, but specific limit-setting choices can only be made through a fair, deliberative process.

What forms of organization – public or private administration and financing – are implied is not a question to which just health provides a unique answer. There is probably an array of "just-enough" institutional structures that can provide the needed protection of opportunity. Similarly, just what kinds of "tiering" or inequalities in services above the basic tier are compatible with protecting opportunity for all? This question not get specific answers from the general theory, though it will clearly supply constraints (see Chapter 9). Reasonable disagreements about these questions should be addressed in a fair, deliberative process.

A Right to Health?

Since just health implies that there are social obligations to meet health needs, broadly understood, does it also imply a right to health or at least a right to health care? In Chapter 1, I claimed that we should not start our account with an appeal to a right to health or to health care. Now that we have developed some relevant theory, what can be said about such a right and its content?

In *Just Health Care*, I argued that we indeed have a right to health care: We should see it as a special case of a right to fair equality of opportunity, since the protection of health it affords helps to protect opportunity. Such a right to health care, I further argued, is properly understood as system relative. The entitlements it involves are contingent claims to an array of health-care services that protect fair shares of the opportunity range under reasonable resource constraints. I resisted, however, viewing a right to health as anything but shorthand for a right to health care (broadly construed to include traditional public health measures). I must modify my position in two ways in light of answers to the second and third Focal Questions. First, since the category of socially controllable factors determining population health and its distribution is clearly broader than just health care, claiming a right to health cannot simply mean that others owe us certain kinds of health care. Does this give us more reason to talk about a right to health? Second, whatever sense we can make out of a right to health (or health care), the specific entitlements it involves can only be determined through a fair, deliberative process, something not taken up in *Just Health Care*. Consider these modifications in turn.

If health needs are broader than the need for health care, should we try to make sense of a right to health? We face an immediate and serious objection. The expression "right to health" appears to embody confusion about the kind of thing that can be the object of a right claim. Health is an inappropriate object, whereas health care is not. If my poor health is not the result of anyone's doing, or failing to do, something for me or to me (or for or to the relevant group of which I am part) that might have prevented or might cure my condition, then it is hard to see how any right of mine is violated. That is what underlay my resistance to understanding a right to health as anything but shorthand for a right to health care.

People who claim a right to health – and here I include myself – should, I suggest, be understood to claim that certain individuals or groups or society as a whole must perform various actions, such as designing certain institutions and distributing important goods in certain ways, that promote or maintain or restore their health and must refrain from actions that interfere with it. The reference to *health* should be construed as a handy way to characterize *functionally* the relevant, socially controllable actions, namely, those that affect population health and its distribution. This gloss on the meaning of a right to health broadens the range of actions from providing health care to meeting the broader set of health needs that arises when we grasp the broader determinants of health. This gloss allows us to see why some advocates, for example of a human right to health, have insisted on a "right to *health*" and not just a "right to (certain) health-care services." They want, and reasonably so, the right to imply that there are obligations to perform a broad range of actions that affect health, even if these actions are not normally construed as health-care services and even if they involve factors outside the health sector, however broadly construed. The gloss makes it clear, however, that a right to health, so understood, is not violated when the socially controllable factors affecting health have been fairly distributed but health fails anyway. We do not have to denounce as confused those who claim that all of their health needs should be met.

Just what entitlements follow from a right to have a broad set of health needs met? The answer is system relative and depends on resource allocation decisions that are made using a fair, deliberative process. To see the point, consider an objection sometimes made to the narrower claim to a right to health care, namely, Fried's (1978) objection that an individual right to health care invites falling into a bottomless pit. Fried is worried that if we posit a fundamental right to have needs satisfied, no other social goals will be able to override the right claims to all health-care needs.

No such fundamental right to have specific needs met is presented on my account. Rather, the rights and entitlements of individuals to have certain needs met are specified only as a result of a fair, deliberative process aimed at meeting population health needs fairly. Typically, not all health needs can be met under reasonable resource constraints. Deciding which needs should be met and what resources are to be used – both within and outside the health sector – requires careful moral judgment and a wealth of empirical knowledge about the effects of alternative allocations. The right to health can yield entitlements only to those needs that we can reasonably try to meet.

We noted earlier some dimensions of the limit setting that must go on. The various institutions that affect opportunity must be weighed against each other. Similarly, the resources required for fair equality of opportunity must be weighed against the needs of other important social institutions. This is true even if we believe that guaranteeing fair equality of opportunity should have (lexical or strict) priority over principles of justice promoting well-being in other ways. The point is that institutions, including health-care institutions, capable of protecting opportunity can be maintained only in societies whose productive capacities they do not undermine. The bugaboo of the bottomless pit is less threatening in the context of such a theory. The price is that we are less clear just what the individual claim involves in general, that is, until we apply the theory to a particular society.

The right to health must be system relative for another reason that is implied by a deeper feature of the theory. I have suggested that what is special about meeting health needs, for purposes of justice, is that it helps to protect individuals' fair shares of the normal opportunity range for their society. This relativity to a society, however, also infects claims about what we are entitled to when a health system is designed. Relativizing the normal range to a society captures an important requirement for a theory of just health care. It is not a feature we should lightly abandon. The importance of meeting specific health needs will vary, depending on facts about a society, and a distributive principle must leave room for such variation. Curing dyslexia might be more important in some societies than others, though it is a form of pathology in all of them.[1]

Our answers to the three Focal Questions have clearly worked together to tell us what we owe each other. We owe measures both inside and outside the health sector that work to protect normal functioning and thus opportunity. Reasonable disagreements about how to meet those health needs fairly wherever they arise mean that we must be accountable for the

---

[1] Suppose that a disease is widespread, even universal, in a society. Suppose that it is a form of anemia that affects all weakens everyone. One might think that the impact on the normal opportunity range will not tell us how important it is to treat this disease, since it hurts everyone equally. But the opportunity account still helps us here, for it is not only a principle governing competitive advantage. This anemia keeps all individuals from adequately carrying out any life plan that otherwise would be reasonable in their society. Remember, the reference point is normal species functioning, not simply functioning in a certain society.

reasonableness of our priority-setting decisions. Even the content of a right to health and health care – the specific entitlements it implies both inside and outside the health sector – cannot be specified except through a fair process that takes specific features of a society into account.

NORMAL FUNCTIONING AND HEALTH NEEDS

What are the limits to our obligation to promote normal functioning, given our answers to the Focal Questions? To explore the implications of our account, consider two cases. In one, we cannot fully restore normal functioning; in the other, we can do much more than promote normal functioning. Specifically, in the former, what do we owe people with disabilities when our medical technologies do not enable us to preserve or restore their normal functioning? The answer to this question about the limits of our medical capabilities carries us outside the health sector. In the latter, do we owe it to people to enhance otherwise normal traits if we have technologies capable of doing that and if doing so would enhance their opportunities?

Opportunity and Disability

Though promoting and protecting health is aimed at preserving normal functioning, sometimes significant impairments of normal functioning cannot be prevented or cured. Chronic illness, both mental and physical, is one important set of examples, but so do physical and mental deficits that interfere with important kinds of functioning and contribute to important types of disabilities. Even if we take reasonable public health and other "upstream" preventive measures, we cannot, for example, prevent or cure all instances of significant sensory deficit, such as blindness or deafness; nor can we prevent or cure significant motor deficits, such as paraplegia or quadriplegia; nor can we prevent or cure various cognitive deficits, such as important forms of mental retardation or deficits induced by brain trauma. All of these count as significant departures from normal functioning on the account we have developed (see Chapter 2).

Our obligation to preserve fair shares of the normal opportunity for individuals does not stop when we encounter such deficits. Sometimes we can provide alternative means that allow individuals to function in equivalent, if not species-typical, ways. Eyeglasses, contact lenses, or corneal surgery are different ways of correcting for a sensory deficit such as myopia, though only the last offers a cure. A prosthesis that replaces an arm or a leg allows an amputee to regain some, if not all, of the motor function the arm or leg ordinarily performs. A motorized wheelchair can restore significant mobility to a paraplegic, and a racing wheelchair allows the paraplegic marathoner to complete the course faster than a runner. Many of these measures, and many others, would presumably be included as health sector interventions on the opportunity-based view we have developed. Obviously, resource allocation questions arise when new measures offer some benefit but at much higher cost. Reasonable people will disagree about how cost-worthy some improvements are and whether they are more important than other things we might invest resources in. Just what health need entitlements follow from our account requires a fair process that establishes accountability for reasonableness.

Our obligation to protect individuals' fair shares of the opportunity range does not stop at the boundaries of the health sector. Often, interventions outside the health sector are key to protecting the range of opportunities open to people. Put quite generally, we can design our institutions so that they are more or less inclusive of people with disabilities (Buchanan et al. 2000), and our obligation to protect opportunity pushes us toward more inclusion. Specifically, the same emphasis on fair equality of opportunity that requires us to meet health needs also supports the design of public spaces so that they are accessible to people with motor and sensory disabilities. It also supports reasonable accommodation of persons with disabilities in the workplace (Daniels 1996b). For persons with a functional deficit that we cannot prevent or cure, if we can minimize the impact of the deficit on opportunities we have an obligation to do so, reasonable resource constraints permitting.

Our account commits us to reasonable accommodation in the workplace (or in public spaces) even where this involves some social costs. In allocating resources to meet health needs, we saw that most people give some priority to meeting the needs of those worst off, even with a loss of efficiency, for example, by foregoing greater benefits that might result from helping those less badly off but easier to help. At the same time, few people give *complete* priority to those who are worst off. Our appeal to fair process was an effort to resolve disputes about how much priority should be given in light of the costs to others. Reasonable accommodation, a feature of the Americans with Disabilities Act, is a similar attempt to find a middle ground in the more competitive environment of the workplace. It too accepts some social cost in order to protect opportunity.

Keeping people with disabilities functioning as close to normally as possible in the workplace may require us to take extra steps to open employment doors. Despite the modest inefficiency that may come, for example, from allowing more break times for someone with a chronic mental disability than for workers without such a disability, that social cost is reasonable if it allows people with mental disabilities to preserve their fair share of the opportunity range. If we had, for example, an expensive but highly effective treatment for those mental disabilities, we would have strong grounds for providing it in the health sector, given its impact on opportunity. Since we do not have it and cannot invest in it there, accepting the cost of reasonable accommodation is a way of extending our obligation outside the health sector to preserve fair shares of the opportunity range. Protecting the health-related opportunity range remains an obligation both inside and outside the health sector.

Treatment versus Enhancement

Consider what might be thought of as the opposite problem. Rather than lacking ways to prevent or restore loss of function in certain disabilities, we have medical interventions that permit us to enhance some otherwise normal traits. Do we have an obligation to provide such enhancements? Specifically, if such an enhancement improves the person's exercisable opportunities, do we have the same reason to provide it as we would to treat an illness? For example, suppose that by using rhinoplasty to provide someone with a more beautiful nose, we could open a new career in modeling. Or, by providing some combination of drugs and therapy, we might make someone who was shy but otherwise normal a better salesperson. Or, by providing growth hormone treatment to a child who is not growth hormone deficient yet will become a very short adult, we can make him a few inches taller. Each intervention arguably improves opportunities. Are we obliged to provide them as we would treatments for pathology?

My account has emphasized our obligation to protect opportunity by protecting and promoting normal functioning. Do we owe people more than normal functioning? Or should we, as the account seems to imply, give some priority to the prevention and treatment[2] of pathology rather than the enhancement of otherwise normal traits (see Chapter 2)? Giving priority to treatment over enhancement underlies what I shall call the "primary rationale" for saying that we are obliged to provide a medical intervention, namely, that it meets an important, objectively ascribable need to prevent or treat significant pathology (see Sabin and Daniels 1994; Buchanan et al. 2000: Ch. 4; and Chapter 2 of this volume).

Of course, the primary rationale is not the only acceptable justification for saying that we owe people assistance through the use of medical technologies; it is not a sufficient condition for ascribing such obligations either. It is not a sufficient condition because we also have to weigh this claim about obligations against other such claims under resource constraints. We may, for example, have to make judgments about which health needs are more important to meet. Nor is meeting such a health need a necessary condition for including a medical service among those we owe each other. Our obligation to protect the equality of women requires us to cover nontherapeutic abortions in public or private insurance schemes. But this rationale clearly goes beyond the primary rationale, since an unwanted pregnancy is

---

[2] I shall use "treatment" to include "prevention."

not a disease or disability; viewing it as a medical necessity is thus inappropriate (see Chapter 2).

The treatment–enhancement distinction and the presumption that we should give priority to treatment (including prevention) over enhancement are widely shared in both our beliefs and our practices in protecting health. The treatment–enhancement distinction, for example, is closely related to the concept of "medical necessity" that appears in public insurance laws in both the United States and Canada and in private insurance contracts. Medically necessary services are those that prevent or treat physical or mental disease and disability or ameliorate conditions deriving from them (but cf. Daniels et al. 1991; Sabin and Daniels 1994). Some medical services may produce benefits for other conditions, but they do not count as medically necessary. For example, insurers will generally reimburse – and in some states, like Massachusetts, must reimburse – reconstructive breast surgery following mastectomy or trauma. But they do not reimburse cosmetic surgery, however strongly a woman may feel that her life will be improved if her breasts are made larger or smaller.[3] Elsewhere, Sabin and I (1994) discuss insurance coverage that was provided for extended psychological therapy for a shy bipolar patient that would not have been provided for a normal but shy patient on the grounds that the shyness might have been an effect of the mental illness.

Some clinicians and some members of the public balk at the line that is drawn here. They may be inclined to say that if suffering is involved, as it might be for short children, shy adults, or people deeply unhappy as a result of their appearance, then we should relieve the suffering with medical interventions funded through insurance. Nevertheless, there is a very good reason why insurers prefer to insist on a diagnosis of disease or disability as an eligibility condition for reimbursement and why they do not agree to reimburse anything that produces a benefit, at least as perceived by the patient or even the therapist. Without the requirement for a disease diagnosis, insurers – whether private or public – would be exposed to what is termed "moral hazard."

Moral hazard refers to the behavioral changes that individuals are likely to make in response to the incentives provided by insurance coverage – specifically, those behavioral changes that make them eligible for benefits to which they would not otherwise be entitled. For example, someone with extensive fire insurance might seek to gain a payoff by setting a fire (here the moral hazard leads to arson and fraud) or by failing to take reasonable

---

[3] Despite the universal public and private insurance exclusion of cosmetic surgery, it is still a tax-deductible form of medical care under U.S. tax law. Perhaps this tax subsidy for nonmedically necessary services can be justified on administrative simplicity or privacy grounds, but otherwise it seems inconsistent with our other policies on what we owe each other in using at least partially collective resources.

precautions against fire. Obviously, insurers do not reimburse people for fire damage resulting from arson arranged by the insured. Similarly, there is no insurance market for reimbursement for the cost of speeding tickets.

If individuals could voluntarily define their otherwise normal condition as one that involved suffering or created an unacceptable disadvantage, given their expectations, then insurance against such suffering or disadvantage would encourage extensive moral hazard. There is no way to predict such freely chosen "events" as having a normal but unwanted condition. An insurance market against certain risks can function, however, only if the risks are measurable actuarially and the market does not create conditions (such as moral hazard) that make the risks unmeasurable. Similarly, even a publicly funded system must be able to match tax revenues against actuarially predictable events.

This point about insurance, especially in publicly funded schemes, is related to a deeper fact about when we feel obligated to assist others, including reducing the effects of an inequality that arises among us. Consider someone who feels very dissatisfied with his appearance: His face is normal but hardly handsome. He feels he might be more successful in romance or in business if his face or hair better matched some social model of handsomeness. To avoid responsibility for his failures, he may blame the "superficiality" of others. The solution, he believes, lies in changing not how he thinks or behaves with prospective social or business partners but his appearance. Are we obliged to relieve his suffering by providing him with the means to obtain cosmetic surgery?

Some may feel so obliged, but most would not. They would complain that the problem here lies in the person's beliefs, attitudes, and excuses. It is his responsibility to rethink his goals and his means of achieving them. If he is unable to do so, it may indicate some deeper psychological problem, and the treatment he may need is psychological counseling, not cosmetic surgery. In part, what we resist here is the idea that an individual can develop very expensive tastes or preferences – for example, for being one of the "beautiful people" – and that others owe him the chance to satisfy those preferences. We resist being held hostage to the expensive tastes of others. If someone wants to spend his own own money to remove what he sees as the obstacle to his success through cosmetic surgery, then let him. We owe him a new face no more than we owe him a Porsche, which he might just as justifiably think would open new doors to him. Of course, we feel quite differently about people who have been disfigured by congenital deformity, disease, or trauma. For them, reconstructive plastic surgery meets a medical need (see MacGreggor 1979; Daniels 1985: 31 n.9; de Beaufort et al., 1996). Obviously, there will be gray areas in which it is unclear whether plastic surgery meets a medical need or simply a cosmetic preference.

The focus on normal functioning and thus on the treatment–enhancement distinction matches many of our beliefs and practices.

Nevertheless, the distinction remains controversial, especially if we move away from cases of unhappiness, as in the cosmetic surgery example, to ones more clearly focused on disadvantage or loss of opportunity. We live, for example, in a "heightist" society in which taller people often gain advantages over shorter people – with evidence of these effects in selection for jobs and offices and judgments about intelligence. When synthetic growth hormone treatments became feasible in the 1990s, many private American insurers covered their use only for children with demonstrated growth hormone deficiency and some other conditions, such as Turner's syndrome and renal deficiency. Yet, some complained, idiopathically short children who did not have such conditions would suffer the same stigma and disadvantage through no fault of their own from being very short as children whose shortness was an effect of some pathology. Indeed, their shortness was just as much a piece of bad luck in a natural lottery for genes and other biological factors as was the shortness of children with pathology. If we are willing to provide expensive treatment for very short children whose condition is caused by pathology, then we should provide it for equally short but otherwise normal children. If they have the same deficit in opportunity, then aren't we obliged to treat them the same way, especially if we say that some health needs are important to meet in order to protect opportunity?[4]

In my earlier discussion of both the capabilities view and the equal opportunity for welfare/advantage view (see Chapter 2), I noted how difficult it is to point to the disadvantage accompanying an otherwise normal trait and to infer that assistance is owed because of that disadvantage (or relative deficit in a capability). The capabilities view, for example, makes no judgments about such singular deficits, considering differences in them to be incommensurable (see Chapter 2). The opportunity for welfare/advantage view risks converting the individual's focus on the specific disadvantage into the hijacking that the construction of the view was supposed to avoid. For these reasons, these views have less divergence than it might seem when we focus on normal functioning. Rather than restate those arguments here, I shall develop a point only hinted at earlier: A view focused on normal functioning is likely to produce more agreement on the proper role of meeting health needs than one that looks to specific enhancements as a means of improving opportunity.

To be useful in making public policy, a distinction such as the treatment–enhancement distinction must pass three tests. Does it make distinctions the public and clinicians regard as fair? Can it be administered in the real

4 In 2004, the Food and Drug Administration approved the use of synthetic growth hormone treatment for idiopathically short children (in the bottom 1.5 percent of projected height) by specialty endocrinologists. The decision prompted criticisms that a social issue – heightism – was being medicalized.

world? And does it lead to results that society can afford?[5] I believe that health care aimed at maintaining normal functioning and giving priority to treatment over enhancement meets these three criteria better than more expansive views.

Consider the first test. We should not let hard cases, such as the growth hormone treatment case, blind us to the way the different accounts converge on the importance of treatments for disease and disability. All developed societies recognize the importance of treating disease and disability; only in a few borderline instances are medical resources used for enhancement. Where disease and disability have a significant impact on opportunity, and where we can effectively provide some form of health care, there is widespread agreement, including among the views discussed in Chapter 2, on the importance of treatment. Thus, where Sen's capability sets would be compromised by disease or disability, so would the individual's fair shares of the normal opportunity range; where disease or disability has such effects, there is likely to be a significant impact on the opportunity for welfare/advantage as well (although disease and disability that we are responsible for create no obligations on the opportunity for welfare view). Conversely, where a disease or disability has little effect on capability sets, it is likely to have little effect on someone's opportunity range, including opportunities for welfare or advantage.

Whereas the alternative views tend to converge on the importance of treatments, at least where the disease or disability has a significant impact on our capabilities, opportunities, or welfare, there is arguably more controversy about enhancements. In the case of treatments, medical and psychiatric sciences provide widely accepted diagnostic categories; clinicians can recognize and more or less reliably identify these disorders and discuss them with patients. For example, although individual cases can pose diagnostic dilemmas, psychiatry has developed publicly accepted methods – currently embodied in the Diagnostic and Statistical Manual of Mental disorders (DSM-IV-TR) – to establish generally agreed-upon diagnoses.[6] Our general desire to treat disease and disability can focus precisely focused on reliably identifiable cases.

The situation is different for enhancements. When is being shorter or shyer or less beautiful than we would like to be a disadvantage that warrants

---

[5] As Robert Cook-Degan points out (personal communication, 1999), a further relevant consideration is whether it leads to stable judgments over time. Advances in science may make some distinctions less useful, including classifications of disease.

[6] Of course, as an examination of the successive revisions of DSM shows, professional agreement at one point in time include many errors, some of which are recognized in later revisions. Which agreements are valid is something we can only determine in light of the overall state of the biomedical sciences.

assistance? Whenever we feel it is? When we cannot adapt to our situation through reasonable efforts? When we have set our hearts on particular goals in life?

If we simply take individuals' assessments at face value, then we – as a society or as insurers – again encounter the moral hazard discussed earlier. If we do not take complainants at face value, how are we to investigate their claims? Have they made reasonable efforts to overcome the condition – participating in social events, asking others for tips on socializing, taking public speaking classes, and so forth? Did they bring it on themselves, as by wishing to consort only with rich, beautiful, and famous people who intimidate them and elicit shyness? We have little idea of how to delve into these questions. And many of us are likely to disagree about how to assess these claims. If we do not investigate, we create substantial risk of moral hazard. But if we do investigate, we find that we have no ability to reconstruct the person's the history of his choices and to assess how responsible he is for creating and sustaining the attitudes and behaviors from which he suffers.

Public support for mental health insurance coverage – historically weak at best and less secure than coverage for physical health – might be compromised further if the public believed that third-party resources were subject to even more moral hazard than exists at present. If the public believed that mental health treatment replaces reasonable efforts to modify one's attitudes and behaviors or to extend one's capacities through learning and practice, support would wane. But this would also occur for physical health care if people saw that scarce medical resources were being diverted into controversial enhancements, perhaps at the expense of clear cases of untreated disease or disability. Our willingness to continue to cooperate depends on our assurance that the terms of cooperation remain fair, but opening the door to moral hazard removes that possibility. It might even be more important to us to to arbitrary in a few hard cases in order to protect general confidence in the fairness of the overall scheme.

Most people understand and accept the moral importance of preventing and treating pathology through shared resources in either public or private insurance systems. There is no comparable agreement on the moral importance of enhancing otherwise normal traits. This suggests that a system that endorsed enhancement and eliminated the priority given to treatment would cause many people to take advantage of shared resources for individual gain. This, in turn, would undermine the basis for sharing risks and benefits in such cooperative schemes.

The importance of treatment rather than enhancement, which most people agree on, has philosophical as well as policy import. The primary rationale, I have argued, for assisting someone medically is that we are preventing or treating a departure from normal functioning. Departure from the "natural baseline" of normal functioning is the primary eligibility condition for claiming assistance to meet health needs. Nevertheless, this use of a natural baseline does not involve attributing metaphysical importance to what is natural, as it does for some strong opponents of enhancement who see it as an affront to human dignity (Kass 2002). We can enhance otherwise normal traits even if we give priority to treatment, and we may sometimes even think we have an obligation to do so (I return to this point momentarily).

People generally agree that this "natural baseline" forms a reasonable and relevant basis for public action despite many other disagreements they may have about other issues of value. Despite many other sorts of comprehensive moral views, people generally agree that maintaining normal functioning contributes in a reasonable and central way to protecting opportunity. The natural baseline has no metaphysical importance: it is not that we must pay some special respect to what is natural, For example, by maintaining or restoring it. Rather, the natural baseline has become a focal point for convergence in our public conception of what we owe each other by way of medical assistance or health protection. To develop fair terms of cooperation, we should not have to resolve our disputes about these comprehensive moral views. Meeting the primary (but not sole) eligibility requirement, however, puts a claim into competition with other eligible claims, and it is in this disputed terrain that fair process is needed to resolve disagreements about what we owe people.

To see that we sometimes may have obligations to enhance an otherwise normal trait, consider the following example. Suppose that an interactive computer game is developed that greatly improves the reading ability of the bottom 10 percent of readers. Suppose further that we can prove that investment in the game is not only cost-effective but also cost-saving in the long run. Further, suppose that the game can improve the opportunity range for a group that is generally worse off than others. We then have good reason to think that investing in this non-health-sector technology is something society should provide.

Now suppose that a drug is invented that is both safe and effective for improving reading in the same population. If we are obliged to provide the computer game, then must we also provide the pill that accomplishes the same result? We have no more reason to call the enhancement health care in the case of the pill than we do in the case of the computer game, even though the pill is a medical technology. The primary eligibility condition and rationale for health care remains treatment (including prevention), not enhancement of normal traits.

RESPONSIBILITY FOR HEALTH

Our answers to the three Focal Questions have focused on the social obligation to maintain and restore health and have said relatively little about individual responsibility to do so. In Chapter 2, I contrasted the extension of Rawls to health and health care, which said almost nothing about individual responsibility for health, with the opportunity for welfare/advantage view. According to the latter view, individuals whose choices worsen their health are not owed (full) compensation or (as much) assistance by others.[7] The emphasis on individual responsibility is appealing, since irresponsible, risky behavior will impose burdens on society that would otherwise be avoidable. Indeed, being silent on this important question may allow critics to say that our account encourages social hijacking. Why should some pay for the risky lifestyle choices of others? There is much evidence that individuals can remain healthy by avoiding smoking, excessive alcohol use, unsafe sex, and certain foods, and by getting adequate exercise and rest. Unhealthy behaviors can give rise to claims on others that more careful people would not make.

Nothing in our approach is incompatible with urging people to adopt healthy lifestyles; far from it. Health education is an essential part of public health on the account developed here. Incentives, and not just education, are also important tools of public health. The harder issue, however, is deciding how to distribute the burdens that result when people behave in risky ways and thus raise the costs of health care. After all, if such behavior is fully informed and truly voluntary, its consequences cannot be easily dismissed as the arbitrary outcome of the natural or social lottery. Should smokers be forced to pay higher insurance premiums or special health-care taxes? Should people be denied care if they contribute to their own illness?

One problem is the task of assigning responsibility. Many risky behaviors, as noted earlier, correlate with other social and economic factors: income, education, ethnicity, religion, gender, and age. Our answer to the second Focal Question thus complicates the problem of assigning responsibility. If a smoking addiction begins in early adolescence and is more difficult to break because of factors associated with low occupational status and education (Barbeau et al. 2004), how much responsibility should we assign to the adult smoker who fails to quit? And in a society where the image of the cool, sexy smoker has become an icon, and where tobacco growers are heavily subsidized, and where tobacco companies have manipulated the addictive properties of their cigarettes, how should responsibility be assigned (Brandt 2007)? If an obesity epidemic affects our children, we may think that they are responsible for what they eat and drink, but we also know that dietary options in their schools and homes, cuts in athletic programs and in physical education in their schools, and poor adult role models all contribute to their behavior. What does holding them responsible really mean? Surely they

---

[7] To be more precise, as the preceding parenthetical phrases encourage us to be, the individual choosing a risky lifestyle is accountable only for that portion of the extra risk that comes from the choice. Since many smokers do not become ill, and since nonsmokers also develop lung cancer and heart disease, the smoker is responsible for only part of the extra risk that comes with smoking.

should not lose their claim on us for assistance because they are responsible for what they eat and drink. Reasonable people will most likely disagree both about assigning responsibility and about the means of doing so. We may all agree that Billy chose the fries over the fruit and in that sense is responsible for what he ate, but little else follows about what we continue to owe Billy if he gets fat and sick. As in other cases, a fair process is needed to resolve such disagreements.

Let us leave aside these obvious problems of assigning responsibility and focus instead on the burdens imposed on others. Should we try to internalize the costs of risky behaviors so that those who engage in them burden others less? For example, if we tax cigarettes heavily and use the taxes to defray the costs of health care, are we holding people responsible for their behavior? Our account raises no objection to such a proposal, even if it does not require it. To be sure, there is some inequity built into such a tax scheme, despite the "dose-response" proportionality between the tax and the burden the unhealthy behavior imposes: There are proportionally fewer rich smokers, and the financial burden on them is lighter than it is on poorer ones. Holding people accountable by taxing them for the burdens they impose on others is not the same thing as saying that others do not owe them assistance for the health problem they create. It is the latter claim about responsibility and what we owe that our account finds objectionable, not holding people accountable for the burdens they impose.

The account we have developed does not punish those who make unhealthy choices by denying them assistance or making it harder for them to obtain it. Sanctions to induce compliance are much more plausible when the health of third parties is at stake, as in efforts to treat drug-resistant forms of tuberculosis or other diseases. In general, meeting health needs, however they arise, is important to protecting opportunity, and is thus important to sustaining the capabilities of free and equal citizens.

DO OUR ANSWERS TO THE FOCAL QUESTIONS WORK TOGETHER?

Each answer to the Focal Questions supplements and yet constrains the others. The special importance of health for protecting opportunity gives us social obligations to promote and protect health. To meet these obligations and to secure equity in health, we must design appropriate policies both inside and outside the health sector. To meet health needs fairly, we should make priority-setting decisions about all these obligations through a fair, deliberative process. Only by combining our answers to all of the Focal Questions can we spell out the entitlements that our right to health and health care includes. Our answers clarify what we owe people when we cannot restore their loss of functioning: Our obligations take us outside the health sector. Our answers also help us establish priorities among the many things we are able to do with medical technologies – we can give priority to treatment over enhancement without drawing metaphysical lines in the sand. Finally, emphasizing our social obligations to meet the health needs of free and equal citizens, regardless of how those needs arise, does not mean that we cannot hold people accountable in reasonable ways for their behaviors. We must temper our judgments in light of what we know about the determinants of health and of risky behaviors, and where we have reasonable disagreements about what to do, we must be accountable for the reasonableness of our decisions.

We have a theory that coheres and gives general guidance to major policy issues. We must now see how it meets some other challenges of the real world and how we can apply it in a range of contexts.

PART II

CHALLENGES

6

Global Aging and Intergenerational Equity

Is the opportunity-based account of just health that I have defended age biased? It might seem so if we think that the opportunities of the elderly are in their past. Isn't it the young, after all, who talk about and care about their opportunities? If opportunity is less important to the elderly, and if health is important because of its impact on opportunity, we should care less about the health and health care of the elderly than we do about the health of the young.[1] In fact, however, most developed countries spend three to four times as much money meeting the greater health needs of the elderly as they do on the young.

In *Just Health Care* and *Am I My Parents' Keeper?* (1988), a later book devoted exclusively to this issue, I responded by reasoning that this objection to my view rested on a misconception of the problem of justice between age groups. Specifically, I rejected the perception of the age-group problem as a problem of competition between groups viewed at a moment in time. I adopted instead a lifespan approach. We should allocate resources prudently

---

[1] On this reading (which I reject), my account of just health shares an age bias with the macroeconomic argument for investing in health (and with the "discounted future earnings" account of valuing lives). According to the macroeconomic argument, investment in health promotes economic growth, but not if we invest heavily in the health of the elderly. If we value health for its contribution to economic growth (or to future earnings), we will value the health of the young more. Many would oppose such views on the grounds that they do not respect people as ends, as entities of value in themselves. Rather, they seem to treat them merely as a means to increasing aggregate income or economic growth. I would take this as a strong objection to my view if it held.

I also distinguish this reading of my view from the fairness arguments of Brock (1989) and Williams (1997), namely, that the elderly have had more opportunity than the young, so protecting fair equality of opportunity ("fair innings," for Williams) requires giving some priority to the young. It also differs from Kamm's (1993) fairness argument that the need for more years is greater for the young than for the old because dying young would be worse than dying old, and we should give priority to those who are worse off. I return briefly to these views when I discuss rationing by age.

to protect health and thus opportunity at each stage of our lives. The basic idea is that, since we all age, we should take as a model for what is fair between age groups what it is prudent for us to do for ourselves at each stage of life. This way of understanding the connection between health, opportunity, and aging avoids the charge of age bias. I further reasoned that if we had institutions that solved the age-group problem in this way, then they could be made fair for the different birth cohorts that pass through these institutions at different times by modestly adjusting the contributions and benefits they make and receive. Such fairness to birth cohorts would help assure stability of the institutions over time.

In this chapter, I modify my earlier response in three basic ways. First, I integrate this account of equity between age groups with what we learned in Part I of this book about the importance of the social determinants of health. Since the lifespan approach is quite general, it should help us think about the distribution of non-health-sector goods over the lifespan and the ways they impact on health. Second, I integrate accountability for reasonableness into the lifespan approach, for reasonable people may disagree about prudent allocation and then must rely on fair process to resolve disputes. I take these to be friendly amendments. Finally, I respond to the real-world challenge of global aging, something not adequately addressed in my earlier work, which largely focused on aging in wealthy developed countries. The challenge of global aging not only makes my assumptions about how to achieve stable solutions to the birth cohort problem seem overly optimistic, but it makes more urgent the need to think about equity between age groups. Accordingly, I begin this discussion with a description of the challenge posed by global aging. That challenge compels me to revisit and more carefully address the problems of equity between age groups and birth cohorts, which I take up next.

THE CHALLENGE OF GLOBAL AGING

Global aging creates what may be the most important public health problem of the twenty-first century. It thus adds urgency to the question of age bias and the just distribution of factors affecting health. Many Americans might assume that aging in their society is simply the result of the large postwar baby boom cohort they so often hear about. But the demographic roots of societal aging go much deeper. A society ages when there is a significant decline in its birth (or fertility) rate and a simultaneous drop in its mortality rate at all ages. Fewer children then are produced, and people live longer. Sometimes, when there is a sudden, temporary increase in the birth rate followed by a significant drop, as in the case of the baby boom, the maturation and aging of that group temporarily accelerate the aging of society. But societal aging can take place without the effect of a superlarge cohort. In its general form, we can depict such aging as the shift from the typical "population pyramid" of earlier periods, wide with many children at the bottom and narrow with

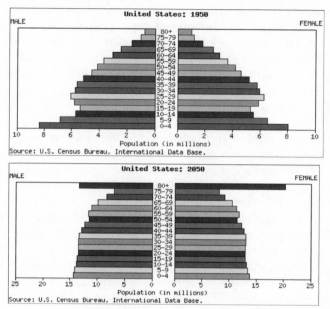

FIGURE 6.1. Illustration of Population Aging in Mexico. *Source:* CONAPO (2004). Proveccioners de la roblacion de Maxico 2000–2050.

few elderly at the top, to a shape that is more like a column or even a column with some bulges at higher ages (representing an enlarged cohort from some earlier period).

Societal, indeed global, aging is treated as a crisis in many recent book titles (which refer to an "age quake" [Wallace 2001], "age wave" [Peterson 1999], or "generational storm" [Kotlikoff and Burns 2004], to note a few), even though it is a result of the *success*, not the *failure*, of long-standing and widely pursued health and family planning policies aimed at reducing mortality and fertility rates. In the United States, the fastest-growing age groups in the country are those over seventy-five and eighty-five. These older age groups will grow even faster when the baby boom cohort reaches those ages beginning in 2020 and "walkers replace strollers" (Kotlikoff and Burns 2004). According to 1996 U.S. census figures, by 2040 there will be more people in the United States over age eighty than there are preschoolers (Peterson 1999). Furthermore, the aging of society is much more advanced in other developed countries. In Italy, for example, the fertility rate (1.2) is well below the level at which the population can reproduce itself (2.1), and the working-age population is already shrinking (as it also is in Japan). Indeed, all the European G-7 countries are below the replacement level in fertility rates. By 2050, half of continental Europe will be forty-nine or older, and well before that, by 2030, one of every two adults in developed countries will have reached retirement age (CSIS 2002).

What may be more surprising to people in developed countries, who are used to seeing mass media pictures of developing countries teeming with children, is that many developing countries are now aging at much faster rates than developed countries did. While the proportion of the elderly in developed countries is due to double over the next fifty years, it is due to triple in East Asia. By 2050, there will be 332 million Chinese sixty-five years of age or over, equivalent to the world's elderly population in 1990 (Jackson and Howe 1999). The 2 billion people over age sixty who will live in our aging world by 2050 will mostly be living in developing countries. Unfortunately, this rapid societal aging is taking place without the wealth and the sophisticated economic institutions that exist in developed countries, so that China will grow old before it grows rich (Jackson and Howe 1999).

The primary effects of societal aging are domestic for each nation, for the changed profile of societal needs it produces requires a national response. But global aging will also have some international effects. When only developed countries faced societal aging, a shrinking labor force could be partly relieved by increased migration of young workers from other countries. (Only in the United States has the scale of such immigration had a significant impact on the workforce and on fertility rates.) But as aging impacts countries worldwide, more countries will have a shrinking workforce. Immigration from younger to older countries may greatly intensify recent changes in immigration compared to those a century ago. In addition, societal aging may affect economic growth rates, leading to shifts in the flow of investment capital internationally. Since all of these factors act as social determinants of health, there can be significant but not easily predictable effects on health.

A Changing Profile of Needs

The graying of societies changes dramatically the profile of health and social support needs. Consider the problem of increased disability and dependency with very old age. Over thirty years ago, Bernice Neugarten (1974) introduced the distinction between the "young old," those ages sixty-five to seventy-four, who are generally quite healthy and free of significant disability, and the "old old," those over age seventy-five, who are more likely to have significant disabilities and require care. The rapid growth in the population of those over seventy-five, unless it is offset by dramatic reductions in the prevalence of disease and disability among that age group, will bring with it increased burdens for the management of chronic disease and long-term care.

Since most long-term care is provided by family members, much of the burden will fall on adult working children. Yet, nearly a quarter of all the elderly in the United States in 1989 had no children, and another 20 percent had only one child. With more women in the workforce, the problem of providing family care is intensified, since women have traditionally been the primary caregivers. In addition, if benefits for elderly retirees are reduced, which is one strategy advocated by many to cope with societal aging in the United States, the elderly will become more economically dependent on their adult children.

The caregiver problem for frail and dependent elderly persons arises in developing countries as well. There, the problem is not the sustainability of the publicly supported social and medical services provided for the elderly in developed countries but the sustainability of informal social structures of support, such as the traditional patterns of care that involve aged parents living with adult children, as in Japan and China. China, for example, must face the consequence of the success of its strict population policy: one child for urban couples, two for rural ones. Like the United States, China will have many elderly persons with no children. It will have even more elderly who have only one child to support them than is the case in the United States. The Chinese refer to this as the "one-two-four" problem: One child must care for two parents and four grandparents.

In 1996 the Chinese government made it a legal requirement that adult children support their elderly parents, obviously anticipating that traditional filial obligations would be strained to the breaking point by the new demographic realities. The law will not solve the problem, given its scale. Instead, China will have to construct public supports that fill the gap left by eroding family supports and do so without further undermining those family supports. China's problem is the problem of all developing countries where rapid aging, extensive urbanization and industrialization, and a lack of existing health-care and income support systems for the elderly all collide with traditional family values.

The point is simple: No aging society, with or without public systems of support, escapes the problems created by societal aging for sustaining and improving institutions that provide care for elderly dependents.

The increase in medical needs with societal aging is much broader than the problem of long-term care for frail elderly people. Aging increases the prevalence of cardiovascular disease, chronic pulmonary disease, diabetes, arthritis, and cancer, as well as Alzheimer's disease and other dementias. The increased cost of treating these more prevalent illnesses imposes great strains on resources and intensifies competition for them in developed countries. The problem will be even greater in the health-care systems of developing countries, many of which have barely begun to gear up to meet the needs posed by chronic diseases. In poorly funded systems, beefing up medical services for the chronic illnesses of middle and older age means stealing resources from primary care and preventive care for the whole population. The prospect of vast unmet health needs for a growing elderly population is the reason I suggested earlier that societal aging may be the greatest public health problem of this century.

The aging of a society also changes the profile of needs that arise outside the health sector and yet affect population health. For example, as people typically live longer, they must plan for income support over a longer retirement period, and they must do so in a global economy that has altered long-standing career patterns and attendant retirement plans. With typically longer lives there may be a need for education beyond childhood and adolescence, including new forms of continuing education for adults. Such education has unknown effects on population health, but if it affects people in the ways education earlier in life does, it may have profound effects on population health.

Sustainability of Institutions and Competition for Resources

Societal aging not only shifts the basic pattern of needs in a society, it also creates problems in sustaining traditional institutions that meet those needs. Those institutions emerged in response to a particular pattern of needs and a particular population age structure. Societal aging, especially rapid aging, strains their adequacy and sustainability.

One way to look at the source of the strain is to measure the change in the ratio of workers to dependents in a society. Actually, we need to look at two distinct ratios: that of workers to retirees and that of workers to all dependents, including retirees and children. A reduction in the number of children, for example, can offset, at least temporarily and partially, an increase in the number of retirees. If retirees are more expensive to support than children, especially if they retire early, live long lives, and develop significant dependencies, then fewer children to support may provide little relief. Moreover, the problems interact: If younger families of childbearing age are heavily burdened with the cost of supporting a large elderly population, it may further reduce their own fertility rates, intensifying the problem later on.

Why think of support for the elderly as a burden on current workers, one that increases as the dependency ratios worsen? The simple answer is that all health-care systems that include the elderly are pay-as-you-go systems. They are funded by some combination of general tax revenues, payroll taxes, sales or value-added taxes, and premiums. Most pension and income support systems in developed countries are funded the same way. The explanation for this fact varies with the good supplied.

With health-care insurance, there is probably no real alternative to pay-as-you-go, since the far greater medical needs of the elderly would make insurance pools stratified by age prohibitively expensive.[2] The same is true

---

[2] Since individual health savings accounts of the sort that have emerged in several countries are usually backed by a shared catastrophic insurance plan, my earlier points would apply to them as well.

for long-term care needs. Private insurance markets for them fail to provide good protection (except for those economically best off) because people would have to buy into them at very early ages in order to spread the risk over their lifespan. Buying such plans late in life, when expected needs are greater, would be impossible for most people because premiums would be too high, given their levels of income and wealth. So, health-care insurance coverage for the elderly – universal coverage for persons of all ages in other developed countries, universal coverage for those over sixty-five in the United States – spreads the risk between younger, healthier workers and older, less healthy retirees, with the promise that the system will remain stable and useful to younger cohorts when they age. In effect, the systems are "actuarially unfair" to the young and an "actuarial boon" to the elderly, but the goal is to make them actuarially fair over the lifespan.[3] The challenge posed by societal aging is whether the system will be stable over the lifespan of younger working cohorts so that they will be supported at benefit levels approximating those they now support for the elderly.

The story is more complicated for pensions and income support, largely because of history and politics. In most developed countries, pensions were introduced through payroll taxes as pay-as-you-go systems in which current workers paid for the benefits of current retirees, expecting in turn to have their benefits paid by later retirees. Such systems offer the political advantage of providing benefits for retirees as soon as the system starts. This was crucial to the political appeal of Social Security in the United States where many older workers who had faced the Great Depression needed support immediately on retirement and could not wait to accrue vested savings over a lifetime of work. In addition, as long as the working population was stable or increasing, as it was throughout most of the twentieth century in developed countries, the ratio of workers to retirees was favorable. Ongoing population growth promised ongoing stability for financing.

Enter population aging. In Italy and Japan, the working-age population is already shrinking. There will be 28 percent fewer working-age Germans and 36 percent fewer working-age Japanese by 2050 than there are today (CSIS 2002). The UN projects that the ratio of working-age adults to elderly in the developed world will drop from 4.5 to 1 today to 2.2 to 1 in 2050. The International Monetary Fund (IMF) estimates the ratios in 2050 for

---

[3] In the United States, we can construe insured workers' health care "premiums" to be the total of their contribution (and that of their employers) to private insurance plus their payroll tax contribution (supporting Medicare) plus their contribution to general tax revenues (supporting Medicaid and public hospitals). They will pay out more than they will receive in medical benefits, on average, which is what I meant by saying that the arrangement is actuarially unfair to them. Retirees, however, pay out less than they receive as benefits, even when we include their high out-of-pocket expenses (thus the "actuarial boon"). Over the lifespan of each, however, the system meets needs and provides approximate actuarial fairness (except that progressive or regressive taxes complicate the point).

Japan, France, Germany, and Italy will be 1.5, 1.4, 1.2 and less than 1 to 1, respectively. Public retirement spending in typical developed countries will grow from 11 to 23 percent of GDP by that year (CSIS 2002).

Other factors also enter, such as the trend toward earlier retirement. In the United States, France, Germany, and Italy, the age of retirement has decreased rather than increased, as one might have expected with people living longer, healthier lives. The combination of a longer lifespan and earlier retirement, along with shrinking working-age populations in countries like Italy and Germany, greatly intensifies the strain on resources in existing transfer schemes. Developing countries, including China, have a longer time period in which to rely on large working-age populations and rapid economic growth rates to prepare for their own health care and income support later in retirement. But the absence of existing institutions to build on, aside from informal family support, will make this a very difficult task.

My point is not to side with critics of pay-as-you-go systems who insist that we turn to systems that rest on vested savings. There are some advantages, outside the context of rapid aging of society, to systems that share risks across cohorts. The well-being of one cohort is less dependent on its own economic history and can be protected against extremely bad luck by sharing risks with other cohorts. The problem is how to stabilize the system in a context of rapid aging. I return to this point later. Here I only address the source of the strain for traditional solutions to the problem of meeting the needs of the old and the young.

INTERGENERATIONAL EQUITY: TWO PROBLEMS, NOT ONE

Aside from some confused calls for intergenerational equity and some passing attention to the threat to traditional familial values,[4] the global aging literature is strikingly silent on basic questions of value, even as it discusses policy steps that are needed. One thing that makes the intensified conflict or competition between the old and the young especially difficult is that the basic needs of different groups are at issue. The old and the young both need health care – often of different types. We are not talking about privileges for one group and necessities for another. Were that the case, justice would easily rule in favor of giving priority to the more important needs. The problem is much harder. What do we do when the competition between the old and the young is for life-extending health care or for income support

---

[4] Traditional rural, agricultural settings with large families supporting their own elderly parents disappeared long ago in developed countries and are rapidly disappearing in developing ones. Migration of adult children to cities for work often involves leaving the elderly behind, sometimes to care for grandchildren. But even where the elderly also are brought to the city, they can no longer engage in productive work in the ways they did in rural settings, so dependency is increased. In addition, there are many fewer children to care for aged parents.

necessary to meet basic needs? Can we choose between health care for the elderly and education for their grandchildren? What is striking about the policy literature is its silence on these issues.

The rest of this chapter is aimed at distinguishing and answering two questions about justice between the old and the young that are often conflated – *equity among age groups* and *equity among birth cohorts*. As we shall see, separate concepts and distinct problems of distributive justice are involved in the appeal to "intergenerational equity." The policy debates about modifying medical and income support systems for retirees require us to be careful in distinguishing these ethical issues. Properly integrated solutions to both problems must also consider the role of the broad determinants of health across the lifespan and the need to rely on fair process in making the many resource allocation decisions solutions involved.

Distinguishing between Age Groups and Birth Cohorts

The question posed by many about intergenerational equity readily leads us to confuse two distinct problems: "What is a fair distribution among age groups?" and "What is a fair distribution among birth cohorts?" Part of the confusion comes from the fact that the term "generation," and thus "intergenerational equity," is multiply ambiguous. When we worry about destroying our atmosphere or oceans or forests, we are concerned about equity between relatively distant generations. Will we leave enough and as good in quality for our great-great grandchildren? I shall not address this problem, important as it is. I shall focus instead on *adjacent* generations, the young and the old in any society, and I shall concentrate on equity in distributing health and health care (though this may require equity with regard to the distribution of other goods as well, as I argued in Chapters 3 and 5). Still, even with the restriction to adjacent generations, there remains an ambiguity: "Generation" can refer to age groups, as in the perennial conflict between the young and the old, or it can refer to birth cohorts, as when we contrast experiences of the World War II generation and the Vietnam War generation. Another source of confusion comes from the fact that the problems interact: A solution to the age group problem must be compatible with a solution to the birth cohort problem, and vice versa.

Despite the ambiguity in "generation," the concepts are clearly different. We individuate them differently. Age groups do not age, but birth cohorts do. The age group comprised of people ages sixty-five to seventy-five is always comprised of people of those ages. The birth cohort of people who are sixty-five to seventy-five in 2010 will, of course, age ten years by 2020. At any given time, an age group consists of one or more birth cohorts, depending how we identify the cohorts. Over time, it consists of a succession of birth cohorts. The birth cohort of people born between 1935 and 1945 that comprises the sixty-five to seventy-five age group in 2010 will be replaced in 2020 by the cohort born between 1945 and 1955. As we age, we pass through different age groups but not different birth cohorts.

A birth cohort is a distinct group of people with a distinctive history and composition. The question "What is a just distribution of social goods between birth cohorts?" thus assumes that we are focused on differences between distinct groups of people. For example, special questions of fairness may arise because of particular facts about the socioeconomic history and composition of particular birth cohorts. In contrast, the notion of an age group abstracts from the distinctiveness of birth cohorts and considers people solely by reference to their place in the lifespan. Consequently, our question about justice between age groups also abstracts from the particular differences between the current elderly and the current young that arise because of the distinctive features of the birth cohorts that happen to make up those age groups. We are concerned with a common problem about justice between the old and the young that persists through the succession of aging birth cohorts.

Equity between Age Groups and Birth Cohorts

Not only are age group and birth cohort different concepts, but we must think about fair distribution differently for them. We should think of fairness between different age groups as a problem of prudential allocation over the lifespan. Institutions that allocate resources in a way that meets needs at each stage of life in a way that makes our lives as a whole go better will treat age groups fairly. Fairness to different birth cohorts, however, requires that cohorts enjoy rough equity in the benefits they receive given the contributions they make as they pass through institutions that appropriately solve the age group problem. Though the concepts and problems of distribution are different, they interact and need to be solved together.

Our tendency to confuse these questions is not simply the result of collective stupidity, including the failure to notice a semantic ambiguity in the term "generation." Rather, the confusion results primarily from our perception of competition between groups. We see the age-group question in competitive terms: The old and the young compete at any given moment for scarce public welfare resources. Whose side should we take? At the personal level, where adult children must care for elderly parents while also raising their own children, the sense of competition is muted by love and obligation. Limits to resources still mean hard choices for many who struggle without adequate societal support.

Still, the perceptions of the age-group problem at both the personal and social levels share a common framework. At both levels, the issue is to determine which transfers of goods should take place between distinct *groups* of individuals, the young and the old, adult children and elderly parents. Which transfers are just or fair? What does one group owe the other? The sharp competition felt at the social level may be tempered by love and a desire to care at the personal level. But the problem is still seen as one between "us" and "them."

This way of construing the age-group problem is reinforced by our tendency to see public policy as something that operates here and now. We scrutinize its effects at a particular time. We rarely think of public policies as operating over long periods of time, indeed, over our whole lifespan. When we do think about the long run – for example, about what life will be like later in this century – we shift questions. We stop thinking about the age-group question and substitute the question about equity between birth cohorts.

In what follows, I reject the perception of the age-group problem as a problem of competition between groups viewed at a given moment and adopt instead the lifespan approach promised earlier.

THE PRUDENTIAL LIFESPAN ACCOUNT

What is a just distribution of resources between the young and the old? The key to answering this question lies in the humbling fact that we all age. In contrast, we do not change sex or race. How are these banal observations relevant?

If we treat blacks and whites or men and women differently, then we produce inequalities between persons, and such inequalities raise questions about justice. For example, if we hire and fire on the basis of race or sex rather than talents and skills, then we create unjust inequalities. If we treat the old and the young differently, however, we may or may not produce inequality between persons. If we treat them differently just occasionally and arbitrarily, then we will be treating different persons unequally. But if we treat the young one way as a matter of policy and the old another way, and if we do so over their whole lives, then we treat all persons the same way. There is no inequality between persons since each person is treated both ways in the course of a complete life. Thus, the banal fact that we age means that age is different from race or sex for purposes of distributive justice.

My account of justice between age groups builds on this basic point: Unequal treatment at different stages of life may be exactly what we want from institutions that operate over a lifetime. Since our needs vary at different life stages, we want institutions to respond to these changes. In many industrialized countries, we defer income from our working lives to our retirement period through some combination of individual savings and an employee or government pension or social security plan. In many such schemes there are no vested savings, but rather a direct transfer from the working young to the retired old. Viewed at a given moment, it appears that "we" young workers are taxed to benefit "them," the old. Similarly, working people pay for far more than the cost of their own health care, for they contribute to the costs of children and the elderly alike, whether in the American mixed insurance system or in universal coverage systems elsewhere. If these systems are stable over the lifespan, then we have designed systems that treat us appropriately – differently – at different ages.

Age groups are treated differently in such schemes. The old pay less and get more, while the young pay more and get less. If this system continues as we age, others will pay "inflated" premiums or taxes that will cover our higher costs when we are elderly. Such a system allows us to defer the use of resources from life stages when we need them less to stages when we need them more. In general, budgeting these transfers prudently enables us to take from some parts of our lives in order to make our lives as a whole better.

Two important lessons emerge about the unequal treatment of different age groups. First, treating the young and old differently does not mean that persons are treated unequally over their lifespan.[5] Second, such unequal treatment may have effects that benefit everyone.[6] These two points provide the central intuition behind the Prudential Lifespan Account of justice between age groups: Prudent allocation among stages of our lives is our guide to what is just between the young and the old.

The lifespan account involves a fundamental shift of perspective. Rather than seeing distinct groups in competition with each other – for example, working adults who pay high premiums and the frail elderly who consume many services – we must view each group as *representing* a stage of our lives. The prudent allocation of resources throughout the stages of life is our guide to justice between groups. From the perspective of stable institutions operating over time, unequal treatment of people by age appears to be

---

[5] McKerlie (1989a,b, 1993) suggests abandoning the standard concern for equality between complete lives and emphasizing instead equality between simultaneous segments of lives. Consider the inequality between simultaneous segments that shows up for Betty and Connie:

Decade	1	2	3	4	5	6	7	8	9
Betty	10	5	10	5	10	5	10	5	
Connie		10	5	10	5	10	5	10	5

Connie has the same pattern of well-being as Betty, but because she was born ten years later, on McKerlie's view, there are thirty-five objectionable units of inequality in decades 2 through 8. McKerlie's view thus runs counter to a basic intuition: Simply changing Connie's birth date, with no other effects on either life, should not make the situation more or less objectionable. I respond more fully to McKerlie's view in Daniels (1996a).

[6] Raising the age of eligibility for Social Security, which arguably is a prudent and fair way to address both the age-group and birth-cohort problems, might leave African Americans, who have lower life expectancy, worse off than whites or Asians. Where such effects occur, they may constitute good reasons for not adopting such a rationing policy, or they might give us reasons to link the rationing to facts about group life expectancy. The general point is that the Prudential Lifespan Account presupposes that solutions to the age-group problem will not disturb more general requirements of justice (see Daniels 1988, 1996a).

budgeting within a life. If we are concerned with net benefits within a life, we can appeal to a standard principle of individual rational choice: It is rational and prudent that a person take from one stage of his life to give to another in order to improve his life as a whole. If the transfers made by an income support or health-care system are prudent, they improve individual well-being. Different individuals in such schemes are each made better off, even when the transfers involve unequal treatment of the young and the old. This means that neither old nor young have grounds for complaint that the system is unfair. Prudent allocation establishes fair terms of cooperation among age groups.

The contrast of age with race or sex should now be clear. Differential treatment of people by age, when part of a prudent lifetime scheme, involves treating people equally over their whole lives. There are no losers. Differential treatment by sex or race always creates inequalities, benefiting some at the expense of others. Losers will have legitimate complaints about unfairness or injustice.[7]

To illustrate the basic idea, consider how I might design a health-care insurance policy that operated over my whole life span. Suppose that I am willing to spend only a certain amount of my lifetime resources insuring myself against health-care risks – health care, however important, is not the only good in my life. In any case, I accept the fact that the benefits I can buy with that lifetime premium will not meet all of my medical needs. Therefore, I must be willing to trade coverage for some needs at certain stages of my life for coverage at others. I also believe that I should give equal consideration to my interests at all points in my life.

Unfortunately, if I know how old I am and think about things only from the perspective of what I consider important at that point in my life, then I risk biasing the design of my insurance package, for example by underestimating the importance of things I will need much later in life. To compensate for this bias, I should pretend that I do not know how old I am and will have to live through all the trade-offs I impose at each stage of my life. For example, I know that if I give myself too much acute health care when I am dying, I do so at the expense of other services, such as long-term care

---

7 Antidiscrimination legislation concerning gender or race in the United States is premised on the idea that unequal treatment, measured by unequal outcomes (as opposed to racist or sexist intent), is prohibited. Antidiscrimination legislation on age is modeled on race and gender legislation, but it must allow for reasonable age-based distinctions in treatment. It accepts as nondiscriminatory age regulation of voting, military service, and alcohol use, as well as eligibility for Medicare and Social Security and for senior discounts. Its prohibition on age-based discrimination in hiring and firing is compatible with the view I propose: These are not prudent features of job allocation over the lifespan but rather arbitrary, often stereotypically driven or economically driven treatment of individuals because they belong to an identifiable group. Whether a prudent lifespan version of compulsory retirement could be defended is a complex issue I leave for another occasion.

services, or preventive services earlier in life, that might improve my quality of life over a considerable period late in life.

Just as individuals set reasonable limits on their lifetime insurance premiums, prudent planners acting on behalf of society in general – using the fair, deliberative process developed in Chapter 4– are limited by what counts as a fair share of health care. This share is not simply a dollar allotment per person. It consists of entitlements to services that depend on our having certain medical needs. Their problem is to find the reasons relevant to allocating this fair share over the whole lifespan. Accountability for reasonableness applies, then, to this lifespan allocation and not simply to setting limits at a given moment. The goal is a distribution that people in each age group think is fair because they all agree that it makes their lives as a whole better than the alternatives. To ensure that our planners avoid biasing the design in favor of their own age group, we shall require them (1) to pretend that they do not know how old they are and (2) to accept a distribution only if they are willing to live with the results at each stage of their lives. Each stage of their own lives thus stands as a proxy for an age group, and they will age from conception to death in the system of trade-offs to which they agree.[8]

Before saying more about application of the Prudential Lifespan Account to health, I want to emphasize that this account is quite general. It gives us a way of thinking about the distribution of many important goods, not just health care. As I remarked earlier, as life expectancy increases and career trajectories change, continuing education or income support for adults may become more important. A prudent allocation of these goods over a lifespan should accommodate such effects of societal aging, especially since both of them are themselves determinants of population health. The Prudential Lifespan Account asks us to think about how planners who do not know their age would allocate a lifetime fair share of entitlements to income support or education to each stage of life. These entitlements are specified relative to what justice in general permits in the way of inequalities among persons.

---

[8] In Daniels (1988: Ch. 3) I give a more detailed statement of these and some other qualifications on the concept of "prudent deliberation" appropriate for solving the age-group problem. Appropriate considerations of prudence require even further restrictions on the knowledge of the deliberators, making them even less like the standard, fully informed consumer of economic theory. For example, they should judge their well-being by reference to all-purpose goods, like income and opportunity, rather than through the very specific lens of the plan of life they happen to have at a given stage of life; otherwise, the design of the lifetime allocation may be biased by a conception of what is good that just happens to be held at a given point in life; see also Buchanan (1975); Rawls (1982b, 2001). In Daniels (1988: Appendix A [reprinted in Daniels 1996a]), I also defend a key feature of classical prudential reasoning, that we value each part of our lives equally ("the requirement of equal concern"), against criticism of this principle by Parfit (1984).

Lifespan Allocation of Health Care

To illustrate the approach, though without the extra complexity raised by the lifespan distribution of such social determinants, consider how the Prudential Lifespan Account might be applied to health care, given the account of just health developed earlier. How should prudent planners think about the entitlements to care that people can reasonably claim at each stage of life, given that meeting these health needs is intended to protect opportunity by protecting normal functioning? Remember, such planners are constrained by pretending that they do not know their own age and must plan for each stage of life on the assumption that they will live through it. Protecting opportunity at each stage of life is especially important since all have a fundamental interest in being able to revise their views about what is valuable in life as they age. Because impairments of normal functioning clearly restrict the portion of the normal opportunity range open to individuals at any stage of life, health-care services should be rationed throughout a life in a way that respects the importance of the age-relative normal opportunity range. With this refinement, the fair equality of opportunity account of just health can avoid the charge of age bias.

Reasonable people will disagree about what this principle means when specific trade-offs must be made. For example, if we allocate resources to prevention early in life in order to reduce the risk of loss of functioning much later on, we may not be able to meet other health needs early or late in life. Versions of the unsolved rationing problems we saw earlier arise in this context as well, even though they take place within stages of a life. Just as reasonable people may disagree about how much priority to give those who are worse off than others, a distribution problem across lives, so too they may disagree about how much priority to give being worse off in health at some stage of life compared to being better off at others.[9] Since we are designing a prudent social scheme, fair, deliberative process is needed to resolve such disagreements so that the outcomes are accepted as fair and legitimate. Just as, in *Just Health Care*, I mistakenly thought that the impact of pathology on normal functioning would be a sufficient measure of the importance of a health need, I also underestimated the sources of disagreement about how to set priorities in meeting needs at different stages of a life by relying on prudence alone. In both cases, we must supplement the opportunity principle – even relativized to stage of life – with fair process.

Depending on the organization of health care in specific systems, this model of prudent allocation over the lifespan becomes either more or less hypothetical. In the United States, where a publicly funded universal

---

[9] Lives containing equal numbers of QALYs may have them distributed differently; reasonable people may disagree about which distribution makes the life as a whole best. Some may be willing to trade away total QALYs against some distributive considerations.

coverage system exists for the elderly but most children and adults are covered by private insurance plans, there is little incentive to apply a lifespan approach to the design of health-care entitlements. Private plans have little economic incentive to invest in preventive measures that will protect the elderly, and decision makers in Medicare never have to reconcile their resource allocation decisions with the needs of younger age groups. In universal coverage systems that fund benefits across the lifespan, the model has a natural applicability.

Consider three specific implications of this application of the Prudential Lifespan Account to health care. Two of these – the importance of meeting children's health needs and the importance of long-term care – are less controversial and I note them briefly; the general problem of rationing by age requires more discussion.

Children's Health

Advocates for children in the United State have long decried the fact that we have uni.:ersal coverage for the elderly but not for children. Proper attention to the health needs of children, within and outside the health sector, has major health benefits over the lifespan. A well-designed system would invest heavily in the health of children, reaping the benefits in the protection of opportunity over the lifespan. In Chapter 3, I noted how important attention to the broader social determinants of health would be in this regard – for example, early childhood interventions that improve educational achievement have health payoffs over the lifespan. Similarly, knowing more about good health in early life will improve health over the lifespan by helping people to avoid unsafe sex, as well as abuse of drugs and alcohol, and by helping them develop good nutritional and exercise habits. A proper approach to children's health must be proactive and not focused simply on treating conditions once they occur. This means proper prenatal and maternal care, well-child visits, attention to sensory and cognitive deficits or disorders, and obviously to nutrition and exercise, as well as comprehensive sex education.

Health systems that cover populations comprehensively at all ages have strong incentives to invest properly in child health. Systems that divide populations by age or employment status lose incentives to invest in these ways. Since most people agree on the importance of children's health, the lifespan model, which emphasizes that importance, should become an aid to planning wherever organizational features of a system do not create obstacles (as they do in the United States).

Long-Term Care

Because the likelihood of needing long-term care increases with age, the aging of society raises urgent questions about the long-term care systems in all developed and many developing countries. It follows from the equality of opportunity account of just health and health care that long-term care is just as important as acute care. Both have the same function: protecting an individual's share of the (age-relative) normal opportunity range. Nevertheless, in many health-care systems in both developed and developing countries, long-term care is undervalued. As a result, the needs of many people with disabilities, regardless of age, have not been met fairly.

Adding the perspective of the Prudential Lifespan Account, two further points emerge. First, it may be prudent to trade some acute care services aimed at a small extension of life for long-term care services that greatly improve the quality of life over a longer period. Second, giving long-term care services that give relief to families, who provide the bulk of long-term care, produces a benefit at two stages of life. It helps both when we provide such care and when we receive it. These considerations suggest that the U.S. system, like many others, has undervalued the importance of long-term care and undersupplied crucial services that benefit us at various points in the lifespan.

In some universal access systems, like the Canadian and some European systems, long-term care services, including many social support and home services, are already incorporated in the benefit package. Rationing health care in these systems will require making explicit how the importance of these services is measured against the importance of existing and emerging acute care technologies. This is exactly where accountability for reasonableness, with its emphasis on deliberation about competing rationales, can educate us over time and can help us learn from the hard choices we must make.

Rationing by Age

In 2006, the Ministry of Health in Thailand considered adding coverage for dialysis within its health insurance plan for people not included in other insurance schemes, which already provided dialysis. One of the hardest questions it faced was: Should there be an age cutoff for eligibility to treatment, and if people were not allowed access to it after a certain age, would it be permissible to stop treatment when people reached that age? There was early evidence (Aaron and Schwartz 1984) of the denial of dialysis to the elderly in the United Kingdom in the 1980s, when it was accessible to the elderly in the United States without limit. Many health systems do not provide certain organ transplants to people over certain ages. If an age cutoff is a proxy for medical risk or likely medical outcomes, then the ethical issue is whether "best outcomes" should be the criterion for allocation and whether age is a good proxy for it (see Chapter 3). Age may be proposed, however, as a criterion for resource allocation when it is not being used as a proxy for another outcome. Is such "pure" age rationing morally permissible? Is it ever required on grounds of fairness?

The issue is a key point of moral controversy. Some critics of rationing by age consider it just as morally impermissible as rationing by race or sex.

They consider age, as opposed to medical suitability, a morally irrelevant basis for distributing medical services. Others advocate rationing by age because they believe that the elderly have a duty to step aside and sacrifice for the young (Callahan 1987). Still others do so because they believe that it is fair for the elderly, who have had the opportunity to live a long time, to forego services in favor of the young, who have had less opportunity to live (cf. Veatch 1988; Brock 1989; Williams 1997). Kamm (1993) argues that we should give priority to the young because they "need" more years of life than the old, being worse off without them than the old are. When the NICE Citizen's Council (2004) considered such questions in the United Kingdom, a majority thought that age was relevant in treatment decisions if it was a measure of risk or potential benefit, but not if it was taken as an indicator for social roles or, as Williams's "fair innings" view (1997) would have it, of the degree to which one has already had experience of life.

In my earlier work on aging (1985: Ch. 5, 1988), I thought that the Prudential Lifespan Account to the age group problem provided a way to resolve this dispute, and I still believe that it offers a reasonable, but restricted, approach to it. I now believe, however, that the reasonable disagreement such pure age rationing faces means that disputes about it, as about many other unsolved distribution problems, must be resolved within a fair, deliberative process such as that described in Chapter 4. Nevertheless, the Prudential Lifespan Account brings an important argument to bear on the deliberation that takes place within such a fair process, and I shall summarize that argument in what follows.

According to the Prudent Lifespan Account to the age group problem, a policy will be fair to different age groups if prudent planners who do not know how old they are would choose it as a way of allocating a lifetime fair share of health care among the stages of life. Under very special conditions of resource scarcity, the following might happen: Very expensive or very scarce life-extending services can be provided to those who have reached a normal life expectancy only by giving fewer services to the young. That is, saving these resources by giving ourselves claim to them in our old age is possible only if we give ourselves reduced access to them in earlier stages of life. With this form of saving, we increase our chance of living a longer than normal lifespan at the cost of reducing our chances of living a normal lifespan. Under some conditions, it would be prudent for planners to agree to ration such technologies by age, making them more available to the young than to the very old. More precisely, if we consider only information about life-years saved, and if rationing by age and rationing by lottery both yield the same life expectancy, it is not imprudent to prefer an increased chance of reaching that life expectancy through age rationing. If we add more information – for example, that years later in life are more likely to contain disabilities, or that earlier years are typically more important to carrying out central projects in life – then we can get the stronger result that age rationing is preferred to rationing by lottery.[10]

Given only two alternatives, rationing by age or rationing by lottery, prudent deliberators with scarce resources might find age rationing prudent and therefore morally permissible. Of course, other alternatives might be more prudent, but if the choice is restricted, then rationing by age would be fair to all persons, treating them equally over their lives, and it would benefit each by maximizing the chances of reaching a normal life expectancy. This argument turns on no prior moral assumptions that life at one age is more *valuable* than life at another. It does not turn on the judgment that it is more important or valuable for society to save the young than the old or that society would benefit more from doing so. Instead, it turns on the

---

[10] In *Just Health Care* I considered two rationing schemes. Scheme A (Age rationing) involves a direct appeal to an age criterion: No one over age seventy or seventy-five – taken to represent a normal lifespan – is eligible for any of several high-cost life-extending technologies, such as some transplant surgeries. Because age rationing reduces utilization of each technology, there are resources available for developing them all, though under this scenario, that development will only be for the young. Scheme L (Lottery) rejects age rationing and allocates life-extending technology solely by medical need. As a result, it can either develop just one such major technology, say heart transplant, making it available to anyone who needs it, or it can develop several such technologies but then ration them by lottery.

Scheme A saves resources – defers their use until later in life – at a lower rate than Scheme L. Scheme L takes more from earlier stages so that later ones may benefit. Specifically, Scheme L involves reducing the chance that the young will reach a normal lifespan because access to life-extending resources has been reduced. In return, Scheme L offers an increased chance of living a longer than normal lifespan to those who do reach a normal lifespan. For instance, though this is an extreme example, Scheme A might offer a 1.0 probability of reaching age 75 (and dying right away), and Scheme L might give a 0.5 probability of reaching 50 and a 0.5 probability of reaching 100. Both yield the same expected lifespan, but they do so differently.

Our prudent deliberators must choose between Schemes A and L. Suppose that they adopted a "maximin" rule of rational choice: Make the worst outcome as good as possible (or as unlikely to happen as possible). If maximin is the correct rule, it is easy to show that Scheme A would be preferable to Scheme L since it makes early death, presumably a worse outcome, less likely. Suppose the deliberators adopt the more common rule of choice – the Standard or Bayesian Rule – that instructs prudent deliberators to maximize their expected net benefit or payoff when they face choices. If the payoff is the number of years lived, the Standard Rule tells us to maximize the expected lifespan. Since Schemes A and L have the same expected lifespan, the Standard Rule instructs prudent deliberators to be indifferent. This tie is an interesting and important result. It tells us that age rationing cannot in general be ruled out on the grounds that it is imprudent and therefore unfair. If we use the Standard Rule and also allow other information – for example, about typical frequencies of disease and disability as we age, or about the degree to which typical plans of life are organized to complete their most important goals before the late stages of life – then without making the judgment that one plan of life is better than another or even, by itself, less prudent, deliberators, familiar with their society and culture but unaware of which conception of the good is theirs, would select Scheme A over Scheme L because they want to increase their chances of living through the middle stages of their lives.

judgment each of us would in effect make, that we would each be better off (or not worse off) from an age rationing scheme. Nor does it turn on prior moral views about the duties of the elderly to the young or vice versa (Callahan 1987).[11]

The Prudential Lifespan Account uses weak assumptions about prudence to make an argument about fairness. Contrast it, for example, with Brock's (1989) suggestion (similar to those of Veatch [1988] and Williams [1997]) that the principle of equality of opportunity states directly that we should give everyone a better chance of reaching normal life expectancy through age rationing rather than give some people an extra opportunity to live much longer. If, however, a young person has had her opportunity enhanced through prior medical treatment, does she still have a greater claim than an old person who has never been so helped? The fair innings view would also be plausible only if it were modified so that only significant differences in the number of years lived was a basis for a fairness claim; it might also have to be qualified depending on the amount of extra time that would be gained by people at different ages. Disagreements about these qualifications might themselves require a fair process to resolve. Part of what is at issue is whether we should judge the equality of opportunity as assured by the outcome (more equal chances at achieving a normal life expectancy) or by a process (more equal chances through a lottery at receiving the life-extending service). Our intuitions pull in different directions on this matter, as did the judgments of the NICE Citizen's Council (2004). My prudential argument, however, makes no such appeal to such intuitions.

The Prudential Lifespan Account does *not* advocate age rationing as a general policy. It supports age rationing only under very limited conditions and only when there is no more prudent alternative. Alternative strategies for allocating resources, more fine-tuned to the conditions of patients and the likely outcomes of treating them, would probably be better.

The Prudential Lifespan Account does not tell us how to ration services over the lifespan (as McKerlie [1989b] and Emanuel [1992] note). Given limited resources, we must sometimes choose to protect the normal

---

[11] Callahan's (1987) argument for rationing by age turns crucially on claims about moral obligations that play no role in mine. The overall structure of Callahan's argument can be captured in the following three-step argument: (1) Life for the old is meaningful only if the old serve the young. Therefore, (2) the old ought to serve the young, e.g., by serving as moral exemplars who surrender claims on lifesaving services in favor of the young. Consequently, (3) the old can be compelled through age-rationing measures to carry out their obligations to the young. This argument is both unsound and invalid. The first premise is false. There are many ways for the old to find meaning in life. But even if the first premise were true, the second one does not follow from it, nor does the third follow from the second. Many things might add meaning to my life, but I am not obliged to do them on either prudential or moral grounds, and many of the things I ought to do are not things that society should compel me to do.

opportunity range better at one stage of life than another or for some groups rather than others. This general problem is the reason I urged the account of fair process or accountability for reasonableness in Chapter 4. It is clear from my brief discussion of alternative views about rationing by age, as well as from the disagreement within the NICE Citizen's Council, that there will be persistent disagreement even about the argument I offer: Reasonable people will draw different conclusions from the moral theories they invoke and the different weight they give to specific moral intuitions. Though I think my argument shows that pure age rationing under very limited conditions is morally permissible, others will strongly disagree and still others will advocate even more permissive forms of it. In practical settings, we need fair procedures in which these diverse views can be brought to bear on real allocation problems. We also need an approach that relies on reasons all can see are relevant, despite lingering disagreements about weights.

EQUITY BETWEEN BIRTH COHORTS

Societal aging on a global scale, we have seen, changes the profile of needs in a society, forcing us to consider a new how to allocate resources to different age groups. The Prudential Lifespan Account, coupled with fair procedures for resource allocation, provides a framework for thinking about how to address the age-group problem. Societal aging, more alarmingly, increases burdens on the working-age population to support a much larger population of people who are retired and elderly, though some of this burden is offset by the decreasing burden of raising children as fertility rates decline. I noted earlier the dramatic decreases in the ratio of workers to elderly in all developed countries and in many developing countries over the next several decades. This demographic change strains resources and intensifies competition for them. It also gives rise to complaints about intergenerational inequity.

A special form of the problem of equity between birth cohorts is the question "Which inequalities in benefit ratios are equitable?" The "benefit ratio" is the ratio of benefits to contributions made over the lifespan to insurance schemes. More generally, what inequalities in the treatment of different cohorts are just or fair as these cohorts pass through institutions intended to provide justice between age groups? Remember, I said that both problems must be solved together.

Since each birth cohort ages, it has a fundamental interest in securing institutions that solve the age-group problem effectively. Unfortunately, institutions or transfer schemes that solve this problem operate under considerable uncertainty. There is uncertainty about population and economic growth rates, as well as about technological change, which further affects productivity. Errors are likely to abound, causing inequalities in benefit ratios between cohorts. Despite these sources of error, institutions that solve the age-group problem must remain stable over time.

The problem goes beyond uncertainty and errors, for we are certain about the strains that rapid societal aging will place on existing transfer schemes in developed countries and the obstacle that aging imposes on establishing new schemes in many developing countries. Transfer schemes, such as Medicare and Social Security in the United States and their analogues elsewhere, must be able to weather the political struggle that will result if errors are allowed to produce unjustifiable or unacceptable inequalities in benefit ratios. They must also be able to weather the rapid aging described earlier, including the emergence of worker/retiree ratios in some developed countries, like Italy, that may require one worker to support one elderly person. In China, which lacks formal transfer schemes and relies on children to support their parents, the problem takes the stark form of the one-two-four problem – one child supporting two parents and four grandparents.

Formal societal transfer schemes will be able to survive the struggle among birth cohorts only if each cohort feels that it has a stake in preserving them. Each will feel that it has such a commitment only if it believes that these schemes work to its benefit within the limits of fairness. Such commitment will be sustained, then, only if the schemes aim for *approximate equality* in benefit ratios.

One objection to this suggestion is that it ignores the fact that some cohorts may be wiser or more prudent than others and may therefore be more productive. Since many believe that people should be rewarded for their contributions, they insist that benefit ratios should reflect *desert*. Specifically, they urge that each cohort should depend on its own savings. But this appeal to desert (contribution) would require disentangling the many sources of change that promote or prevent good economic fortune. It would not justify relying on individual or cohort savings alone, for they result from many factors other than moral desert.

Since it is hard to see how a stable system could incorporate such factors in its scheme of benefits, it seems reasonable for cohorts to aim for approximate equality in benefit ratios and to seek other ways of persuading each other to act prudently over time. Each cohort, after all, has an interest in securing stable institutions that solve the age-group problem. Cohorts must therefore cooperate to achieve such stability. But cooperation will require some *sharing of risks* across cohorts. In general, the burdens of economic declines and of living through unfavorable retiree/employee ratios must be shared, as must the benefits of economic growth and favorable retiree/employee ratios. This suggests again that approximate equality in benefit ratios should be the practical target of public policy, if not a hard-and-fast rule. This does not mean that where there are purely pay-as-you-go schemes, no effort should be made to supplement them with vested savings. For health care, however, it seems necessary to find ways to make pay-as-you-go schemes stable.

This solution to the birth cohort problem is open to another important objection. Birth cohorts, some argue, cannot be trusted to abide by a transfer scheme that ideally solves the age-group problem through intercohort transfers, because, as they age, they will use their increasing political power to revise the scheme in favor of their old age, benefiting heavily at both ends of the lifespan. Thomson (1989) suggests that a particular cohort has been greedy in just these ways in New Zealand and that similar distortions have occurred in transfer schemes elsewhere. His argument is compatible with the view that this behavior is just the result of the special circumstances or opportunities of a particular cohort. But a stronger version of this objection insists that the pattern is general or inevitable. For example, some public choice theorists (e.g., Epstein 1988) argue that large state-managed transfer schemes are sitting ducks for the self-interested behavior of aging cohorts as their political power increases.

Note that not all cohorts behave this way. More important, the alternative is not obvious. If we avoid schemes that depend on intercohort transfers of the sort that take place in the U.S. Social Security system, then we still have to answer the question "How can social institutions facilitate adequate types and rates of savings?" We are back to the age-group problem, but we must now solve it by relying only on the resources of one cohort. Moreover, we are ruling out an important advantage offered by a system with intercohort transfers, namely, that it tends to share risks more widely over time. Rather, we should take advantage of the fact that an equitable form of risk sharing would be much better than the results of "privatizing" the age-group problem for each cohort.

Objections to unequal benefit ratios should not lead us to eliminate intercohort transfer schemes, at least not on the grounds that equality will then result. Making each cohort solely responsible for its own well-being over the lifespan will by no means assure that different cohorts will do equally well. Inequalities will come about because of uneven economic growth rates. It is not at all obvious that unequal benefit ratios in intercohort schemes will generate worse forms and greater degrees of inequality than the inequalities that result when each cohort must depend on its own resources and good luck. Cooperation may be better than a go-it-alone strategy, and the problem then involves designing institutions and securing a long-term commitment to schemes that are fair.

Several strategies are available for adjusting benefits to achieve approximate equality in benefit ratios despite demographic shifts and other sources of uncertainty and error. One strategy is to build a cushion of unexpended benefits while the ratio of workers to retirees is still relatively high. This has been done in financing reforms of the U.S. Social Security system, though there is always a risk that these benefits will be targeted by politicians seeking to relieve budget deficits. In the 2000 U.S. presidential election campaign, both candidates said that they would not break into the "lockbox" of enlarged Social Security funds that were needed to make the U.S. system stable through the baby boom retirement period. But the budget deficits created by the Bush administration's tax cuts and Iraq war expenditures clearly threaten that lockbox.

A second strategy is more basic, for it involves rethinking some of the retirement policies that have dominated developed welfare systems in recent decades. Many current policies provide considerable incentives for older workers to choose retirement well before any disability makes it necessary. It is also difficult for older workers to find flexible, part-time employment that can reduce the need to draw on income support benefits. Underlying these incentives and policies are both economic and moral considerations. Pushing older workers out of the workforce in periods of unemployment when large numbers of young workers are seeking employment may have seemed an acceptable way to ration jobs by age, or it may have seemed an appropriate way to make room for better-educated and potentially more productive workers in technologically advancing economies. These economic considerations may have been reinforced by the view that the elderly want to enjoy more leisure time. They should be reassessed.

The health status of the elderly remains quite good well into their mid-seventies. Millions of elderly persons who would be happier with some form of meaningful work, at least on a part-time basis, are forced to retire. At the same time, as I noted, both in the United States and in other developed countries, there is a surprising trend toward earlier retirement despite better health and longer life expectancy. With shrinking workforces and earlier retirement, many European economies face a shortage of workers in the next few decades. Under these conditions, it may well be wise to consider revising the benefits and incentives that lead workers to retire early. The new shape of a life, with vigorous and healthy years extending well beyond the standard retirement age, means that we must revise our concept of the typical course of life.

In the United States, compulsory retirement ages have been raised or eliminated, at least for large categories of employment; similar legislation is being considered within the European Union. This development may encourage reassessment of the employability of older workers. It may not be enough, however, simply to eliminate legal or quasi-legal barriers to the employment of willing elderly workers. Rather, we may have to encourage companies to design flexible employment practices that accommodate the needs of older workers. Such practices may become an increasingly important way of assuring the welfare rights of an aging population.

It is interesting to note that health-care savings schemes (Medicare in the United States and universal coverage schemes in other developed countries) face comparable problems of birth cohort equity. First, as with income support schemes, there will be a bias in favor of early entrants. This bias is hard to avoid in immature schemes – an important point to keep in mind for developing countries that may introduce them.

There is also an opposite bias in the case of health care. Consider a scheme involving some form of age rationing of new technology, as in our earlier discussion of rationing by age. Elderly people might complain about a scheme that denied access to a given technology at a certain age by saying that it is not fair to their cohort: Their cohort never had the benefit of increasing its chances of reaching a normal life span because that technology (say, heart transplantation) now being denied was not available in its youth.

Two points might be made in response to this complaint. First, each birth cohort is nevertheless treated equally in the following way: At some point in their lives, members of each cohort will be denied the best available life-extending technologies, but at all other points in their lives they will have a better chance of receiving them (whatever they then are). To be sure, the particular technology that is denied them late in life may not be the one they had a better chance of receiving early in life, but there is fairness in the exchange. Still, if technology improves very rapidly, as it has in recent decades, then the bargain is not as favorable from a prudential perspective as it seems when we ignore the rapid rate of technological advance.

A second point is more general: Some such changes, for example in technology, are at least as difficult to project as the other factors that lead to error (replacement ratio differences) in savings schemes. Indeed, in general, we may be even more prone to error in the health-care setting than in the income-support setting. Given the overriding importance of stability in such schemes, considerable tolerance for error must obtain.

INTERGENERATIONAL EQUITY AND HARD CASES

My main thesis in this chapter has been that there are two problems of intergenerational equity, the age-group and birth-cohort problems, that interact and must be solved together. The solutions must also be integrated with a broader view of health needs and with the use of a fair, deliberative process to address disagreements about distributive fairness. To solve the age-group problem, we should think about prudent allocation over the lifespan of the good in question. For health care, that means protecting the age-relative opportunity range for individuals by promoting normal functioning at each stage of life. Yet, a scheme that aims to do that must be sustainable and must be fair to different birth cohorts passing through it, assuring them roughly comparable benefit ratios. In a period of rapid societal aging, both are especially difficult to accomplish.

What do these general solutions to the distributive problems tell us about the challenging problems faced by a rapidly aging developing country like China or a developed country with a shrinking working-age population like Italy? These are hard cases in which to achieve and sustain intergenerational equity, but they illustrate the challenge to my view that comes from global aging. In what follows, I shall highlight the ethical constraints on policies imposed by my account of intergenerational equity; I save for another occasion a more detailed analysis of how different policies fare ethically within these constraints.

Case 1: Italy

Unlike China, Italy is a relatively wealthy, developed country with a universal coverage health care insurance scheme funded largely by taxes on workers. It has a developed pay-as-you-go income support system for retirees and relatively few fully funded pension schemes. It is important to remember that income support for the elderly is an important social determinant of health, and so it is important to consider it along with access to medical services in thinking about health protection across the lifespan. In many ways these schemes are typical of developed countries, except that the United States, Japan, and to a lesser extent Great Britain have developed some funded pension schemes.

For health and health care, the Italians have an institutional structure that offers a framework for solving the age-group problem. If fair process is implemented, and if there is careful deliberation about prudent allocation across the lifespan both within and outside the health sector, Italians can meet the following key implications of my proposal regarding equity between age groups: (1) they can allocate resources in ways that protect the age-relative opportunity range, meeting key needs at each stage of life; (2) their decisions can be assessed to see if they pay adequate attention to health-care services especially important later in life, such as chronic care, long-term care, and preventive care throughout the lifespan; (this late stage of life is now typical for a society with considerable longevity, so these needs must be met in a prudent scheme); (3) they can integrate their long-term care and social support systems for the elderly with socially appropriate reliance on filial obligations, taking into account the dramatic structural changes that occur in families when the birth rate falls below the replacement rate; and (4) they can adjust the distribution of important determinants of health, such as education, job structure, and income support, so that they better protect the opportunity range across the lifespan. Italy was famous in the twentieth century for its strong, extended families and a culture that celebrated them. By the middle of the twenty-first century, Italy will find itself with greatly reduced kinship relations on which to draw for mutual support. Against that changing structure, the burden on public resources is greater.

Though these general implications of the age-group problem may be easy to state, they are not easy to conform to. If resources are severely constrained in a population with a shrinking workforce and an increasing elderly population, rationing across the lifespan may become more stringent, and this will be resisted by groups or individuals who stand to lose benefits. Systems that do not achieve legitimacy for necessary limits, including adjustments to benefit ratios, through a fair process will be at special risk. To ease the burden, some changes outside the health sector may he necessarly: for example, delaying rather than hastening retirement and providing flexible work rules that accommodate better part-time work by the elderly or flexible hours to allow for increased care of dependents. Creating incentives for pro-natal policies that can stabilize or increase the fertility rate – including more flexible work schedules, adequate day care, and educational incentives for children – are all non-health-sector interventions with health consequences. Providing more education later in life will be necessary so that work can remain meaningful and rewarding to people over a longer period. It may be necessary to relax immigration rules to encourage an influx of younger workers, despite the cultural tensions diversity sometimes produces. None of these changes is easy to achieve politically, yet without them, generous health systems may be unsustainable and justice in health across the lifespan may be impossible.

One point that makes Italy a hard case is that it is on the leading edge of societies with a shrinking population that nevertheless have social and ethical commitments to meeting population needs for health and income support. We simply have no experience that tells us how best to address the problem of worker/retiree ratios approaching 1:1 or worse. In that context, there is a grave threat to the forms of institutional solidarity and equity that exist in Italy.

Given intense competition for resources across age groups and between cohorts, one proposal is to shift pay-as-you-go systems to fully funded ones. I am not prepared to debate the economic implications of these proposals on savings rates and investment and therefore economic growth. However, with no major improvements in economic growth (difficult in a shrinking population in any case), the impact on sustainability and equity across cohorts is largely perceived, not real. If cohorts are each responsible for financing their own income support in old age, as well as their health care through some form of lifelong medical savings account, then each cohort will have only the benefits it can pay for. If a population is stable, because it can replace itself, but it is relatively old, at least compared to experience when current institutions were developed, then pay-as-you-go is no more demanding than paying for oneself (cohort by cohort).

In a shrinking population, however, younger cohorts may not have confidence that a system will deliver to them what they are asked to deliver to an older cohort.[12] Under such conditions, transitional mixed systems may be necessary, with pay-as-you-go universal coverage aimed at meeting basic

---

[12] Dickson and Shepsle (2001) examine several patterns of contributing to and benefiting from ("working and shirking") schemes in which overlapping generations participate. The stability of contribution to such schemes depends on the expectation of subsequent benefits. Consequently, as the public goods generated by such schemes are threateneded, cohorts that are expected to contribute lose faith in the assured participation of others.

health needs and reducing poverty, and with funded systems relieving the political pressure on the system to deliver more benefits than people can sustain with their savings. The ethical constraint on such transitional systems is that they continue to meet obligations to those already retired: Some recent proposals in the United State for privatizing Social Security have failed to consider the burden of funding those already retired. This does not mean that existing benefits can never be reduced: Making benefit ratios equitable over time may require some reductions where cohorts enjoyed greater than fair benefits.

Despite these complications, the main point is clear: General solutions to the two problems of intergenerational equity do not rule out relying on mixed systems. Such systems may be necessary to address severe limits to the sustainability of otherwise reasonable solutions to the age-group problem. To maintain intergenerational equity, however, we must not abandon any particular cohort, and we must make sure that pursuit of equity between cohorts does not mean abandoning plausible institutions for meeting the age-group problem.

Case 2: China

Consider briefly our other hard case, China, as an illustration of a rapidly aging developing country. What does the Prudential Life Span Account say that China must do?

China must develop a health system and an insurance scheme that can meet health needs across the lifespan. As the lifespan is extended, and as typical lives will include periods of higher risk of chronic illness and disability later in life, health systems in developing countries must be prepared to meet those needs. In China there is a poorly funded urban health-care insurance system and an even less adequately funded rural insurance system. Neither insurance system is prepared to provide the chronic care needed in later life. Without appropriate insurance that shares risk widely over the population, individuals will be forced to cover very high medical costs, and families with ill elderly relatives will face terrible choices about health care versus falling into poverty.

China will have to expand its health system capacity to meet the chronic health needs of an aging population. It cannot simply allow the hospitals to expand services in ways that maximize revenues without attention to unmet needs. Otherwise, major inequities will emerge between people with different conditions. Confidence in the private sector to plan prudent lifespan allocation is misplaced, a lesson China should have learned from its dramatic failure to meet rural health needs through purely private financing.

Especially problematic will be the intense burdens of caring for the frail elderly – burdens traditionally met by adult children, generally living in extended households, largely in rural settings. As family structures in China have shifted to single households, with fewer elderly parents living with adult children, the strain of providing care is much greater. Earlier I noted that nearly a quarter of elderly Americans have no adult children to depend on. Given the strict population policies in China over several decades, the same will be true of elderly Chinese.

Fair treatment across age groups means that there is a societal responsibility to provide this care. Responsibility cannot simply be dumped on families, especially when they do not exist, or where they are too separated geographically to provide care, or where changed family structures mean that cross-household transfers cannot substitute for the internal transfers that sustained the elderly in earlier times, when they lived in multiple family structures. China, like other countries that have strong cultural traditions of filial obligation, cannot simply demand that families care for their elderly. Instead, it must develop a universal care system that assures all elderly persons that a lack of dependents will not cause them to be abandoned by society in old age. The delicate policy task is to integrate such a solution with informal familial supports so that family support is made less burdensome – through incentives rather than sanctions – at the same time that all are protected. This policy approach will be prudent for the young as well as the old, making it easier for the young to carry out family obligations despite complex internal migration patterns. Just what form these policies should take depends on existing social structures. In some developed countries, forms of adult day care or respite care that relieve adult children of the burden part of the time have been found to lead to better and more sustained care for the elderly.

China, despite rapid aging, still has enough time to develop institutions to meet these needs. It can even do so in a way that remains fair to different cohorts. Indeed, any system that is developed now, in anticipation of the retirement of the postrevolution Chinese baby boom generation, should be seen as meeting the interests of all cohorts. The huge Chinese workforce that will now be saddled with the cost of financing that insurance scheme will itself be drawing benefits from it only it if is put in place now in a way that can be sustained for the decades after 2015, when that cohort starts to retire, and after 2029, when China's population will peak and the number of workers will clearly start to shrink. Once the very large working-age population begins to shrink, relative to the elderly, it will be much harder, if not impossible, to develop a system in which that working-age population helps prepare for its own old age. Nevertheless, it is not easy politically to do so now: For current workers to prepare for their own retirement in a period when fewer workers will follow them, they must contribute to savings (or pay taxes) at very high rates, rates that will be resisted.

Some policy proposals call for China to develop a mixed system, with pay-as-you-go universal coverage for basic health and income support protections, combined with fully funded schemes to provide more sustainable income support for an elderly retired population. As I noted earlier, my solutions to the two distributive problems do not rule out or in specific combinations of financing for institutions. The solutions do, however, impose ethical restrictions on what is done.

The hard cases posed by global aging do not, after all, show that it is impossible simultaneously to address the age-group and birth-cohort problems fairly. Still, the challenge they pose is difficult, in part because political discussion is not adequately informed by the kind of lifespan view of population health presented here. Properly integrating approaches to the challenge with accountability for reasonableness can create the social learning curve that improves political discussion and the resulting institutions.

7

Consent to Workplace Risk and Health Protection

Is our account of just health, with its emphasis on equitably distributing the risks through preventive health measures, incompatible with individual liberties? In *Just Health Care* I addressed this question by examining what rationale might justify stringent occupational safety and health standards and still respect individual liberty to consent to risk. In this chapter, I consider a more recent challenge to such stringent regulation that derives from the disability rights movement. Since people with disabilities have historically been denied the opportunity to work by employers who invoke stereotyped claims about risks, they have insisted on their individual right to consent to workplace risks as a way of avoiding such undue paternalism. Recent legislation and some case law support this approach. This new challenge to stringent health protection thus appeals not only to individual liberties but also to a potential conflict with the same notion of opportunity that grounded the need for such health protection. Can just health address this challenge? I argue that it can. In addition, the ability of our integrated theory to address issues of moral disagreement about priority setting allows us to respond to moral disagreements about what we owe people with special sensitivities to risk.

To protect opportunity, we saw in Chapter 5, justice requires preventive health measures that go beyond individual interventions such as medical screening and vaccination to include broader safety and health regulation outside the health sector itself. Such measures include environmental regulation to preserve clean air and water, transportation regulation to protect against road accidents, food and drug regulation to assure safety, quality, and efficacy, and other forms of product safety regulation (IOM 2006). A paradigm case of such protection is the focus of this chapter, namely, regulation to reduce the exposure of workers to health hazards in the workplace. Indeed, without such protection, workers will be exposed to risks that others do not face, creating health inequalities that are arguably unjust. Legislation and subsequent litigation set a very high legal standard for such protection

in the United States, namely, protection to the degree that it is "technologically feasible" to reduce risks (OSHA 1970).[1]

Such stringent measures to protect the health of workers, despite their
apparent support within our theory of justice and health, have been challenged on the grounds that they unfairly restrict the liberty and opportunity
of the workers they aim to protect. One recent challenge comes from advocates for workers with disabilities who supported a worker named Echazabal
against a Chevron-owned oil refinery that refused to hire him because of
the medical risks he faced.[2] According to his initial medical tests, Echazabal
had a disability, compromised liver function, that made him particularly sus-
ceptible to risks from the chemicals he encountered at work. His advocates
nevertheless argued that disabled workers like him should be permitted
to consent to risks even when other workers cannot take such chances with
their health because of the stringent standards. Only by relying on their own
consent to risk can such workers be protected against discriminatory, malev-
olent stereotyping by employers who historically "protected" them against
(imagined) vulnerabilities to risk, thus denying them the opportunity to
work. Letting employers like Chevron use stringent workplace health standards to deny employment to disabled workers restores their paternalistic
cover. Individual consent to risk, they claim, is a necessary protection against
discrimination masquerading as justifiable paternalism. As we shall see, the
issue goes beyond workers with disabilities and concerns women as well:
They too have been victims of discrimination parading as paternalism.

Even if this defense of individual consent to risk is restricted to workers
with disabilities and women, it poses an obstacle to stringent public health
regulation. In the case of Echazabal, it would mean that society must refrain
from protecting the most vulnerable workers. Under such conditions, less
vulnerable workers might then complain that they are subject to unjustifiable paternalism, since they are less at risk than Echazabal and yet have less
liberty to consent to risk-taking while his liberty is protected. The challenge
raised by Echazabal thus becomes a challenge to the very foundations of
stringent health hazard regulation.

What are, after all, the grounds for restricting the liberties of workers to
consent to risks in the workplace in exchange for higher pay – hazard pay?
A striking feature of public interventions in the domain of lifestyle choices –
at least since the Prohibition era in the United States – has been the concern not to run afoul of individual liberty. Self-affecting behaviors, however
harmful, tend to be seen as matters of individual liberty, with the singular

---

[1] The Occupational Safety and Health Act of 1970, Pub. L. No. 91-596, 84 Stat. 1590, is
   codified at 27 USS pp. 651–78 (1976). A legal standard, however, is only as effective as its
   enforcement, and enforcement requires greater agency funding than has been provided for
   much of the period since the law was passed.
[2] *Chevron U.S.A., Inc. v. Echazabal*, 536 U.S. 73 (2002). I describe the legal features of this case
   more fully later in the chapter; here I highlight the ethical issue it illustrates.

exception of mind-altering or addictive drugs. Is stringent health protection compatible with the liberty and opportunity of workers in general? And if we can find such grounds in the general case, how can we protect workers with disabilities or women against discriminatory stereotyping if we deny them the right to evaluate risks for themselves? Is stringent health protection that is justified in the name of protecting opportunity actually antithetical to protecting the opportunity of vulnerable classes of workers?

In this chapter, I shall examine the considerations of justice involved in these challenges to stringent protection against workplace risks. First, I shall review and modify slightly the defense of such stringent protection that I developed in *Just Health Care*. That defense turns on the fact that typical workers facing health hazards in the workplace may have unfairly restricted choices, and if they do, we may be justified in protecting their health (and thus their opportunity) even if they might be willing to trade it for better pay or job security. In effect, what seems like intrusive paternalism may be justified as a way of avoiding exploitation or at least the consequences of unfairly restricted opportunities. Once we see what rationale can be offered for stringent health standards, we can then consider whether it stands up to the new concerns raised by Echazabal about the value of individual consent to risk, at least for some vulnerable groups of people. I shall thus be concerned with the coherence of our account of just health with broader concerns about individual liberty and special concerns about the opportunity of people with disabilities. Since our account of just health helps explain why we must protect the opportunities of people with disabilities, this potential conflict of one form of opportunity protection with another needs to be addressed.

RISK, LIBERTY, AND OPPORTUNITY IN THE WORKPLACE

Promoting and protecting opportunity, we have seen, requires both the treatment and prevention of significant pathology. Nevertheless, there is an important asymmetry between them. Although society is obliged to protect health by providing reasonable medical services that people have claims to when in need, they do not have to use these services. They may decline to accept this protection, and society cannot compel their treatment if they are competent. Indeed, before undergoing treatment, individuals must give informed, voluntary consent. Our right to medical care is thus mediated by our specific intention to exercise that right and press our claim on specific services. Individual consent to the benefits and burdens of risk-taking is thus fully respected and in no way challenged when required medical services are provided. Deep strands of liberal political philosophy coalesce to form a protected space within which individuals are sovereign in their self-regarding decisions.

With regulations to prevent exposure to risks in the workplace (and elsewhere), however, individual consent to risk-taking is preempted and replaced by social mandates. Our right to health protection through preventive measures is not mediated in the same way by specific intentions to exercise the right. Indeed, our right to consent to the benefits and burdens of risk-taking, at least with regard to regulated risks, is eliminated. This asymmetry lies at the heart of the issue we must address in this section, namely, whether protecting health and thus opportunity through stringent preventive measures is compatible with protecting individual liberties to take and to benefit from taking risks, or at least is compatible under certain conditions.

Does our opportunity-based justification for preventive measures unfairly threaten the liberty of workers and employers to contract, through hazard pay, to distribute the benefits and burdens of risk-taking to their mutual advantage? Stringent regulation may seem unduly paternalistic, perhaps valuing workers' health more highly than workers themselves value it. To illustrate the problem, we shall consider a specific form of stringent regulation, the "technological feasibility" standard embodied in U.S. law (OSHA 1970) and supported by subsequent litigation. This standard may be viewed as an upper bound on stringent regulation. If it can be shown to respect individual liberties, then it is plausible to think that the opportunity-based account we have developed will be consistent with those parts of the general theory of justice that protect individual liberty.

The Technological Feasibility Standard: Beyond Market Regulation

The Occupational Safety and Health Act of 1970 requires the U.S. secretary of labor to specify permissible exposure levels and require various practices, like wearing air masks, and means, like monitoring devices, to assure that exposure does not exceed these levels. The criterion it specifies for acceptable standards is that a standard should "assure, *to the extent feasible,* on the basis of the best available evidence, that no employee will suffer material impairment of health." The Occupational Safety and Health Administration (OSHA) has taken "feasibility" to mean technological (or technical) feasibility. A standard must protect workers to the degree that it is technologically feasible to do so, though with a modest concession to economic considerations: The costs of compliance with the standard should not result in putting a whole industry out of business, though it may drive out marginal producers. The U.S. Supreme Court decision in *American Textile Manufacturers Institute et al. v. Donovan* (commonly referred to as the "Cotton Dust Case") upheld the technological feasibility criterion against the demand of textile manufacturers that OSHA employ a cost-benefit analysis to demonstrate the economic feasibility of the cotton dust standard.[3]

---

[3] The reasoning in the ruling, namely, that Congress had already conducted a cost-benefit analysis and decided that the technological feasibility standard was cost-beneficial, does not address the issues we must consider.

The technological feasibility criterion moves OSHA beyond the role of mere "market adjustor." A widely held view is that governments should intervene to "correct" markets only when they depart in specifiable ways from the conditions that define ideal or fair market conditions. In this view, market exchanges are fair (and efficient) if they are made under certain conditions. For example, the market model presupposes that employers who buy risk-taking with hazard pay provide workers with adequate or full information about the nature of the risks involved. If relevant information is systematically withheld, or is provided in a systematically unequal way, then regulation is needed to ensure that only informed exchanges take place. Uncertainty would otherwise undermine both efficiency and procedural fairness.

Similarly, markets will be efficient and procedurally fair only if the commodities are priced at their true social cost. If the costs of health damage to workers are externalized and not priced in the health hazard market, because the bill for illness and disability is picked up by society as a whole, the market will be neither efficient nor fair in its outcomes. Such a "free" market would embody a form of freeloading. Advantageous bargains would be made between workers and employers at the expense of nonconsenting third parties outside the market. To restore the market to ideal conditions would require a mechanism compelling the internalization of the externalized costs.

In this market view, OSHA would have a major role as a market adjustor wherever the health hazard market fails to provide for informed exchanges and fails to price all factors of production at their true social cost. Specifically, OSHA would have to guarantee that information is provided to all parties involved in the exchanges. OSHA would also have to make sure that the market properly priced the commodities exchanged in it. Of course, there are many possible ways to internalize of externalized costs: Instead of standards defining permissible dose exposures, forcing the costs of cleanup on the company (at least initially), relevant employers might be taxed and, the revenues earmarked for the externalized costs. Presumably, these taxes would no longer be available to employers and workers as part of the pie that they divide among themselves. But another way of internalizing costs might be to use a cost-benefit criterion in the design of protection standards. Such a criterion would force the internalization of externalized costs only when, and to the point where, further internalization was not potentially beneficial.

It should now be clear just how the stricter feasibility criterion pushes OSHA well beyond the role of mere market adjustor or regulator. The effect of the standard is to eliminate completely the market in which risk-taking is exchanged for hazard pay, at least for all hazards that it is technologically feasible to eliminate. Ideally, there would be no hazards left to bargain about. Why single out this market for such drastic intervention, indeed elimination? Why not allow exchanges within the modified, adjusted market that would result from a weaker OSHA, one that merely provided information and internalized externalized costs?

Too Much Protection?

I noted earlier that advocates for workers with disabilities (and women) have insisted that they can protect their opportunities to work only if they retain the right to consent to workplace risks. Only then can they avoid discriminatory stereotyping that masquerades as paternalistic concern. Does this objection generalize to other workers? Cannot all workers say that the technological feasibility standard values their health more than they themselves do, for they might prefer to preserve a right to consent to risks, at least once they know what they are and the costs of their choices are internal to their hazard pay negotiations? The more stringent criterion, with its greater compliance costs, might mean fewer jobs and less job security than would be possible in a market that allowed employers and workers room to negotiate a distribution of burdens more congenial to them. Can't they also complain that the technological feasibility standard is overly paternalistic?[4]

Indeed, the restriction is completely out of keeping with many other practices regarding autonomy and the regulation of risks. People take risks with their health, and are allowed to do so, in other contexts – in work, in play, and in everyday living. Many workers, ranging from specialists, like stunt drivers and test pilots, to policemen, firemen, and ironworkers, face great risks in their work. They are permitted to negotiate hazard pay for the full range of these risks, and no government agency intervenes to insist that risks be eliminated to the extent technologically feasible. Of course, there are safety rules and regulations in most of these contexts, some imposed by the government, some initiated by unions. But no such restrictive standard as the technical feasibility criterion plays a role.

In addition, many lifestyle choices bring with them far greater health risks than risks from many workplace health hazards. Yet, people are not prohibited from smoking, drinking excessive alcohol, failing to exercise, or eating too much fatty meat. Nor are they prohibited from hang gliding, scuba diving, driving without seat belts (in many states), or sunbathing. The very workers we refuse to allow to face even modest exposure to carcinogens in the workplace we still allow to drive to work with cigarette in mouth and seat belt unhooked (even if we require auto makers to install the belts).[5]

---

4 Of course, most workers actually sought stringent government regulation (Berman 1978) and did not complain about the threat of government regulatory paternalism. Nor did employers historically try to protect most workers against real or imagined risks, as people with disabilities and women complain they did. I pursue the question of too much protection hypothetically, as a way to examine the underlying ethical issues, recognizing that some workers might actually hold such views.

5 The Johns-Manville company banned all smoking by workers at all of its asbestos facilities in an effort to reduce synergistic effects. But the U.S. Court of Appeals struck down the ban

Any rationale for the strict feasibility criterion must be consistent with the autonomy we allow in these other contexts.[6] One response would be to restrict autonomy in the name of health protection in these contexts as well. But such intrusive and extensive paternalism would be difficult to justify, at least to reconcile with other widely held views about autonomy. Nor should we say that the issue of paternalism does not arise at all because the strong feasibility criterion is Congress's response to the will of the majority of workers in the affected workplaces. If the majority wants such stringent regulation, and if the regulation is passed in response to that majority will, then the minority is not being protected paternalistically at all. The (libertarian) minority is being protected, despite its own wishes, but for the sake of others, not itself. This claim that the restriction is not paternalistic ignores, however, the libertarian insistence that the autonomy of the minority is a fundamental liberty, a right, not a privilege so easily suspended at majority whim.

Autonomy and Risky Lifestyle Choices

Most of us would agree that promoting healthy lifestyles is an important social goal, but we are justifiably hesitant about permitting too much social intrusion into individual decision making about lifestyles. We resist the suggestion that there is only one acceptable conception of the good life – for example, that there is just one reasonable degree of risk aversion. Nevertheless, even a view that allows individuals to be the best judges of their purposes and interests rests on important assumptions about the information available to them, their competency to judge risks and benefits, and the voluntariness of the decision. When these assumptions do not hold, however, we may think that paternalism is justifiable because true autonomy is not possible.

Individuals who value their autonomy must nevertheless realize that sometimes their competency to make rational decisions is temporarily or permanently undermined. It would be rational for them to insure themselves against the harmful outcomes of incompetent decisions by authorizing others to act on their behalf, even contrary to their expressed wishes, when specifiable failures of competency make rational choice impossible (Dworkin 1972). The conditions for paternalism must be well defined and involve the inability to make competent decisions or threats to the voluntariness of the decisions.

---

at its Dennis plant as a violation of a collective bargaining agreement. It also stated that nothing in the OSHA regulations requires such a ban and that "the danger is to the smoker who willingly courts it" (*Johns-Manville Sales Corp. v. International Association of Machinists, Local 1609*, 621 F. 2d 759 (5th Cir., 1980)).

[6] Indeed, it is often argued that OSHA standards are assessed by a more stringent criterion than is used in other health and safety regulative contexts, e.g., by Consumer Product Safety, the Environmental Protection Agency, the Nuclear Regulatory Commission, etc. Whether there really is inconsistency here, despite differences in the standards, is a complicated question.

Many health-threatening behaviors – smoking or not wearing seat belts – are not themselves evidence of diminished capacity for rational decision making. Many such behaviors are associated with desired natural effects – the relaxation of smoking, weight loss – that individuals may value differently. To intervene in such behavior requires independent evidence that the behavior is the result of diminished capacity to make decisions or is in some specifiable way involuntary. Even where there is such evidence, the intervention must be restricted, where possible, to restoring the decision-making capacity; it should not involve permanent prohibition of the behavior. Of course, people may not be competent to judge the rationality of these behaviors if they lack relevant information about them (Brandt 1979: 110ff.). But then the preferred intervention is to provide the information in an effective manner. Only if it is impossible to assure that information will be accessible can we impose more stringent restrictions. For example, stringent safety standards imposed by the U.S. Consumer Product Safety Commission can be justified because, even if we could inform purchasers of risks, we cannot be sure that all users of products are aware of them.

Sometimes, when the voluntariness of choices is diminished, paternalism may also be justified. We saw in Chapter 5, for example, that there is reason not to hold people responsible for some risky lifestyle choices because we are unsure how voluntary they really are: Teenagers who begin smoking may be caving in to strong peer pressure; they may be too strongly influenced by tobacco company advertisements; they may be under the influence of class- or culturally based views about macho or otherwise cool behavior; or they may simply be trapped by the addictive powers of nicotine, something tobacco companies can manipulate to entrap adolescents (Smith 2006). If the voluntariness of choices in OSHA-regulated workplaces is reduced, then we may have reason to give their autonomy less respect.

Even if we ought to preserve autonomy in general, we are not bound to preserve the illusion of autonomy. We do not compromise autonomy in the workplace if workers' "choices" about risk-taking generally fail to be informed, competent, or truly voluntary. Rather, we are protecting ourselves against the harms that would result from living with the illusion of autonomy.

Finding a Path

Our discussion of autonomy and paternalism suggests the path we must follow if we are to find a defense of the technological feasibility standard. A plausible defense should turn on finding something distinctive about either (1) the type of risk-taking involved in OSHA-regulated contexts or (2) the contexts in which these choices would be made. The distinctive feature should then explain why we may restrict autonomy to the degree we do in OSHA-regulated workplaces but not elsewhere. Specifically, the risks or the contexts must allow us to question the competency of typical workers to make judgments about these risks or the voluntariness of their choices. Though our path is generally clear, it is easy to wander into some dead ends. We might be tempted to think that OSHA-regulated risks are generally less "visible" or "graspable" than risks we generally do not regulate. If risks are less visible or less easily grasped, then, arguably, workers are less competent to assess them. Chemical workers, for example, face risks from toxins or carcinogens that are not visible in the same way that the risks to a fireman of building collapse or smoke inhalation are (Ashford 1976: Ch. 7). The latter risks are clear in the work situations; no special knowledge or information is needed to make one aware of them. Connected to the difference in risk graspability is a potential inequality in access to information about them. Moreover, several decades of psychological literature have shown that we are notoriously unreliable and inconsistent "rational deliberators" about the kinds of risk-taking decisions imposed on us by invisible, long-term risks (see Tversky and Kahneman [1981] and the extensive literature on bounded rationality that follows it). Consequently, to rely on individual decision making in a hazard pay market for these risks would be to rely on a competency we have definite reason to think is diminished.

This argument proves too much. Invisible, indirect, "low-graspability" risks, like problems of bounded rationality, are part of the fabric of our everyday lifestyle choices. Decisions to accept the risks of smoking, or not exercising, or eating too much fatty meat all seem to involve decisions very similar to the risk-taking involved in exposure to cotton dust or benzene. We are on the wrong path.[7]

Another false path is the claim that risk-taking that we should not prohibit or stringently regulate is intrinsically rewarding, whereas OSHA-regulated risks are not. For example, some find smoking pleasurable; others think that facing the risk of being a "first responder" is morally desirable or psychologically gratifying. In contrast, breathing benzene or cotton dust is neither pleasant, nor morally desirable, nor deeply gratifying, even if it involves the extrinsic award of hazard pay. Such exposure is unlikely to be thought a "calling," as some see firefighting (McCarthy 1981: 779–80).

The contrast between intrinsic and extrinsic rewards cannot take us down the right path. A system of hazard pay establishes rewards that are clearly motivating – more money or more job security. The only way to save the argument for paternalism here would be to show that these extrinsic rewards

---

[7] The same point about inequality in information is also a dead end, since it could also be applied to consumers of cigarettes, alcohol, high-cholesterol foods, and so on. Indeed, it seems more likely that we could take steps to ensure equality of access to information in the employer–employee relationship, as we do in the doctor–patient relationship, where we rely on informed consent, than we could do so in the highly diffuse relationship between cigarette manufacturer and consumer

are suspect in a way that the more direct, desirable consequences of other risks are not. And whatever the grounds for such suspicion about extrinsic rewards, the argument must leave room for the fact that risk-taking also involves extrinsic rewards in cases where the intrinsic rewards are demonstrably greater – for example, the high pay of Hollywood stuntmen.

If we cannot characterize the nature of the risks in a way that leads us down the path to our desired rationale for stringent regulation, perhaps we should focus instead on the context and specifically on the idea that hazard pay negotiation, at least for a broad class of workers, involves risk-taking that is not truly voluntary (Ashford 1976; 333–6; McCarthy 1981: 780). Shortly, I shall defend a weak version of such an argument, but first, it is important to see that hazard pay offers are not true instances of coercion. It is tempting to look for an argument showing that coercion is present in any such hazard pay market. This would clearly imply the diminished voluntariness needed to justify the paternalism involved in OSHA's strong feasibility criterion. Coerced responses are paradigmatically not autonomous, and clearly we are not bound by then.

Consider a central case of coercion, the mugger who threatens, gun in hand, "Your money or your life!" The standard analyses all agree that the coercion consists in the fact that (1) the mugger changes the range of options open to the victim, and (2) the change makes the victim much worse off than he would be in some relevant baseline situation.[8] Defining coercion is difficult because of the problem of specifying the relevant baseline. Consider a worker who has a "clean," nonrisky job. His employer wants to change the work process and says, "Accept hazard pay for these increased risks or lose your job." Is the proposal coercive? Our first problem is to specify the "normally expected" course of events. Shall we understand the normal course of events locally, as the continuation of the clean job now held by this worker? Or should we understand it more broadly, by reference to a more global baseline, the normal practices and prerogatives of employers, including the powers to hire and fire in accord with decisions about profitability?

If we construe the baseline locally, the proposal seems coercive. The employer's proposal changes the worker's options in a way that makes the worker much worse off. But this result depends strongly on the alternatives (and their utilities) open to the worker. It does not depend just on the employer's action. If the worker can get a comparable clean job elsewhere, and changing jobs entails no great losses of benefits, pensions, and so on,

---

[8] Other conditions concern the relative payoff of the alternatives. In general, the utility of a victim's doing the coerced act will have to be much greater than his suffering the consequences of not doing it. Thus, the victim generally much prefers paying to dying. There are complexities here that I shall ignore. In this section, I am indebted to David Zimmerman (1981) and Alan Wertheimer (1987); also see Nozick (1969).

then this may just be a case of an unpleasant, not a coercive, offer. The "lose your job" part of the employer's proposal loses much of its sting, and the employer has not really seriously altered the worker's options for the worse. That is, conditions (1) and (2) of the standard analysis do not obtain, so the proposal is just an (noncoercive) offer, however unpleasant. However, if the alternative is "Starve your family (go on welfare) or accept hazard pay for cancer risks," then the proposal meets conditions (1) and (2) and may well be coercive. In contrast, if the worker was already unemployed, and the proposal was "Accept hazard pay or stay unemployed," then conditions (1) and (2) are not met.

Should the coerciveness of the offer so depend on whether the employer is proposing unemployment that is new or merely continued? According to the dominant view (Wertheimer 1987), the employer's firing rather than not hiring is crucial since coercion requires a threat.[9] To be sure, the proposal to the already unemployed worker might be judged exploitive, even if it is not coercive. For our purposes, if we could agree that the offer was exploitive, we might have grounds for viewing it as morally objectionable in ways that might provide a rationale for the strong feasibility criterion (Wertheimer 1996). But then the argument would turn on showing why the exploitive conditions undermine autonomy and not on the narrower, more direct judgment that the employer's offer is coercive.

Suppose we attempt to make the baseline less sensitive to such arguably irrelevant details as whether new or continued unemployment is threatened. Then proposals that are no more coercive than these practices will be camouflaged and will not appear coercive at all. To illustrate this point about the baseline, Nozick (1969: 450) discusses a slave owner who beats his slaves daily. One day he proposes that the slave can avoid his usual beating if he does something disagreeable that the slave master wants done. The proposal seems coercive, but we cannot show that it is by appeal to a baseline of normally expected options. Here the change from the baseline is welcomed by the slave. This is the kind of example that seems most relevant to our case: The offer of hazard pay for facing cancer risks is most likely to be welcomed by the otherwise unemployed worker.

The approach that Nozick and others (Wertheimer 1987) adopt is to suggest that we need a second baseline that is specified by what is morally

---

9 Suppose that normally workers are presented with the choices embodied in the employer's proposal to the employed worker because employers normally make decisions about profitability that require such proposals. Though our employed worker now faces an unhappy choice, between taking unpleasant risks and being unemployed, and though his particular options are worse than the ones he enjoyed before the proposal, they are not worse than the normally expected options specified by a more global baseline. That is, workers normally have such poor options, and employed and unemployed workers are treated similarly. However, conditions 1 and 2 are not met in either case, and the offer is not coercive on the standard account.

required. In the slave example, it is morally required that the slave not be beaten or not be a slave at all. By reference to this preproposal baseline, the master's proposal is coercive even if the slave welcomes the offer. Where, however, the two baselines conflict and yield different judgments about the presence of coercion, we need to know which baseline to use, which is problematic in some cases.[10] More important is the fact that the two-baseline theory makes the concept of coercion intrinsically moral (Zimmerman 1981). We cannot decide whether a proposal is coercive or not unless we can agree on other judgments about what is morally required.

This point about the baseline applies to our hazard pay example. For a strict libertarian like Nozick, the normal, unregulated hiring and firing practices of employers do not violate the morally required baseline since they are within the employers' rights, as specified by Nozick's (1974: 263) view of individual rights (Zimmerman 1981: 121–2, 129–30). If, however, the distribution of income or other social goods, like opportunity, is not fair or just (see Part I), then hazard pay proposals will make workers worse off than what is morally required. (The background injustice, however, may not be the result of actions by the particular employer making the proposal: They are systematic and institutional in origin.) By making coercion a moral notion, we are required to make judgments about justice. As a result, we cannot hope to appeal to agreement on coerciveness, and its prima facie wrongness, to undercut or short-circuit moral disagreement about these other issues.

A Rationale for the Technological Feasibility Criterion

In hazard pay offers, employers do not meet the standard definition of coercion. Specifically, their proposals do not worsen the condition of workers compared either to a baseline defined by normally expected conditions (the ordinary, unregulated practices of employers) or to a moral baseline defined by the rights of employers, especially as Nozick (1974) would define them. If, however, typical workers facing such offers have an *unfairly* restricted range of opportunities – say because of an unjust distribution of such goods as education and job training (which themselves are social determinants of health) – then in an intuitive sense they are not as free as others to choose from among a reasonable or fair set of options. Their exercisable opportunity range is unfairly reduced – in Sen's (1992) terms (see Chapter 2) they

---

[10] For example, Nozick (1969: 451) considers the example of the drug dealer who proposes that he give an addict his usual dose for $20 only if the addict, in addition to paying, performs a disagreeable task. Nozick suggests that the proposal is a threat because here the addict prefers the normally expected baseline (the $20 dose), not the morally required baseline (no drug). We need to know why the addict's preference is here (always?) decisive. See Zimmerman (1981: 129).

have unfairly reduced capabilities to do or be something, and there is a loss of positive freedom.

In *Just Health Care*, perhaps misleadingly, I termed offers that take advantage of this unfair loss of options or positive freedom "quasi-coercive." I was trying to emphasize that what matters morally in coercion is the (unjustifiable) *loss in the range of options* and not simply whether the agents (employers) making such offers actually make the situation worse or are doing what they are not entitled to do. It is the unfair lack of options in the context, and not simply the role of the employer, that matters.

What may be misleading about the terminology, however, is the manner in which it implies a loss of voluntariness: If coerced actions are the clearest example of involuntary acts, then quasi-coerced ones must involve diminished voluntariness. I welcomed that implication since paternalistic risk regulation would readily be justified if voluntariness is reduced. Wertheimer (1987), however, argues persuasively that reducing the choice space does not by itself diminish the voluntariness of actions. Many restricted choices are voluntary. The term quasi-coercion would then be misleading if it implies that the mere restriction of choice spaces by background conditions (rather than employers) makes the choices less voluntary. What should be emphasized is that it is the *unfairness* or *injustice* of the restriction on options – whatever its source – that justifies discounting such choices. Wertheimer allows an important exception to his claim that restrictions on choice spaces do not automatically reduce voluntariness: If an agent is not entitled to restrict certain choices through an offer, then the offer can count as coercive. Analogously, I am saying that if restrictions on options are unfair, even if it is not the employer who restricts them unfairly, then the choices are quasi-coerced and we have reason to discount the validity of the consent to risk in those circumstances.[11] The central normative claim, then, is that we have morally adequate grounds for questioning the autonomy of decisions made when options are unfairly restricted, even if the decisions are not the result of coercive offers.

The argument that follows gives a plausible rationale for OSHA's strong feasibility criterion while successfully sidestepping widely held concerns about unjustifiable paternalism. The rationale for not relying on consent to risk in the typical workplace is that choices are unfairly restricted and it is reasonable to protect people against having to accept proposals under such

---

[11] We do not have the direct, invasive intrusion into the individual's choice space that is present in the central cases of coercion – for example, when the mugger exceeds his rights by pointing a gun at my head. Similarly, we do not have the employer actively preventing the worker from being in a preferred preproposal situation. Instead, we have an indirect, yet pervasive, erosion of that space as a result of unjust or unfair social practices and institutions. In both cases, the restriction is socially caused. It is not the kind of restriction that results merely from nature or misfortune; it is an act or institution of man, not God or nature, that produces it. Moreover, there are just, feasible alternatives.

conditions. The argument could be characterized as an argument from justice, namely, the need to avoid exploitation, and not a claim about justifiable paternalism, strictly understood. Strictly understood, for an intervention to be paternalistic, it must be aimed at the best interests of the worker who is denied the opportunity to consent to risks for hazard pay. But if the rationale is to protect other workers from exploitation, then the denial of consent is not paternalistic. It may, however, feel quite paternalistic to the worker who truly believes she would be better off facing the additional risks for hazard pay. We can better respond to that perception of paternalism by saying that unfairly restricted options are an adequate reason for discounting the validity of consent. In effect, justice and justifiable paternalism converge here.

The argument of OSHA's strong feasibility criterion can now be stated as follows: (1) Hazard pay proposals for technologically reducible risks in the contexts regulated by OSHA are quasi-coercive or would tend to be over time. (2) Eliminating such proposals (and the market for them) protects workers from harmful consequences, namely, the destruction of their health at a price that only someone under quasi-coercion would accept. (3) Though hazard pay proposals of the sort involved here may be welcomed by certain workers, the autonomy embodied in accepting them is only illusory, for quasi-coercion undermines true autonomy in much the same way that coercion does.[12] (4) Just as people would reasonably contract to permit paternalistic interventions that protect them against the harmful decisions they would make when they are not, or cannot be, adequately informed, competent, or free to decide independently, they would reasonably contract to protect themselves against quasi-coerced decisions of the sort involved here. Thus, (5) OSHA's strong feasibility criterion can be viewed as a social insurance policy against quasi-coercive proposals to trade health for other benefits.

To succeed, this argument must cover the right cases. Does it, for example, help us see why OSHA regulates hazards like toxins in the workplace but not the risks taken by stunt drivers or even firemen protecting lives or property? The choice to be a fireman or stunt driver is exceptional, reflecting a high degree of self-selection: These workers could readily have chosen many other kinds of work. In contrast, the choice to be a miner, mill worker, or industrial worker facing health hazards subject to OSHA's strong criterion is typical. For a large class of workers, these are the primary forms of available employment. Indeed, these are the typical options, or the sole or most attractive ones, for a class of workers with few options. Workers' options are restricted by various factors: limited educational opportunity,

---

[12] Like the slave in Nozick's example, people who usually suffer from an unfair or unjust restriction of their options may welcome a quasi-coercive proposal since it may advance their interests. Moreover, its quasi-coerciveness may even seem invisible.

few marketable skills and talents, accidents of geographical location, or limited money for financing job mobility.

Nothing in this argument for strong OSHA regulation implies that we should intervene similarly in lifestyle choices affecting health, even though by doing so we might prevent comparable harms. Like the stunt driver's choices, these lifestyle choices are also not generally or potentially quasi-coerced.[13] Earlier I expressed some worries about the voluntariness of certain lifestyle choices, noting, for example, the effect of strong subcultural influences. But these threats to autonomy are different from quasi-coercion. Arguments based on these more diffuse kinds of influence are not likely to justify comparable interventions. Indeed, if we respect diversity, they are just the sorts of influence we fear undermining.

Although our rationale for the technological feasibility standard explains why stringent regulation is appropriate for typical workplace situations, it has important limitations. It justifies overruling consent to risks only where consent is quasi-coerced. In a more just world, where workers' opportunities are more fairly distributed, it would not find a foothold. This limitation would not satisfy some public health advocates. The rationale also justifies correcting for a consequence of unfairly distributed opportunities without eliminating the more basic injustice itself – and it does so by further limiting the options of the vulnerable workers it protects. In this regard, it is not an ideal solution since it leaves a deeper problem in place. Such an ideal solution would, however, be achieved if society conformed with the Rawlsian principles of justice as fairness discussed in Chapters 2 and 3. Finally, our philosophical rationale is politically incorrect, for it rests on grounds – the unfairness of workers' options – that Congress would never admit as a basis for the legislation.

RECONCILING STRINGENT REGULATION WITH THE OPPORTUNITIES OF VULNERABLE GROUPS

In order to protect health, and thus opportunity, in the workplace, I have offered a limited defense of the kind of paternalism that some people complain underlies the stringent health hazard regulation provided by the technological feasibility criterion. Some people view such regulation as unduly paternalistic because it bars workers from consenting to risks that are similar to those they have the right to consent to elsewhere in life. Specifically, these are the residual risks that would be addressed in hazard pay negotiation once workers are given proper information about them and once the costs they impose are built into the transaction. Such stringent regulation is justifiable because typical workers are unfairly restricted (quasi-coerced) in

[13] The poor elderly who have to eat dog food may be a case of quasi-coercion.

their choices. Accordingly, we may discount their willingness to face certain risks. As I said earlier, this is a case where justice and justifiable paternalism converge. The regulation expresses society's determination to value the health of these workers more than they themselves might value it in hazard pay negotiations. So, the regulation is paternalistic, but it is justifiable only if workers' options in this situation are typically unfairly restricted, and thus it is a matter of justice as well.

This rationale, however, conflicts directly with another strand of justice-based concerns about protecting the opportunities of vulnerable workers. In order to protect opportunity in the workplace for traditionally excluded groups, such as people with disabilities and women, civil rights advocates have argued vigorously against paternalism. Such paternalism, as I noted earlier, has often "protected" workers against stereotypical, imagined risks, denying them real opportunities and disguising employer bias and self interest.

How shall we understand and resolve this apparent conflict that arises through different ways of protecting opportunity? In what follows, I first pursue a strategy of narrowing the conflict. If disability rights advocates confine their antipaternalist insistence on consent to workplace risks to people with bona fide disabilities, without extending their objection to other cases of special sensitivities to risk or to hazard regulation in general, then it may be possible to defuse the conflict either with individual medical assessment (as the Supreme Court proposed) or with exceptional consent to risk if medical assessment proves discriminatory in its effect. But this strategy of confinement presupposes that it is acceptable to exclude from the workplace people with special sensitivities who are not otherwise disabled. I conclude this chapter by examining that assumption more carefully and argue that reasonable people may disagree about what protections are owed such workers, given the resources that can be devoted to prevention through regulation. This reasonable disagreement, like others we encounter in protecting health, must be addressed by a decision-making process that is accountable for its reasonableness. When I initially examined this issue about individual variation in sensitivity to risk in *Just Health Care*, I was baffled by the possibility of such ethical disagreement. *Just Health* provides an account of fair process needed to resolve such disputes.

Protecting Opportunity by Rejecting Paternalism

We should admit from the start that there are strong grounds for rejecting paternalism regarding certain social groups. Historically, women and people with disabilities have been the victims of discrimination in job settings because of stereotypical views about the risks they face or impose on others. These stereotypes form the basis for an insidious paternalism that disguises discrimination while pretending to protect people with disabilities.

(Somewhat ironically, such paternalism toward women was the basis for the infamous *Lochner v. New York* [1905] U.S. Supreme Court decision that allowed a maximum work week to be legislated for women while male bakers were denied the same protection.)

The courts, interpreting civil rights legislation, have rejected this kind of unsupported paternalism, at least in the case of gender. Most notably, the Supreme Court ruled that Johnson Controls, which makes batteries using lead, could not require women of childbearing age to prove that they had undergone sterilization before they could work in an environment that posed special risks to a fetus (*Automobile Workers v Johnson Controls, Inc.*, 499 U.S. 187 [1991]). Rather, women, as a protected class under civil rights legislation, have the right to consent to such risks and to control their own reproductive decisions.

The Americans with Disabilities Act (ADA) and the case law preceding it also aim to eliminate the (apparently) paternalistic protection of people with disabilities. Historically, paternalism denied people with disabilities jobs on the grounds that they faced greater risks to themselves or imposed greater risks on others. The paternalism involved infantilizing attitudes toward those with disabilities. Employers (and schools and other institutions) had determined what was best for people with disabilities, masking their prejudice and narrow economic interests as paternalism. In short, paternalism in this context had undermined opportunity and worked only to the benefit of the discriminatory employer.

To counter the harmful stereotypes and the unacceptable paternalism, advocates for people with disabilities argue that there should be expert scientific assessment of the real risks people with disabilities face or impose on others. They also argue that these individuals should be allowed to determine for themselves – through their own consent – what risks are acceptable to them. Insisting on individual consent to risk is the best defense against the prejudice buried beneath paternalism.

There is a further moral underpinning to this argument aside from the need to avoid the harms of misdirected paternalism. Individuals with disabilities have been deprived of the opportunity to assume the standard workplace risks accepted by other workers. They have a right to be treated just like other workers who agree to accept standard risks. The case is very different, however, where there are real, not exaggerated, risks to third parties. Where individuals with disabilities pose risks to others who have not chosen to accept these risks, excluding them from ADA protections is justified as a way of preventing the imposition of unfair burdens.

What happens when the risk to a vulnerable, protected group is real and not just the result of unfounded stereotypes? The *Johnson Controls* case involves just such a significant and real risk to fetuses from lead exposure. There is also, however, a real and significant risk to future children due to the effects of lead on sperm, and not just on eggs or fetuses. Johnson

Controls imposed no comparable constraints on men. This mismatch – the real risks to both men and women and the requirement that only women be sterilized – demonstrates unjustifiable discrimination disguised as paternalism. Women, the Court concluded, should be allowed to consent to the reproductive risks they face, just as men do. This strong endorsement of consent to risk – even to real risks – crystallizes the antipaternalist stance that civil liberties advocates endorse and wanted extended to people with disabilities as well.

Civil rights laws go beyond simply ruling out baseless or unfounded stereotypes. They prohibit an employer from "rational discrimination" against protected races or classes, those groups with a history of discrimination, exclusion, and subjugation. It might, for example, be rational for an employer to estimate (correctly) that customers would prefer that he not hire blacks and to infer that he will be at a competitive disadvantage if he does, but such rational discrimination is still prohibited (Bagenstos 2004). Arguably, people with disabilities have suffered comparable exclusion. Full civil rights protections for people with disabilities, then, should protect them in the same way against even rational discrimination, which involves real additional health risks they may face, as well as against baseless stereotypes. Affording that protection, if we extrapolate from the *Johnson Controls* case, would mean allowing the worker with a disability to consent to a (real) risk and not paternalistically refusing her the option of facing it.

The issue comes to the fore in the case I noted earlier, *Chevron U.S.A. Inc. v. Echazabal* (2002). (I leave issues of legal interpretation to those more qualified to make them, concentrating here on the ethical issues involved.) Echazabal, an oil refinery worker with hepatitis C, claimed that Chevron violated his rights under the ADA when it withdrew a job offer to hire him because medical evidence showed him to be at high risk for exposure to workplace toxins (the evidence was not in question in the case). Chevron argued that significant risks to Echazabal's safety ("threat to self") disqualified him from ADA protection, just as risks to the safety of others ("threat to others") would, since under OSHA legislation, Chevron has strong obligations to protect worker safety and health. Specifically, Chevron argued that its action was in keeping with the Equal Employment Opportunities Commission's (EEOC) ruling that permitted employers to refuse to hire workers who might face a significant risk. This determination had to be based on an individual assessment and could not rest on stereotypical assumptions about classes of workers.

In *Chevron v. Echazabal*, the Supreme Court decided that the ADA does not require an employer to ignore risks to an individual's health where a disability exists. In so doing, it upheld the EEOC's interpretation of the ADA and rejected the antipaternalist views of those who had championed its enactment. The Court argued there was a way other than individual consent to risk to protect workers with disabilities against discrimination, namely, through an individual medical assessment. Since Echazabal had had this assessment, there was no basis for the concern about stereotyping.

Critics of the Supreme Court ruling argue that the language of the ADA explicitly noted risks to third parties as acceptable grounds for disqualifying workers from ADA protection but deliberately omitted any mention of risks to the individual with a disability. The intention behind the omission was to exclude consideration of such risks. Allowing claims about risks to the individual to be considered would open the door to the kinds of stereotypical assumptions about people with disabilities that had unfairly reduced their employment opportunities. A primary intention of this law was to prevent stereotyping, all agree. Consequently, there was every reason to view the specific mention of risks to third parties as a way of excluding considerations of risk to the disabled workers themselves. According to critics of the Supreme Court ruling, the EEOC guidelines, which the Supreme Court upheld, thus eviscerate the antipaternalistic intent of the ADA itself.

Chevron and its allies argued, however, that congressional intent could not have precluded individual medical assessment of risks to the individual. How could the ADA force Chevron to ignore worker protections imposed by OSHA when these protections create a business necessity to consider worker safety?[14] Congress could not have intended that the ADA language exclude compliance with OSHA safety standards and EEOC regulations. Risks to the self were therefore not excluded as grounds for disqualifying a worker from the ADA simply because only risks to others were explicitly mentioned as an example of such grounds in the ADA.

Let us assume, at least for the sake of argument, that the facts show that Echazabal faces significantly higher risks of serious illness or death from exposure to toxins because of his hepatitis, that Chevron has met the OSHA-mandated technologically feasibility standard, and that Echazabal's extra risk could be avoided only by transferring him to a job that did not entail exposure.[15] Nevertheless, his advocates argue, we should allow him to consent to those higher risks because he is "otherwise qualified" in that he does not impose risks on others, only on himself. (It is a red herring to say that if Echazabal is at risk, then so are all workers and the workplace should be made clean enough to protect them all since we are supposing that workers without Echazabal's condition are protected to the level that is technologically feasible. We cannot do more for them in order to help Echazabal.) To put the conflict I am outlining bluntly, on this interpretation, the ADA says that we should trust what may be a quasi-coerced decision to

---

[14] The irony of large corporations standing up for stringent worker protections is noted by Ron Bayer (2003).

[15] The *Echazabel* case relied on the initial medical tests, but later testing called this factual basis into question; the ethically interesting issue turns on the case as tried, not the late finding of facts.

avoid the burden imposed by discrimination, whereas the OSHA standards upheld by the Supreme Court discount consent to such risks and disallow such risk-taking.

One way to reduce the seriousness of the conflict regarding consent to risk is to limit its scope. Consider a case in which another worker is not disabled in broader life functions, as Echazabal is, but has a supersensitivity to a specific toxin in a particular type of workplace. Suppose that the consequences are a high risk for serious illness or death. (I am supposing that a window washer who develops acrophobia is not disabled, since many other jobs are open to him and the acrophobia does not interfere with a major life function; the same holds for this hypothetical supersensitivity or allergy to the toxin.) Suppose further that the workplace meets OSHA standards for that toxin and that all workers are screened for this supersensitivity. Those failing the screening test are not hired – even though some or all of them would consent to the risk. Should we accept the willingness of supersensitive workers to take the risk or should we exclude them because of the high risk to their own health?

The supersensitive workers cannot be protected, as most workers can, by the technological feasibility standard. Their level of risk is what would have been faced by most workers in a much dirtier workplace than the OSHA standard allows, even had they wanted to consent to those risks. If advocates for Echazabal insist that we rely on consent to risk for these nondisabled but supersensitive workers, then they are in clear conflict with the ethical basis of OSHA legislation. If, however, their insistence on consent to risk for Echazabal rests completely on his status as a worker with a bona fide disability, the conflict with OSHA is more limited. Their concern is only to avoid the paternalism that harms people with disabilities, not to insist that we always accept consent to risk for all workers, even those who are quasi-coerced. This more limited conflict is less problematic and may be resolvable.

If the Supreme Court in *Chevron v. Echazabal* had accepted the argument that a threat to the self was excluded as a ground for not hiring a worker, as advocates for Echazabal wanted, it would have prohibited a form of rational discrimination against people with disabilities. That is, although he faced an admitted risk that it was rational to consider, the Court might have accepted the argument that rational discrimination is prohibited because the threat of misguided paternalism is so great. The Court would have been saying that we could not rely on individual medical determination of risk as a way of avoiding bias disguised as paternalism. Occupational health advocates would probably have considered this exception ill-advised, for the reasons noted earlier, but the appeal to individual consent would have been limited to clear cases of traditionally excluded groups needing special protection. Because of that limit, the general rule in favor of strict regulation would be preserved.

Instead, however, the Court found that individual medical assessment provides adequate protection against harmful stereotyping. Advocates for the ADA believe that such assessment can itself be abused, allowing people with disabilities to be excluded. Some of these advocates reject individual assessment because, in abandoning individual consent to risk, the Court failed to give the same civil rights to people with disabilities that it had given to women in the *Johnson Controls* case. Arguably, however, the cases are different, since men were exempted from the restrictions imposed on women by Johnson Controls. We need a hypothetical case to consider a true analogue to Echazabal.

Consider the following case. We discover that a sex-linked gene, *gx*, is extremely common, and when it is present on both X chromosomes, as in nearly all women, it produces a supersensitivity to XOX, a chemical found not in nature but in the manufacturing process in a certain industry. Because men have only one such gene, they are not supersensitive. Manufacturers want either to exclude women from the workplaces where XOX is found or, despite the cost, to screen women, find those who have only one copy of *gx*, and allow them to work.

Would it be consistent with the *Johnson Controls* decision for the Supreme Court to allow the screening and selective exclusion of some (actually, most) women rather than just allowing their of individual consent to risk? I think it would. The cases are different because the screening program allows scientifically based worker protection that is properly tailored to those at risk – unlike the Johnson Controls policy that exempted men who were at similar risk to women. In this hypothetical cases of gene *gx*, I assume that people with double copies do not qualify as disabled according to the ADA and case law following it. They are not impaired in a range of life functions, and their impairment at one job with special conditions is not a generalized impairment at work. (I leave aside the uncontested judgment that Echazabal was disabled as a result of his hepatitis C; I take that condition to be a true disability, whereas having double *gx*, which has no effects except in the unnatural environment that contains XOX, does not qualify as a disability.)

My strategy in reconciling stringent protection of worker health with fears of paternalism has been to limit the conflict as much as possible. If the antipaternalism is restricted to genuine disabilities and not extended to isolated supersensitivities, then the conflict is at least limited in one direction and is less of a direct confrontation with health hazard regulation. In addition, there may even be room to qualify the antipaternalism in the case of civil rights, as my XOX case suggests, provided that we can rely on an objective assessment of grave risk.

There remains, however, a direct area of conflict, as in the *Echazabal* case. Should we rely, as the Supreme Court proposes, on individual medical assessment to avoid discriminatory stereotyping? In theory, this does not seem implausible. In practice, however, medical assessment could itself become a form of discrimination aimed at particular groups of vulnerable workers. Where such discrimination exists, it would be preferable to allow workers with disabilities to rely on informed consent than to subject them to known discrimination. The exemption from the more stringent regulation would still seem anomalous, but it would be a next-best solution since individual medical assessment fails to avoid discrimination.

Individual Variation in Sensitivity to Risk

In the previous section, I assumed that supersensitivities to particular workplace toxins are not by themselves disabilities warranting the same protection we give workers with disabilities. Since such workers have faced no discrimination comparable to that of workers with disabilities or women, individual consent to risk in their case lacks appeal as a defense against exclusion disguised as paternalism. My strategy for confining the conflict between my rationale for the technological feasibility criterion and the antipaternalism of advocates for women or people with disabilities turns on that lack of appeal.

Nevertheless, further ethical examination is nededed, because the assumption marks an important moral disagreement about what kinds of health protection and what kinds of protection of workplace opportunities we owe each other. Because there is no history of discrimination against such workers, I shall leave standing the part of the assumption most relevant to my confinement strategy, namely, that allowing such workers to consent to higher risks is not a good defense against discrimination. But this still leaves the question of whether we owe such workers some form of compensation if we exclude them from settings safe for most workers but unsafe for them.[16] On this point there is considerable moral disagreement (although, as we saw in *Chevron v. Echazabal*, the Supreme Court concluded that legally we owe no such compensation, even to a worker with a true disability). Since the resources available for preventive measures in the workplace are limited, just as those in the medical sector are, this disagreement about priorities in preventive health involves a decision that must be accountable for its reasonableness.

I shall examine two ways of thinking about supersensitivity to risk and highlight the moral disagreement that can be raised about each. The first involves the way in which we pool risks in thinking about preventive regulatory measures and the analogy in pooling medical risks in treatment

---

[16] The concern here is different from the literature on genetic screening that focuses primarily on the discriminatory effect of tests that have only modest predictive value. Even if we have a highly sensitive test, we must still decide whether we owe excluded workers some kind of compensation.

(insurance). The second considers whether we should think of "normal durability" – the absence of supersensitivity – as a marketable trait, or whether we should think of supersensitivity as analogous to such protected or morally irrelevant traits as gender, race, or disability. Moral disagreement in both contexts translates fairly directly into disagreements about policy.

The problem posed by supersensitivity to workplace hazards is part of a far more general issue. After all, people also vary in their susceptibility to disease and thus in their probable claims on curative parts of the health-care system. Being at high risk for disease has many sources: genetic background, past disease or trauma, or other environmentally induced sensitivities, including those (somewhat) voluntarily imposed, say through smoking. When we cannot distinguish individuals by the risks they face, all individuals will appear to be in the same risk pool. But if we can distinguish individuals by risk actuarially and divide them into subgroups with distinct susceptibilities, then we face a general moral question: What is the moral relevance of detectable individual variation in susceptibility to disease? The question about the moral relevance of individual susceptibility to workplace hazards seems to be just a special case of this more general question.

In curative contexts such as the design of medical insurance schemes, we generally pool people with detectably different actuarial levels of risk. Employee group plans, for example, do not separate risk subgroups, say by careful screening using good predictors of disease or disability, before admitting people to group health plans, although employer screening of prospective workers may have some of this effect, if not this intention. (Of course, private insurers may try to market their coverage selectively to low-risk populations, but this is a different issue.) Similarly, in national health insurance schemes, there is a common risk pool and no differential tax or premium rate depending on differences in susceptibility to disease. Pooling risks in this way means that low-risk subgroups subsidize high-risk subgroups. In effect, detectable variation in susceptibility to disease is treated as a morally irrelevant basis for financing curative health care. We saw in Part I the justification for such risk pooling in our social obligation to protect opportunity by protecting health.

The technological feasibility criterion is primarily a strategy of cleaning up the workplace rather than selecting a workforce that is highly resistant to risk. The strategy combines all workers into a common risk pool without drawing actuarially relevant distinctions among subgroups that face different risks. This community rating of the combined risk pool increases the costs of making the workplace safe for workers who are at lower risk. Thus, lower-risk workers, and society as a whole, pay a higher premium, which includes a cross-subsidy, to ensure that the workplace is safe (for any given level of protection), than would be required if we agreed to insure only the most resistant, durable workers. Though the insurance costs of meeting

this obligation are initially borne by the employer, they are largely trans-
ferred to broader segments of society through tax deductions, consumer
price increases, and reduced wages to the workforce, which can no longer
negotiate hazard pay except for a few ineliminable risks.

The strategy involves making minimal distinctions among workers so that
we have to know less about each worker. It blends diverse workers into an
average worker, who is the given or fixed variable held constant while the
workplace is modified. Consequently, we do not need to risk invading the
privacy of individuals to gather the biological information needed to select
the most durable workers.

In protecting the work opportunities and health of workers with normal
sensitivity to risk, have we committed ourselves to providing extra protection
to supersensitive workers? After all, we insulated the workplace from the
strategy of hiring the most durable workforce. But does this mean that are
cannot exclude supersensitive workers? Or, if we are permitted to protect
their health by excluding them, must we then compensate them for their
loss of work opportunities in some way, say by placing them in other positions
or by offering them job retraining? Moral disagreement surfaces in answers
to these questions.

Excluding a supersensitive worker without offering compensation to protect workplace opportunities still gives that worker all the preventive health
given to others. Just as in curative contexts, where we pool risks and share
their burden, in this preventive context we are protecting workers at greatest
risk from workplace hazards. The fact that such workers also pay a price in
workplace opportunity is too bad, but the technological feasibility standard
already imposes higher costs to protect a normal range of worker opportunities. Arguably, that is all it is reasonable to expect us to spend to protect
both health and work opportunities.

The alternative view is that more is owed to the supersensitive worker,
who is disadvantaged, we may suppose, through no fault of his own. We are
under a moral obligation to protect a fair share of the opportunity range,
and using resources for this purpose should not be restricted to health
care or health protection alone. For example, we spend a lot of money to
improve the education and thus opportunity range of people with many
learning and cognitive disabilities. We should think of supersensitivity as an
analogue to a learning disability and spend money to protect opportunity
for these workers.

Let us leave unresolved this moral disagreement about how to spend our
money to protect opportunity in various areas – health, education, and work.
Instead, I shall examine the issue from a different perspective. Should we
think of normal durability – the absence of supersensitivity – as a marketable
trait relevant to hiring and firing? Or should supersensitivity be protected
against market forces in the way we protect race, gender, and disability?

Here too there is moral disagreement, and our philosophical models pull in two directions.

Race and gender are traits that we think of as morally irrelevant to job placement. They have no bearing on the proper grounds for placement in jobs and offices, namely competency, based on talents and skills, to perform the tasks. Using irrelevant traits thus is a direct conflict with protecting equality of opportunity. Disabilities and special sensitivities to workplace risks fall in between. If physical or mental disabilities nevertheless leave a person otherwise qualified to perform the essential tasks or functions of a job, there is moral agreement, reflected in law, that these disabilities are a morally irrelevant traits. A disability is relevant only when it directly prevents the competent performance of a job – we then say that the individual is not otherwise qualified. As I noted earlier, however, there is an important proviso on the applicability of the law: If a disability interferes with the safe performance of a job or if this individual cannot tolerate the conditions of the work environment, then, according to *Chevron v. Echazabal*, there are special grounds for giving the individual a job with less risk or even not hiring him.

For any job, must individuals have normal ability to withstand workplace hazards? We ordinarily take it for granted that each person has the requisite capacity to perform safely. We make this requirement explicit only when there are special reasons to think that individuals have certain physical or mental handicaps. This classification method assumes that the "talent" of being in the normal range for safe performance is a relevant trait for job assignments. So, the decision to exclude someone lacking this talent does not deny him equal opportunity. The individual's fair range of opportunities is defined by his talents and skills, and he lacks the talent to perform certain jobs safely.

Alternatively, we may deny that sensitivity or durability is a talent at all. We may believe this because sensitivities resemble such morally irrelevant traits as sex and race; they are unrelated to the standard skills or talents required for a given job. Workers with special sensitivities to an environmental toxin are still competent as judged by the usual standards of competency. Their special sensitivity does not mean that their performance is compromised in any obvious way, but ability to produce the standard work product (or provide a service) is just what we think of as most central to employer decisions about placement.

Sensitivities resemble race, sex, and physical handicaps in another way. There are costs to protecting equality of opportunity even for the traits we have mentioned that should play no role in job placement. For example, there are indirect costs associated with integrating the workforce that result from poor cooperation due to racist or sexist attitudes. Or the costs may be direct ones, like the costs of affirmative action programs designed to redress past discrimination. In general, these costs are likely to be minor and to diminish over time. More significant costs may be involved in bringing the workplace, or educational and other public institutions, into compliance with the laws guaranteeing equal opportunity to people with disabilities. But even here these costs, though initially paid directly by some employers, are eventually distributed to society in general through higher prices or special uses of public funds. Such costs are the social price of guaranteeing equality of opportunity, especially in a society with a history of denying it. Although the costs of protecting the equal opportunity of workers with special sensitivities would be higher, they resemble in principle the extra cost of establishing a stringent lead standard, rather than relaxing it and removing more workers permanently from the workforce.

When we ignore race or gender in hiring and placing workers, treating them as morally irrelevant, we do workers no harm, only the good of respecting equality of opportunity. In contrast, ignoring supersensitivities – in the name of equal opportunity – will harm the very workers whose opportunity we are protecting. This difference between sensitivities and race or gender is a good reason for thinking that they are not really similar. Still, it does not push sensitivities into the category of talents and abilities either. It does not mean that we need not be concerned about compromising equal opportunity.

Different policies aimed at protecting the opportunities of sensitive workers would have different costs. If we allow such workers to consent to their extra risks, then the cost of protecting their equal opportunity is the cost of allowing them to work in risky environments. These costs may involve workplace modification or special insurance policies to cover their increased health care. If we reject this option because we are still concerned that such consent might be quasi-coerced, then we have other policy options. We might offer supersensitive individuals special training programs to expand their opportunities as compensation for excluding them. Or we might give them priority placement in other low-risk jobs. The costs of these or other compensatory programs are the price of protecting equal opportunity in this setting.

Adopting such special policy options is morally necessary, given the argument we are considering, only if sensitivities ultimately resemble race or sex more than talents and abilities. Unfortunately, philosophical considerations pull in two directions, and reasonable people will disagree about their force. Of course, further philosophical examination may show that one set of considerations is decisive, and such investigation certainly should be encouraged. That is true of many of the disagreements that led us to invoke fair process in Chapter 4.

Nevertheless, we must resolve disagreements about how to spend our resources for protecting opportunity, with its built-in conflict between health protection and job opportunity. We must do this in real time, using procedures that confer legitimacy on the resulting decisions. In *Just Health Care*, I was forced to point to the disagreement and leave it unresolved. Here we have further resources. Accountability for reasonableness gives us the framework to set priorities for prevention, just as it does for medical treatment, although embodying it in the complex institutions that regulate workplace health is a task that cannot be discussed here. The integrated theory I have been elaborating thus has the scope and power to address an issue left hanging in my earlier work.

8

Medical Professionalism and the Care We Should Get

Is medical professionalism compatible with the requirements of justice for population health and fair treatment within a health system? In this chapter I explore selected aspects of this question, focusing in particular on two issues that pose the potential conflict in a very sharp form. Can physicians reconcile their professional obligations to an individual patient under treatment with the fair treatment of all patients? Do physicians owe treatment to people in need even when they face great risk to themselves, or are professional obligations more limited? (Despite the importance of nurses in delivering care to patients, I shall focus on physicians because of their primary role in determining what services are to be delivered.)

Both questions arose as actual challenges because of events and policies in the past two decades. During the late 1980s and early 1990s, fearing contagion from patients with human immunodeficiency virus/acquired immune deficiency syndrome (HIV/AIDS), medical professionals questioned their obligation to face such risks. The issue arose even more dramatically a decade later when the severe acute respiratory syndrome (SARS) epidemic infected health workers in several countries at an alarming rate. Refusals to treat obviously lead to problems of access to care, both for very sick individuals and for a public facing an epidemic.[1] What does medical professionalism require, and is it compatible with what our account says justice requires?

---

[1] I leave aside other issues of access raised by American professional codes and their accommodation to U.S. insurance arrangements. For example, physicians must give priority to the welfare of their patients over their own interests (the Primacy Principle). At the same time, American physicians are free to decide that they will not take on particular individuals or groups as patients provided that their exclusion is not a form of "invidious discrimination." They are also free to consider their economic and other interests in patient selection. Consequently, American physicians are free to decide that they will not take Medicaid patients and be subject to Medicaid's historically low levels of reimbursement – with obvious consequences for access to care.

Also in the 1980s and 1990s, in the United States and elsewhere, physicians bridled at efforts to control medical costs by requiring them to act as gatekeepers. Many physicians believe they are required to be dedicated advocates for their own patients; they also believe that preserving clinical autonomy is necessary if they are to do the best they can for their patients. Consequently, they resist the role of gatekeeper or steward of medical resources, even if this promotes fair distribution. Can we reconcile what our theory of justice requires for meeting medical needs in a population with physicians' professional obligations?

PROFESSIONALISM AND THE DUTY TO TREAT

To assess these conflicts between professionalism and justice, I need to clarify the nature and scope of professional obligations, since I have already said what I mean by justice and health. Where do professional obligations come from? How do professionals acquire them? How stringent are their demands? I shall argue against attempts to derive professional ethics from the mere concept of the profession or from some idealized conception of the doctor–patient relationship, abstracted from history and institutions. Instead, the physician's obligations and powers should be seen as the result of a social negotiation (Daniels 1991a). When the negotiation is distorted by special interests, including those of some medical professionals, or when the design of the health system ignores important requirements of justice, tensions emerge between the requirements of justice and what many professionals believe to be their obligations and powers. When that negotiation is guided by considerations of justice and by reference to the design of the institutions shaping population health, professional ethics will be compatible with justice.

Professionalism and Moral Exceptionalism

What is philosophically interesting and distinctive about professional ethics, medical or otherwise, is the idea that some occupational roles should be governed by distinctive ethical norms. People who undertake these roles acquire duties or obligations, as well as privileges and powers, not required of or granted to others. Characterized in this way, professional roles appear to involve a form of "moral exceptionalism."

Professional ethics requires exceptions to our ordinary, more universal moral point of view, suggestive of an earlier conception of morality in which our station or status in life determined what was right for us. For example, morally and legally, we require ordinary individuals to say what they know about others in certain circumstances (e.g., if we are pursuing a matter of criminal or even civil justice), but we exempt physicians and lawyers from saying what they may know about their patients or clients. We exempt them even if doing so imposes costs or burdens on others. Instead, we require confidentiality of lawyers and doctors, for different reasons in each case, insulating them from concerns about the welfare or even rights of others, that is, from having to consider reasons that ordinarily would be of the greatest moral relevance. In contrast, though we generally exempt ordinary people from a duty to assist others when they themselves are at risk, we expect physicians and other health professionals to take certain risks – for example, the risk of infection in treating certain patients who seek their aid. In ordinary transactions where goods and services are exchanged for money, we expect honesty, but also we expect people to pursue their economic advantage without criticism. Physicians, however, are bound by the Primacy Principle to elevate patients' interests above their own financial interests.

One justification for the special duties and prerogatives of physicians preserves the universality of our moral perspective, in effect converting the exceptionalism into a special set of requirements of general morality. Of course, theorists with different views of morality will tell different stories about how to ground these exceptional roles within general morality. Consequentialists, such as utilitarians, will try to show how goodness (or net utility) in the world is maximized if professionals behave in the way professionalism requires. For example, they might argue that the best way to promote (aggregate) population health is to institutionalize a system of responsibilities, powers, and prerogatives for medical professionals. Alternatively, nonconsequentialists, such as certain rights theorists or contractarians, will try to show how rights are better protected if professionals behave professionally. For example, the adversarial ethic of the lawyer might be defended (I leave aside how successfully) on the grounds that it elicits the best arguments and evidence on both sides and thus makes it more likely that trials will be fair – a result that either the consequentialist or the nonconsequentialist might aim for. Similarly, one would have to show that a range of patient rights, including the right to health, are best protected in a system that establishes a particular professional ethic.

Another justification involves thinking of these special moral requirements and permissions as examples of what we recognize as virtuous behavior for professionals. The good or virtuous doctor or lawyer behaves in these ways. Rather than thinking of these professional virtues as exceptions to ordinary morality, we should think of morality as consisting of the virtuous behaviors we should exhibit in the different (often multiple) roles we occupy. These virtues, on this view, are the bedrock out of which we construct our understanding of morality, not exceptions we must make in order to promote other moral objectives. Adopting this justification is another way of rejecting the idea of moral exceptionalism.

In what follows, I explore a few issues that bear on this broader debate, but I narrow my focus to the relationship between justice and professional ethics.

The Duty to Treat Despite the Risk of Infection

Do physicians and other health-care workers have a moral duty to treat HIV patients despite the risks of contagion? If so, what are the grounds of this duty? How dependent is the duty on the level of risk? What about the greater risks of infection for health workers posed by the SARS epidemic of 2003? In the late 1980s, a world-famous heart surgeon proclaimed that he would not operate on HIV-positive patients. He was not alone. As the National Commission on Acquired Immune Deficiency Syndrome (1990) remarked in its report to President George H. W. Bush, "a shocking number of physicians are reluctant to take care of people living with HIV infection and AIDS."[2]

State professional organizations and medical boards disagreed about the duty to treat. For example, in 1987, the Board of Medical Examiners in New Jersey proclaimed that "A licensee of this Board may not categorically refuse to treat a patient who has AIDS or AIDS related complex, or an HIV positive blood test, when he or she possesses the skill and experience to treat the condition presented" (Annas 1988: 30). A diametrically opposed position was taken by the Arizona Board of Medical Examiners, and James Mann, the chairman of the Texas Medical Association's Board of Counselors, defended its decision that there is no moral or professional duty to treat as follows: "We didn't agree that a physician who diagnoses AIDS is mandated to treat the patient. I don't think it can be called discrimination when it's a matter of a guy [sic] laying his health and career on the line" (Annas 1988: 30)

Nationally, though the American Nursing Association strongly defended the duty to treat in its 1986 ethics code (Freedman 1988), the American Medical Association's (AMA) 1986 statement on the issue left the door wide open to refusals to treat: It allowed physicians who were "emotionally" unable to care for AIDS patients to refer them to others (Freedman 1988). In late 1987, the AMA issued a new statement that seemed to close that door:

A physician may not ethically refuse to treat a patient whose condition is within the physician's current realm of competence solely because the patient is seropositive. The tradition of the American Medical Association, since its organization in 1847, is that: "when an epidemic prevails, a physician must continue his labors without regard to the risk to his own health." . . . Physicians should respond to the best of their abilities in cases of emergency where first aid treatment is essential, and physicians should not abandon patients whose care they have undertaken. (AMA 1987, cited in Freedman 1988)

---

[2] Fortunately, the situation has changed, in part because there are better preventive measures against nosocomial infections and treatments, but also because there is much better understanding of the risks and experience that reduces the early fear raised by the epidemic. The debate about the issue, however, remains relevant since other epidemics with greater risks have emerged.

In contrast to the AMA, some professional organizations of surgeons, such as the American Academy of Orthopedic Surgeons, did not insist that surgeons have a duty to treat HIV patients. Of course, when the ADA was passed a few years later, it legally prohibited discrimination against AIDS patients, and much of the debate about the duty to treat patients with HIV/AIDS abated.

Why was there so much *professional* disagreement about whether there was a professional duty to treat?

If we examine the AMA position, two sources of controversy in the 1987 statement become apparent. First, the statement says that doctors must treat "without regard to the risk." This claim cannot be taken at face value. It implies that physicians have consented, simply by becoming medical professionals, to face *any level of risk, however high, including certain death.* No one believes that, and no one should. We even ask soldiers to volunteer for especially risky or suicide missions. Historically, various societies negotiated special contracts with doctors during plagues; they did not assume that all physicians had agreed, merely by becoming physicians, to accept a very high risk of death.

The second source of disagreement is clear in the following:

Principle VI of the 1980 [AMA] Principle of Medical Ethics states that "A physician shall in the provision of appropriate patient care, except in emergencies, be free to choose whom to serve, with whom to associate and the environment in which to provide medical services." The Council has always interpreted this Principle as not supporting illegal or invidious discrimination.... Thus, it is the view of the Council that Principle VI does not permit categorical discrimination against a patient solely on [the basis of] his or her seropositivity.

This conclusion is open to an obvious reply: Refusal to treat HIV patients is not invidious discrimination but merely self-protection (Charen 1989).

To save the AMA position, we might flesh out its implicit argument as follows:

1. Refusing to treat HIV patients is discriminatory, because physicians have a duty to face the standard level of risk associated with their profession.
2. The risk of HIV infection and its consequences do not exceed that level and are comparable to other risks physicians willingly take.
3. Consequently, appealing to self-protection in the case of patients with a high risk for HIV is discriminatory.

This argument is both valid and sound. The risks of HIV infection are comparable to other risks physicians normally accepted in the 1980s, such as the risk of death from hepatitis infection. This argument leaves open, however, the case of significantly higher risks, to which I return later.

The Duty to Treat and Consent to Risks

What is the basis for the duty asserted in the first premise of this argument?

Justice generally treats *consent* as the appropriate mechanism for distributing the benefits and burdens of risk-taking, as we saw when we examined the stringent technological feasibility standard in Chapter 7. Consequently, if physicians have a duty or obligation to take certain risks, it must be the result of their *agreeing* to do so, just as firefighters and police officers agree to take certain standard risks when they train for and enter their occupations. It is standard for firefighters to distinguish acceptable risks when property is at stake from the higher risks they accept when life is at stake. And some risks are clearly above the call of duty and are left to heroes and heroines.

Because justice requires consent to the risks involved in a duty to treat, there are constraints not only on the scope or content of such a duty, but also on its justifications. Professional obligations are acquired, and acquired obligations in general result only from actions or roles one undertakes consensually. (An interesting exception may be filial obligations.)[3] Nevertheless, some have claimed that the very concept of being a medical professional implies a duty to treat despite nosocomial risks – those risks involved in treating patients (Zuger and Miles 1987; Emanuel 1988). Others have tried to ground the duty in appeals to what history tells us were once the standard virtues or duties of such professionals (Arras 1988).

One reason for seeking such a transcendent duty to treat is so that we can ignore the kinds of denials of consent that were common in the early years of the HIV/AIDS epidemic. Some insisted, "I may have consented to some risks on entering the profession, but not to *those* risks," or "Maybe earlier practitioners consented to risks of infection, but I entered the profession during the age of antibiotics, when there were few such risks, and so I did not consent to them." On the view I have been defending, these denials of consent have to be taken seriously. Taking them seriously entails gathering evidence about the types of risks people knew about and then inferring that the risks HIV poses for most physicians do not exceed the risks to which they consented on entering the profession. The defense of a duty to treat that traces it to consent is thus cumbersome and inelegant, resembling the analysis of a specific contract. More conceptual justifications avoid such detailed analysis of the institutional context in which physicians enter the profession.[4]

---

[3] Goodin (1985), however, argues that special obligations derive more generally from dependency relations and not simply from consensual undertakings.

[4] A mistaken inference underlies another objection to basing professional obligations on considerations of justice. I argued some time ago that if individuals have a right to health care, there must be a corresponding *social* obligation that guarantees that appropriate health

By examining some of these alternative justifications briefly, I aim to show that either they incorporate consent to risk without acknowledging it or they fail to provide a foundation for a duty to treat. I also draw some lessons from these accounts that point to a plausible model of professional obligations in general.

Virtues and the Duty to Treat

John Arras (1988) articulates two distinct "virtue ethic" accounts of the duty to treat – one conceptual and the other historical. Abigail Zuger and Stephen Miles (1987: 1927) typify the conceptual approach and trace their view to Scribonius, a first-century Roman physician: "To be in a profession implied a commitment to a certain end (*professio*), and thus an obligation to perform certain functions or duties (*officia*) necessary to attain that end. In the case of medicine, the *professio* is healing, the *officia* is treatment of sick persons presenting for care. Professional virtues are the attributes of character needed to honor the commitment to healing." Because physicians have voluntarily committed themselves to healing, they are obliged to undertake the duty of caring for HIV patients; physicians who refuse to treat "are falling short of an excellence in practice implicit in their professional commitment."

This conceptual approach errs by assuming that physicians have committed themselves to *healing in general.* Yet, obviously, each physician cannot treat everyone who needs or even seeks healing; that is not achievable. What *would* be an achievable goal is to treat the patients one chooses to take on, or the patients assigned to one in an insurance program, or the patients one can squeeze into a forty-hour week. This is roughly how the Principle VI of AMA Code, for example, construes the commitment. Physicians have a right to choose whom to treat, provided that no morally objectionable or illegal discrimination is involved. We cannot infer whom healers must treat from the Scribonian concept of a healer.

Properly understood, the conceptual approach fails to show that we need not worry about consent to risks. Rather, this approach contends that physicians have already consented to all nosocomial risks because they have adopted the unrestricted end of healing, and having that end logically commits physicians to facing all nosocomial risks. But it simply does not follow that if I have a goal of healing people, then I have that goal regardless of any obstacles to carrying it out. I might have the goal of healing people *provided that doing so does not become too dangerous.* Such a proviso does not introduce

care is provided, but this social obligation does not mean that each physician or provider must deliver that care (Daniels 1981, 1985). Instead, society might be able to guarantee the delivery of all necessary care by letting physicians contract individually to deliver whatever care they choose. From this fact, some then mistakenly infer that justice provides no basis for an individual duty to treat despite risks. Earlier, I made a different argument from justice.

a logical or conceptual inconsistency between my goal of healing (some) people and my concerns about my safety.

In discussing the AMA view, we concluded that those who consented to becoming physicians accepted some standard level of risks and a duty to treat in the face of those risks. Physicians learn to distinguish standard from exceptional risks through medical education, clinical training, and observation of role models in various institutions. Nothing about the risks or their consent to them is inherent in the concept of a physician.

For reasons similar to these, Arras rejects the conceptual approach and instead suggests that we try to abstract from the historical record a pattern of virtuous physician behavior to which physicians appear to have been committed. At least in the past century or two, he concludes, professional organizations and society as a whole have expected physicians to be willing to face significant risks of contagion or infection in times of epidemics. Virtuous physicians would feel an obligation to treat even at risk to themselves.

Yet, the historical approach also faces problems that Arras acknowledges. First, the historical record is spotty. Many physicians in epidemics have not been paragons of virtue, often requiring strong incentives to treat instead of flee. Second, even though virtuous physicians behaved one way under conditions existing long ago, we cannot conclude that they must do so now. Many things about medical practice have changed: the understanding of disease, the product it delivers, the institutional framework involved. Since everything else is so altered, why think that the virtues are unchanged?

Acknowledging that the virtues are not immutable and depend on the context, Arras suggests that ongoing negotiation[5] between the profession and society is responsible for a historically determined model of the virtuous physician. Virtues are "fragile" (Arras's term). Society and the medical profession renegotiate the virtues that physicians should exhibit as conditions and institutions change. Therefore, obligations that derive from past virtues are binding now only if we still subscribe to those virtues. If contemporary physicians (or their professional organizations) insist that they have not consented to the risks past physicians accepted, then renegotiation is clearly already underway.

Given the fragility of virtue, the historical basis for a duty to treat ultimately must rest on consent. The ideal of a good physician responds to changing conditions in medicine and in the health-care system. The historical version of the virtue ethic does no more than set the stage for consent. History makes it possible to be explicit about the virtues that people entering the

---

[5] The metaphor of "negotiation" is intended to suggest various forms of interaction between professional organizations and broader political institutions. It may lead to such specific legal arrangements as ceding monopoly privileges (licensing restrictions) in return for monitoring of competency and other professional obligations, or there may be broader understandings that emerge from public debate about specific issues.

profession have incorporated through their education, their training, and their emulation of the role models of good physicians. But this involves consent, and thus the picture of how the virtues of the good physician are articulated and become internalized is consistent with my central point: Consent to risk acts as a (justice-based) constraint on any account of the foundations for a duty to treat. Dissecting the virtue-ethic account, we find consent at its core.

Socially Negotiated Professional Obligations

The following picture of professional obligations emerges from this discussion: The socially negotiated ideal of the good physician is constrained by, but not limited to, what justice requires; it is thus a relatively fixed conception from the point of view of any individual. The individual entering a profession must consent to adopting this conception, but he or she cannot custom design consent by picking and choosing among the obligations. Although becoming a doctor means accepting *this* set of obligations, the ideal is not immutable and is renegotiated as conditions inside and outside medicine change.

This model of professional obligations leaves room for the kind of controversy that surrounded the duty to treat HIV patients in the early 1990s. There can be, and has been, disagreement both about the level of standard risks covered by a duty to treat and about whether the nosocomial risks of HIV exceed that level. Where evidence is complex, reasonable people may disagree, but the ground is also fertile for unreasonable biases and fears to produce dogmatic positions.

This account of professional obligations also fits quite well with the antidiscrimination requirements of the ADA of 1990. The ADA prohibits discrimination against HIV patients in many settings, including health-care settings, reinforcing the AMA's injunction against "invidious discrimination." (The AMA Code in effect converts what is now a legal obligation not to discriminate into a professional obligation.) But the empirical issue remains: Are the risks imposed by patients "significant" risks to others within the legal language of the ADA? My argument about professional commitments to a standard level of risk suggests that HIV patients offer no significant extra risks beyond those that physicians standardly face, for example, from hepatitis B (Centers for Disease Control 1989). If I am right, then the ADA and the position I have developed here about professional obligations complement each other. If the risks imposed by HIV patients *were* significantly higher than evidence shows them to be, however, then both professional and legal obligations would need modification – and in similar ways.[6]

[6] I discuss the actual levels of risk posed by nosocomial infection from HIV/AIDS in Daniels (1991a, 1995). It is important to remember that in the late 1980s, HIV/AIDS had no effective

The Duty to Treat and Higher Risks

The duty to treat HIV/AIDS patients turns on whether there is a rough understanding and agreement about what constitutes the standard level of risk for medical professionals. Should we include in that standard level the significant spike in risks facing some health workers when a new epidemic, such as SARS, emerges and spreads? Or is the standard level exclusive of the elevated risks posed by such epidemics? Indeed, the SARS epidemic revived, at least in a weak form, the debate about the duty to treat of health workers.

The SARS epidemic posed significant new risks to health workers. According to WHO (2003a) figures, there were 8,427 probable cases in twenty-nine countries between November 1, 2002, and July 11, 2003, when new cases stopped (except for a brief but contained outbreak the next year in China, with 813 deaths) – with a mortality rate of just under 10 percent. Though health-care workers were 20 percent of those infected overall, in Canada and Singapore over 40 percent of those infected were health workers (Editorial 2003). The high but variable rate of infection of health workers was the result of several factors: the difficulty of initial diagnosis, failure to use appropriate protective measures, and unpredictable variation in the ability of individual patients to spread the disease. Thus "superspreaders" infected large numbers of persons in some hospitals, including in Toronto, but in the United States, infected patients seemed to spread the disease very little (SARS-FAQ 2003).

In several countries, health workers treating infected patients were called heroes by the government and the media – but heroism is generally thought to involve action above and beyond the call of duty. In Taiwan and elsewhere, where some hospitals were quarantined and sealed off, health workers were confined with their patients. As one commentator noted, some of these workers were at best reluctant heroes (Hsin and Macer 2004).

Were health workers duty bound to treat these patients? Some health workers in several countries refused to show up for work. Many health workers were torn between a sense of duty to their patients and solidarity with other health workers and their fear of transmitting the disease to their own families. In some countries, some health workers protested against inadequate protective equipment and training for its use. In Canada, health workers may refuse to work if they face special risks, but they must use the procedures provided by the Occupational Health and Safety Act. One Canadian nurse who refused to work on the grounds that protective equipment

treatment and was perceived as a death sentence. In addition, the response to the disease was biased by the stigma attached to both of the populations first affected by it: gay men and intravenous drug users. It is tempting in retrospect, especially in light of the much weaker version of the duty-to-treat debate in the SARS epidemic, that much of the earlier response was based on homophobia and contempt for drug users, but hard information about nosocomial risks was slow to come and infection was tantamount to death.

did not fit well lost her job, suggesting that health workers were being given little leeway to refuse assignments.

At the same time that a duty to treat was being affirmed in various countries facing the SARS epidemic, thoughtful statements about it coupled the professional duty with a societal duty to provide the resources – appropriate equipment, training, patient management, and planning (Singer et al. 2003; University of Toronto Joint Center for Bioethics 2005). The professional duty to treat depends on providing an institutional context that ensures worker and patient safety and public health. If those societal obligations, which are required by justice, are not met, the professional obligation would be unduly burdensome. In effect, affirming it while not meeting societal obligations would be asking one party but not the other to abide by the terms that were negotiated.

Though the risks were significant and clearly higher than for the HIV/AIDS epidemic, no professional association stated that there is no duty to treat SARS, as some U.S. professional associations asserted for HIV/AIDS in the late 1980s and early 1990s. It is tempting to think that this confirms the view that the earlier behavior regarding HIV/AIDS was primarily the result of bias – invidious discrimination indeed – whereas the SARS epidemic had no association with sexual behavior or drug abuse. But the difference may also have been the result of seeing the SARS epidemic as a looming threat to any city or country, one from which there was no way to hide. At the same time, evidence quickly demonstrated that the epidemic could be controlled, that infections could be isolated through appropriate public health measures, and that risks to health workers could be controlled and lessened by proper procedures and equipment.

The SARS epidemic in 2003 and the threat of avian flu in 2005, involving the H5N1 virus, demonstrated that worldwide epidemics are not a thing of the past but are facilitated by globalization. In addition, weak health systems in the developing world and systems not committed to full transparency, including the public reporting of cases, pose a threat to public health in wealthy developed countries. Public health is only as strong as the weakest link in the public health chain. If that is true, then exposure to spikes in risk from such epidemics should be seen as one of the standard risks that health workers face in a globalized world. Obviously, some very special cases – and SARS bordered on being one, as would an airborne avian flu – might pose such novel and significant risks that we would have to rethink the claim that health workers, especially physicians, have already consented to facing them on entering the profession. We may need to develop special teams of health workers to meet health needs in such cases. These teams would clearly be volunteers who have consented to serve as the front line in such cases. Such a division of labor might be an effective way to contain emerging epidemics, and it would help us clarify the scope of a duty to treat. Alternatively, if society prefers all health workers to face such risks, it must train them and supply them with the means to reduce the risks to a reasonable level. The institutions we construct to manage these threats to public health will require a form of ongoing negotiation with various health professionals about what constitutes standard risks facing the profession and what constitutes exceptional risks.

TWO HISTORY LESSONS

The obligations that physicians undertake on training for and entering the profession reflect a process of social negotiation that reconciles societal and professional interests. Two lessons from history illuminate that process. The first lesson is an observation about why those societal and professional interests changed dramatically in the past century. The second suggests that the form of reconciliation reflects specific facts about the power and vested interests of the professionals and not some idealized conception of the professional–patient relationship. Together these lessons support my central claim that professional ethics must be constrained by justice.

The Changing Relation to Production for Physicians

Over the course of the twentieth century, there was a dramatic transformation in the product that we call health care, in the way it is produced, and in the relationship of physicians to that means of production. This transformation, the result of many social forces, has profound implications for how we should think about professional roles. It explains why those roles, including their obligations and prerogatives, are the subject of ongoing social negotiation.

Until well into the twentieth century, the "means of production"[7] of the product (medical care) that doctors could deliver to their patients was contained in their heads, their hands, their hearts, and their little black bags. Physicians clearly owned and controlled the means of production. Their control was strengthened with the emergence of licensing laws and the monopolies they established. Any account of the professional norms that governed physician behavior early in the twentieth century should reflect that basic fact about the relation of physicians to the means of production. For example, only the physician needed information from the patient, and only the physician had an obligation to respect patient confidentiality. (Leave aside the company doctor and, for other reasons, leave aside the legal obligation to report certain infectious diseases that pose public health problems.) Similarly, access to care depended on being able to pay the physician's fees. The good of the community could then be served by

[7] I do not intend to carry any other theoretical baggage into the discussion other than Marx's apt terminology when I talk about means of production and the relation to production.

a sliding scale of fees or at least by some pro bono work by physicians. The virtuous physician was one who did not exclude the poor from services but cross-subsidized them. We might view this obligation as a quid pro quo for the income guaranteed by licensing regulations.

As the twentieth century progressed, and especially in its last third to half, the means of production radically changed, as did physicians' relation to it. As medical technology advanced, society – or specific institutions and agents in society – became capable of affecting health outcomes in many ways that were not possible earlier. Physicians play a crucial role in helping to orchestrate the delivery of this product, but what they deliver is often owned and controlled by others – in terms of either skills possessed or drugs, facilities, and equipment owned and controlled by others. Many people thus have a stake in the product that physicians deliver to patients; it is not simply the product of what the physician does or has. This transformation in the relation of physicians to the production of the good they help deliver is far greater than any similar transformation in the analogous relation to production of lawyers.

This changing relation to production is often not correctly understood and described. It is often noted that doctors could do very little for patients a century ago, and that limited capability is contrasted with what they or medicine, presumably embodied in physicians – can do today. But it is not the same "they," for physicians can deliver the goods today only if other stakeholders in those goods make them available and cooperate in their production and delivery. Similarly, the changing relation to production is more fundamental than the common observation that physicians were once solo entrepreneurs and today they often work in more complex institutional arrangements. Many physicians still work primarily as solo entrepreneurs or small group partners, both in the United States and elsewhere, but that does not alter the fact that they have a very different relationship to the means of production than they did earlier in the twentieth century. Here and elsewhere, regardless of the differences in the corporatization of medicine or the methods of financing insurance, physicians stand in a similar relation to the means of production. They can deliver a good to patients only if others who have a stake in the means of production cooperate to deliver that good with them.

Public discussions of the threats to professionalism from the emergence of business and markets in American medicine sometimes confuse the result of a fundamental change in physicians' relations to production with more optional or discretionary changes in institutional form, or even with the mere fact of rising costs.[8] Physicians' obligation to keep patient

---

[8] Rising costs are indeed a motivating factor in institutional change, but they are an effect of the changing health-care product and the means of production. The relation to production and the product could conceivably have changed without driving up costs, for example, had

confidentiality means one thing where no one else is involved in health-care delivery, but it means another when many are involved in its production and financing and have a legitimate interest in knowing about the patient's condition. This point is true regardless of whether the many others involved belong to a private managed care plan or a public insurance entity. Professional norms regarding confidentiality remain important but take a different form given the changes in health care production and delivery. Markets can and do threaten patient-centered values unless we recognize clearly how professional norms should be modified.

If the goods that physicians can deliver to patients are solely the result of knowledge and skills physicians possess, then the "agency" role of physicians seems fairly straightforward. If, however, these goods are not owned and controlled physicians alone, but physicians play a key role in determining which of those goods are needed and authorizing access to them, then the agency role of physicians became more complex. Professional norms must reflect that complexity. This claim is true whether the physician is surrounded by private market arrangements, by public ownership of the goods and services involved, or by some mixture thereof. The controversy we examine later about conflicts between professional obligations to advocate for patients and societal concerns to conserve resources and distribute them fairly must be addressed by rethinking – renegotiating–professional roles and obligations.

Negotiating Power

Our second history lesson – actually three mini-lessons in one – draws on Paul Starr's (1982) classic account of the way the American medical profession acquired and exercised the cultural authority and power it now enjoys. The first point is that the features of the institutional arrangements and the powers American physicians have acquired are not due to the inner logic or nature of the physician–patient relationship but are the results of an historical and idiosyncratic struggle of the medical profession to protect its interests. Physicians did not acquire their cultural power merely because they were healers, and society has always revered healers. Rather, physicians resisted "capture" by hospitals and other emerging institutions because hospitals in the United States remained dependent on physicians for referrals. In contrast, in many European countries, physicians were often salaried employees of hospitals from an early period. Consequently they too had an interest in undercutting the independence of non-hospital-based physicians. U.S. physicians and their professional associations and lobbies

we immediately developed more cost-reducing technologies (the polio vaccine was cheaper than the iron lung) than cost-increasing ones. Even in such a case, changes in the relation to production will alter professional roles and norms.

also resisted capture by institutions developed to improve access to health care through new financing and insurance schemes. For example, when Medicare and Medicaid were established, physicians retained the power to determine whether they would treat such patients and how many they would treat. They also retained the retrospective fee-for-service reimbursement system common to private insurance schemes. If we add to this physician control over where they locate their practices and what specialties they enter, we arrive at a unique pattern of physician autonomy and power, one that has blocked access to care for important subgroups in the population. The details of this history undermine any inclination we might have had to believe that the autonomy and power granted American physicians are based either on the requirements of the physician–patient relationship or on a reasoned social calculation about how to guarantee equitable access to high-quality care at acceptable costs.

The second point to emerge from Starr's (1982) history is that physicians misused appeals to professional ethics to bolster their claims that certain institutional arrangements had to be preserved. To illustrate this point, consider how some American physicians, presumably sincerely, made explicitly ethical arguments in favor of the broad institutional powers and authority they sought. The code of ethics the AMA adopted in 1934 claimed that it was "unprofessional" for a physician to permit making "a direct profit" from his work: "The making of a profit from the medical work is beneath the dignity of professional practice, is unfair competition with the profession at large, is harmful alike to the profession of medicine and the welfare of the people, and is against sound public policy." As Starr points out, it was unprofessional only for someone *other* than a physician to make a profit from the physician's work. It was acceptable, however, for another physician to make such a profit! How exquisitely refined this principle of professional ethics is! The first of ten principles for medical service adopted by the AMA in 1934 (current codes are less explicit about converting economic considerations into ethical ones) says, "All features of medical service in any method of medical practice should be under the control of the medical profession." The fifth claimed that the "medical profession alone can determine the adequacy and character" of the institutions involved in medical care, which should be construed as "but expansions of the equipment of the physician." Starr remarks, "the doctors took professional authority, patient confidentiality, and free choice to require a specific set of economic relations." For example, "However the cost of medical service may be distributed . . . the immediate cost should be borne by the patient if able to pay at the time the service is rendered." Thus, as Starr concludes, "the AMA insisted that all health insurance plans accept the private physician's monopoly control of the medical market and complete authority over all aspects of medical institutions," and it did so by deriving these controls from its view of professional ethics.

The third point in this history lesson is that the social negotiation in which the American medical profession engaged was not guided by justice at all. Physicians not only sought power and autonomy at the expense of other stakeholders in the production of health care, but their professional organizations opposed institutions required by justice, including universal insurance coverage. One of their weapons in this negotiation was a misleading appeal to professional ethics itself. In view of this history, we must not assume that important, morally desirable features of medical decision making can be preserved only if we maintain familiar institutional arrangements. These arrangements are not necessarily the historical product of respect for any transcendent moral core of the physician–patient relationship.

Our history lessons support my central claim. The shape of professional relationships, and thus the scope and content of professional ethics, should depend on what kinds of institutions are needed to guarantee the just distribution of the goods provided by those relationships. It is justice that should be primary here in designing social institutions, including professional roles and their norms. Professional ethics should govern roles circumscribed by just institutions and should not be the tail that wags the dog. Ludicrous professional codes, such as the 1934 AMA principles discussed by Starr (1982), are but an extreme result of reversing appropriate priorities. This central claim is a generalization of my earlier argument about negotiating, with justice as a guide, the specifics of a duty to treat, including the standard level of risk to which physicians consent on entering the profession.

PHYSICIAN AUTONOMY AND IDEAL ADVOCACY

How should justice guide the social negotiation of the components of physician autonomy included in an acceptable professional ethic? There are four main dimensions of autonomy traditionally claimed by U.S. physicians: (1) whom to treat, (2) where to practice, (3) what to specialize in, and (4) how to treat. Arguably, assuring equitable access to care of the sort guaranteed in many universal coverage systems would lead to changes in the choice space and incentives open to U.S. physicians in the first three dimensions. It might mean restricting the power of physicians to choose whom to treat, what specialties they will enter, and where they will locate. These powers can be modified in ways that violate no fundamental liberties of physicians (Daniels 1981), though realistic options open to them would clearly differ from what they are now.

I focus in what follows on dimension (4), how to treat, because it is the only one whose rationale rests primarily on patient rather than physician interests. Autonomy in treatment decisions is constrained by what might be called an "ethic of advocacy." The autonomy we grant physicians is necessary precisely if they are to act in their patients' best interests, and for this reason I also include some constraints on physicians. Clinical decisions must be (A) competent, complying with professional standards of care; (B) respectful of patient autonomy; (C) respectful of patient rights, such as confidentiality; (D) free from consideration of physicians' interests; (E) uninfluenced by judgments about patients' worth.

The competency constraint (A) is enforced by peer review and by tort law (how effectively it is enforced I leave aside; see Brennan et al. 1991; IOM 1999). The four other constraints are special features of the fiduciary relationship between a physician, with his greater knowledge and skill, and the patient, for whom the physician acts as an agent or advocate. I shall not comment on constraints B and C because they have less to do with the problem of distributive justice and have been the focus of much recent clinical medical ethics. But the "purity" constraints D and E are at the heart of the issue. Constraint D requires that physicians not allow their economic or career interests to influence patient treatment. Constraint E is interpreted by some to mean that physicians should not decide how much it is worth to save or extend a particular patient's life. More narrowly interpreted, constraint E bars physicians from considering facts other than medical need or likelihood of treatment success in making clinical decisions for a particular patient. I shall call the Ideal Advocate model the view that physicians should pursue their patients' best interests through autonomous clinical decision making while adhering to the ethic of advocacy.

Some people believe that the Ideal Advocate is necessarily also an Unrestricted Ideal Advocate. That is, physicians should have no external constraints on the treatment they can provide for their patients. Because pre-cost-containment, fee-for-service arrangements – typical when physicians owned and controlled the means of medical production – seem to embody the virtues of the Unrestricted Ideal Advocate, many physicians may think of them as the form medicine must take if it is to be morally acceptable. Because current cost-containment measures introduce a concern about resource limitations through incentives that threaten the purity constraints D and E, it is easy for physicians to overgeneralize and to think that any challenge to the Unrestricted Ideal Advocate must also undermine the Ideal Advocate (Daniels 1986, 1987).

Physician Incentives and Agency

How should we think of the physician's agency role in light of the changed relation to production and in light of what justice requires?

Prior to the transformation of the physician's relation to the production of medical goods, the problem of physician agency focused largely on the asymmetry in power and knowledge between the patient and the physician. The physician produced and owned the good that was to be delivered and possessed whatever knowledge existed about the patient's condition and the available care. The patient was completely dependent on the physician not to abuse that situation and to pursue the patient's interest. Other patients would not be affected in any way by what the physicians did (except insofar as the physician spent time with one patient and not another), and almost no one else was called upon to contribute when the doctor delivered his care.

In this context, it seems natural to think of the physician as the only fiduciary agent of the individual patient. The main threat to that relationship is the physician's fee-for-service incentive to take advantage of the power and knowledge asymmetry, famously captured in George Bernard Shaw's (1911) attack on the trustworthiness of physicians. If, however, physicians accept the Primacy Principle, which requires putting patient's interests before their own, then fiduciary agency is preserved. In effect, no one else's interests are at stake, and physicians can accept this agency role with no concern that they might then be in conflict with the interests of others – a nice situation.

After the transformation of the physician's relation to the production and delivery of medical goods, there remains an asymmetry between physician and patient with regard to knowledge and power, and we still want the physician to act in the patient's interests. Now, however, what physicians think it is best to do for a given patient requires the cooperation of many others in the medical system. In addition, in the cooperative schemes we have developed for delivering complex and costly care, whatever is done for one patient must be fair in light of what is done for others similarly dependent on that cooperative scheme. Here agency seems much more complex.

Many commentators have suggested that physicians can have only one master, that they can only be the agents of their patients. They suggest that ethical rules acknowledging that physicians are also accountable to other providers and patients in a cooperative health-care scheme, or that there may be other stakeholders who are also accountable for delivering care fairly to patients in a covered population – that is, any "collective" ethic – threatens the physician's professional role. On this view, the physician must remain the patient advocate, unfettered by concerns about other patients or the system as a whole.

There is a deep problem with this traditional view. Consider the analogy to lawyers as their clients' agents. Defense lawyers are advocates only if they are also *adversaries*. They are adversaries of the prosecutor, and perhaps of the public that the prosecutor represents, and they may be adversaries of lawyers representing other defendants in the same case. All of these adversaries must then be heard by a neutral jury of their peers. That jury must decide whether appropriate standards of evidence are met in what they hear and see.

There is a significant disanalogy with the medical case. Although we like the idea that our physicians should pursue our best interests, we do not want them to become adversaries against other physicians representing other patients whose interests may conflict with ours. In any case, there is no neutral jury of our peers to adjudicate the dispute among adversaries that would result. The legal analogy breaks down. Moreover, it is not obvious that patients would trust physicians more if they acted as "hired guns," adversaries of whomever they are not treating at the moment. Physicians too would not want to end up with the public distrust that lawyers now enjoy (though that distrust may not solely be the product of lawyers' adversarial role).

Our task, then, is not to articulate professional obligations that convert patient advocates into adversaries of other patients. Instead, we want professional obligations that provide fair, reasonable protections for individual patients and at the same are compatible with what we want from our cooperative health-care schemes, namely, the protection of population health under reasonable resource constraints. Such obligations will, of course, reflect the altered relationship of the physician to the means of producing health care; they will also recognize the many who have a stake in a cooperative scheme that is fair to all.

Providers inevitably find themselves in a framework that restricts the resources for treating certain conditions to provide a more equitable distribution of resources overall. There will be some things that providers cannot do for their patients. Providers will not be able to be unrestricted advocates of their patients, but will have to do the best they can for them under systemic restrictions. In a just system, those who make decisions about these limits will be accountable for the reasonableness of their decisions (see Chapter 4). We can now state how the Ideal Advocate model must be qualified: Physicians should be the advocates of their patients, abiding by the ethic of agency, within the limits imposed by a fair allocation of resources. Ideal Advocates may not do things that would be unfair or unjust to other patients. This is the sense in which justice is primary or provides the framework for professional ethics.

Stringent – but just – rationing schemes need not threaten the ethic of advocacy. The purity constraint (D), which requires clinical decisions to ignore the physician's interests, is perfectly compatible with the just rationing of limited health-care resources. British physicians, for example, who deny beneficial care that may be available to patients in the United States, do not do so because of economic incentives that directly reward them for denying care. It is possible to construct institutions in which physicians pursue their patients' best interests and respect fair resource limitations without their incentive for denying care deriving from economic incentives to them. Some years ago, James Sabin and I interviewed Canadian primary care physicians who had to assign their patients a level of urgency to place them on a queue for computed tomography (CT) scans. We asked them why they did not exaggerate the urgency of their own patients in order to advocate more vigorously for them. They replied that they could not do that without being unfair to their own patients. If they acquired the reputation for exaggerating patients' status, the physicians administering CT scans would discount their ratings, and then they would be hurting their own more urgently ill patients.

Similarly, physicians constrained by fair resource limits are not violating the constraint about making judgments of social worth (and so are not violating constraint E). Physicians acting as gatekeepers are abiding by a just social decision when the limits imposed on them result from a fair process. Physicians can still advocate effectively for their patients within the limits imposed by justice. That is all that constraints D and E require.

Now we can better see why American cost-containment measures seem so threatening to the idea that physicians must be Ideal Advocates for their patients. Constraints on physician autonomy embodied in current cost-restraint measures have no such justification grounded in requirements of justice. In the United States, there is no assurance that when a patient is required to forego beneficial treatment, the resources saved are used for other patients whom justice requires that we treat instead. Rather, services that might benefit patients are foregone simply because, say, it is not profitable to treat them compared to others, and the system of incentives has no guiding principle other than the intention of reducing "unnecessary" services. Indeed, decisions about the use of new technologies are made without considering opportunity costs at all, let alone a principle of justice.

In the United States over the past two decades, physicians have faced relatively novel incentives aimed at getting them to modify their clinical decisions. I have in mind various kinds of "withholding" of fees and capitation arrangements with physician groups in the 1980s and 1990s. We need to understand just what threat, if any, these incentives pose to professional obligations (such as the principle requiring physicians to keep patient interests primary). Theory tells us that these incentives are likely to pose a serious threat if they put too much of a physician's income at risk and if the risk is immediately felt because the risk pool of physicians and patients is too small. But we have very little actual evidence about the outcomes or the effects of variations in these incentives. Without that evidence, we do not know how to respond to the distrust caused by these incentives. The institutions that have negotiated these incentive schemes with physicians have not provided convincing evidence and arguments to assure patients and the public that these schemes are reasonably designed (see Daniels and Sabin 2002). They are examples of uncontrolled social experiments of the sort discussed in Chapter 9.

The standard analysis of the problem posed by these incentives is misleading, and the standard response to it is inadequate. The standard analysis is that these incentives pose a conflict of interest for the physician, pitting the individual patient's interests against the physician's. The ethical guidelines respond that physicians – or their plans – should disclose at least the general features of these incentive schemes, at least to those who ask about them.

The standard analysis is misleading because there are interests other than those of the physician and a given patient. Many others – patients and providers – have legitimate interests in how shared resources are used; specifically, they have a legitimate interest in their being used fairly and reasonably. An incentive system for physicians should reflect a reasonable balance among these various interests. It should provide some incentive to practice good stewardship, thus protecting patients' interests, but should also provide some assurance that individual patients' interests will be supported.

The appropriate way to address this complex problem is to analyze incentive schemes carefully so that we learn how they actually work. It is not enough to suggest that the problem of their appropriate design can be solved simply by plan disclosure or even physician disclosure. Disclosing the features of schemes without providing evidence that they do not lead physicians to treat individual patients unfairly is simply misleading, for it implies that we know how to evaluate the schemes once they are disclosed. Unfortunately, the AMA code calls only for such simple disclosure.

Having an adequate analysis of how to support physicians in their obligations to individual patients and patient populations (remember that physicians have obligations to the community and not just to individuals) requires an institutional ethic that is generally missing. Specifically, institutions – and physicians working with them – must be *accountable for the reasonableness* of their limit-setting behavior. They must be willing to show that the direct limits they set, as well as indirect ways of setting limits such as incentive schemes, are reasonable. They must publicly show that the decisions about these limits rest on reasons that all consider relevant to meeting the health needs of a population under reasonable resource constraints.

To preserve what is valuable in professionalism and professional norms, we must pay careful attention to the ways in which the complex institutions that deliver our health care work and not simply focus on the ethic of the individual professional. Both must fit together.

PUBLIC HEALTH PROFESSIONALISM

Physicians should play the role of Ideal Advocates, doing the best they can for their patients, keeping in mind a just distribution of health and health care. The advocacy role aims to protect particular individual needs so that they are not lost sight of in a system of rules and decisions that promote population health. This picture may give us some insight into how we should think about the professionalism of public health workers, including public health physicians.

It is tempting to think of public health professionals as advocates for population health and its fair distribution, including the fair distribution of risks to health. They may have to resist special pleading by individuals or interest groups whose demands would work to the disadvantage of population health. They must push back against those demands, but they, like physicians, are constrained by justice as well. They must be attentive to individual rights and liberties, even as they pursue public health and marshal police powers of the state to do so. It is one thing to protect public health by resisting vested interests, such as those who would pollute the air or water or profit from unsafe workplaces or food distribution, but it is another to ignore important individual rights, including privacy and confidentiality rights, in the pursuit of a public good.

This analogy between the Ideal Advocacy roles of medical professionals and public health professionals may illuminate important questions about what professionalism means for those in public health, but I shall not pursue the topic here. Neither advocate is unconstrained. The physician resists the tendency of systems to ignore individual differences, but she does so within constraints on fair distribution that justice requires. The public health professional resists the tendency of individuals or groups to pursue their own interests while posing risks to population health, but here too justice, in the form of individual rights and liberties, constrains the pursuit of public goals. This division of labor could well be an assignment of professional obligations that promotes justice overall, even if each professional may feel in some tension with the requirements of justice. The resulting division of labor and assignment of professional obligations are compatible with and help secure justice and population health.

PART III

USES

9

Fairness in Health Sector Reform

The theory of justice and health developed in this book should help guide our understanding in practical ways about the just design of health systems. Our beliefs about the acceptable design of health systems should also have a bearing on what we think is just health and health care. After all, ethical theory should help guide practice and, conversely, acceptable moral practice should constrain ethical theory. We should look to such a "reflective equilibrium" between different levels of moral belief and practice as a source of justification in the ethics of health policy, just as we should more generally (Rawls 1971; Daniels 1996a). In Part III, we explore applications of the theory elaborated in Part I and defended in Part II in order to examine the adequacy of the theory to the demands of our practice in health policy.

The main goal of this chapter is to show how the theory of just health developed in earlier chapters can guide our practical concerns about health systems in both developed and developing countries and how our beliefs about just institutional arrangements constrain the theory. I do this by describing a tool, the Benchmarks of Fairness, that I helped devise for monitoring and evaluating the fairness of health sector reforms (Daniels et al. 1996; Daniels, Bryant, et al. 2000). The Benchmarks translate central ideas about justice and health into an evidence-based approach to improving health policy. By bridging theory and practice in this way, they also help us assess the adequacy of the theory.

One central motivation for developing the Benchmarks, especially for their use in developing countries, is the widely held belief that many health system reforms imposed on developing countries in the 1980s and 1990s were not evidence-based policy proposals; in any case, they carried important risks as well as promised benefits. Moreover, many countries were induced to accept these reforms because they were tied to international loans that the countries desperately needed. Improving the capacity of developing countries to evaluate the anticipated effects of such reforms, and to monitor and evaluate their actual effects, was a central objective in developing the Benchmarks.

This reason for developing the Benchmarks becomes more urgent if we pursue the troubling suggestion that many health reforms should be considered as social experiments conducted without adequate scientific or ethical review (Daniels 2006). Domestic and international examples of such experiments abound. Attempts to control costs in the U.S. health-care system aim at changing either physician or patient behavior in utilizing health services. Over two decades ago, diagnosis related groups (DRGs) were introduced as a way of shortening hospital stays for Medicare patients without review of the risks imposed, though many physicians and hospitals protested that patients would be discharged early in ways that imposed great risks on them (Daniels 1986, 1987; also see Chapter 8). During the 1980s and 1990s, capitation and other physician reimbursement schemes were introduced to change physician utilization behavior, again without review of the risks to patients or knowledge of the actual effects of these mechanisms, despite complaints about the risks of undertreatment (Daniels and Sabin 2002: Ch. 8). Currently, insurers aiming to change patient demand are introducing novel deductible structures. Despite warnings about risks to some patients and to insurance markets themselves (Rosenthal and Daniels 2006), there is no provision for ethical or scientific review.

Social experiments without ethical review are common in developing countries, where reforms are often initiated by external agents, such as the International Monetary Fund (IMF) or the World Bank (WB), that offer loans only if certain measures are used. A classic example from the 1980s and 1990s is the requirement that systems in developing countries introduce user fees as a way of providing new resources for underfunded public systems. Despite exemptions for the very poor, user fees in many places decreased access and created opportunities for corruption (Gilson 1997a,b). Similarly, many countries were induced to seek efficiency by expanding their private health sector. Unfortunately, weak state regulation led to a sector of questionable quality that pulled personnel from the public system and undermined equity in various ways (Bennett et al. 1997). Decentralization was advocated as a way of improving local control over resource use and making systems more responsive to local needs, but in many places this has created serious problems for the delivery of public health services (Bossert 1998). There are also problems of sustainability (Berman 1995; Berman and Bossert, 2004). These social experiments now create special ethical problems for international efforts to scale up antiretroviral treatments (ARTs) in high-prevalence countries: User fees are barriers to access, personnel drawn to private clinics are not available for public delivery systems, and weakened public health structures make delivery of ARTs more difficult (McCoy 2003; Daniels 2004, 2005; see Chapter 10). Reforms may thus not only fail to accomplish their avowed goals, but their long-lasting effects can make it more difficult to implement better reforms.

Social experiments should be subject to ethical and scientific review before implementation and ethical and scientific monitoring and evaluation afterward. This thesis may at first seem perverse. Health system reforms are not intended as research aimed at new knowledge. They aim instead to improve population health through better delivery of medical and public health services. Nevertheless, reforms have important similarities to clinical research. They often use measures of unknown efficacy. They may impose health risks on population subgroups much greater than those involved in typical clinical research. Like clinical research, reforms trade on the credibility of science and the medical or public health establishment. Both raise issues about governance, including the control people can exercise over what happens to them in the pursuit of societal goals. Finally, both aim at desirable social goals – new knowledge or improved health delivery; review should not make their pursuit too difficult.

A second goal of this chapter, then, is to suggest that the Benchmarks – or something modeled on them – should be used as the basis for the ethical and scientific review of such social experiments. Some adaptation of the Benchmarks could address all three key elements of such a review: (1) an examination of the rationale for the goals of the reform, (2) an assessment of whether the measures it includes are likely to achieve those goals and what the risks are if they do not, and (3) an evidence base emerging out of ongoing monitoring and evaluation so that the reform can be modified if it does not meet expectations or imposes unanticipated risks. Such a review would supplement, not replace, the political accountability that reforms ordinarily have or should have.

The argument of this chapter is that the Benchmarks provide an important application of my account of justice and health to the design and performance of the health sector. Subsequent chapters in Part III describe other applications, both actual and potential, of the theory of just health. Chapters 10–12 examine the applicability of accountability for reasonableness to a range of pressing issues in global health – the scaling up of ARTs for HIV/AIDS, the reduction of unjust health inequalities, and efforts to increase right to health. The concluding chapter, Chapter 13, poses a challenge and suggests where more work must be done if just health is to be applied successfully to the problem of international health inequalities.

BENCHMARKS OF FAIRNESS

I have been involved in developing the Benchmarks of Fairness, an evidence-based policy method for evaluating the fairness of health sector reforms, for well over a decade (Daniels et al. 1996, 2005; Daniels, Bryant, et al. 2000). Through this project, I have sought to make the connection between theory

TABLE 9.1 *Fairness as Equity, Efficiency, and Accountability in the Generic Benchmarks*

Benchmark		Concern of Fairness
B1	Intersectoral Public Health	
B2	Financial Barriers to Equitable Access	
B3	Nonfinancial Barriers to Access	EQUITY
B4	Comprehensiveness of Benefits and Tiering	
B5	Equitable Financing	
B6	Efficacy, Efficiency, and Quality Improvement	
B7	Administrative Efficiency	EFFICIENCY
B8	Democratic Accountability and Empowerment	
B9	Patient and Provider Autonomy	ACCOUNTABILITY

and practice. The Benchmarks of Fairness translate many of the general ideas developed earlier in this book into an integrated view of how we should seek *equity, accountability, and efficiency* in health policy. By combining an operations research methodology with an integrated ethical framework for assessing the effects of reforms on aspects of fairness, it is possible to provide an evidence base for evaluating health policy and improving it.

Each of the nine Benchmarks marks out a central objective of fairness in health policy. For example, Benchmarks B2 and B3 (of the generic developing country version; see Table 9.1) concern the reduction of financial and nonfinancial barriers to access to health care. Each Benchmark contains several main criteria, which mark out components of this objective of fairness or key means to achieving them. For example, Benchmark B3 focuses on reducing geographical maldistribution of resources, gender barriers, cultural barriers, and discrimination or exclusion as key criteria of equitable access. For many of the criteria, more detailed subcriteria are described. For example, reducing cultural barriers to access would mean providing care in appropriate languages, educating people about preventive and curative health practices, including the problems of uninformed reliance on traditional healers, and providing services in ways sensitive to cultural attitudes in particular ethnic groups or classes.

The nine generic Benchmarks integrate the goals of fairness as follows: B1–B5 address equity; B6 and B7 consider efficiency; and B8 and B9 concern accountability (see Table 9.1). Rather than seeing efficiency as conflicting with fairness, improving efficiency means that more needs can be met fairly. Accountability is valued both intrinsically, as a matter of fairness in governance, and instrumentally, since it is difficult to achieve efficiency or equity without accountability.

To convert the generic Benchmarks into a tool for evaluating reforms in a specific context, they must be adapted for that purpose by a local interdisciplinary team. An evidence-based application aims to refine the generic criteria, specify indicators appropriate to local conditions, and achieve agreement on how to evaluate changes in these indicators. Applying the Benchmarks then enables planners or community groups to evaluate the impact of health policies. By providing an evaluation methodology that rests on locally accessible information, teams can modify current practice, which often involves little evidence-based evaluation of proposals to improve the health of disadvantaged people (Machenbach 2003).

In what follows, I shall focus first on how the theory of just health provides a coherent account of the central ideas underlying the construction of the Benchmarks. Then, after briefly describing the development of the Benchmarks and contrasting it with another approach to measuring health system performance, I describe in more detail the generic developing-country version of the approach and briefly discuss several applications of it to demonstrate its relevance to health policy. I then apply the benchmarking approach to the problem of social experimentation.

Why Equity, Efficiency, and Accountability?

The theory developed in this book helps clarify both the content and the relationships among equity, efficiency, and accountability in just health systems. I shall elaborate on its implications shortly, especially for the concept of equity. But first, it will be useful to say more about why all three objectives must be addressed in an integrated way if a health system is to be fair to those affected by it.

In answer to the first Focal Question (Is health of special moral importance?), I argued that health, and thus health care, is of special moral importance because keeping people functioning normally helps to protect the range of exercisable opportunities (or capability sets) open to them (see Chapter 2). If we have social obligations to protect opportunity, a claim on which several egalitarian theories tend to converge, either because we want to give priority to those with the worst opportunities or because we support a concept of fair equality of opportunity, then we have an obligation to protect normal functioning in a population. This obligation means that we must distribute as *equitably* as we can not only the risk of becoming ill but also the means of overcoming illness. To distribute the risks of illness and, consequently, health equitably, we must distribute the social determinants of health in a just way (Chapter 3). That answer to the second Focal Question (When is a health inequality unjust?) means that we must look beyond the health sector as it is ordinarily (and narrowly) construed.

Benchmark B1, we shall see, takes steps to promote an intersectoral focus on public health and risks to health. It forces us to consider how other sectors – transportation, education, taxation – impact population health. In addition, we must provide *equitable access* to the full range of health services people need – preventive, curative, rehabilitative, compensatory, acute, chronic, physical, and mental (Benchmarks B2–B4). Since this is a social obligation, we must assure *equitable financing* of these services (Benchmark B5). I shall say more about the crucial concept of "equitable access" shortly, but its importance to the theory of just health is apparent from earlier chapters.

Similarly, the importance of accountability and efficiency is clear (see Chapter 4) from our answer to the third Focal Question (how can we meet needs fairly under resource constraints?). Under reasonable resource constraints, we will not be able to meet all health needs. To meet needs fairly, we should establish accountability for reasonableness in the institutions that make decisions about priorities in resource allocation and limits to health care. In effect, we need *accountability and democratic empowerment* if we are to have justice in health policy. Just health, like the Benchmarks, requires us to address problems of accountability along with problems of equity in the pursuit of just health policy. Since the Benchmarks require accountability in resource allocation decisions as well as in all matters of system performance (Benchmarks B8 and B9), I shall say more shortly about how this broader notion of accountability can be accommodated by the theory of just health.

Regardless of how fairly (and accountably) we allocate limited resources to meet needs, if we do so inefficiently we will do less well at meeting population health needs. Since health is not the only good we must pursue justly, resources are always limited. Because my theory of just health implies that we have obligations to promote population health and distribute it fairly, our health systems must be *clinically and administratively effective and efficient*, that is, they must get value for money (Benchmarks B6 and B7). I shall say more about how the theory forces efficiency into the service of equity shortly, but the point here is that it must be integrated into any account of the goals of a just health system.

Putting these points together, the answers provided earlier to our three Focal Questions of justice and health mean that we must attend to *equity, accountability,* and *efficiency* in an integrated way if we are to have justice in health policy and health system design. Together, these ideas provide a coherent rationale for the detailed integration of these ideas built into the Benchmarks of Fairness. The Benchmarks establish operational criteria against which we can assess progress in a health system toward establishing equity, accountability, and efficiency. Health sector reforms should aim at fairness, and their contributions to the components of fairness can be monitored and evaluated once proper criteria and indicators of their satisfaction are constructed.

Equity

I begin with the concept of equity of access to personal medical services (Benchmarks B2–B4). I draw on the health services literature on this topic, but my concern is conceptual and moral and I undertake no systematic review here. Unfortunately, this empirical literature on equity of access is complex and confusing, and it does not yield a clear consensus on what counts as equitable access.

There are three central reasons for this divergence. First, access is itself a complicated notion, a composite of many factors. As a result, determining when access is equal, let alone equitable, is not a trivial problem. In some cases, considerations about equity already play a role in our judgments about equality, for we may care little about some inequalities and greatly about others. For example, if I have an aversion to the color of the coffee room near our offices, but you do not, and I get less coffee there than you as a result, I might still agree that we have equal access to coffee. If coffee met a basic need, and not simply a preference, however, I might judge equality of access differently, caring more about how burdensome it was to obtain it because of my preferences or sensitivities.

Second, health-care services are nonhomogeneous. Some have more important, more basic, or more urgent functions than others. Judgments about equity will depend on the weights we give to these diverse functions. Third, divergence on what counts as equitable access derives from divergence on more basic moral questions about distributive justice. If we think health care is a commodity like any other and has no special moral importance, then we will make different judgments about equitable access than if we think that (some of) it has moral importance because it meets an important need and protects opportunity.

Historically, three seminal accounts of equitable access, each reflecting an underlying ethical stance on more basic questions, dominate the health policy literature: a use-per-need-based account (see the seminal works by Aday and Andersen 1975; Aday et al. 1980), a process variable account (Sloan and Bentkover 1979), and a modified market account (Havighurst 1977; Enthoven 1980; and various successors). A classic statement of the use-per-need account is this: "The greatest 'equity' of access is said to exist when need, rather than structural (for example, availability of physicians), or individual (for example, family income) factors determine who gains entry to the health care system" (Aday et al. 1980: 26). The normative proposal, then, is that "Inequity in health service distribution occurs when individuals receive services primarily according to their place in the social structure, their enabling characteristics, or the characteristics of the health system ... [all of which can be measured to see if they are important access variables] ... instead of according to their need (Aday et al. 1980: 43). Of course, if older people use services more than younger ones, then the inequity is only apparent since need varies between the groups.

There is a good fit between the use-per-need view of equity and the argument earlier in this book about the importance of health needs. Meeting health needs is of special moral importance because it protects opportunity, which we have obligations of justice to protect. In contrast, meeting preferences for other goods, or for medical services such as cosmetic surgery that do not meet health needs, might pose no problem of equity if access was determined by income.

Nevertheless, use-per-need seems to ignore effects other than health outcomes that matter to people, such as longer-versus shorter-term mental therapy (supposing that both are equally effective). Should we limit our concerns about equity to cases involving objective health outcomes? In addition, differences in some process variables may impose burdens on health service users that do not show up as differences in utilization (or use-per-need) rates, such as (let us suppose) waiting times. Does this matter only if it interferes with use-per-need? One response to these objections is a second account of equity of access: We have equity of access only if there is equality in (at least some important) "process variables" (Sloan and Bentkover 1979).

The equity issues raised by objections to the use-per-need account and by advocates of the process variable account are best resolved by an appeal to accountability for reasonableness in resource allocation decisions. Reasonable people may disagree about how much to weigh concerns about patient satisfaction that are not reflected in measurements of differences in efficacy or health status outcomes. More general principles of distributive justice may be less helpful in setting this kind of disagreement than we would hope, and we must rely on fair process. The Benchmarks are eclectic on this issue, leaving it open to include indicators that focus on use-per-need and on process variables. Indeed, sometimes we only have indirect evidence about some differences in process variables, and we have to assume that they are likely to be important for use-per-need as well, though we cannot measure that directly.

If we think of health services as commodities like any other, as proponents of the market view of equity of access might insist, then we are less troubled by departures from equity viewed as use-per-need. A moderate version of such a view holds that we have equity when there are no information barriers, financial barriers, or supply anomalies that prevent access to a decent minimum of care (Havighurst 1971, 1974, 1977; Enthoven 1980).[1] Much depends on how the notion of a decent minimum is characterized. Unfortunately, proponents of the market view shy away from developing a full justification of the focus on a decent minimum, perhaps because doing so may undercut the idea that health care is a commodity like any other. Some proponents characterize the minimum simply as a list of categories of service (Enthoven 1980: 128).[2] Others say that the decent minimum is what

---

[1] The Enthoven (1980) proposal to have "managed competition" among health plans influenced the design of the Clinton administration's plan to establish universal insurance coverage in 1993.

[2] Enthoven (1980) suggested that the list of basic services in the Health Maintenance Organization (HMO) Act of 1973 constitutes the minimum.

might be provided by a low-cost or average-cost benefit package in the existing insurance market. But neither a list nor appeal to a market-determined package tells us why this is what justice requires.

The fundamental problem is that the market view gives us no account of why either version of that package is something we owe each other as a matter of justice. Both versions may include many things we do not owe each other and exclude many we do owe each other, at least as judged by any plausible *functional* analysis of the role of health care. Our opportunity-protecting account of the function of health care, in contrast, gives a rough guide to thinking about categorical inclusions and exclusions of services. Accountability for reasonableness explains how we should set limits under resource constraints while still aiming for that opportunity-protecting goal. But an unjustified list, or an appeal to low-cost or average-cost packages, provides no foundation for the claim.

Our account of just health is compatible with allowing multiple tiers in the health-care system, provided that the basic tier protects normal functioning as much as possible under resource constraints. If market-based upper tiers do not undermine the lower tier, then the theory of just health does not bar them (Daniels 1998d).[3] In very resource-poor settings, it may not be feasible to provide such a robust basic tier universally, but doing so remains the goal, over time, of health reform (and this is reflected in Benchmark B4).

As we shall see in the discussion of the Benchmarks that follows, there is no explicit appeal to the account of just health developed earlier. The Benchmarks proceed more pragmatically, reflecting widely shared judgments about specific inequities in risks and in access to services. The barriers to access, both financial and nonfinancial, are generally obvious, and the gradual progress to reducing tiering is seen as a clear objective. The Benchmark criteria do not insist on ideal outcomes, but rather on progress toward the reduction of agreed-upon barriers. The account of equity that follows from the theory developed here, however, provides a coherent rationale for the Benchmark criteria, even if that rationale was not explicitly appealed to in developing the generic international version of them.

I shall comment further, though briefly, on equity of financing when I discuss Benchmark B5. Here I want to clarify one point that emerges in discussions of private insurance markets; though these markets are small in many developing countries, they have often been encouraged by external agencies promoting various forms of privatization. Private insurance markets encourage risk stratification and risk rating of medical insurance. If insurers can find those at lower risk for various medical conditions, they can

---

[3] In Daniels (1998d) I argued that one could structure a tax on a supplementary insurance scheme that worked above a public insurance scheme so that it maximally supported additional benefits in the public sphere, thus making others as well off as they could be while allowing some additional health-care protection for those willing to pay for it.

provide coverage at a lower cost, potentially increasing the market share. When premiums reflect specific risk levels of purchasers in this way, they are called "actuarially fair." In contrast, if people whose known risks are at different levels pay premiums that reflect average risk in the community, the premiums are said to be "community rated."

It is important not to confuse actuarial fairness with equity in financing, as some promoters of risk rating do (Daniels 1990b). Actuarial fairness means that people with predictably greater health needs pay more for medical insurance. If it is a social obligation to protect normal functioning, and thus opportunity, by providing health insurance, then financing must be by ability to pay, not level of expected medical need. Actuarial fairness is not fairness or equity, at least for health care. In other areas of insurance, where we think of people buying primarily economic security – for example, against the risk of fire or theft – we may think it reasonable to charge people according to their levels of risk: A brick house with new wiring that is closer to a fire hydrant may be at lower risk of fire damage than one made of wood that is located far from water. But where we aim to protect opportunity, and have a social obligation to do so, we attempt to share risks in a way that does not burden those at greater risk (Daniels 1995).

Accountability

In Chapter 4, I provided a defense of the importance of a fair process in limit-setting decisions and described the four conditions (Publicity, Relevance, Revisability, and Enforceability) that assure accountability for reasonableness (also see Chapters 10–12). The Benchmarks include the criteria for accountability for reasonableness (in Benchmark B8), but a broader concern about accountability must be pursued in the Benchmarks overall. I do not think that the theory of just health, aside from the focus on accountability for reasonableness, provides any specific rationale for the broader appeal to accountability in the Benchmarks, though the theory is quite compatible with that appeal.

Accountability, as the Benchmarks use the notion, is a relation between (1) an agent or institution, (2) a task or goal it is responsible for performing, and (3) an agent or group or institution to which it is responsible for carrying out that task or achieving that goal. For example, a health clinic may be responsible for delivering certain primary health-care services to a population in a given area; that is one of its tasks or goals. It is responsible both to that population and to the authorities that manage the system for carrying out that task. The authorities, and the public that controls the authorities through democratic institutions, hold the health clinic personnel accountable for carrying out the tasks by requiring performance reports on the operations of the health clinic, by measuring the quantity and quality of the services delivered by that clinic, and by taking steps to improve performance, including imposing incentives or sanctions on clinic personnel. In turn, the authorities to whom the clinic is accountable are themselves accountable to the public whose health they are responsible for protecting by, among other things, assuring that health clinics perform well. The public can hold those authorities accountable for overseeing the health clinics by asking for transparency in the performance reports regarding the clinic, by demanding specific changes in its performance, and by sanctioning the authorities through the actions of advocacy groups and other democratic measures.

These broad notions of accountability are part of good governance in any set of institutions (Lowenson 2002). The rationales for them derive from broad notions of good governance that are not specific to our account of just health, although they are compatible with them, and no doubt these rationales would be required by these ideas about good governance had we developed a full theory of justice rather than an account of just health. For example, the focus on transparency in the Benchmarks is a presupposition of democratic controls over institutions that affect fundamental aspects of well-being in a society, as health care institutions do. This idea is not only a presupposition of democratic governance in general, but also a specific requirement of justice in some general theories of justice, such as Rawls's social contract theory, which affirm that the terms of social cooperation must be ones that people can generally agree on. That requirement implies that people must also have access to the information that lets them determine if those terms of cooperation are satisfied by the functioning of specific institutions. This sort of theory makes accountability in the functioning of basic social institutions, such as health systems, something of intrinsic moral value: We value knowing how systems fundamentally affect our well-being because *we* ultimatly are responsible for what they do for us and because their performance must conform to the constraints we have set. Accountability is thus of intrinsic moral value or importance even if it is also of instrumental importance through its contribution to the efficient functioning of institutions.

We shall see shortly just what is involved in specifying criteria that capture elements of accountability in a measurable way.

Efficiency
The theory of just health developed here makes it clear why efficiency alone cannot tell us what justice requires in health. Our account is not equivalent to maximizing health benefits (however measured) at the margin, regardless of who gets them; nor is it more generally equivalent to a notion of Pareto superiority or optimality.[4] Nevertheless, just health requires the efficient functioning of systems that aim to promote normal functioning. Efficient

---

[4] Arrangement A is Pareto superior to B if someone is better off in A than in B and no one is worse off. An arrangement is Pareto optimal if there is no arrangement that is Pareto superior to it. See Ch. 2, p. 54, n. 33.

use of any given level of resources means that we can meet more of the important needs that give rise to claims on us. The task is to put efficiency to work in promoting just health, not to see it as being generally in conflict with equity (though it sometimes is). In this sense, one system is more efficient than another if it achieves the same fair distribution of health outcomes with fewer resources as inputs or if it achieves a fair distribution of a better set of health outcomes with comparable resource inputs.

In Chapter 4, I explained that we must sometimes make trade-offs between maximizing health benefits and distributing lesser benefits more fairly. I also explained that reasonable people will disagree about how those trade-offs should be made in various circumstances. We need accountability for reasonableness in deciding what is fair treatment in those cases. In effect, some decisions about efficiency will have to be made in the context of fair procedures for resource allocation. Efficiency is important to achieving goals of just health in general, but we do not pursue efficiency for its own sake. We pursue equity and balance efficiency with equity by making decisions accountable for reasonableness. This picture may not seem simple and clean, but it reflects the complexity we face in pursuing just health

Development of the Benchmarks

The central ethical concerns of the Benchmarks – equity, accountability, and efficiency – are properly grounded in our account of just health. Though they can be understood in this way as an effort to translate theoretical ideas into a practical tool that informs health policy, their development actually involved a more complex process than mere inference from theory. To understand better the tool and how it is used, it is necessary to reflect briefly on the process of developing it.

The original Benchmarks of Fairness were developed to assess and promote discussion about comprehensive medical insurance reforms proposed in the United States in the first Clinton administration.[5] The original Benchmarks focused heavily on reforming a technologically advanced but inefficient and inequitable system that lacked universal coverage. Despite this specific narrow focus, the original Benchmarks addressed basic questions about access to needed services, efficiency in delivering them, and accountability within the system that must be asked about *any* reform. Because of

---

[5] Drawing on a discussion of "design principles" for health reform (Daniels 1995), the Ethics Working Group of the Clinton Health Care Task Force, after considerable discussion, developed "principles" to govern the Clinton proposal (Brock and Daniels 1994). Don Light, a sociologist, proposed developing these principles into a matrix for assessing competing reform proposals (Daniels et al. 1996). During 1993 we worked with congressional staff and other sources to estimate the degree to which satisfaction of criteria concerning access, efficiency, and accountability would emerge from the main types of competing health insurance reform proposals before the 103rd Congress.

this generality, the Benchmarks became an appropriate starting point for thinking about a matrix for use in developing countries.

In the development of the American version of the Benchmarks, my thinking clearly went from theory to practice. I had asked what "design principles," derived from concerns about justice, should play a role in evaluating health insurance reform. I then worked with collaborators to operationalize those ideas. In developing the international adaptation of the Benchmarks, however, we worked largely in the opposite direction. The generic Benchmarks were developed by focusing on case studies of health policy practice in several developing countries, examining what had been attempted, what had worked and not worked to improve fairness, as judged by the collaborating teams, and generalizing from these cases to produce the benchmarking criteria on which there was consensus across sites. I highlight this difference in methodology here because, in a rough way, it exhibits the interactive view between theory and practice that I referred to earlier as reflective equilibrium (see also Daniels 1996a; Rawls 1971, 1974).

To adapt the Benchmarks for use in health systems in countries at different levels of development, teams of collaborators from four countries – Colombia, Mexico, Pakistan, and Thailand – were formed.[6] Teams used each country as a case study for which appropriate Benchmarks were developed. By successively reviewing the work of previous workshops across sites, the teams produced a modifiable scheme of generic Benchmarks appropriate to all countries. Despite the different cultural and social histories and levels of development in the collaborating sites, the teams arrived at a generic matrix for assessing the fairness of reform efforts. Specifically, the teams agreed upon the nine main Benchmarks (see Table 9.1), described earlier.

The emergence of a consensus on the concept of fairness in such diverse sites was surprising to many, since we had been cautioned that cultural diversity would produce disagreement, not consensus. Two factors in our process may explain the agreement. First, we began with the experience of successful reform and failed reform in each system, and it turns out that there was great agreement about common features, despite differences in social history. The agreement was not only about the facts of the situation but also on judgments about the fairness and unfairness of the features of the cases. We were then able to generalize from this shared experience and shared

---

[6] In 1997, I proposed to a World Health Organization (WHO/CIOMS) conference in Geneva on equity in health that the benchmarks of fairness be adapted for use in developing countries (Daniels 1998b). John Bryant, then at Aga Khan University in Karachi, Pakistan, invited me to do some pilot work with the idea. At nearly the same time, Julio Frenk, later to become director of the evidence and policy group at WHO and then minister of health in Mexico, proposed that I adapt the Benchmarks for use in Latin American developing countries and invited me to discuss the idea with researchers in Mexico. The Rockefeller Foundation agreed to support an effort to combine these Asian and Latin American proposals regarding adaptation.

evaluations of it to the criteria involved in the Benchmarks. Second, we did not take up the standard problems in bioethics that generate considerable cross-cultural controversy, such as termination of treatment and euthanasia, organ transplantation, or abortion. A related point is that our method took us from agreement on beliefs about practices to criteria of fairness, not from abstract theoretical issues to concrete instances of them. We avoided debate not only about the controversial bioethics topics noted, but also about competing theoretical frameworks for talking about justice that might have sparked complaints about cultural bias. Had we, for example, tried to discuss the social contractarian foundations for concerns about equity or accountability, we might have found considerable disagreement that was not present in our judgments about the cases.

What is of some interest is that the two approaches, from theory to design principles in the U.S. origins and from case studies to mid-level criteria in the international adaptation, converged on very similar structures. To be sure, the U.S. framework was introduced as a point of departure in the international adaptation process, but rather than being rejected outright as a form of cultural imperialism, it was readily modified to reflect developing-country experiences and beliefs about fairness. I have already noted that I see the convergence of these directions of reasoning as a form of reflective equilibrium that emerged in the overall development of the Benchmarks.

The results of the international adaptation were announced at the same time that the WHO presented a framework for assessing health system performance (World Health Organization 2000; Murray and Evans 2003). The Benchmarks of Fairness, however, serve a different purpose from the WHO's index of health system performance. The WHO framework combines measures of health outcomes and system responsiveness and the distribution of financial contribution into an overall index of performance. The five dimensions measured are assigned weights derived from a survey of experts. The index was used to rank the overall performance of countries, presumably to motivate those that performed less well. The methodology behind the indexing approach was extensively criticized, and a commission evaluating it proposed various improvements (Blendon et al. 2001; Braveman et al. 2001; Navarro 2001; Anand et al. 2002). I comment here only on the contrast in purpose with the Benchmarks.

The Benchmarks are not intended for cross-country comparisons. In developing the benchmarking method, we believed that there may be various ways to trade off changes in each Benchmark and that these trade-offs might be decided differently in different countries. This was a special instance of the point noted earlier, that there may be more than one fair, or fairest, arrangement. Accordingly, there is no attempt to rank the Benchmarks in terms of their importance to produce a single index number. The Benchmarks aim instead to show the complex pattern of the effects of a reform on fairness. Since the goal is to guide evaluation and further deliberation about improving the local situation, the pattern is more informative than what results from compressing information into an index. These features make the benchmarking approach attractive to collaborating sites.

The Generic Benchmarks for Developing Countries

Earlier I suggested how the key concerns of the Benchmarks are connected with the account of just health developed and defended in Parts I and II. Before explaining how the generic Benchmarks may be adapted for local purposes in monitoring and evaluation, it will be helpful to describe in more detail how these Benchmarks are structured. (See Daniels, Bryant, Castano, Dantes, Khan, and Pannarunothai, [2000] for the subcriteria that fall under the main criteria described in the Benchmark-by-Benchmark description provided here.)

Benchmark B1: Intersectoral Public Health

I noted earlier that the rationale for this Benchmark is that social determinants and other risk factors "upstream" from the point of health-care delivery affect population health (see Chapters 3, 5, and 7). The first criterion in Benchmark B1 asks for estimates of the degree to which a population benefits from reductions in exposure to a comprehensive set of risk factors as a result of the reforms under consideration. The comprehensive list includes standard public health concerns such as clean air and water, sanitation, workplace hazards, basic nutrition, housing quality, literacy and basic education, health literacy, public safety, and violence reduction. Though not all reforms will affect all these factors, the list of risks is comprehensive because reforms would make systems fairer the more inequalities in exposure they eliminated. The criterion encourages gathering information on these exposures and disaggregating it to measure equity in exposure.

The second criterion in this Benchmark calls for developing an information infrastructure to measure and monitor health inequalities and to study the most effective ways to reduce them. The third criterion evaluates health sector reforms for their cooperation with other sectors and for their involvement of communities and vulnerable groups in these efforts. Country-specific differences require country-specific adjustments of the Benchmarks. For example, in some countries it may be crucial to focus on reducing of violence or accidents, and in others on clean water or other factors.

Benchmark B2: Financial Barriers to Equitable Access

Fairness requires reducing financial and nonfinancial barriers to equitable access to needed services. The concept of equitable access discussed earlier is operationalized in Benchmarks B2–B4, though all of them focus on moving the system progressively from wherever it is with regard to these barriers, that is, from the baseline of the status quo, toward better compliance with criteria that call for the reduction of specific agreed-upon barriers.

Benchmark B2 recognizes the large, "informal," nontaxable employment sector in many developing countries, often including 60–90 percent of the population. Since workers and their families in the informal sector generally include the poorest part of the population, services must be provided fully or largely through general tax revenues. The larger the informal sector, the greater the need for public financing but the smaller the tax base to provide it. Stringent resource limits in many countries will produce skeletal essential benefit packages that not only fail to meet many needs, but drive people into poverty when they try to cover the costs of illness out of pocket (Knaul et al. 2006). Benchmark B2 encourages a long-term strategy aimed at moving as much of the population as possible into the formal sector and then into insurance schemes that can be built on broadly based general tax revenues, social security payments, or employer-based contributions. (Benchmark B4 also requires gradual expansion of the benefit package in the informal sector, ultimately aiming for comparable benefits for all.)

Benchmark B2 also specifies interim goals in both sectors. Because public resources are scarce in the informal sector, a crucial issue is whether the most important services are available to all. Benchmark B2 encourages reforms to specify a basic package of services that all will receive by a specific target date and then to improve that package over time. This Benchmark concentrates on two aims of reform of the formal sector besides increasing the size of the sector: producing uniform and more adequate benefits across all groups of workers and integrating the various schemes that involve these workers.

Benchmark B3: Nonfinancial Barriers to Access

The four main criteria in this Benchmark single out what collaborating teams agreed were the central nonfinancial barriers to access to care. The case-study method led teams to these conclusions, though the relative importance of each varied from country to country. The first criterion evaluates reforms according to the measures they take to address the poor distribution of drugs, supplies, facilities, and personnel common in all four countries. Where the reform relies on local fund-holding and decentralization, the criteria also examine specific goals and accountability for them (see also Benchmark B8). The second criterion addresses gender barriers, which are especially important barriers to primary care in many countries. An example is the squatter communities of Karachi, Pakistan, where studies of children at high risk of death from diarrheal disease and pneumonia suggest that lack of maternal autonomy is a key risk factor (D'Souza and Bryant 1999). The third criterion includes a variety of cultural barriers, including language and conceptions of illness. The fourth criterion focus on discrimination.

Benchmark B4: Comprehensiveness of Benefits and Tiering

The rationale for this Benchmark is that all people, regardless of class or ethnicity or gender, have comparable health needs and there are similar social obligations to meet them. Inequalities in the coverage and quality of care (tiering) reduce the fairness of systems. Some kinds of tiering are worse than others, and some may be justifiable (Daniels 1998d). It is less serious if a small but wealthy group does better than others, provided that the others do well (e.g., private-sector insurance in the United Kingdom), than if a poor group is worse off than the rest of society (e.g., failing to insure the working poor in the United States [Daniels 1991b] or failing to deliver a minimal benefit package to the whole informal sector while the top 5 percent of the population has excellent private insurance). Some tiering is also unavoidable in systems with severe resource constraints and a large informal sector (Gonzalez-Pier et al. 2006).

The criteria focus on differential treatment of people by class within a system, not only between the public and private sectors but also within the public sector. Residents of Sultanabad, a squatter locality of Karachi, remarked that "the tradesman will do better than the labourer in a public hospital," suggesting a widespread perception of tiering in the system, where the poor commonly wait four to five hours to be seen in a hospital and then get five minutes with the physician, while well-to-do patients can just walk into private facilities and be seen right away. Tiering exists in the benefit packages available to different subgroups in the formal sector in most developing countries, including the four – Thailand, Pakistan, Colombia, and Mexico – that developed the generic Benchmarks. In Thailand, for example, civil service workers and other formal sector workers have better access to hemodialysis than those covered by the insurance scheme for the informal sector. In Pakistan, some multinational employers provide better coverage than the social security schemes, and the military in Pakistan has the best coverage of any group. Mexico's recent reforms aim at closing this benefit gap in an evidence-based way (Frenk et al. 2006; Gonzalez Pier et al. 2006).

Benchmark B5: Equitable Financing

This Benchmark rests on the idea that financing medical services, as opposed to access, should be according to ability to pay. Three main sources of funding are involved in most systems: tax-based revenues, insurance premiums, and out-of-pocket payments. The Benchmark distinguishes primarily between tax-based and premium-based parts of the system, noting that in both there are still out-of-pocket payments for care. Tax-based schemes are more equitable if their structure is more progressive (higher-income people pay more than lower-income people). Premium-based schemes are more equitable if they are community-rated rather than risk-rated. Risk rating shifts the burden to those at higher risk of illness. The same inequity is involved in out-of-pocket contributions in both tax-based and premium-based systems. A good measure of progress must combine all financing systems (Kakwani 1977).

Substantial out-of-pocket costs for health care are common in nearly all developing countries. These payments make the financing of these systems highly regressive by shifting the burden to the sick. Cost recovery measures (user fees) in many countries, a feature of reforms that were pushed by the IMF and the WB, make the system more regressive, since exemption policies for the very poor generally work poorly.

Benchmark B6: Efficacy, Efficiency, and Quality Improvement
The rationale for this and the next Benchmark is that, other things being equal, a system that gets more value for money in the use of its resources is fairer to those in need. Distributive justice and fairness are issues because resources are always limited. A key criterion in Benchmark B6 is primary health care for community-based delivery. This criterion rests on the judgment that such care is one of the most efficient forms of delivery in a population, and the features of community care, including its focus on outreach, reflect the Alma Ata Declaration (1978) goals. Reforms aimed at improving primary care must assure appropriate training, incentives, resource allocation, and community participation in decisions affecting delivery. Emphasis was placed on a population focus and on the need to integrate different parts of the health system, such as referrals. Community participation ideally involves an interactive relationship that goes beyond mere outreach.

The second main concern of Benchmark B6 is promoting evidence-based practice in all areas of services, including preventive, curative, and management practices. To advance this, the criteria call for the development of an information infrastructure and database, as well as for health services research to support evidence-based practice. The third main criterion concerns measures to improve the quality of services in the system, including professional training, continuing education, accreditation, and community participation in evaluating the quality of care.

In all of the systems we examined, there are problems with referral mechanisms and with the role of primary care gatekeepers. Dissatisfaction with primary care services causes many people to turn to higher-level hospitals for primary care, leading to considerable inefficiency. Similarly, there is no control of efficacy or quality since people will often abandon the public sector primary care services for completely unregulated private sector services. Establishing good referral systems is a critical element in the efficiency of care, but the restrictions to such systems also reduce the kinds of choice or autonomy assessed by Benchmark B9. To justify restrictions on autonomy, there must be qualified practitioners doing the diagnosis and referral, clear, accessible routes to higher levels of care, and general knowledge of the importance of such a system.

Benchmark B7: Administrative Efficiency
Benchmark B7 seeks efficiency in the management of the health-care system. Addressing these problems, however, also requires greater accountability, including transparency; consequently, Benchmark B8 must be used together with Benchmark B7 to achieve real improvement.

The criteria included in Benchmark B7 were based on many examples from the four collaborating country teams that developed the generic Benchmarks. Key areas of common concern were various sources of administrative overhead (inappropriate technology acquisition, inefficient use of personnel, high transaction costs), costly forms of purchasing, cost shifting, and many types of abuse and fraud (shadow providers,[7] drug sales and self-referrals, inappropriate promotion of drugs and devices).

Some general points emerged that cut across the local differences. In all countries, public sector practitioners receive very low pay; this is a reason for many of the abuses that create efficiency and accountability problems (noted in the next Benchmark). Lack of integrated financing schemes means that there are incentives to shift costs from one part of the system to others. In Thailand, where unions are weak, civil service work rules prevent efficient personnel allocation. In Latin America, strong unions and their work rules create the same obstacle to reallocation of personnel.

In the public sector of all the systems there are common complaints: Bureaucratic practices and corruption lead to great inefficiencies in the purchase of supplies and equipment, failure to enforce rules about personnel, favoritism and hiring on grounds other than competency, and other highly inefficient practices. In all these contexts, there is talk about "decentralization" as a solution, but decentralization helps only if there is careful planning and regulation to make sure that decentralized units have similar goals. There are also concerns that decentralization may weaken the delivery of some public health measures.

Benchmark B8: Democratic Accountability and Empowerment

Benchmark B8 emerged as critically important in all four countries involved in developing the generic Benchmarks, since without democratic accountability, reforms are unlikely to succeed in any area. The rationale for including accountability is that health systems are responsible for improving population health in an equitable manner, and those affected by decisions and policies that influence well-being in such fundamental ways must understand and have ultimate control over that system. Such control requires accountability for reasonableness in decision making about allocation and other matters. Such accountability includes transparency, global budgeting (where possible), involvement of relevant stakeholders, fair appeals processes, adequate privacy protection, and measures to enforce compliance with rules and laws. Ultimately, the criteria require a strengthening of civil society, so that people understand the problems and are empowered to try to improve the health sector.

---

[7] Shadow providers collect public salaries but fail to show up for many of their clinic hours.

One important criterion, originally proposed in the Latin American work-shops, evaluates reform for its attempt to stimulate the growth of advocacy groups, clearly a matter cutting across sectors. This criterion is important because of the crucial role such groups play in countries with developed democratic traditions of pushing public authorities to attack problems in both public and private sectors. In Pakistan and Thailand, this idea was expanded into the criterion "strengthening civil society," which has two components: establishing an enabling environment for advocacy groups and stimulating public debate about health policy measures. Many aspects of this Benchmark go beyond merely holding health-care institutions account-able to the public; they actually increase the power of the public to remedy problems.

Benchmark B9: Patient and Provider Autonomy

This is the Benchmark that most directly addresses a culturally variable issue. How important is autonomy or choice? In some market-based approaches, informed choice is necessary if quality is to be improved and true preferences met. But how much choice, and what kinds of choices? Similarly, provider autonomy is widely sought by professionals. Planners, however, often see such autonomy as an obstacle to the efficient use of services, since profes-sionals and provider institutions are influenced by incentives to utilize what they can supply.

For these reasons, it is important to emphasize how Benchmark B9 may conflict with other Benchmarks and that people in the same or different cultures may disagree about weightings. Consequently, there may be no one fairest system, but rather many fair designs. Benchmarks allow for cultural and other variations, but they encourage discussion about the grounds for designs that value some Benchmarks over others.

A clear example of the conflict between Benchmark B9 and other Bench-marks involves referral systems and the restrictions on patients they involve. Benchmark B6, for example, may approve of restrictions on autonomy in order to achieve a primary care focus and the efficiency that results from letting primary care physicians control access to other levels of care, but Benchmark B9 is concerned with loss of choice. Similarly, choice of alterna-tive providers will undermine efficiency and quality if there is no adequate evidence-based assessment of credentials or alternative forms of treatment. Practitioner autonomy may be essential if the practitioner is to address the health-care problems of individual patients, but this presupposes high levels of competency and knowledge of appropriate practices.

Adapting and Using the Benchmarks

The generic Benchmarks described here and in Daniels, Bryant, Castano, Dantes, Khan, and Pannarunothai (2000) are a proposal for a policy tool.

Since 2000, we have demonstrated that these Benchmarks can be adapted and field tested for local uses. These adaptations have focused on both national (Mexico) and subnational applications (Cameroon; Thailand), and they have been adapted to evaluate both comprehensive health sector reforms (Mexico, Cameroon, Thailand) and the impact of more specific policies (Guatemala, Ecuador, Yunnan Province, China, the Philippines).

To convert the generic Benchmarks into a tool for evaluating reforms in a specific context, as I said earlier, they must be adapted locally by an interdisciplinary team. A typical interdisciplinary team consists of policy makers, academics, health system personnel, clinicians, and stakeholders. The breadth of the Benchmarks compels people with different types of training to look across disciplinary boundaries and brings together people from various levels in the health system to understand their different views.

The local purposes and level of application (national or subnational) determine how the team will modify the generic benchmarking criteria. The Guatemalan team, for example, ignored some Benchmarks, combined features of others, and developed criteria that concentrated on the delivery of public health services. Familiarity with specifics of the local reform mechanisms also affects the selection of criteria. Developing appropriate criteria for some improvements in efficiency or accountability, for example, requires knowledge of the kinds of community structures involved in health unity management. The adaptation process encourages stakeholders to take ownership of the resulting tool.

The team must also pay attention to the sources of information for different indicators. In many cases, there are good data for traditional indicators of some measures of health outcomes and some kinds of utilization. For indicators bearing on accountability, intersectoral cooperation, and quality measures, countries have had to use nonstandard sources of information or qualitative techniques. The goal of selecting appropriate indicators is to develop an evidence base for judgments about whether the reforms are reaching the goals of fairness or not. In this way, the Benchmarks lead to evidence-based policy.

Constructing an Evidence Base Using the Benchmarks: Two Strategies
One strategy for developing the evidence base consists of selecting indicators to measure the change in satisfaction with the adapted criteria and developing a set of rules that assign indicator scores to an ordinal scale, say from -5 to $+5$. Suppose that the operationalized criterion is household access to clean water. If the baseline measure is that 50 percent of households in the area have access to clean water where the goal is 100 percent, then adding 10 percent more households would score one point on such a scale. When indicators have no such endpoint, degrees of improvement would more obviously reflect judgments about ordinal rank.

This approach has the advantage of giving clear operational content to points on the evaluation scale. Objectivity is achieved by being able to convert judgments into obtainable measures. Disagreements might arise about whether the scoring rules were appropriate or the indicator faulty, but these disagreements can be settled by objective methods. A limitation of this approach, however, is that only the interdisciplinary team has constructed the measures and scale, and the scale might be challenged for possible biases.

The Thai team used an alternative strategy for developing an evidence base (Pannarunothai and Faramnuayphol 2006). It asked focus groups to judge the fairness of reform-induced changes after providing them with specific evidence about changes based on selected indicators. Statistical analysis of group responses provides evidence about perception of the fairness of reforms.

The advantage of the alternative approach is that it allows broader and more varied inputs into the evaluation process than the first strategy. The disadvantage of this approach is that the basis of people's judgments is less clear. Why one group considers a change to be less fair than another is less clear than if the content of the judgment were more specifically operationalized. Disagreements between groups with differing evaluations may be harder to resolve. One question for further research is whether the strengths of the two approaches can be combined while avoiding their weaknesses.

Illustrative Adaptations

Since 2000, the generic Benchmark framework has been adapted for local use in countries on three continents. In Mexico, a national application was made using most of the generic criteria and indicators that could track changes from 1995, when reforms were introduced, to 2000 (Gomez-Dantes et al. 2004). Most other country teams have undertaken more extensive framework adaptation for local use for specific purposes.[8] I offer recent examples from Guatemala and Ecuador to illustrate how the Benchmarks can be used to inform the reform process.

In Guatemala, a team of academics and members of the Ministry of Health adapted the Benchmarks to focus on the effects of reforms aimed at decentralizing, financing, and improving access to public health services, especially reproductive and maternal health services. In their adaptation (Daniels and Flores 2004; Daniels et al. 2005), they used criteria and indicators to focus on important nonfinancial barriers to care, such as language

---

[8] In Zambia, the adaptation focused on the equity of ARTs at the district level; in Yunnan Province (China), the adaptation measured the impact on minority populations of the new rural insurance program; in the Philippines, a WHO project examined maternal and child health programs; in Mexico, an application looked solely at cervical cancer screening programs (Gómez-Jauregui, Daniels), and Reichenbach 2004).

and the distribution of trained personnel. They were able to document the virtual absence of trained medical personnel (physicians, nurses) speaking indigenous languages in the districts with high concentrations of non-Spanish-speaking populations. They documented the fact that there was underreporting of low-birthweight infants in deliveries that did not have trained birth attendants, which suggests an understating of the problem of low birthweight in this underserved population.

More importantly, they were able to construct indices for evaluating the equity of resource allocation and the reform measures intended to solve some resource allocation problems. The indices use readily collected information that is not adequately analyzed, showing that the available evidence base for policy was stronger than many had realized. For example, to compare health needs by district with resource allocation by district, a specific measure of equity in resource allocation, two indices were constructed, one measuring the shortfall in delivering important health care services (immunization, antenatal care, and supervised deliveries) and another measuring health expenditures. Equity requires that districts with a higher priority receive more resources. In fact, there is great mismatch between actual resource allocation and the priority that a district should have, given its shortfall in providing key health services. That suggests a significant inequity in the resource allocation policy (although the mismatch does not rule out other possibilities, such as greater efficiency in the districts providing better services).

A specific reform proposal was introduced to address this mismatch. It involved using community volunteers to make up for the deficit in resources in the government plan to contract outside the public sector for some essential services. The Guatemalan team constructed an index to measure the availability of such community health workers by district. They found that the districts that should have the highest priority for resources, but were not getting them, were also the districts that had the worst potential for using community health workers to compensate for resource deficits. The benchmarking approach thus showed that this problem would not be solved by the reform measure being proposed. This is a good illustration of the real-time feedback that a properly implemented Benchmarks project can bring to deliberation about reform measures and their adequacy.

The Ecuadoran team built a coalition that included the provincial level of the Ministry of Health, local government, nongovernment organizations (NGOs), and civil society organizations. By including civil society stakeholders from the beginning, in contrast to what was done in Guatemala, it was easier to keep pressure on the Ministry of Health to make data available and pay attention to the outcomes of the monitoring and evaluation. The team's adaptation of the Benchmarks emphasized indicators related to maternal and child health and reproductive health services that were supposed to be free under a new reform. The adaptation showed that treatment for acute respiratory infection, one of their indicator conditions, was subject to charges even though it was supposed to be free and clinics were being reimbursed under the reform for the same services. These findings were presented to health authorities, and some of the civil society groups requested an investigation of the charges and immediate action to stop them.

To evaluate improvement in the quality of services for the target groups, the Benchmark team used the ratio of medical to administrative staff in health facilities. The survey found that on average, public facilities have seven administrative staff for every ten medical staff, whereas NGO facilities have a ratio of 3 to 10. Public hospitals varied considerably on this indicator, ranging from one administrative staff for every five medical staff to one administrative staff for every two medical staff. This (admittedly) rough efficiency indicator shows the need for further investigation and action. The coalition secured agreement from provincial authorities from the Ministry of Health to study public staffing issues and modify policy where necessary.

Lessons Learned
The projects in developing countries on three continents, including Latin America, show that local interdisciplinary teams can construct a method for using evidence to evaluate the fairness of reforms, though the method remains a work in progress.

First, such teams can agree upon what changes would make the system more or less fair in specific ways. Agreeing on a framework for analysis is a first step in developing an evidence-based approach to policy that invites deliberation about values and the trade-offs that must occur among them. Although the generic benchmarking approach showed that considerable agreement could be reached across different cultures, the country-specific projects allow for different sites to emphasize aspects of fairness in a way that reflects local deliberation.

Second, teams can work across disciplinary boundaries and levels within the system to bring evidence to inform their evaluation of implemented reforms and policies. This effort must accept the weakness of the standard information infrastructure so that the teams can use information of modest quality, which is often the best available in some developing countries. Further, teams must address the lack of standard measures within or outside health systems for examining important elements of fairness, such as accountability, transparency, and encouragement of civic advocacy. In constructing locally useful if nonstandard measures, teams develop the capacity to deliberate about the fine structure of reforms and whether they embody mechanisms that can achieve goals.

Third, these projects show that appropriate coalitions can perform an evaluation despite the political tensions that arise when parts of the system would prefer less scrutiny. For example, though the Ministry of Health staff involved in the Guatemalan project initially resisted making certain information available, they realized that it would enable them to improve the delivery of service and produced the information. The potential contribution of this approach to civic advocacy is also significant, and some projects have specifically aimed at involving advocacy groups in its application. For example, the Thai evidence showed that nonhealth experts had a lower estimate of the fairness of reform efforts than health experts. This shows the value of the approach for advocacy groups, who may be better equipped to hold managers accountable to the goals of reform.

Fourth, the projects show the need for cooperative research that can share the lessons of the individual efforts across sites. A network of researchers regionally or even globally can generate a catalog of appropriate indicators for nonstandard criteria and contexts in which information is poor. The catalog would enable new sites to adapt the Benchmarks more easily and effectively.

Finally, local interest in this method confirms the importance of the goal of the benchmarking approach. The goal is not to produce cross-country comparisons of fairness, but to enable each country to use evidence to improve the fairness of its system from its original baseline.

The Benchmarks project suggests that the theory of just health can give practical guidance to health policy and health sector reforms. At the same time, that practical experience suggests that key features of health practice are compatible with central elements of the theory. The complex adaptation process, however, shows that translating ideas about justice or fairness – such as equity, accountability, and efficiency – into measurable features of health systems is itself difficult.

HEALTH SECTOR REFORMS AS SOCIAL EXPERIMENTS REQUIRING ETHICAL REVIEW

One motivation for adapting the Benchmarks for use in developing countries is to improve the local capacity to evaluate health reforms – viewed as social experiments on a population. Now that we have seen how the Benchmarks combine an integrated ethical framework with a methodology adapted from operations research, we can assess whether it can achieve the main purposes of an ethical and scientific review of such social experiments. Such a review must assess its goals and expected outcomes, the appropriateness of its design given its goals, and its governance (Daniels 2006). This discussion leaves open the question of who should undertake such a review, those who develop and implement policy or some independent agency. Institutional forms will clearly vary with different political systems and different types of agency, such as domestic versus international agencies or NGOs.

Justifying Ethical Review

Experiments on human subjects require proactive ethical and scientific review to ensure that they meet standards set by domestic (United States

National Commission 1979) and international commissions and accords (Nuremburg Code 1949; World Medical Association 1964 [with subsequent revisions]). The review assesses the rationale for the research and the proposed experimental design, as well as compliance with principles governing how subjects consent to the experiments and are treated while in them. Leave aside the mechanisms for such review (Institutional Review Boards), since they are inappropriate for health system reforms, and focus instead on why some form of review is needed. Research generally imposes risks on relatively small groups of subjects in order to achieve a societal goal advancing knowledge and technology without benefiting those subjects directly. Generally, we think we must ethically justify policies or actions that deliberately benefit some at the expense of others.

Ethical review of clinical research is required from diverse ethical perspectives. People who believe that the rightness of an action is determined solely by its consequences, such as utilitarians, require a careful assessment of the effects of imposing risks on some in order to benefit society. Are the risks minimized to the extent possible? Is the experiment designed well enough to achieve its objective, or are there other designs more likely to succeed with less risk? Do we preserve the trust people have in scientists or science by making sure that they do not perceive themselves as manipulated or deceived or exploited? Assuring informed voluntary consent is one way of minimizing those perceptions in clinical research.

People who believe that the right thing to do is not simply determined by assessing the consequences of an action also have good reason to conduct proactive ethical review. Some people, agreeing with Kant (1785), believe there is a fundamental ethical rule that we not use people merely as means to an end. The fact that imposing risks on research subjects leads to knowledge does not justify the research, even if the risks are minimized and the knowledge gains are significant. Unless those at risk make it their own goal to pursue that knowledge by giving informed consent to the risks, we would be using them merely as a means to gain knowledge.

Health system reforms often use unproven measures to improve the delivery of medical or public health services. These measures impose risks on population subgroups. For example, decentralization of health systems risks undermining the delivery of immunizations or tuberculosis treatments. Successful reforms teach us that certain measures work. Unsuccessful reforms teach us that some measures do not work or were not properly implemented. Though knowledge may not be the main goal of reforms, it is a desired result that we acquire by imposing risks on our fellow citizens.

If we have good reason to carry out an ethical review of the scientific design of clinical experiments and to insist that the people involved in them are not merely guinea pigs but appropriately govern their own actions, then we have a reason to review proactively efforts to transform health systems and to monitor and evaluate their effects so that we can minimize the harms they may impose. Labeling health system reforms as "operations" or "managerial prerogatives," not social experiments, ignores the fact that we are often as much in the dark about the safety and efficacy of reforms as we are about drugs in clinical trials.

One objection to the analogy between clinical and social experiments is that mechanisms other than proactive ethical review already assure public accountability for harmful decisions in health sector transformation. Even internationally instigated reforms are matters that the public can hold domestic officials accountable for through democratic processes, or through tort law, where it is developed and enforceable, or even through negative market effects, if private sector reforms prove harmful. Ethical review is an unnecessary extra layer of bureaucratic interference with necessary reforms that it is already difficult to initiate.

Where the democratic process and tort law are well developed, they work after the fact to hold authorities accountable for harms imposed. Where they are effective, they offer an incentive to avoid mistaken and dangerous reforms. Unfortunately, they are often not available or effective in the developing countries where externally imposed social experiments are most common. Even where these after-the-fact protections are in place, it is better to give authorities a tool, such as a framework for ethical and scientific review, that will help them to avoid problems before they are created.

Ethical Evaluation of Goals and Outcomes

In the ethical and scientific review of clinical research, a key question is whether there is a plausible scientific rationale, given the scientific literature, for pursuing this line of research in this way. Analogously, in the review of a social experiment, it is important to inquire whether the objectives of the reform have an appropriate ethical and scientific rationale.

What are the ethically acceptable objectives of health sector reform? One approach does not advocate a specific set of principles or values but calls for reformers to clarify their value commitments (Roberts et al. 2004). Arguably, all key aspects of health system transformation involve ethical commitments that reformers should make explicit. For example, equity in access to services and financing of services has to be weighed against different views about what justice requires and different views about the importance of efficiency or other goals of reforms.

The Benchmarks of Fairness methodology offers a more explicit framework for assessing the goals and outcomes of reform than the demand for values clarification. Together, the Benchmarks address the complaint that "it is unfair" when the system treats some patients differently from others with similar needs, when some needs are not met because of administrative or other inefficiency, or when people have no say in how the system treats them. Fairness involves various claims about what people are owed as a matter of justice. This integrated ethical framework responds to health system reform efforts imposed by external agencies on developing countries. Initially, many reform efforts focused only on enhancing efficiency, while critics complained that there was little attention to the sacrifice of equity. Recently, there has been increased interest, especially in the WB, in issues of equity and more recently in governance and accountability.[9] The Benchmarks framework integrates these various goals and assesses the trade-offs among them. In addition, one Benchmark points to the importance of intersectoral planning in determining population levels of health and its distribution.

The benchmarking approach shares with the more modest call for values clarification two key points. First, there must be local weighing and balancing of values within a reform effort. Only then can various stakeholders be clear and explicit about the commitments of the effort, providing public accountability for the goals of the reform that enhances their legitimacy. The Benchmarks avoid cross-country comparisons and embody local deliberation about how to improve fairness in reform.

Second, there usually is a range of fair ways to make reasonable trade-offs among the central goals of reforms. Most people engaged in health system reform have a central goal of improving population health. Many reformers also have the goal of distributing the benefits of reform equitably, for example, by reducing unjustifiable health inequalities. Even so, as we saw in Chapter 4, reasonable people will disagree about what equitable distribution involves. They may disagree, for example, about how much priority to give to those who are worse off or about how much weight to give to achieving best outcomes as compared to giving people fair chances at some benefits. Fair procedures for resolving these disagreements may yield a range of legitimate proposals.

Ethical Evaluation of the Appropriateness of Reform Measures

An ethical and scientific review must assess the appropriateness of the design of the reform to the goals of the reform. Further, it must examine whether measures taken to achieve one goal interfere with achieving others. User fees in developing countries were advocated by external agencies promoting reform because they might increase the resources available in underfunded systems. Where such fees prevent access to services for the very poor, they frustrate the goal of fair access even if they improve system sustainability. In general, the review would ask: How good is the evidence that measures

9 World Bank, "Multi-Country Projects on Equity, Poverty, and Health." Available at http:// www1.worldbank.org/prem/poverty/health/library/guide/proj14.htm. For WB projects on governance, go to http://web.worldbank.org/WBSITE/EXTERNAL/TOPICS/ EXTPUBLICSECTORANDGOVERNANCE/0,,menuPK:286310~pagePK:149018~piPK: 149093~theSitePK:286305,00.html. Also see Public Sector Group (2000).

being advocated will work if implemented? Are there adequate plans for implementing reforms? How sensitive is the estimate of benefits or harms to key features of the local situation? Have relevant stakeholders been asked to help implement the reform? The benchmarking methodology illustrates one way to organize this kind of ethical evaluation.

A more comprehensive review of evidence, even in systems not well equipped to provide it, can provide some ethical oversight of the design of reforms. In the Benchmarks work in Guatemala, careful assessment of the possible use of community volunteers in contracting for the delivery of essential services showed that this could not fill the gaps in the reform. This evidence could be used immediately to revise the reform proposal. In conducting such a comprehensive review, we must understand that some improvements may take time to implement. Mechanisms may produce worse outcomes until they are fully in place or until responses to the change stabilize in the system. Ethical review must therefore be both proactive and ongoing, relying on monitoring and evaluation to make sure that the risks to a population are understood and can be minimized by the timely modification of reforms.

If developing countries acquire the capacity to conduct such a review, they can better resist the ill-conceived reforms imposed on them by external agencies. Moreover, their review imposes a form of accountability on such agencies. Another source of such accountability on these external agencies would be independent ethical and scientific review of the reforms they propose and fund.

Ethical Evaluation of the Governance of Health System Reforms

In clinical research, ethical review enforces standards of informed consent so that research subjects can affirm the goals of the research and avoid manipulation, deception, or exploitation. Ethical review also ensures that subjects will be given medical care that meets certain standards during and perhaps after trials. Subjects are assured that adequate surveillance of outcomes, including risks, is done so that harms can be minimized or benefits optimized. The ethical review of the governance of health system reforms should include analogous components.

In a political process, where reforms are implemented by democratically controlled agencies, the analogy to informed consent is democratic oversight of the reform process. Unfortunately, this analogy may not hold wherever democratic control of institutions is weak, whether in developed or developing countries, and wherever powerful external agencies offer large incentives and are not themselves held accountable for the reforms they impose. The remedy, however, is not to mimic clinical research by imposing requirements for some form of informed voluntary consent by the affected public. Instead, countries must develop improved mechanisms of accountability for external and domestic agencies and must empower civic society when they are undertaking reform. In addition, countries undertaking reform must learn how to monitor and evaluate the reforms in order to gain the evidence needed for the ethical and scientific review.

The Benchmarks of Fairness illustrate one kind of ethical and operations research framework for assessing the governance of reform. Participants in the international adaptation process leading to the benchmarking method claimed that Benchmark B8, Democratic Empowerment and Accountability, was the most important Benchmark because it addressed key gaps in many developing-country systems. Unfortunately, there is little prior experience in measuring how systems establish transparency, accountability, and fair process in making resource allocation decisions. Benchmark B8 also encourages the development of civic society groups that can sustain pressure on ministries of health to implement appropriate reforms; unfortunately, it is notoriously difficult to measure the effectiveness of such groups. Despite these obstacles, improving accountability and fair process in reform has been judged important to one internationally promoted health reform: the effort to scale up ARTs for HIV/AIDS. WHO endorsed an appeal to accountability for reasonableness in its guidelines for achieving equity in its program designed to treat 3 million people by 2005 (see Chapter 10).

A key gap in developing countries is the lack of capacity to conduct research on health systems reforms and to monitor and evaluate the effects of reforms. Without this capacity, and the evidence it produces, ethical and scientific review of reform is not locally feasible. Fortunately, international attention is now focusing on this gap. The WHO Alliance for Health System and Policy and its Global Forum focus on the 90–10 gap in research capacity – 10 percent of the world's research focuses on 90 percent of its population.[10] A Ministerial Summit on Health Systems Research held in Mexico in November 2004 was aimed at encouraging ministries of health to develop the capacity to do research that can form an evidence base for policy and its evaluation.[11] The Benchmarks illustrate one approach that can be developed further in these efforts.

An Agenda for Action

To carry on ethical and scientific review of social experiments involving health system reforms, we need to do the following. First, we need to develop a framework that captures and integrates the ethically desirable objectives

---

[10] The "90–10" formula ignores the epidemiological transition that has made noncommunicable disease the major burden of disease in most developing countries, with the exception of parts of Africa and South Asia.

[11] Global Forum for Health Research, "Statement on Health Research for Equity in Global Health. Mexico City," 2004. Available at htp://www.globalforumhealth.org/forum8/Statement.html.

of reform and that can, with thoughtful local adaptation, be accepted in various settings. Second, we must develop an evidence base to assess the appropriateness of the measures or means used in system reforms. There must be both research, capacity to provide that evidence prior to reforms and a commitment to ongoing monitoring and evaluation of reforms; this will provide an ongoing evidence base to reevaluate what is being done. Third, the tools for evaluating reform efforts must include ways of assessing the key elements of governance involved in deciding on reforms, implementing them, and modifying them if they do not go as planned or expected.

The Benchmarks of Fairness illustrate what one such ethical framework might look like. They also illustrate how such a framework might be used for prospective or retrospective assessment of the fit between reform measures and reform objectives, and how the Benchmarks might also be used to evaluate governance and accountability in designing and implementing reforms. Moreover, they provide a tool that can be used by policy makers or by external reviewers, leaving open the decision about who should conduct such a review. Still, the Benchmarks are at best only a work in progress. Much more needs to be done with the Benchmarks or with other, better approaches in order to meet these needs.

Ethics and social science must join in developing appropriate tools, and funding institutions must invest in relevant research capabilities. Health system transformation is a far more complex process involving many more objectives than typical clinical trials. Its ethical review is a more complex task than the review of clinical research. We do not want to wait for social experiments in health system transformation to produce atrocities like those that made clear the need for review of clinical research. However, we also do not want to create insurmountable obstacles to needed reforms.

10

Accountability for Reasonableness in Developing Countries

Two Applications

Being accountable for the reasonableness of our decisions about limits in health policy requires us to develop an account of the reasons that fair-minded people can agree are relevant to meeting their health needs. It requires us to publicize the grounds for those decisions while viewing them as revisable in light of new evidence (see Chapter 4). Does this approach to priority setting, originally developed by examining decision-making processes in the decentralized and private U.S. medical insurance context, have more general applicability? Can it apply where it may be most urgently needed, in developing countries with the most dramatic resource allocation questions?

My goal in this chapter is to show that accountability for reasonableness provides a way of establishing legitimacy and fairness in two different developing-country contexts in which resources are severely limited. First, I shall describe the way in which accountability for reasonableness can address moral controversies about patient and site selection in the global effort to scale up ARTs for HIV/AIDS in low-income, high-prevalence countries. Then I shall describe how accountability provides a framework for introducing a fair, deliberative process in determining the benefit package in the new Mexican catastrophic insurance plan. That scheme is part of Mexico's recent national health reform, the Seguro Popular, aimed at incrementally providing universal coverage to a previously uninsured and underserved half of

I thank Jim Sabin and Russell Teagarden for helpful comments on the original work on the 3 by 5 program. Alex Capron and Andreas Reis provided me with useful sources for that work as well. I also thank participants in the WHO and UNAIDS consultation on Equity in the Three by Five Program, Geneva, January 26–7, 2004. Cf. Daniels (2004, 2005). The work on the Mexican application could not have proceeded without the assistance of Secretary Julio Frenk, Dra. Mercedes Juan, Eduardo Gonzalez Pier, Cristina Gutierrez, Octavio Gomez Dantes, Dr. Guilliermo Soberon, and other members of the working groups assembled to develop and implement the process described. I also thank Jason Lakin, with whom I am preparing a case study of the development of the process.

the Mexican population (Frenk et al. 2006). In both contexts, either international or national agencies have endorsed the approach as a key feature of programs or reforms in progress. Indeed, WHO (2006a) used accountability for reasonableness in a case study evaluating the decision-making process used in Tanzania to develop a plan for scaling up ARTs.

Unfortunately, neither example provides evidence that priority setting is thereby improved or is judged to be more legitimate or fair. Such evidence would, of course, be most welcome. In Mexico, however, there is a plan to monitor and evaluate the implementation of the fair process so that such evidence may be obtained. Despite the current lack of such evidence, both examples at least show that relevant authorities consider the approach to be a plausible and feasible way to address important resource allocation problems.

ASSURING EQUITY THROUGH FAIR PROCESS IN THE WHO "3 BY 5" PROGRAM

In 2003, WHO, in collaboration with the Joint United Nations Programme on HIV/AIDS (UNAIDS), launched its 3 by 5 program to facilitate the ART of 3 million HIV/AIDS patients by 2005 in high-prevalence countries.[1] In addition to this ambitious target, nearly a tenfold increase in treatments, WHO's program goals specified that treatment must be accompanied by improved delivery of preventive measures against HIV and must not undermine the ability of health systems to address other urgent preventive and curative needs.[2] Given the large, rapid infusion of donor resources needed, and given the fragility of many of the health systems where the incidence of HIV/AIDS is the highest, success was by no means assured;[3] in fact, by the target date, only about 1.2 million patients were under treatment. The program also carried the risk of inadvertently impairing HIV prevention programs or other components of health systems (Potts and Walsh 2003).

---

[1] An archive of documents relating to this program can be found at http://www.who.int/3by5/en/, accessed October 8, 2006.

[2] Dhaliwal et al. (2003: 10) *"ARV treatment should be planned and implemented as an integral component of the continuum of care, treatment and prevention.* Planning and implementing ARV treatment programmes must be based on responding to the community's care, treatment and prevention needs. It will also be important to *situate ARV treatment programmes within existing health systems.* Although most health systems in resource limited settings tend to be underdeveloped and overstretched, situating ARV treatment programmes within such health systems can be an opportunity to strengthen them [emphasis in the original]."

[3] "... [T]here are signs that targets set for resource generation will not be met. As of March 2002, the projected annual costs of the Fund [Global Fund for AIDS, Tuberoulosis, and Malaria] were less than the pledges received from donor governments and corporations, and the money promised by donors at the end of this year [2003] is $1,371m less than the money that the Fund needs" (McCoy 2003: 13).

Even in its statement of a target, the 3 by 5 program raises a daunting ethical issue: *Only 3 million* people will be given life-extending drugs *out of 6 million* who could benefit from them, by WHO's own criteria for patient selection. Thus, 3 by 5 is equivalent to 3 out of 6. While the former poses an inspiring logistical challenge, the latter states a grim ethical challenge. *Is there a fair way to select the fortunate 3 million?* Without an approach that establishes *legitimacy* for the selection decisions that are made, what could be a great achievement risks becoming a focus of angry resentment. When people win millions of dollars in a national lottery, they are viewed as very lucky. No one resents their winning, provided that the lottery is itself fair. If the lottery is rigged or appears to be rigged, reactions are very different and very intense. Fairness matters. Fairness matters even more when the stakes are millions of lives.

Competing Principles and Considerations: Four Examples

Though moral controversy surrounds nearly every decision about patient selection in scaling up ARTs, I shall limit my comments to four key issues. Reasonable people can and do disagree about each of these issues. Persistent disagreement about moral issues in these cases, including the principles underlying these conclusions, makes plausible my appeal to accountability for reasonableness.

Cost Recovery for ARTs
A central question in scale-up policy concerns what charges, if any, should be made for drugs or services involved in treating HIV /AIDS. There is considerable evidence that even very low prices for antiretroviral drugs and treatments are a major deterrent to very poor families. There is also evidence that programs exempting the poor from user fees often do not work as planned and allow corruption, as does the sale of treatments itself (Gilson 1997a). So there are strong equity considerations that weigh against cost recovery, and many insist that no charges should be required. Nearly all agree that if charges are made, they must not be allowed to prevent access, though how to implement this principle is not clear in light of failed efforts at exemption schemes.

At the same time, proponents of cost recovery argue that it permits resources to be stretched further, perhaps saving more people, and that it improves sustainability. Some also argue that fairness or equity requires some systems to recover costs, since those systems already charge user fees for other medical services. It would be unfair to exempt people with HIV/ AIDS from the obligations imposed on other kinds of patients who also have serious illnesses. Other people might reply that no one with serious illness should have to pay user fees that prevent access, and that a system is more fair if fewer people face that problem. On this view, insisting on consistency may be politically useful, but it does not increase fairness.

These maximization and fairness considerations are weighed differently by different people. Ministry of health officials in systems that have implemented costrecovery feel strongly about the inequity between disease conditions and the importance of sustainability. Providers take both sides of the question. Advocates for people with HIV/AIDS strongly oppose charges. This clearly is a moral disagreement that requires careful deliberation. Moreover, it is an issue that arises at both international and national levels: International donors could influence national decisions if they adopted a strong position on equity, and yet these organizations have little inclination or incentive to use a fair process in their own decision making. In any case, national decision makers must take their own position, ideally through a fair process that provided accountability for reasonableness. In addition, each level of decision making calls for the same.

Medical Eligibility Criteria

WHO (2003c) recommendations for medical eligibility suggest that patients with CD4 counts (a measure of immune system capability) below 200 receive treatment; alternatively, if testing is not possible, those with clinically diagnosed AIDS should be treated. This guideline leaves it to national programs to decide whether to treat patients earlier in their illness – for example, those with CD4 counts below 350. In resource-rich countries, some practitioners urge earlier treatment since it avoids waiting until patients are much sicker, though there is controversy about whether overall survival time is increased. In making its recommendation for resource-poor countries, the WHO guideline sets eligibility at the 200 CD4 level. The WHO claims that benefits at that level are well demonstrated – ignoring the possibly greater benefit to less ill patients – and that treating sicker patients will permit resources to benefit more people – which may not be true.

This recommendation about medical eligibility incorporates both technical medical judgments about clinical benefits and value judgments. One interpretation of the criterion involving the lower CD4 count is that WHO is giving preference to more urgently ill patients. One reason for doing so might be to try to save more people: Saving the sickest first means that there is more time to save less sick people later. This presupposes that resources are temporarily, not permanently, scarce (Kamm 1993), so that new resources will be available later to save those not treated first. If this is the rationale, the governing principle seems to be promoting best outcomes, not giving priority to the sickest, but that rationale is plausible only if resources are expanding. If, however, resources are not increasing, then less ill patients who then do not qualify on the WHO criterion might argue that they will do better if given the drugs before they met the criterion than they will once they meet the criterion. They might argue, and some providers in richer countries would agree, that they are denied the potentially greater benefit in order to give a lesser benefit to others who are more urgently ill. Clearly, the choice of criterion is not a simple technical judgment but involves value judgments that must be carefully assessed.

Consider a second feature of the treatment protocols that is presented as if it is primarily a technical matter, although it too rests on value assumptions. The WHO proposals require some way to assure patient compliance with drug regimens. This may involve community-based workers, but in some places there has also been a discussion of the importance of family support or psychosocial measures of patient readiness to comply with drug regimens, such as regularity of clinic visits. The requirement would mean that some who lack family, perhaps because of prior AIDS deaths or because of other choices or misfortunes, will be denied any benefit at all, as Macklin (2004) notes.

Two reasons might be given for such measures: They assure better outcomes for patients and they reduce the risk of emerging drug resistance. Both are not simply technical but involve value judgments that should be made explicit. If the reason is to select patients with better outcomes, then some patients will be denied a fair chance at any benefit in order to favor best outcomes. This is an instance of one of the unsolved rationing problems discussed in Chapter 4. If the reason is to avoid a risk of emerging drug resistance, a clear threat to third parties, then an ethical judgment is being made that the risks to third parties outweigh the denial of care to, say, those without family assistance. Again, this is a denial of a fair chance to a significant benefit in order to avoid possible significant harm to third parties. Reasonable people will disagree about how to weigh this risk against the claim of having a fair chance at some benefit, giving us another version of the fair chance/best outcome problem discussed in Chapter 4.

My point in articulating the ethical controversy that surrounds the CD4 count criterion and the patient compliance criterion is not to insist that these criteria are unacceptable or unwarranted. Rather, *it is to point out that they are not just technical.* The controversy deserves to be addressed by a fair, deliberative process at the very high level of program development within WHO. That process should not just involve technical experts, though it should also include them.

If the WHO process can be seen as fair and appropriately deliberative about the ethical issues, then the eligibility criteria may later be defended in case they are apposed on ethical grounds at other levels of implementation in 3 by 5. The same point applies to national implementation of those criteria and additions to them. For example, a community that had lost many people to AIDS, and therefore could not provide family supports in many instances, might object that barring victims of the AIDS epidemic was unjustifiable and that they should not be further harmed in this way. That objection has great force and may be grounds for reconsidering exceptions to the eligibility requirements.

This objection might well mean that WHO must view its eligibility criteria as based on decisions that are revisable in light of new evidence and arguments, and its deliberative process should allow for that. Or perhaps the deliberation about this exception should take place at the country or local level and discretion should be granted to the local decision makers.

Siting of Treatment Facilities

The location of ART treatment facilities, as well as the degree of their integration into existing health systems, will clearly influence who has good access to care. To reach rural populations, which traditionally have the worst access to care, rural sites have to be developed. The same point can be made for vulnerable groups, such as ethnic minorities, who often have had worse access to care.

Health planners developing programs for scaling up ART, however, argue that locating initial ART sites in urban tertiary care facilities, often a university hospital where diagnostic equipment and better-trained personnel already exist, is a more efficient way to reach large numbers of patients quickly. Moreover, as training permits and scaling up becomes possible, other sites at the provincial, district, and even peripheral levels can then be added. Thus, in Zambia, the first phase of the effort located sites in Lusaka and Ndolo, but in the second phase, sites in all nine provinces were included, with plans to extend these to district-level treatment centers as scaling up proceeds (WHO 2003b).

If planners develop siting plans for scaling up ART that follow this argument from efficiency, which is also the path of least political resistance, then 3 by 5 efforts will replicate the existing inequities of facilities, and of personnel and resource allocation in those health systems, at least for the time frame of the 3 by 5 program and possibly will beyond. The argument from efficiency that is invoked to justify this approach – more patients treatable in less time using fewer new resources – entrenches existing inequities in the system. It clearly risks leaving more rural areas and special groups with traditional vulnerabilities underserved, perhaps to be catered to in the distant future, if at all.

In a stirring argument for a different approach to siting, David McCoy (2003) says that distributional equity should carry the day at both national and provincial levels in each country. Governments should take advantage of the flow of new resources from the Global Fund and elsewhere to move health systems toward a sustainable, equitable distribution of care. Instead of focusing on the most resource-rich sites and areas, the 3 by 5 and other programs should make a special effort to reach out to rural and other underserved populations from the beginning, putting the necessary resources into training and infrastructure that can later mean better health for traditionally underserved populations.

Obviously, the balance between efficiency (in the short run) and equity is a matter for deliberation at the country and subnational levels, as well as for international donors. This too is not just a technical issue; it is also a value-laden question. It involves trade-offs between long- and short-term results, and between underserved and better-served populations. There is no set of principles that tells us what the proper balance point is in general or even in specific situations. Rather, the weight given to different considerations may vary from country to country and even from province to province. Ignoring either equity or efficiency would probably be unacceptable, but just where to find a balance is a matter for deliberation in a fair process that gives legitimacy to the result.

Priority to Special Groups

Macklin (2004) identifies several special groups that have been candidates for special priority. I shall concentrate solely on granting special priority to health workers because the discussion well illustrates my central point. Reasonable people will disagree about whether to give priority to health workers and about when to do so, if at all. The disagreements involve deep moral issues that are unlikely to be resolved in the time frame for the 3 by 5 program. The case well illustrates the need for an account of fair decision-making process.

Those who would grant priority to health workers say that an adequate number of such workers is essential to the sustainable delivery of ARTs. If the supply of such workers is low, or if it is threatened by the AIDS epidemic itself, as well as by international market forces draining trained personnel from developing countries with a high incidence of HIV/AIDS, then granting priority to health workers may provide some protection against an increasing scarcity of health workers.

The pro-priority argument can be seen as a choice between two options. Suppose that both options have the same resources – personnel and drugs – initially available. In the Priority Option, we grant priority to health workers who meet the medical eligibility requirements. In the No Priority Option, we take people on a first-come, first-served basis, presumably barring favoritism for health workers. If granting priority means that there are enough health workers, then we may suppose that more people will be saved by ARTs over time. Note that in the short run, the number of people treated and saved will be the same: Favoring health workers does not mean saving more lives initially, only over time.[4]

Of course, this claim rests on empirical assumptions. One assumption is that the available health workers cannot be adequately protected by other

---

4 Macklin (2004) refers to this as a "utilitarian consideration," since it maximizes health benefits, but I note that maximizing the effectiveness of such workers might have the overall goal of reaching underserved parts of the population or of reducing inequalities in access to ARTs rather than maximizing net health benefits. In this case, equity itself may be undercut by not giving such priority to health workers, at least under some conditions.

measures (e.g., increased training). Another assumption is that any new funds made available for increased training will increase the number of personnel available more in the Priority Case than in the No Priority Option, because in the No Priority Option attrition will be greater. Both assumptions are relevant if the number of health personnel directly determines the number of patients treated. Where there is an adequate supply of personnel, or where the number of personnel does not limit the number of possible treatments, then the empirical assumptions in favor of the Priority Option are not met and the argument for it is not sound. For example, in developed countries that are rich in personnel, arguments for giving priority to health workers fail to satisfy the empirical assumptions their premises depend on.

One argument against giving any priority to groups, like health workers (or teachers), who arguably provide an essential social service, including saving additional lives, is that doing so is unfair. There are several ways to argue for its unfairness. Suppose we think, as John Broome (1989) argues, that fairness involves *claims* people have on others, say as a result of facts about them such as their degree of medical need. We may have other reasons for treating people differently – say health workers as compared to other people with AIDS because of the additional consequences of treating the health workers first – but doing so ignores the claims other people with AIDS have by virtue of their need. It remains unfair to them that they be so treated and their claims ignored when others are treated who have no greater claims.

Another argument for the unfairness of granting priority to health workers is that we are not treating people with equal respect or as being of equal moral worth (Kamm 1993; Brock 2003). One way to give content to the idea of equal respect is the Kantian view that we should not treat people merely as a means to the ends of others but always as ends in themselves. By not giving equal priority to nonhealth workers, we are treating them as a means to our social end of saving more lives.

Similarly, by looking to the *indirect* effects of treating health workers first, we risk abandoning the view that people are of equal worth or should not be treated merely as means. If they are of equal worth, and that is the basis for equal treatment, then some people should not be considered more worthly simply because they have some trait, such as training, that allows them to make an additional social contribution. Notice that in all of these arguments from fairness, whether from claims, from not treating people as means, or from equal worth, the rightness of what we do is not simply a matter of the most lives saved over time. Here the divide between different moral views is deeply rooted.

Nevertheless, some philosophers and others who respect nonconsequentialist constraints might still favor support for the Priority Option (Brock 2003). For example, Kamm might extend an argument she has given about a hypothetical case[5] in this way: Though we "do not do with our resource [ART drugs] whatever will result in as much good as possible . . . we [do] try to achieve the best outcome for which our resource was specifically designed." Since the health worker and the extra patients they will give the drugs to all have the same need for ARTs as the patients who fail to get priority, the drugs are being allocated for the purpose they were designed to serve. Brock would reach the same conclusion, though this is not the occasion for a full discussion of these philosophical controversies.[6]

Reasonable people will disagree about acceptable policy in the Priority Option, as in the previous issues. Different people will give different weight to the empirical considerations, especially since they may give different weight or emphasis in their moral judgments to the principle of equal respect, which prohibits social worth judgments in medical context. Some may feel that priority can be given only when scarcity is worst, for only then will the social worth aspects of giving priority be framed by a specific consequence of not granting it; others may be moved even when scarcity is less pressing. Some may also be troubled by the suggestion that health workers are generally better off than many of the patients they treat, so that giving them priority may seem to be a matter of socioeconomic privilege, especially if health workers grant the privilege of priority to themselves or even administer it.

Because reasonable people will disagree about when priority is warranted at all, and if so about how much, it requires a fair deliberative process. It is not an issue on which principles we all agree on give us clear determinations about the right course of action. It is also clear that different groups of people may arrive at different conclusions, even when the facts are comparable. For various reasons, perhaps cultural, perhaps experiential, members of some social groups may tend to weight these factors differently. Fair process may then yield somewhat different answers, depending on who the deliberators are. In different systems, such variation may itself be objectionable to different degrees.

[5] Kamm (1993) argues that saving a surgeon with a drug, because the surgeon can then use her skills to save others, would be unfair to anyone in need of the drug who is passed over in favor of the surgeon. But saving someone who could run fast to deliver a drug to save a second person in need would be fair because we are using the drug for the purpose for which it was designed.

[6] Kamm and Brock both conclude that one does not violate a Kantian injunction against treating people as means in a case like our Priority Option, though for somewhat different reasons. This suggests that at least some nonconsequentialists might agree with consequentialists about acceptability of the Priority Option, even if they would disagree about the reasoning underlying their conclusions. Brock's and Kamm's reasoning about health workers would not extend to teachers, however, though consequentialists might see the two issues similarly. Nothing emerges in the subtleties of this philosophical debate that challenges my claim that reasonable people will disagree on these cases.

Fair process is a way to produce agreement, or at least to narrow disagreement, among a group trying to justify decisions to each other. But that may not eliminate all conflicting results of deliberation across decision contexts. (I argued in Chapter 4 that getting different decisions from different groups applying fair process does not violate a *formal principle of justice*, namely, that we treat like cases similarly.) In her discussion of ethical principles that might bear on the issue of priorities among patient groups, Macklin (2004) notes that some groups may be viewed as more deserving than others, or at least as having a special claim of compensation. For example, people who became infected during vaccine trials might be considered special victims, and though they were not promised any compensation, they are owed it because of their effort to contribute to society. Similarly, people who were infected by contaminated blood, or who are victims of rape, might be thought to deserve special compensation because they are the victims of social neglect, or of negligence, or of a failure to provide basic security that is owed to all.

At the 2004 Geneva consultation on equity in 3 by 5, the Chinese defended the view that special priority should be given to the many people infected by improperly screened blood. Others objected, however, that singling out this group for special priority risked increasing the stigma against other infected groups. The stigma problem is exacerbated by the illegal status of intravenous drug users and sex workers. Giving priority to the innocent or victimized group would thus make it harder to treat the epidemic in other groups and in the population as a whole. The Chinese were not moved by the objection and received some support from others about the special compensation owed the targets of the Chinese policy. This ethical controversy requires more careful deliberation under conditions that assure fair process.

Everyone can recognize the relevance of these concerns about special treatment or special compensation. Still, how much weight is given to them may depend on other moral views that people hold and on the costs involved in giving them priority. My goal here is not to resolve these issues but to suggest that they require careful deliberation in the proper setting. For a decision-making process about setting priorities to be fair, it must encourage the kind of deliberation that allows these arguments to be considered. That is the way in which communities tend to air and resolve moral disagreements or, even if they cannot resolve them, to find a way to cooperate despite residual disagreements.

WHO/UNAIDS Endorsement of Accountability for Reasonableness

In its Guidelines on Equity in the 3 by 5 program, WHO/UNAIDS (2004) recognizes that controversy surrounds patient selection and siting decisions, such as the ones we just reviewed. The Guidelines then call for a fair, deliberative process that abides by the conditions specified in Chapter 4. None of these conditions is novel or surprising in the international or even national settings where scaling up is being discussed. Transparency and publicity are widely recognized features of good governance, and they have been emphasized by various international agencies, including the WB, with its recent focus on governance. Involving stakeholders in evaluating the rationales underlying a policy – a modification of the relevance condition that I shall comment on shortly – is also widely believed to improve deliberation and assure people affected by decisions that their voices have been heard. Indeed, it was a crucial feature of primary health care reform proposals throughout the 1980s, when local communities were encouraged to participate in the governance of health clinics. Revisability is a way to assure due process to those who may be affected by decisions that are bad for them. Enforcement is an assurance condition for all.

Applying Accountability for Reasonableness

To see what this application of accountability for reasonableness would mean in practice, consider the steps that might be taken to address the controversy about siting treatment services.

A Hypothetical Application to Siting Decisions
The siting of treatment centers for ARTs is determined primarily by countries and their subdivisions (provinces, districts), though external funding may be tied to approval of siting plans. In that case, external agencies may have general guidelines that involve concerns about equity of access and efficiency of delivery. For example, at a very general level, the "guiding principles" for scaling up ARTs suggest a "political commitment to working towards a universal access to ARV treatments" and "situating ARV treatment programmes within existing health systems," though with a "phased approach for scaling up ARV treatment" in ways that preserve "equity" (Dhaliwal, Okero, Schilleisoort, Green, Conway, and Jain 2003: 9). If these general points are made more specific as recommendations to national and subnational decision makers, then the recommendations will have to be based on a consultative, deliberative process involving various stakeholders.

Let us suppose in what follows that only general guidelines about siting are issued to countries by external agencies. Suppose that the guidelines state that goals should include equitable access, with full respect for international agreements about human rights. Funders then allow countries to make specific siting decisions that take into account sustainability and the capacity of the system to train personnel in a phased effort to scale up. We saw earlier that the trade-offs involved reflect controversial value judgments – conflicts between efficiency and equity of access. These are not simply technical decisions based on empirical evidence.

Though values and facts are both involved, the empirical background must be taken into account. Appropriate evidence must be gathered about the capacity of the system to undertake ARTs and to integrate them with appropriate preventive measures in a way that does not undermine the rest of the system. The capacity to monitor CD4 counts and to train personnel to deliver standardized first- and second-line treatments at different sites must be assessed. Knowledge of surrounding communities must be good; planners must know about their ability to develop family and community supports for sustaining drug regimens in different settings. Countries must assess how these measures can be integrated with other components of the health system in ways that strengthen it rather than pull resources away from it. The needs of different subpopulations must also be determined, including their access to different potential treatment centers.

This information base provides a background for the ethical deliberation about how to prioritize among goals, but it does not determine those priorities. Knowing that certain existing centers, say some tertiary care facilities connected with universities in large cities, have the capacity to scale up treatment to patients if drugs are available is a fact that the evidence gathering can make clear. What is not clear is how to use that fact to phase in broader access to ARTs. Given existing inequalities in access, siting treatment where the highest capacity already exists means better-served populations will again benefit more and those least well-served will have to wait for much later phases of the scaling-up effort, assuming they actually occur.

Should priorities be changed to correct existing inequities, even if that means slower scaling up to start with and fewer patients reached immediately (with more dying), in order to save more people from underserved groups where the need may be greater sooner? This kind of trade-off in planning must reflect deliberation about values. It is not simply a matter for experts but for all stakeholders affected by the decision – people with HIV/AIDS in the various communities, clinicians who must treat them or turn them away, planners whose facilities are affected by the decisions, and communities whose children are being orphaned and whose survivors are driven deeper into poverty. All are affected by the priorities that are set.

To illustrate the problem involved in these trade-offs, note what happens if traditional inequalities in the system are taken as a given. The rationale for building on existing strengths is that resources are already in place for beginning ART delivery in certain central tertiary care facilities. Scaling up will be more efficient, some then conclude, if those strengths are utilized. In Zimbabwe, for example, the Ministry of Health and the University of Zimbabwe directed "the setting up of treatment initiatives in the main cities, away from the areas of greatest need," presumably because those are the sites where scaling up poses fewer logistical and personnel problems (Ray and Kureya 2003: 5). But "district hospitals, including mission hospitals that have already developed the infrastructure required for community based [voluntary counseling and testing] VCT, home based care and prevention of [parent-to-child transmission] PTCT . . . [are] preferable sites . . . closer to areas of greatest need" (Ray and Kureya 2003: 5). Zimbabwe thus risked replicating in its ART effort a common pattern of inequity in health services, namely, that richer population subgroups, often located in cities, derive far more benefit from public sector services than the poor (McCoy 2003: 26).

There is another important dimension to the problem of siting decisions: Are treatment sites *well integrated into the delivery system* or are they separate silos, removed from efforts to improve equity more generally in the system? The problem is well illustrated in the case of Malawi (Kemp et al. 2003). In a national plan to improve equity in health services, an Essential Health Package (EHP) was developed by the Malawi Ministry of Health in 1999. The siting issue is whether ARTs are included in an expanded EHP and their delivery is tied to developing the infrastructure needed to assure universal coverage for the EHP, or whether ART treatment is promoted in ways that motivate health workers to abandon the EHP effort and to follow the new resources to ART treatment centers, thus weakening an already fragile system with inadequate personnel.

This aspect of the siting decision is not merely technical but involves value-based trade-offs. It should be given just as careful attention in deliberations about fair process as the issue of urban versus rural siting. Unless the decision making includes the deliberative, inclusive process described here, the result will be to disguise value issues as merely organizational and technical ones. Losers will then feel that they have been treated unfairly. In this instance, the losers will not just be those who would benefit from ART but do not receive it, but also those who need access to EHP but do not get it. In Malawi, as in other countries, a central obstacle to equitable scaling up is the great scarcity of health care personnel. This problem must be addressed in scaling-up plans; it is not a fixed determinant of them.

Given these facts, deliberation is needed to arrive at an acceptable valuation of the trade-offs involved. A key issue, then, is, what stakeholders are invited to join the national and provincial decision-making process about siting? Siting does not just mean location, but also integration with existing facilities. The claim that the decision has broad effects implies that the involvement of stakeholders must also be inclusive.

A basic guiding principle in scaling up, noted earlier, is the inclusion of stakeholders and the community in planning. But this inclusion must extend to the process of setting priorities around which the planning occurs. The point of such involvement is to broaden the deliberative process and to ensure that value questions are addressed, not submerged as merely technical issues about capacity in the existing system. In many countries, effective scaling up will require coordination with the public sector and key components of the private sector, including NGOs of various sorts. This fact implies some broadening of official consultation and planning. This broadening should include all the stakeholders affected by the siting plan: providers of different types from different levels of the public system and from the private sector, advocacy groups, and representatives of diverse community groups. The intention is not to stimulate lobbying, but to provide a context in which arguments about needs and the consequences of different siting arrangements can be assessed.

Uganda's effort at scaling up involved establishing a National Advisory Board to make various recommendations based on an assessment of needs for ARTs (Okero et al. 2003). The Board was also to recommend objective criteria for people who should participate and suggest how the scaling-up effort could improve the health care infrastructure. Key to this approach was the Board's inclusion of a range of specialists and stakeholders, including representatives of people living with HIV/AIDS. In addition, the Ministry of Health appointed a National Committee on Access to ARV Therapy. It was multidisciplinary, including representatives of various international and bilateral agencies, faith-based and other NGOs, and people living with HIV/AIDS. One of its tasks was to oversee the development of "technical guidelines" for ART. With some elaboration of its consultative activities, this kind of committee could play a role in making priority-setting decisions regarding siting and other issues in scaling-up. Think of it as involving practical first steps toward the elements of fair process, which are elaborated in what follows.

In seeking agreement on relevant reasons, it is important to include a broad range of stakeholders affected by the decisions. This inclusion can take different forms, provided that some of them do not become labeled or perceived as tokenism. Focus groups may be needed in some cases since involving some types of stakeholders in the more centralized process may not be feasible. However, this kind of consultation should not be seen as a process in which the "experts" talk to "consumers" but are not really bound to listen to what they say.

There is no one formal structure or institutional arrangement that must be used to achieve a deliberative, fair process. Various institutional structures can be integrated: public hearings, testimony from various groups to a commission, focus groups or other community and other stakeholder investigative approaches. Local traditions may make some forms easier and more acceptable than others. The central conditions described earlier – publicity, involving stakeholders to seek agreement on relevant reasons, allowing for revisability, enforcement of the process – are general enough to be compatible with many arrangements.[7]

Siting decisions may be made at various levels in a health system: national, provincial, district. Deliberation may require different degrees and formats

---

[7] There are checklists for each component of accountability for reasonableness; see Daniels (2004).

of stakeholder involvement at different levels. But the rationales for all decisions must be publicly accessible, regardless of the level, and each rationale must be constrained by agreement on relevant reasons. Each must be
revisable in light of better evidence and arguments from other levels that
impact it.

In some countries, existing community structures can be adapted to play
the role described here; others have begun to build them into scaling-up
proposals. For example, in Cameroon there are "dialogue structures" that
involve community representatives (in theory and sometimes in practice)
in governing local health units. Such structures can supply representatives
for both local and provincial or national efforts at deliberation.

In Zambia, a multidisciplinary Task Force on ART in the Central Board of
Health (CBOH) includes people from different disciplinary backgrounds
who work part-time on ART program development. However, the Task Force
does not include a broader set of stakeholders needed for the kind of deliberation proposed here (WHO 2003b: 8). Each province in Zambia has an ART
Selection Committee "comprised of a physician, a social worker, a counselor,
a religious representative and a psychologist (where one exists). Inclusion
of a representative of people living with HIV/AIDS has been suggested and
is being considered. It is responsible for selection of patients to be put on
treatment, following set criteria" (WHO 2003b: 8) Such a structure could
be expanded to deliberate about the "set criteria" used in patient selection.
Nevertheless, its professional focus implies that the set criteria are largely
technical or medical and that the sole issue is who meets them.

Lowenson (2004) argues that there is a strong connection between stakeholder involvement – various forms or types of participation in the priority-
setting process – and accountability. Participation builds understanding of
what has to be done and encourages a sense of control. Fostering that understanding and sense of control in civic groups creates an organized pressure
to keep decision makers and providers on track for doing what they have
agreed to do. This relationship does not require that stakeholders, including
community organizations, actually have *control* or exercise a *delegated power*,
though such strong forms of empowerment may exist at very peripheral
levels. Those strong forms of participation may be desirable and feasible in
some settings, but they probably will not occur without strong political forces
working both from above and below, a relatively rare event. Nevertheless,
joint planning and *advising in a formal way*, rather that simply being consulted
on occasion or receiving information after the fact, are forms of participation that generate accountability. They are also the forms are also essential
to establishing a fair process in which relevant reasons can be agreed to by
affected parties.

It is also important to recognize that participation can be encouraged in
theory and on paper without actually being achieved. The Zimbabwe Health
Review Commission (cited in Lowenson 2004) points to various factors
that undercut official positions supporting participation. They include poor

health worker appreciation of the value of participation, poor health worker skills in facilitating community involvement, weak methods for improving that appreciation and the needed skills, weak political commitment to participation, and lack of stable planning structures for joint planning between communities and health services. If fair process is to succeed, it must include active stakeholder involvement, so these obstacles, common to Zimbabwe and many other countries, must be overcome in institutions that set selection criteria.

An important feature of fair process is the opportunity to revise in light of new evidence and arguments, and especially to reconsider cases based on complaints of unfair treatment. A national and provincial decision-making process for determining appropriate ART sites must be open to complaints by areas that consider themselves underserved. What is needed is a process open and sensitive enough to distinguish cases of (temporarily) unavoidable inequality from those of unjustifiable inequity.

Specifically, rationing decisions will generally have losers – people who are given lower priority than others. But not every such case is one of inequity. What matters are the grounds for establishing the priority and the process used. Every rationing decision may leave some groups of people relatively worse off, but if the decision involves due consideration of all ethical issues, there may be no way to eliminate the disadvantage without equally disadvantaging others. If no one is worse off than others would be or than anyone need be under the conditions, the complaint about equity may be unfounded. The goal is to eliminate all patterns of inequity, but where not all needs can be met, there is no way to eliminate inequality.

What is crucial is that lower levels of a system must have a way to raise complaints and higher levels must be willing to listen to those complaints to see if there is an inequity that must be addressed. Decision makers at higher levels must then address it. They must consider revising the recommended siting pattern accordingly.

The challenging point is that many of these arrangements – especially the proposals about a fair process that extend these preliminary versions – are novel to most health systems and even to most forms of public deliberation in any government structure. The striking ethical challenge of distributing ARTs fairly provides an opportunity to introduce accountability for the reasonableness of priority setting into systems more generally. Just as the argument supporting the scaling-up effort makes the point that this is not a solo program but an effort to improve the functioning of health systems beyond the use of ARTs, so too the deliberative, fair process that equitable scaling up requires should be translated into ongoing procedures in the system as a whole.

Beyond Hypothetical Applications
So far, I have discussed a hypothetical siting decision to illustrate key features that a fair decision-making process should include. Nevertheless, the

applicability of accountability for reasonableness to this problem goes beyond what is merely hypothetical. In Malawi, for example, the National AIDS Commission (2004) issued a consensus report on equity in the 3 by 5 program in 2004. The report recommended that ARTs be given free of charge in public settings and subsidized in private ones; that treatment centers be located in all districts; that access be on a first-come, first-served basis, despite the bias in favor of better-educated and better-off subgroups; that health promotion of ARTs be aimed at strategically important and vulnerable groups; and that strong emphasis be placed on integrating ARTs with essential health services. The report includes a full discussion of the rationales for the recommendations and reasons for rejecting minority views on some of the issues. The report also recommends monitoring for equity throughout the scaling-up process.

These recommendations take a stand on some controversial issues. For example, the rationale for the first-come, first-served policy favored better-off, better-educated people, but the concern that was given weight in the recommendation was that the policy avoided making front-line providers act as gatekeepers for controversial priority decisions. Similarly, the rationale for free delivery at public sites, combined with subsidized delivery at private sites, was motivated by the concern that few Malawans would be able to pay any significant fees and would increase the risk of the emergence of resistant strains.

At least as important as the recommendations themselves and the transparency in announcing their rationale is the process used in reaching them. To my knowledge, the Malawi Commission operated without any direct appeal to the framework developed here, yet the process they used reflects its key elements.[8] This suggests that these key features constitute a realistic and feasible way to describe a coherent process. Specifically, in July 2003, a national meeting of stakeholders and the ART working group were given a technical paper about the issues. Following this meeting, a team of five panelists conducted three live phone-in programs on Malawi radio and two panel discussions on television. Feedback was invited from listeners, and then six meetings with various stakeholders were held; these served as focus groups. A study was also commissioned in seven districts. All of this input into the National AIDS Commission provided the basis for the recommendations.

It remains to be seen whether these recommendations are implemented in the scaling-up process, so the full effects of a fair process are not measured by this initial work. It also remains to be seen whether the process implemented in Malawi yields proposals to global funders that reflect local

---

[8] The process was probably influenced by the work of Equinet, an advocacy group active in southern Africa that emphasizes the connection between equity and stakeholder involvement in decision making.

concerns and express resistance to the sole goal of maximizing the number of treatments – which may be the focus of global funders.

Another important piece of evidence about feasibility is provided by work in Tanzania. Demonstrating an ongoing commitment to the relationship between equity and a fair process, the WHO (2006a) published a case study of decision making about the scaling up of ARTs in Tanzania. The study examines how well the requirements of accountability for reasonableness – publicity, relevant reasons, and revisability conditions – were met by the decision makers. The study concludes that each requirement, aided by consultation with a variety of relevant stakeholders, was largely satisfied. There was some tension with external funders: Consultations with many stakeholders are not only time-consuming, but sometimes they lead to modifications of decisions that donors do not prefer. Nevertheless, the conditions required by accountability for reasonableness were thought essential to the development of a Tanzanian national plan that had "buy-in" from relevant groups.

As the WHO endorsement shows, and as actual practice in two low-income countries, Malawi and Tanzania, also shows, accountability for reasonableness moves us beyond theory to an important area of practice. It builds on features that are already present in various cultures and provides a coherent rationale for adhering to them. In the next section, I describe how accountability for reasonableness is embraced by a middle-income country, Mexico, as a solution to the hard problem of incrementally expanding the benefit package of its catastrophic insurance plan.

ACCOUNTABILITY FOR REASONABLE DECISIONS ABOUT CATASTROPHIC INSURANCE BENEFITS IN MEXICO

In 2003, Mexico passed new legislation establishing a national health reform, the Seguro Popular, to provide insurance coverage to the half of its population, some 50 million people, in its informal sector.[9] These are people previously promised personal medical services through publicly owned clinics and hospitals. Serious underfunding of these services and facilities meant, however, that only a few essential services were covered, despite successive reforms aimed at expanding that benefit. As a result of the inadequate public sector coverage, over 55 percent of payments for medical services were out of pocket, making Mexico a relatively poor performer on WHO measures of the fairness of health system financing (WHO 2000). The Seguro Popular greatly increases federal government financing of the system. The funding increase allows the government to provide a much bigger essential benefit package that includes relatively low-cost but high-utilization services. The Seguro Popular also includes a Fund for Protection

---

[9] See Chapter 9 for a discussion of the Benchmarks strategy for reducing financial barriers to care in both the formal and informal sectors of the economy.

from Catastrophic Expenses (FPGC) that covers high-cost treatments for certain conditions. Since resources for this voluntary catastrophic insurance plan depend on the level of enrollment of the uninsured population in the Seguro Popular, new conditions can be added to the catastrophic benefit package only incrementally as increased revenue from premiums permits.[10]

This stringent resource limit creates the need for a fair process to set priorities for coverage. In what follows, I describe the progress that has been made toward institutionalizing accountability for reasonableness to address this problem. To start, consider the difficulty of the problem.

Why Fair Process for Coverage Decisions?

The General Health Council was charged with making recommendations for coverage. Based on work from clinical and economics working groups, it initially developed a list of sixty conditions (later expanded to sixty-four and then sixty-eight) that were candidates for coverage. But how should choices be made among them? Considered in the abstract, the problem was daunting. All were serious conditions affecting various numbers of people at different stages of life, and all had very high treatment costs. Should the General Health Council always give priority to a more prevalent condition than to a less prevalent one? If so, helping the most people means giving people with less prevalent conditions no chance of receiving a significant benefit. Should the General Health Council give more weight to the prevalence or the seriousness of a condition? Should it consider the age at which the condition occurs? How should it weight cost-effectiveness against seriousness or prevalence? Should it give weight to pressure from civic advocacy groups? The law authorizing the plan provided only very general criteria, such as social acceptability, conformance with ethical norms of the medical profession, and cost-effectiveness, but these criteria might conflict with each other and are vague, and no priorities among them were built into the law itself. The difficulty in choosing fairly was one clear reason for introducing a fair decision making process.

A second reason for implementing a fair process was the awareness that some initial coverage decisions were made with no clear criteria or process in place. This posed a potential political problem, especially in the transition between administrations that would take place at the end of 2006. For example, some of the initial decisions – to cover ARTs for HIV/AIDS and childhood leukemias – were in part the result of ongoing advocacy by civic groups before the FPGC was implemented. By making this an initial coverage decision, these groups became supporters of the insurance plan. Another initial coverage decision was also not controversial, for cervical cancer is a

---

[10] For a comprehensive overview of the Seguro Popular, see Frenk et al. (2006), Gonzalez-Pier et al. (2006), and Knaul et al. (2006).

preventable condition that is screened for but not treated. Lack of coverage for treatment after promoting screening was difficult to justify. Other early decisions were more troubling: An NGO promised partial funding if coverage for cataract surgery were provided, even though this condition did not meet other standards of catastrophic cost. Similarly, lysosomal diseases, relatively rare enzyme deficiency conditions that cause early childhood death and are treatable only at very high cost, were considered after significant lobbying by an advocacy group supported by a broader child advocacy group.

The secretary of health was thus vulnerable to lobbying and public pressure. Clearly, decisions in the transition to a new government would be defensible only with a decision process that was perceived to be objective and fair. The concern was not only that specific decisions might be challenged as arbitrary or political, but also that the whole catastrophic insurance plan might be at risk if it was considered unfair. Designing a fair process was thus important both to produce fair outcomes and to protect against political attacks that might build on a perception of unfairness.

Adapting Accountability for Reasonableness

In March 2006, I conducted workshops with various key personnel from the Ministry of Health and the Seguro Popular to explain the need for implementing a fair, deliberative process for making coverage decisions in the catastrophic plan and to describe the features of such a process. Following these workshops and various high-level meetings with the secretary of health and other key personnel, the secretary of the General Health Council was authorized to implement an appropriate process for decision making. The first step involved writing a manual describing the process and providing a basis for its implementation. At the initial workshops, it was suggested that the process should include the efforts of four working groups. A clinical group would provide important information about the clinical course of the disease and the effectiveness of treatments. An economics group would provide information on the costs and cost-effectiveness of the treatments. Since conformance with ethical norms and social acceptability were also criteria mentioned in the law, an ethics working group, with assistance from the National Bioethics Commission, and a social acceptability working group would contribute to the deliberative process.

The first draft of the manual, however, converted the proposed process into an attempt to produce an algorithm for making coverage decisions. The draft called for each group to evaluate all sixty-four disease–treatment pairs on a set of criteria it would select, ranking them on an ordinal scale of 1–5 so that a decision that aggregated these numbers would be used to make selections. The problem with such a method is that it assumes that the two groups giving normative inputs could work in the same way as the clinical or economic groups, which can divide each disease into five categories of prevalence, or rank them by mortality rates or by the cost-effectiveness of their treatments. But the ethics group would not be able to come up with criteria that were amenable to such straightforward scaling. In a workshop in August 2006, the ethics group engaged in an exercise that made the problem clear: Members deliberated about hypothetical diseases that varied in prevalence, seriousness, and age of onset. When members thought about the trade-offs that might be made among these criteria, it became clear that the group would not be able to scale diseases in the way the manual proposed. Instead, members concluded that they should analyze the conflicts in choosing among specific candidate diseases and make a recommendation about how to rank them. The process of developing agreement on the design of a fair process included consideration of conclusions about criteria and methods from each proposed working group.

In August 2006, the key leadership of the effort to design a fair process agreed that the two groups assessing values, the ethics group and the social acceptability group, would have to function in a different way from what the algorithm required. As a result, the following process was proposed to a large meeting of relevant Ministry of Health officials: The clinical and economics groups would evaluate a group of disease–treatment pairs on criteria that included prevalence, seriousness (mortality rates), course of the disease, and cost and cost-effectiveness. The ethics group would then base its analysis of the ethical issues on this information, and it would make its recommendations accordingly to the General Health Council. The General Health Council would consider inputs from these three groups and make its own preliminary recommendation. It would then interact with stakeholders assembled by the working group on social acceptability. Its final recommendation would include its deliberation about the input from those stakeholders.

This proposal was refined in October 2006 after further consultations with the working groups on ethics and on social acceptability. The ethics group requested that the General Health Council develop criteria, in consultation with the other working groups, for selecting a "next group" of candidate diseases. Applying these criteria would begin the whole process in a manner all could accept as reasonable. The process was also modified so that a subcommittee of the General Health Council, the Committee on Priorities, would make a preliminary recommendation about coverage and interact with the stakeholders assembled by the working group on social acceptability. After that consultation process, it would make a final recommendation to the General Health Council, which, in turn, would make a recommendation to the National Commission that oversees the FPCG. In short, the empirical rankings by the clinical and economics groups are subject to an ethical evaluation; then recommendations resulting from that analysis are subject to assessment from a group of stakeholders that give input on its social acceptability. Any recommendations that are finally made

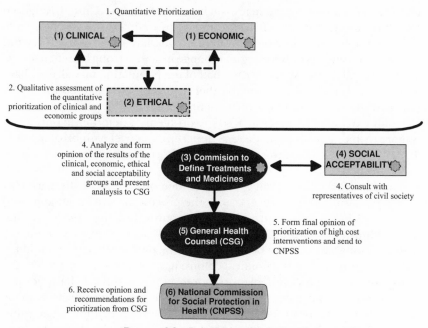

FIGURE 10.1. Proposal for Prioritizing High-Cost Interventions.

to the National Commission, as well as the Commission's own decisions, must be made public, including full rationales for them that provide reasons and evaluations of alternatives.

The approved process embodies all four features of accountability for reasonableness. The publicity condition is met because all rationales for recommendations and final coverage decisions will be publicly available on a website. The involvement of an appropriate group of stakeholders and the successive deliberations by various groups give some assurance that the rationales are based on reasons that the parties consider relevant. The decisions are revisable in light of new evidence, for example, about new treatments and their impact on cost-effectiveness. Conformance with these three conditions is enforced by the authority of the Ministry of Health, the General Health Council, and the National Commission overseeing the Seguro Popular.

This process is a bold step. If it is implemented and survives transitions in the government, it will be the first example of accountability for reasonableness being used to solve a unique priority-setting problem. The problem is unique because no other government has faced such a dramatic limit-setting task: determining how a very small but incrementally expandable pool of resources should be used to cover treatments with catastrophic costs. Some elements of accountability for reasonableness are incorporated in other public decision-making agencies, such as NICE in the United Kingdom (Rawlins 2005). But for NICE, the task is to evaluate specific new technologies for coverage in a system where no one has access to them yet and where the addition is only a marginal change in a very strong benefit package available to all. In the Mexican case, half of the population may already have access to such treatments through other insurance coverage, so the equity issues are glaring. In addition, the benefit package is weak but is being incrementally expanded from scratch, so the problem of determining priorities is more visible. The Mexican process undertakes a novel path-breaking task. To evaluate the process and its impact, a monitoring and evaluation program is also needed.

The Mexican effort is not a complete demonstration of the feasibility of implementing such a process, since the process has only been approved and its full implementation will require approval of the new leadership in the Ministry of Health. Nevertheless, the ideas central to accountability for reasonableness have been embraced by public officials in a middle-income country where the political culture has not always been open to the transparency the process demands. Moreover, these officials have not just embraced ideas but have approved establishing an institution to embody them. These facts are strong evidence of the feasibility of applying accountability for reasonableness in developing countries facing hard choices about limits to care.

11

Reducing Health Disparities

No Simple Matter

It is a commonplace in recent public health discussions that we should give some priority in our policies to reducing health inequities between social groups. This theme has become important in the United States, where race "disparities" (a euphemism for "inequities") are significant and generally thought to be unjust (IOM 2002). It is a more developed feature of public policy in Europe, where a Health For All strategy has evolved (WHO Europe 1999). In the United Kingdom, health inequalities by class, and more recently by ethnicity, have been the subject of major reports leading to policy initiatives both within the health sector and across sectors aimed at narrowing the health gap (Department of Health 1999, 2003; Secretary of State 1999: 5, cited in Graham 2004a,b; Graham and Kelly 2004). These initiatives address the social determinants of health and the ways inequalities in their distribution produce health inequalities across social groups. In Sweden, special attention has been paid to limiting social inequality as a way of reducing health inequalities (Ostlin and Diderichsen 2001). In Europe more generally, reducing health disparities has emerged as a major policy theme (WHO Europe 2002). Globally, WHO and some of its regional organizations have made equity in health central to its agenda.[1]

In Chapter 3, I argued that a health inequality between social groups is unjust when it results from an unjust distribution of the socially controllable factors affecting population health. The claim is not a tautology because Rawls's justice as fairness is used to illustrate what a just distribution of those socially controllable determinants of health would be. In this chapter, I consider whether that account also captures our concerns about race or gender inequalities in health. If it does generalize from the focus on SES in

---

[1] For example, the Pan American Health Organization (PAHO) highlights work on equity at http://www.paho.org/English/AD/GE/Ethnicity.htm. The WHO (2006b) *World Health Report 2006* emphasizes work in reducing health inequalities: See http://www.who.int/hrh/whro6_consultation/en/index9.html, accessed October 19, 2006.

Chapter 3, it gives a clear meaning to the claim that a health inequality is unjust. It also gives us good reason to want to reduce the inequality.

Life is not so simple, however, even where injustice is involved. In this chapter, I argue that policy makers face unexpected complexity when they aim to reduce injustice in this way. Many policies that would reduce inequities between groups encounter the same issues of distributive justice that we identified in Chapter 4 as unsolved rationing problems: the priorities problem, the aggregation problem, and the best outcomes/fair chances problem. These unsolved distributive problems, so common in medical resource allocation contexts, describe the baseline distributions of health neutrally. Though some people are clearly in worse health to start with than others in the priority problem, for example, no judgment is made about whether that inequality is itself unfair or unjust. The baseline is taken as a given, without prior moral judgment about how it arose.

This moral neutrality regarding the baseline may carry over from the neutrality that seems appropriate in medical contexts. In those contexts, we properly focus on the medical need and not on a moral account of how the need arose. Thus, emergency medical personnel treat beating or gunshot victims whether they initiated the attack or were innocently caught up in it. Doctors set the broken leg whether it comes from a fall while fleeing the police, from skiing, from a mugging, or from a slip on the ice. In these contexts, there is a deliberate detachment from moral evaluation of the baseline.[2] Similarly, the unsolved distribution problems focus on relevant health needs without the complication of a moral account of their origin.

It is the morally problematic features of the baseline that transform health inequalities into inequities. Inequalities in the prevalence of some diseases between blacks and whites are the result of the unjust distribution of many socially controllable factors, including income, job opportunity, education, housing quality and location, and racial discrimination. Other inequalities in the health outcomes for specific diseases, where many other factors are controlled for (education, insurance coverage, income), appear to be the result of racially distinct utilization decisions by clinicians – perhaps because of conscious or unconscious stereotyping. Similarly, the higher prevalence of HIV/AIDS among young females compared to males in southern Africa is the result of an unjust distribution of property and marriage rights, extreme poverty leading to transactional sex, and the lack of empowerment of women to control their sexual and reproductive choices. Justice opposes the health inequality – the health inequity – in all these examples.

---

[2] In Chapter 10 I noted that the Chinese government decided to expand ARTs for HIV/AIDS patients but gave priority to people who were infected by contaminated blood. Since, giving priority to these innocents wronged by the state can reinforce the stigma attaching to people infected by sex workers or intravenous drug use and make it harder to fight the epidemic, there are strong public health reasons for not deviating from some cases of moral neutrality.

The unsolved rationing problems interact with efforts to reduce health inequities. Suppose that we can improve the condition of the worst-off groups, say those victimized by racism, only by targeting interventions for them in ways that reduce significantly the benefits we can deliver to others. To give a high priority to reducing an unjust racial inequality in health, we may have to forego using resources more effectively to improve the health of larger numbers of other people. What price in aggregate health should we pay in order to reduce unjust health disparities? Does the answer depend on the type or degree of injustice? On the relative gains and losses to the different groups? In either case, reasonable people are likely to disagree about the fairest policy. As in Chapter 4, we must appeal to fair process to legitimize decisions of this sort.

The trade-off between reducing health inequalities and promoting population health results from well-intentioned policy. Frequently, measures intended to improve health in general have a differential impact on population subgroups. A stop-smoking campaign may be more effective for better-off groups, say professionals and groups with higher income and higher educations levels, than for manual workers or lower SES groups (Barbeau et al. 2004). Since smoking levels are already higher for lower SES groups, the inequality in smoking rates may increase, along with attendant health effects. What should we do when efforts to improve population health increase health disparities? Does it matter if we think that the initial disparity is unjust, and we therefore make it worse while trying to improve health? Is it fair if better-off groups improve more and increase their relative advantage as long as worse-off groups improve somewhat?

Our task in this chapter is to examine this troubling conflict between reducing unjust health disparities and promoting population health fairly.

RACE AND GENDER INEQUITIES ILLUSTRATED

It is important in what follows to have clearly in mind some examples of health inequalities between groups that we agree are unjust.

Consider the following examples of health inequalities that most people would consider unjust:

A. *Race inequity in access:* Controlling for type of payer, treatment site, and clinical condition, physicians underutilize important treatments, such as cardiac catheterization (Schulman et al 1999) and renal transplantation (Epstein et al. 2000), in blacks as compared to whites. The Schulman study used black and white male and female actors in videotapes. They were dressed similarly and had matching educational and occupational profiles and were given identical clinical descriptions. Blacks were offered catheterization less than whites, and women less then men, with black women receiving the lowest referral rate. The Epstein study noted that there was overutilization among whites even while there was underutilization for blacks.

Whether we think there is overt racism among providers, or subconscious stereotyping that has no malicious intent, the effect is an inequality of access to crucial, even lifesaving, interventions. This inequality of access by race (as well as by gender, in the Schulman study) makes this an example of a health inequity. Significant research is needed to uncover the exact features of provider beliefs about patients that contribute to these differences (van Ryn 2002), though we know that there is negative perception of blacks and lower SES patients on such important issues as intelligence, affiliation with patients, and the likelihood of patient compliance (van Ryn and Burke 2000). Understanding the source of the discrimination will be important to devise interventions that remedy the problem.

B. *Health inequity directly induced by the experience of racism:* There is substantial evidence for direct negative health effects of the experience of racism. A comprehensive review of recent literature (Williams et al. 2003) found that a majority of studies showed a strong association between the experience of discrimination and (1) psychological distress, (2) major depression, and (3) physiological measures of stress, such as blood pressure (Harrell et al. 2003). With regard to the last, there is some evidence that people who internalize rather than resist discrimination have higher blood pressure, so coping strategies moderate the effects of discrimination for some people (Krieger and Sidney 1996; Noh and Kaspar 2003). Since racism has many sources, remedying the health inequity that results from it is likely to be more difficult than altering the discriminatory behavior of providers, as in the catheterization and renal transplant examples.

C. *Health inequity resulting from cumulative exposures to health risks as a result of institutional racism:* In 1990, black men at age twenty could expect to live forty-seven more years, nine with some level of disability. White men at 20 could expect to live 54.6 more years, with at least a year less of disability (Hayward and Heron 1999). Compared to white males, black males ages fifty-one to sixty-one have a higher prevalence of hypertension, stroke, diabetes, kidney and bladder problems, and stomach ulcers; whites have a higher prevalence of cardiac and chronic obstructive pulmonary disease, high cholesterol, and back and eye problems. All told, blacks have a higher mortality rate and a higher rate of disability in middle age.

SES explains most of the aggregate black–white differences in health, but we should not infer that only class and not race is to blame. The broad legacy of racism, overt and institutional, in American society disproportionately confines blacks in lower SES groups. As a result, merely pointing to the significance of SES in explaining racial disparities in health understates the unfair social and economic disadvantage suffered by blacks. This is true even if we cannot counter racial inequalities without simultaneously addressing class inequalities (Kawachi et al. 2005).

Despite the importance of SES, at each SES level the health of blacks is worse than that of whites (House and Williams 2000). In addition, segregation – including hypersegregation and other severe forms of segregation – is associated with multiple risks factors for blacks as compared to those of whites (Acevedo-Garcia et al. 2003). These health risks accumulate over a lifetime, beginning with infancy and early childhood, so that much of the middle-age increase in black mortality rates as compared to those of whites must be understood as one of cumulative disadvantage and exposure to a wider range of health risks.

Though risky individual behaviors contribute to health inequality, all the major health behaviors (smoking, excessive drinking and eating, lack of exercise) explain only 10–20 percent of SES inequalities in health. If, however, all SES-associated risk factors, including environmental exposures, and stress factors from economic vulnerability and weaker social supports, lower control over work and life, a much larger proportion (50–100 percent) of SES-associated health inequalities can be explained, suggesting a broad pattern of accumulated risk over childhood and adult life. Since the health inequalities produced by SES and race vastly exceed in scope those produced by inequalities in access to health care, broad intersectoral efforts will be needed to reduce these health inequalities.

D. *Gender inequity in the HIV/AIDS epidemic:* Girls and young women (ages fifteen to twenty-four) have a significantly higher incidence of HIV/AIDS than males of comparable age in sub-Saharan Africa (UNFPA, UNAIDS, and UNIFEM 2004). A variety of factors contribute to this difference. Although young girls have some biological vulnerability to HIV, the key determinants of health inequality are diverse: widespread poverty, which induces transactional sex at an early age, including to pay for school fees; gender inequalities in property rights and marriage and divorce rights, which give women little room to protect themselves from unsafe sex; and early marriage to much older men who may well be HIV positive. Reducing the health inequality would require not only preventive efforts in the health sector, but also educational and legal reforms that eliminate the inequality in power between genders and give these women a variety of human rights that would protect them in this epidemic.

These examples are all relatively uncontroversial instances of health inequities. In addition, each would count as a race or gender inequity in health on the account provided in Chapter 3, since each involves an unjust distribution of the socially controllable factors affecting health. This claim is true if we are talking about access to needed medical services, as in A. It is true if we are talking about the immediate health consequences of discriminatory practices that violate protections of equality of opportunity, as in B or C. And it is true if we are talking about violations of both basic liberties and the protection of opportunity, as in D.

In each of these cases, we have clear reasons of justice to intervene to reduce the health inequality. In some cases, the point of intervention may be clearer: Perhaps we can change provider utilization decisions in A, and thus access, more easily than we can reduce the exposure to racism and its bad direct effects on health in B or indirect ones in C. Whatever we do, reducing inequities requires an investment of resources. We turn to the distributive implications of such investments now.

ENCOUNTERS WITH UNSOLVED RATIONING PROBLEMS

Pursuit of the health-related Millennium Development Goals (MDGs) provides an interesting example of how unsolved distributive problems arise within efforts to reduce health inequalities. Unlike the examples of race and gender just discussed, and to which we return shortly, the MDG goal of inequality reduction is not based on the explicit judgment that the inequality is unjust. Still, it moves us beyond the moral neutrality of the medical rationing cases because it assumes that the inequalities are unacceptable and should be reduced. Five of the eight internationally negotiated MDGs directly reduce inequality, since their targets aim at reducing poverty or providing primary education to those who lack it. The three health targets, however, apply to the whole population, that is, as an aggregate, such as the under-five child mortality rate.

David Gwatkin (2002) models two extreme approaches to these aggregate health goals. A maximizing approach seeks rapid achievement of the target goal by directing resources to those population subgroups who are already better off but easier to reach and improve. It will increase intracountry inequality, yet is likely to be attractive to international donors aiming to show rapid progress. From their perspective, the maximizing strategy may also reduce embarrassing inequalities across countries more rapidly. In contrast, an egalitarian approach aims to help those who are worst off (within each country) first, then the next worst-off, and so on. It sacrifices some aggregate health benefit in order to give priority to those who are worse off and whose child under-five mortality rate may be harder to improve. But how much priority? How much sacrifice of aggregate mortality of children under age five should we accept in order to give greater benefits to the worst-off groups? The problem also can be posed as a conflict between best outcomes and fair chances. Best (aggregate) outcomes involve getting the numbers up quickly. But should we not give the worse-off groups a fair chance at significant benefits instead? If we pursue the maximizing strategy, the worst-off groups have little chance at some benefit.

In the Gwatkin example, nothing explicit is said about the injustice of the baseline inequality, although the MDG goals imply that high levels of poverty and avoidable child mortality are unacceptable. Nevertheless, reasonable people may still disagree about the trade-offs involved and give weight to different policy alternatives. If the worst-off group with regard to under-five child mortality happens to be an ethnic minority that has long suffered exclusion and discrimination, then Gwatkin's example more closely resembles cases of inequity discussed in the previous section. Similarly, if the next worse-off group lives in a very poor agricultural region that has been underserved by public health and medical interventions, their disadvantage also counts as an inequity. Does making the injustice of the baseline more explicit affect our thinking about what trade-offs between equity and maximization we would consider acceptable?

How Much Priority Should Be Given to Reducing Existing Health Inequities?

Consider the problem by focusing on an actual clear example of a health inequity. When we understand the determinants of the gender inequality in HIV/AIDS prevalence among people ages fifteen to twenty-four in southern Africa, there is no question that the inequality is an inequity that should be redressed. With an international effort to provide ARTs underway, we might think that one indicator of fair access to treatments would be to match prevalence to treatment rates. That is, in this age group, we should treat more women than men. Suppose that this would be difficult because of the social stigma facing infected women. Accordingly, suppose that efforts to enroll proportionally more women for treatment involve treating fewer people overall because it is easier and quicker to enroll men.

Of course, higher rates of treatment will not redress the inequality in prevalence itself. That would require changing gender-biased divorce and marriage laws, eliminating gender inequalities in property rights, eliminating school fees so that young girls would not have to resort to transactional sex to pay them, and so on. It would also involve public health measures that reduced sexually transmitted diseases and provided effective education about safe sex.

An international agency understanding this situation might conclude that it could use its resources for treating HIV/AIDS patients more efficiently if it maximized the numbers treated and did not invest heavily in trying to break down the gender barriers to treatment. Maximizing the numbers treated, rather than seeking treatment proportional to prevalence, is a best outcomes strategy. It does not give priority to the worst-off groups. Others, perhaps advocating from a human rights perspective, would accept lower treatment rates in order to invest in a more equitable policy. Reasonable people would disagree about how to make the trade-offs between health maximization and health equity. And this would happen even if all agree that the gender bias against women, and the resulting health inequity, demand redress on grounds of justice.

A similar problem can arise in the case of racial inequality in access to renal transplantation or cardiac catheterization. Suppose that we think that unconscious stereotyping explains the different utilization decisions by race (and gender, in the case of catheterization). Some might then propose addressing the problem by intensive sensitivity training of all relevant personnel, hoping to reduce the stereotyping and its racist effects. Suppose that this strategy would have its biggest impact by increasing access for blacks and women, especially black women. An alternative strategy might involve a much broader retraining effort aimed at giving all practitioners a better grasp of relevant practice guidelines. Arguably, this training might have a better aggregate impact on population health – for example, addressing the overutilization among whites of some interventions – though it may have a less focused impact on the stereotyping and would not target as directly the underutilization by blacks. Reasonable people may disagree about how to make this trade-off in effects, despite agreement on the racial injustice involved.

With these examples in mind, what can be said about the priority problem? There is considerable force to the claim that we should increase the priority we grant to those whose health is worse if this is a result of racist or sexist social policy or individual acts of racism or sexism. After all, we have a social obligation to avoid racist or sexist treatment of people, whatever its effects, and we also have a social obligation to try to preserve normal functioning in the whole population. The latter would apply even if the baseline were morally neutral, but we now owe remedy to the worst off for two weighty reasons of justice, not one. This fact of extra reasons might mean giving them more priority than they would otherwise have had.

In addition, suppose that the better-off groups were partly responsible for the discriminatory practices. Suppose further that they also derived benefit from them. Arguably, this may be somewhat the case in the gender disparity in HIV/AIDS example. (Some argue that whites benefit from racism in the United States, but although whites are better off than blacks and often have obtained privileges that blacks lack, there is strong reason to think that racism prevents blacks and whites from uniting to seek better conditions for all [Kawachi et al. 2005].) We might, on these suppositions, have further reason for increasing the priority given to those who are made worse off as a result of discrimination by those who benefit. We might think, for example, that the latter forfeit some of their claim to have their own health needs met because they compromised the health of others. In any case, we should not be complicit in sustaining the advantage they acquired illegitimately by refraining from giving more priority to those they have harmed.

But how much more priority? We should not give complete priority in the sense of redressing the effects on health of racism regardless of the sacrifices involved in the health of others. Even if the average health status of blacks is worse than that of other groups, as it clearly is in our examples, it seems wrong to meet first the health needs of blacks whose health status is not as bad as that of more seriously ill members of other groups. We should not completely override our concern to meet more serious health needs before less serious ones, which is part of our obligation of justice to promote normal functioning, just because the additional, but less important, health needs were the results of racism.[3]

Similarly, if devoting all the resources necessary to eliminating the race gap in health status to a group that is only 10 percent of the population means that a much larger proportion of the population foregoes aggregate health benefits that vastly exceed the gains to the minority, we are most likely assigning too much priority to the worst-off group.[4] Our concern to rectify intergroup inequities, reflected in giving some additional priority to meeting their needs and closing the gap, should not lead us to ignore other considerations of equity across individuals and should not lead us to ignore the aggregate impact on population health. Even if we increase priority to the group that is worst off as a result of injustice, we cannot ignore the individual or aggregate health needs of better-off groups.

The burden of responsibility or complicitness in racist or sexist practices might give us additional reason to address first the health gap of those who are victimized. Nevertheless, knowing that some groups that are largely responsible for racist or sexist health policies are the ones that also enjoy a relative health advantage as a result does not imply that we may ignore their health needs altogether. In general, we do not believe that the proper punishment for even criminal misdeeds is the denial of medical care. For example, if the physicians who are involved in reducing the access of blacks to renal transplantation and cardiac catheterization all belong to a professional group whose health status is superior, proper remedy of their misdeeds would not include denying them proper medical treatment.

Though we may give additional priority to meeting a group's health needs if they are the result of unjust social practices, we cannot give their needs complete priority. We are back to the main features of our unsolved rationing problems: Extreme views, such as either no priority or complete priority to those worst off, are implausible. Reasonable people will continue to disagree about how much additional priority to grant. Some of this disagreement may be the result of the original disagreement about how to make the trade-offs

---

[3] Temkin (1993) makes a similar point when he emphasizes the importance of focusing on individuals, not groups, in making comparisons from an egalitarian perspective.

[4] Kubzansky et al. (2001) (in Evans et al. 2001) distinguish the population impact of a policy from what happens to worse-off groups and suggest that policy should address both issues.

in the morally neutral distributive problems. But some of it may be the result of disagreements about how much weight to give to the underlying fact of injustice, be it race or gender based.

Should it, for example, matter whether the denial of treatments in the renal transplantation or cardiac catheterization examples is the result of conscious racist attitudes or simply the result of stereotypes that have a racist impact and are readily absorbed in our culture? If we suppose that the effect of either mechanism is the same – we get the same health inequity – should it matter how much we should blame those responsible? We might think that it matters because we want to single out explicit racism for special sanction. But giving more priority to blacks is not a sanction against the attitudes of the providers; rather, it is felt by other patients competing for needed services. Whether the advantage enjoyed by the white patients competing for these resources is the result of explicit racism or merely stereotyping that has racist effects seems not to matter. We want to reestablish fair access for all to needed services.

In sum, the following points have emerged from our discussion. Knowing that the health inequality between two groups is unjust may justify giving some extra priority to the worst off or may add to our concern that the worst off be given a fair chance at some benefit. There are, however, limits to the sacrifices in population health that would be acceptable as a result of attempting to reduce the health inequity. Other people also have claims of justice on measures that protect their health. In addition, although we find racism and gender bias reprehensible forms of injustice, this does not mean that those who may be complicit in them, or derive some benefit from them, lose all claim on health protection themselves. In short, reasonable people will disagree about how to make the trade-offs involved.

Improving Health at the Expense of Worsening Inequities

So far, we have been discussing contexts in which we face an existing health inequity, we have reasons of justice for reducing it, and yet we encounter other questions about distributive fairness in trying to do so. We encounter conflicting claims about fairness as well as conflicts between concerns about equity and concerns to promote aggregate population health. Similar issues arise in an even broader range of health policy contexts. Consider now cases where we aim to improve population health, but our methods either create or exacerbate health inequalities, some of which may be admittedly unjust.

David Mechanic (2002) notes that some interventions that improve population health avoid generating inequalities but others do not. The kind of intervention that improves population health while not increasing health inequalities is relatively unusual and has distinctive properties. Fluoridation of water, for example, improves the health of all who must use the water supply, independently of their demographic and behavioral features.

Other interventions – smoking cessation, for example, as we noted earlier – improve population health while disproportionately helping groups who have higher income and education.[5] In vaccination campaigns in developing countries, better-off groups seek out vaccination at higher rates than poorer, less well educated, and geographically more remote groups do. Unfortunately, many measures have this property.

Mechanic (2002) notes that black infant morality rates (IMRs) in the United States were 64 percent higher than white's in 1954 but were 130 percent higher in 1998, even though white rates dropped by 20.8 per 1,000 and black rates dropped by 30.1 per 1,000. One issue is how we make the racial comparison: Should we focus on the more rapid decrease in black IMR, which emphasizes improvement, or on ratios between black and white rates, which emphasize the gap? This is not a real choice, since both matter. In this and other cases, Mechanic concludes that it is reasonable to accept *increasing* health inequalities (as measured by the ratios) that result from policies that improve population health as long as the health of all groups is being improved. Accordingly, there should be no real complaint about the ongoing (and increasing, from the perspective of ratios) inequality, given the fact of improving black rates.

Mechanic's conclusion requires more careful consideration. Suppose that we have two interventions (in any sector and involving any novel technology) that both raise the health of all groups. If intervention A does less for those who are worse off than B but much more for those who are much better off, then both satisfy Mechanic's criterion, which fails to tell us how to choose between them. We may have strong views about whether to pursue A or B, depending on further facts about the magnitude of the effects or other facts about the sizes of the groups and thus the total impact of the programs. In addition, if the initial inequality is one that society is responsible for causing through unfair policies, there may be, as we noted, a special obligation to give more weight to equity than to maximizing aggregate population health. If those who are better off are in part responsible for the inequality, or even if they simply benefit from it, there may be even more reason to trade some benefits to them in favor of a policy that emphasized giving priority to those unjustly worse off. But just how much sacrifice of benefits to others we should make is something reasonable people will disagree about.

In addition to the problems of magnitude – how much inequality is generated by alternatives and how much improvement is sacrificed if greater equality is pursued – there are issues about speed. Historical injustices that underlie many health inequalities, as in our racism and gender bias examples, are long-standing. Surely we owe some reasonable rate of progress

---

[5] There is some evidence that lower-status groups try to stop smoking as frequently as higher-status groups, but they are less successful (Barbeau et al. 2004).

toward eliminating them – let alone not increasing them (Held 1973). But how fast is fast enough? Here too people are likely to disagree, in part because they may disagree about how much current responsibility society has for the historical injustice, but also because policies involving different rates of progress will include new versions of the same distributive problems we have been discussing.

Some of our difficulty in addressing these issues comes from our lack of precision in quantifying how the strategies or interventions we pursue will affect population health as a whole and that of various subgroups. We cannot, for example, simply look at the IMR record and identify the interventions most responsible for aggregate or disaggregated changes. Some other measures might offer greater promise of doing that – perhaps cardiac mortality or morbidity rates, since we may be able to note points at which specific interventions, including smoking cessation, dietary changes, introduction of screening measures, introduction of aspirin, statins and other treatments, had an impact and try to quantify that impact. We might then have better illustrations of the magnitude of effects in the aggregate and across groups so that we can better model our discussion of hypothetical differences using actual evidence. This may help us think about these issues more clearly in light of what matters most. This intersection of a social science and an ethical agenda is clearly suggested by our discussion.

Mechanic's criterion, in short, has the same distributive problems we have been considering. Reasonable people will disagree about which policy, A or B, to pursue. The scope of the problems due to these unsolved rationing problems is very great: They go well beyond medical resource allocation for individuals and pose dilemmas for population health. They pose these dilemmas regardless of whether the baseline distribution is described in morally neutral terms or is a clear case of injustice. They pose these dilemmas whether we are trying to reduce health inequities or whether we are trying to avoid making them greater.

THE COMPLEXITY OF INEQUALITY ITSELF

Another source of complexity in the problem of reducing health disparities derives from what Larry Temkin (1993) has identified as the "complexity of inequality." Temkin gives a schematic description of situations in which two or more groups of individuals differ in their levels of well-being. He then asks, "Which situation has the worse inequality?" The question is normative, not descriptive, for he is not asking which has more inequality. Specifically, someone who is worse off has a complaint, he argues, about the unfairness of the inequality. The strength of that complaint, however, depends on whether we compare those who are worst off (1) with those who are best off, (2) with all those better off than they are, or (3) with the average to determine the magnitude of their complaint. To determine when one inequality is worse than another, we must not only assess the strength of each complaint, but we must aggregate those complaints within each situation. Here too there are three approaches to aggregation: We can adopt a maximin egalitarian view of how to sum up complaints, an additive view, or a weighted additive view.[6] The nine combinations of these bases for judging inequalities better or worse yield somewhat divergent judgments about cases, including ones with multiple groups and ones involving welfare transfers among groups. Though all nine approaches, for example, might prefer to make the worst-off individual or group better before giving comparable benefits to any of the other individuals or (equal-sized) groups, they will differ on judgments about many other cases.

Temkin argues that none of these nine combinations can be dismissed outright as inconsistent or otherwise completely implausible. If so, then reasonable people – even egalitarians – will often disagree about which situation is worse with regard to inequality than another. This source of disagreement is likely to be present in our thinking about alternative scenarios for reducing admittedly unjust inequalities in health as well. Some such inequalities will be judged worse than others, and yet reasonable disagreement about how to make that judgment will persist.

Disagreement in judgments about when one inequality is worse than another may be part of what underlies disagreements about how much priority to give the worst-off individuals or groups. After all, how much priority we might want to give may vary with how strong we think the claims of the worst off are, and that in turn may depend on whether we compare them to the best off, to the average, or to all who are better off. It may be, however, that the disagreement about how much priority is independent of some of the disagreements is about when an inequality is worse. That would be the case if the concern that underlies the judgment about priorities is not primarily egalitarian but, say, some other consideration of justice.

Temkin and I agree that the kind of disagreement he analyzes does not imply that the concept of inequality is inconsistent, incoherent, or even ambiguous. Accordingly, I conclude that the reasoning behind the disagreements needs to be addressed using a fair, deliberative process. Temkin believes that although unfair inequalities always count for *something* when we make judgments about the best outcome and the best thing to do, all things considered, equality is only one of many considerations. Since other values must be considered, different people, including different types of egalitarians, may assign different weight to the purely egalitarian consideration given their different views about other values. In short, reasonable people will disagree. Temkin's seminal work on inequality and egalitarianism

---

[6] The additive view simply sums up complaints; the weighted additive view weights complaints by seriousness before adding them; the maximin egalitarian view aggregates the complaints of those who are worst off. See Temkin (1993: Ch. 2).

thus opens the door to a reliance on fair, deliberative process for resolving disagreements about how much to weigh equality against other values, at least in real time and under the pressure of pragmatic considerations.

Despite this potential point of convergence between Temkin's egalitarianism and the account I have developed, there is an important difference as well, for my version of health egalitarianism is not the strict egalitarianism Temkin argues for. To see the point, consider an implication of the account of health as normal functioning developed earlier. Health, understood as the absence of departures from normal functioning (or pathology, as in Chapter 2), is a finite or limited concept, unlike income or wealth. This conception matches the way health is viewed in the actual work of medicine and public health, where it is treated as a threshold (or, better yet, a ceiling) that we strive to reach but not exceed. In this regard, it is unlike money: We can always have more, without limit.[7] As a result of this fact about health, the ultimate goal of what I think of as health egalitarians and health maximizers is identical: Make all people completely healthy. Nevertheless, health egalitarians – who pursue just health as I have described it – and health maximizers clearly differ in their strategies for achieving this ultimate goal. The former, but not the latter, pursue some forms of equity in the distribution of health, even at the expense of aggregate population health. At the same time, my health egalitarians are not strict egalitarians of the sort Temkin defends; nor are they strict prioritarians (Parfit 1995), at least not ones who give strict priority to those who are worst off. This middle ground needs some clarification.

My health egalitarians are not strict Temkin-style egalitarians because they would not consider it better in any way to "level down" the health of those in better health, such as those with sight, to create more equality with those who have worse health, the blind. Specifically, they would not see that situation as in any way better because more people, rather than fewer, would now fall short of full health, the health egalitarian's ultimate goal. (In contrast, if we forego some health benefits to those with better health in order to give some priority to those who have worse health, as my health egalitarians would, the leveling down is offset by benefits to those with worse health.[8]) Of course, Temkin does not view such leveling down as better, all things considered, but only better with regard to equality, which for him is one (important) value among others. My health egalitarians are also not strict prioritarians – or maximiners of health – who insist on maximizing

---

[7] Nevertheless, some enhancements might make us superhealthy, for example, because we have better resistance to disease; some subjective views of well-being, such as welfare-based ones, may involve psychological limits, making it a limit concept as well. Still, if well-being is a composite of various objective and subjective components, and income or wealth is included, then it shares the fate of income and wealth.

[8] This is not a real leveling down since only a potential health gain is not delivered and no group's health is actually reduced.

health for those in the worst health before making any effort to improve the health of others. Indeed, it is because of the reasonable disagreements about *how much priority* to give to those who are worse off (among other disagreements) that we must rely on accountability for reasonableness to arrive at fair and legitimate decisions. Health egalitarians, as I am using the term to characterize those pursuing just health, fall in between strict egalitarians à la Temkin and strict health prioritarians. Although I here retain the term health egalitarian, even though my health egalitarians might well be considered prioritarians, I do not want to quarrel about the term. My account is a claim about what justice requires – and here that falls in between strict egalitarianism and strict prioritarianism.[9] We need fair, deliberative process to find an acceptable middle ground.

REASONABLE DISAGREEMENTS AND ACCOUNTABILITY FOR REASONABLENESS

The central argument of this chapter has been that reducing unjust inequalities faces unexpected complexity in the pursuit of justice. Even where health inequalities between groups are clearly unjust and we have good reasons of justice for reducing them, we still encounter unsolved distributive problems. We identified three sources of reasonable disagreement: (1) preexisting disagreements about how to address the priorities, aggregation, and best/outcomes fair chances problems that arise in all resource allocations, including these decisions aimed at reducing health inequalities; (2) disagreement about how much to weigh the injustice of the baseline against

[9] Justice, on my view, agrees more with some versions of egalitarianism that Temkin distinguishes (some approaches to judging inequality better or worse) than with others. Given the ultimate health egalitarian goal of making all people fully functional over a normal life span, it makes sense to judge the magnitude of the complaint of those in ill health by comparison to the standard of the best-off group. (This comparison with the best-off group is similar to the method used in one important summary measure of population health intended to measure the total burden of disease in a population. DALYs measure the loss of health compared to a standard of what the best-off group in the world, the Japanese, actually enjoys.) Adopting this perspective makes just health agree more with one of the forms of egalitarianism Temkin distinguishes than with others.

To see the point, consider a health version of what Temkin (1993: 27) calls "The Sequence" (here I substitute health status for welfare). The Sequence consists of a set of situations that differ from each other in the following way: In the first, ninety-nine people are completely healthy and one is in poor health. In the next, two are in poor health and ninety-eight are completely healthy. Each successive situation adds one more to the number of those in poor health and subtracts one from the group in good health. The last situation has ninety-nine in poor health and one who remains completely healthy. Temkin argues that from the egalitarian perspective of judging how bad each situation is, three views remain plausible: It gets worse and then better; it gets worse and worse, and it gets better and better. From the perspective of my view of justice and health, however, the situation gets worse and worse – in agreement with what some but not all types of egalitarians might believe.

other issues of fair distribution posed by these distributive problems; and (3) Temkin-type disagreements about when one inequality is worse than another, which may interact with the second disagreement about weighing injustice. These three sources of disagreement arise in the more common case where we are not setting out to remove injustice but only to improve population health, and we discover that our interventions tend to sustain or increase health inequalities, many of which are unjust. In short, the problem is both complex and pervasive.

How can we make decisions in the face of these controversies? My answer should hardly be surprising, in light of the discussion in Chapters 4 and 10. We need to make these resource allocation decisions in real time and in a way that is perceived to be fair by all affected by them, despite the underlying moral disagreements. As in the simpler case of the distributive problems taken alone, we must resort to a form of procedural justice. In the absence of prior agreement on principles that can resolve our disputes, we must make decisions using a process that is fair to all. The outcome of the fair process can then be accepted as fair.

I shall not repeat the points made in earlier chapters about the features of accountability for reasonableness and the rationale for them. Instead, I conclude by emphasizing the work that still must be done if that process is to be implemented. First, there must be a body of research on how those features can best be achieved at the different institutional levels at which decisions are made about improving population health and reducing health disparities. Second, as I noted earlier, we are woefully ignorant of the actual magnitudes of the trade-offs involved in one type of intervention rather than another. Our deliberations about options should be informed by the best evidence and arguments, but that is hard to do if we do not clearly understand what actually moves and how far when one or another lever is pulled. I see integrating these two bodies of research with clear normative thinking as a major challenge facing the bioethics of population health.

12

Priority Setting and Human Rights

The broad effort to improve population health and its distribution through the international legal framework of human rights is one of the most promising movements in international health.[1] What I shall refer to as a "human rights–based approach" (see "Key Features of a Rights-Based Approach to Health") has several great strengths. It establishes specific governmental accountabilities for promoting population health by articulating a right to health and related rights. It broadens the arena in which health is pursued by including various rights to a broad range of environmental, legal, cultural, and social determinants of health. It emphasizes the importance of setting specific goals and targets for achieving the rights that bear on health and then monitoring and evaluating progress toward those goals and targets. It insists on good governance, and so it stresses the importance of transparency and inclusion or participation in efforts to secure these rights. In all these respects, there is considerable agreement between the practical implications of the account of just health we have been examining and the requirements of this international legal framework.

KEY FEATURES OF A RIGHTS-BASED APPROACH TO HEALTH

In what follows, I shall understand a rights-based approach to health to include these key elements, adapted from Gruskin et al. (forthcoming):

1. *Stakeholders, including government officials, recognize the legal imperative to respect, protect, and fulfill human rights relevant to health and to the delivery*

---

[1] Although the international human rights community invokes, persuasively or not, natural law as a foundation for at least some of the human rights embodied in international law, I shall view the approach as a positive legal framework.

I draw in this chapter on collaborative work with my colleague, Sofia Gruskin, who has kindly agreed to let me use our joint work as a basis for this chapter and who has provided useful comments as well.

of health care. A broad cluster of rights is related to health, including rights to nondiscrimination, education, security, basic liberties, and political participation. A rights-based approach thus reaches beyond the health sector to emphasize the responsibility of a government in securing the health and well-being of its population.

2. *Primary responsibility rests on government officials, working with various stakeholders, to determine which interventions are most important to pursue because of their impact on population health. This requires a thorough evidence-based assessment of the epidemiological, social, economic, cultural, and legal features of the local situation and an evaluation of how different programs will help achieve the rights that impact on health.*

3. *Governments are responsible and accountable not only for the impact of decisions on the health and well-being of affected populations, but also for the manner in which decisions are made.*

4. *A rights-based approach is directly concerned with equity in the allocation and utilization of resources. Because this approach focuses on the legal and policy contexts in which interventions occure, it examines whether and how laws and policy constrain or support not only health and well-being in general but also any intended intervention. The approach provides support for accountability, transparency, and equitable resource (re)allocation through monitoring and evaluation mechanisms.*

Philosophers who complain that we lack adequate philosophical foundations for the broad range of human rights recognized in international law are right. Developing such foundations, if possible, is a worthy task, but it is not my purpose here. Instead, I build more modestly on the practical strengths of the human rights movement by addressing and trying to eliminate what I believe has been one of its important blind spots: the problem of priority setting in the face of the unsolved rationing problems discussed earlier (Chapters 4, 10, and 11). These distributive problems in part explain the difficulty of a rights-based approach in establishing priorities among claimants to different rights as well as among competing claimants to the same rights. These unsolved problems are thus at the core of a central feature of the human rights doctrine: the claim that economic, social, and cultural rights are "progressively realizable" since resource limits mean that they cannot be fully satisfied in most countries.[2] For example, the right to "the highest attainable level of physical and mental health" proclaimed in international law (ICESCR 1966) "takes into account both the individual's biological and socio-economic preconditions and a State's available resources." Signatory governments with different levels of resources are required to set benchmarks and targets against which progress toward realization of this right can

---

[2] Human rights proponents more recently have extended the notion of progressive realization to all human rights, but in this chapter we are concerned with social and economic rights.

be measured.[3] Progressive realization implies priority setting, and priority setting, even within a human rights framework, encounters the distributive problems we faced in earlier chapters.

Some philosophers insist on searching for proper philosophical foundations for human rights. They believe that only with such a theoretical underpinning can we understand better how to resolve conflicts among some of these rights that have a bearing on health. They may also believe that such foundations will enable us to set priorities in trying to realize these rights better when compliance is partial. If they are right, then the approach I take here, whatever its practical strengths, is limited by the lack of such foundations.

I am skeptical, however, that proper philosophical foundations will resolve these problems of conflict and prioritization. Instead, I see the problem of priority setting, among conflicting rights and among the means of realizing them, as structurally very similar to the priority-setting problem addressed in earlier chapters. Just as a plausible general theory of justice for health and health care leaves us with unsolved resource allocation problems, so too a theory that provides foundations for the broad range of human rights that are relevant to population health will leave us with the same unsolved problems, for they are perfectly general and apply to the distribution of many goods governed by various human rights. I do not argue for this strong claim in what follows, however, settling for a more modest task.

My goal in this chapter is, first, to show how the priority-setting problem we addressed in Chapter 4 also arises in the context of human rights. A human rights approach to health encounters reasonable disagreements about priorities in designing institutions that improve compliance with human rights under nonideal conditions, including severe resource limits. A human rights approach to improving population health must resolve those disagreements in a way that makes the outcomes legitimate.

My further goal in this chapter is to show that the shared problem has a shared solution. Accountability for reasonableness, the account of fair, deliberative process discussed in Chapter 4, strengthens a human rights approach to health. It specifies the conditions under which negotiations among rights proponents, various stakeholders, and governments about progressive realization should be carried out. It provides a coherent rationale for those conditions. Accordingly, it adds legitimacy to the priority setting that must go on as the details of progressive realization are worked out. As

---

[3] The UN Commission on Human Rights (2003/28) specifically "Urges States to take steps, individually and through international assistance and cooperation, especially economic and technical, to the maximum of their available resources, with a view to achieving progressively the full realization of the right of everyone to the enjoyment of the highest attainable standard of physical and mental health by all appropriate means, including particularly the adoption of legislative measures."

we shall see, accountability for reasonableness also enables human rights advocates to respond to an important criticism: that the vagueness or inde-terminacy of progressive realization allows some states to hide their unwill-ingness to improve population health behind claims of severe resource limits (Chapman 1997; Chapman and Russell 1998; Torres 2005). Since a human rights approach already contains features that fit well with the key require-ments of accountability for reasonableness – an emphasis on transparency, on stakeholder involvement, and on good governance – this account of fair process is by no means an alien graft from work in distributive justice. In addition, human rights proponents have considerable experience in estab-lishing government accountability for specific goals. This can strengthen the general approach embodied in accountability for reasonableness.

MORAL RIGHTS AND HUMAN RIGHTS TO HEALTH
AND HEALTH CARE

There is an important difference between the approach taken in this book to justifying a moral right to health and the positivist legal approach to human rights that is embodied in international law.[4] In Chapter 1, I argued that moral rights should not be considered a starting point for thinking about what we owe each other in terms of protecting health – as legal rights are in international agreements about human rights. Rather, they should emerge from broader work in political philosophy. Accordingly, I used the observation that protecting normal functioning helps to protect fair equality of opportunity to ground my view that the moral right to health and health care is a special instance of a broader right to fair equality of opportunity (Chapters 2 and 5). If we have a social obligation to ensure fair equality of opportunity, we have an obligation to promote normal functioning, and our moral right to health and health care is the corollary of those obligations.

Obviously, this account of a moral right to health and health care does not provide a foundation for the much broader range of human rights that are included in international agreements. My focus is on just health. My account also arguably fails to provide a foundation for a *human* right to health and health care, one that arises simply because we are human. Rather, the moral right to health I have discussed is tied to the terms of fair cooperation that

---

4 The human right to health and health care is affirmed inter alia, in article 25, para-graph 1, of the Universal Declaration of Human Rights, article 12 of the International Covenant on Economic, Social and Cultural Rights, and article 24 of the Convention on the Rights of the Child. See http://www.unhchr.ch/Huridocda/Huridoca.nsf/TestFrame/267fa9369338eca7c1256d1e0036a014?Opendocument (accessed August 23, 2005). See also Convention to Eliminate All Forms of Discrimination Against Women (CEDAW) at http://www.un.org/womenwatch/daw/cedaw; see also the International Convention on the Elimination of All Forms of Racial Discrimination (CERD) at http://www.ohchr.org/english/law/cerd.htm.

are justifiable within a society of free and equal individuals. Its claim to universality, as a human right independent of the social relationships that exist in a state or society, is not thereby established. (We shall see some implications of that restriction in Chapter 13.) As attractive as the idea of human rights seems to many people, my account is narrower in both scope and justification.

Because of this narrower scope and justification, the moral right to health and health care that I defend has a specific content only relative to the conditions in a specific society. The specific content of a right consists of the entitlements it includes. Those entitlements are determined by the reasonable choices made by appropriate agents in that society when they decide how to promote normal functioning under resource constraints. As I suggest in Chapter 5, those entitlements should be specified by decision makers who are held accountable for the reasonableness of the limits they set.

This restriction on how we specify the content of the right to health means, for example, that we cannot directly infer from (1) the moral fact that Jack has a right to health care and (2) the empirical fact that an experimental pancreas transplant offers him his only chance at survival that (3) Jack is entitled to that transplant. Jack's medical entitlements – given his right – depend both on his condition and on the array of interventions it is reasonable to provide the population of which he is a member. That reasonable array in turn depends on what we know is effective, what resources we have, and what priority should be given to meeting his need compared to those of others. If pancreas transplants are of unproven efficacy, or if their cost or cost-effectiveness makes their inclusion in a benefit package unreasonable, given what else it would be better to include, then coverage for such transplants may be denied for Jack and others. Although a moral right to health is grounded in the general idea that we have an obligation to protect opportunity by promoting normal functioning, its specific content is in this fundamental way system relative.

We might think, in contrast, that Jill's human right to the "highest attainable standard" of health has a specific content, that is, it gives rise to specific entitlements, independently of the features of the state in which she lives. After all, isn't it a *human* right and not just a moral right of citizens of a just state? It should not matter where Jill lives; she should have the same entitlements as humans anywhere. For example, we might think that if the highest attainable level of health is what she might get in Japan, where she would be entitled (we may suppose) to a pancreas transplant, then that sets the standard and specifies what Jill is entitled to as a human with this right in, say, Malawi. That thought would be mistaken.

Despite the contrasting universality that comes from declaring certain rights to be *human* rights (rather than, say, the moral rights of citizens), in practice the content of the rights that emerge similarly depend on the conditions in a specific state. Signatory states have an obligation to "respect, protect, and fulfill" these rights relevant to health (CESCR 2000). Consequently, the actual entitlements that follow from an individual's human right to health and health care – and thus what claims that individual can make on relevant authorities and providers – similarly depend on the resources, including the political resources, available in those states. This is what progressive realization of a right to health means. Of course, those resources may be expanded as a result of cooperation among signatory states and their contributions to those who need assistance.

Progressive Realization of a Right to Health

The doctrine that a right to health and health care is progressively realizable recognizes that full realization of a right to health is beyond the capacity of many states. Accordingly, decisions will have to be made about what entitlements a right to health actually assures under existing limits. The problem goes beyond low-income developing countries. Even wealthy states may not be able to provide every treatment that has some efficacy to all citizens who need them, let alone aid persons in other states to get them, regardless of cost, as the troublesome queues in some universal coverage systems in wealthy countries attest. Consequently, as in the case of the moral right, we cannot infer that because Jill has a human right to health and health care, as recognized by her state, she is entitled to whatever treatment may improve her health, such as the pancreas transplant, regardless of what it is feasible and reasonable for the state to offer.

This point about specific entitlements is not a challenge to the claim that the right to health and health care is a right of individuals. That remains the case for both the moral right argued for in Chapters 2 and 5 and the human right agreed to by international proclamations and treaties. Rather, it is a challenge to the idea that Jack's or Jill's having a moral right or a human right to health and health care implies that they are entitled to every intervention that might improve their health.[5] How we specify those entitlements is the problem of priority setting, and it lies at the core of the idea of progressive realization of the human right to health.

The example of the pancreas transplant should not mislead us into focusing narrowly on medical services. Assuring the progressive realization of the right to health and health care recognized in international law, like the satisfaction of the moral right to health discussed earlier, is a complex task that

---

[5] This point has implications for litigation aimed at securing a specific treatment for an individual or a group when that treatment is not covered within a public (or mixed) insurance system but the system is governed by a legal "right to health care," whether it derives from a state's constitution, legislation, or international agreements. Arbitrary or discriminatory exclusions might violate that right claim, but I am suggesting that in general it is not the court's role to determine the content of a benefit package to which individuals have entitlements.

cuts across all sectors (see Chapters 3 and 7). A key strength of the human rights approach is that it emphasizes that realizing the right to health is closely related to and depends on the political and legal satisfaction of other rights, including rights to food, housing, work, education, nondiscrimination, privacy, access to information, and freedoms of association, assembly, and movement, as well as adequate resources and a properly functioning public health sector (CESCR 2000). In considering how to improve realization of that right from any given starting point, complex decisions and choices have to be made about the distribution of the many determinants of population health.

In a human rights approach to health, negotiation among various stakeholders, with particular responsibility on the part of government officials, is necessary to determine which interventions may have the biggest impact on health or meet the most important health needs, thereby moving a system closer to providing what a right to health or health care requires. There will be reasonable disagreements about how resources can most effectively be used and about what kinds of partial improvements – for example, in access to care – should be emphasized. Decisions about these issues will create winners and losers. Consequently, it is important to establish that all are being treated fairly and that the outcome of the negotiation is perceived as legitimate.

In setting priorities across all the interventions that might improve realization of the various rights, we must assess complex epidemiological, economic, technical, and other information. Reasonable people may disagree even about these empirical matters. Setting priorities, however, as we have seen, generally gives rise to moral disagreements as well. It is not always clear which actors are most appropriate in resolving them. Consequently, a legitimacy problem arises even for advocates of human rights and for the government officials they negotiate with. The legitimacy problem concerns not only *who* can resolve these disputes, but also *under what conditions* the resolution becomes legitimate. For example, what are the grounds for setting priorities in a way that emerges from this negotiation? Are those grounds publicly accessible to people affected by the decisions? Are they based on public health needs and an adequate consideration of alternative reasons and evidence? Can they be revised in light of new evidence and arguments? The legitimacy of decisions (as noted in Chapter 4) depends largely on being able to answer these questions appropriately.

The moral disagreements across sectors and within the health sector involve the same kinds of distributive problems that we encountered earlier in this book. How much priority should we give to the worst-off individuals or groups? When does aggregating modest benefits to larger numbers of people outweigh providing significant benefits to fewer people? Must we give all people a fair chance at some benefit rather than favor allocating resources only to those with the best outcomes? We saw that a straight

health-maximizing view raises ethical issues in all of these distributive problems, and we saw that most people do not support straight maximizing
approaches, however traditional they may be in thinking about public
health.

The simple health-maximizing approach is rejected by both human rights
advocates and distributive justice advocates for the same fundamental reason. Both focus on individuals' or groups' claims to goods and services that
protect their health, and not simply on maximizing some good (health or
welfare) in the aggregate for the whole population. Consequently, these
unsolved rationing problems lie at the core of disputes about implementing
rights. Strikingly, as we saw in Chapter 11, these distributive problems must
be addressed even when we know from the start that some health inequalities are unjust and violate the right to health or health care of the worst-off
groups. The problem is the same from the point of view of distributive justice
or a legal perspective on human rights. Since we also do not know how to
weight the injustice of the initial distribution against the other distributive
considerations, we have a doubly complex priority-setting problem.

THE RIGHTS-BASED APPROACH TO HEALTH AND PRIORITY
SETTING: A GENERIC ILLUSTRATION

To illustrate how a human rights–based approach to health unavoidably
encounters a difficult priority-setting problem, I shall describe a hypothetical
context that is typical of many settings where this approach is attempted.
To give this generic illustration some of the texture of a real case, I also
provide some fictional background information. The fiction unfortunately
approximates reality in many countries.

Background Information about Maternal and Reproductive Health

Suppose we are working in a country of some 60 million people with a gross
domestic product per capita (GDPpc) of $4,500, better than that of the
Philippines ($3,200 GDPpc) but worse that than of Iran ($5,500 GDPpc).
With a sizable portion of the population living on less than $2 per day,
poverty remains a major problem. An increasingly stable democratic government shows some concern about rights, and a minister of health is especially
determined to improve maternal and child health.

This task is large and complex. According to Demographic and Health
Survey (DHS) figures for 2002–3, the national infant mortality rate is 35
per 1,000, while the maternal mortality rate is very high, 310 per 100,000
births. Only 62 percent of deliveries are attended by skilled personnel. Disaggregating these figures reveals considerable regional variation: In one
province the estimated maternal mortality rate is 225, while in another it
is 635 and in yet another it is a staggering 950. Disaggregating in another

way, adolescent girls and young women have maternal mortality rates two to four times those of older women in a country where 10 percent of women have children before age twenty.

One aspect of the problem is access to relevant services and interventions. By government stipulation, only legally married women can use family planning services. Emergency obstetric services are concentrated in urban centers, posing significant geographical barriers to many women with complications in pregnancy, such as obstructed labor. Funding higher-level care in urban tertiary-care centers absorbs a significant part of the health budget, leaving other services poorly funded. Some NGOs provide reproductive health services that supplement government services. In addition, cultural attitudes favor the use of traditional birth attendants rather than trained personnel even when the latter exist.

Cultural traditions in many parts of the country push girls into early marriage without free and full consent. Although a marriage law states that marriages must be agreed to by both partners and that the legal age of marriage for women is sixteen (nineteen for men), a loophole in the law allows children under age twenty-one to be married with the consent of their parents. As a result, communities often support the marriage of young girls under age sixteen: Over 15 percent of the women in one province were married before age sixteen. The lack of cultural and legal support for the empowerment of women can be seen as key factors in poor maternal health and high rates of maternal mortality.

Available Program Options

The government and its partners must assess several new proposals intended to resolve certain problems of maternal and child health. Each of the following proposals would contribute to progressive realization of a right to health and health care. Some are the immediate responsibilities of the health sector; others fall to other sectors of government, such as by promoting broader empowerment of women. We shall see that reasonable disagreement about priorities among them will arise for a rights-based approach in much the same way that it does for our account of just health.

1. *An outreach program to deliver family planning services to married women, including education about the advantages of trained birth attendants:* This preventive program addresses both the relatively high fertility rates in some areas and the cultural barriers to using skilled birth attendants. It does nothing by itself, however, about the relative lack of skilled birth personnel in some areas. It also favors older married women, because adolescent married women have little autonomy and are hidden at home. Accordingly, this program may reduce aggregate rates of maternal and child mortality even as it increases inequalities among

subgroups. Targeting younger married women requires overcoming the cultural barriers to reaching them, say with a program that relies on community-based health workers who can reach them at home.

2. *A program to invest more heavily in emergency obstetric facilities, siting them in ways that address more underserved populations, at least in urban or semiurban areas:* This program is expensive and would compete for resources with preventive programs. It directly addresses, however, the problem of obstructed labor and other birth complications that contribute significantly to the high maternal mortality rates, whereas the outreach program does not. Moreover, some of the proposed sites would be in extraurban areas, though in districts with better infrastructure that allows easier access. The program does little to address the geographical barriers to access to these services, for it does nothing about poor roads or missing transportation services in many rural areas. Even the proposed extraurban sites are in districts with lower maternal mortality rates than many other extraurban areas, so the program allocates scarce resources for better-served populations.

3. *A program to provide trained attendants at all peripheral centers:* This program addresses the gap in services left by the outreach program described in Program 1. Some NGOs and the Ministry of Health (MoH) agree on the importance of this program, but they disagree on a primary component. The NGOs want to make access to birthing services free, whereas the MoH is committed to assessing user fees, which are charged for nearly all other services except vaccinations. The NGOs argue that the poorest and most vulnerable groups will revert to traditional birth attendants instead of using facilities with trained workers if user fees are retained. The MoH insists that the widespread use of such fees as an important source of revenue would be undermined if fees were waived for this service alone. The MoH is even resistant to NGOs launching their program without user fees while the MoH program contains them for fear of its larger effect on the population.

4. *A proposal to strengthen the marriage law by closing the loophole that allows families and communities to permit marriage at a very early age:* Closing this legal loophole that now allows cultural traditions to disempower women is crucial to work upstream from the health system itself. Unfortunately, it will be difficult to secure the political commitment needed to confront the cultural forces that support the status quo. Though many NGOs and even groups within the MoH support this legal strategy, critics argue that it will mean spending so much political capital that other measures may suffer, including those focused on the health sector, where there is substantial political support for other measures. In addition, this legal strategy may take years to pass and implement: Assuring its enforcement would provide a rallying point

for cultural conservatives, delaying its impact for a long time and possibly sidetracking measures that might produce more immediate effects.

5. *A program to increase the enrollment of girls in secondary school:* A system of incentives for families that send their girls to school through the secondary level is another, longer-term way to change the social determinants of the problem. If families are rewarded for keeping girls in school longer, it will delay the age of marriage, enable women to wield more influence within the household, and give them more opportunities outside it as well. In addition, better-educated women provide better health care for their children, a fact observed across many settings.

The Priority-Setting Problem

Ideally, were resources available, all these programs would be initiated together since all have considerable promise. But resources are limited and priorities must be set, as the concept of progressive realization implies. What should they be?[6]

A key element of a rights-based approach involves analyzing which rights and which population groups are positively or negatively impacted by each intervention. Specific attention must be paid to who benefits most, and in what ways, from each intervention and who would be left out. Thus, the importance of Program 5 in providing a right to education for girls speaks in its favor, and the potential long-term impact of reducing early adolescent birth rates and the complications of such births would have to be estimated. Program 4 would make similar contributions outside the health sector by empowering women to improve their own reproductive health over time. But neither of these programs addresses the immediate needs of women at greatest short-term risk of complications from unattended childbirth. Women whose right to health is compromised by their lack of access to appropriate treatments are more directly affected by Programs 1, 2, and 3 than they are by Programs 4 and 5. In addition, the most vulnerable group and those most at risk, young unmarried women, are not served by any of these programs, creating serious problems of exclusion and discrimination.

---

[6] The priority-setting problem in the hypothetical situation arises from the perspective of the opportunity-based account of justice and health developed earlier. Like the rights-based approach, just health requires both health sector and non–health sector efforts to promote normal functioning. Accordingly, all five programs find support within such a theory. Both the health sector approaches (Programs 1–3) and the non–health sector approaches (Programs 4 and 5) have an impact on health and thus on opportunity. Some of them, like the education program or the program on family and property law, also impact opportunity in other ways. Like the rights-based approach, the opportunity-based account finds grounds for supporting each program but less of a basis for choosing among them.

Even young married women are hard to reach through any of them because of cultural barriers.

A rights-based approach must assess the relative impacts of each program on maternal health. However, this only *identifies* the different claimants competing for resources that would lead to better satisfaction of different rights. It does not determine which program should take priority since there is no basis for saying that claimants to one right have priority over claimants to another. We thus have an unsolved priority-setting problem across different rights.

There is also an unsolved problem of setting priorities among claimants to the same right. The issues posed by Programs 1, 2, and 3, for example, point to conflicts among claimants to the right to health care itself. One division among these competing claimants is the group that would benefit from preventive measures in the health sector (Program 1) as opposed to those who need treatment (Programs 2 and 3). Another conflict can arise among claimants served by the same program. Thus, locating resources in urban or rural areas will help different people, all of whom have reasonable right-based claims to have their health-care needs met through either preventive or curative interventions.

Attention to rights identifies these claimants and some of the issues that should be considered, including the magnitude of the benefits they might get. But it does not establish priorities among them. Noting that one program helps more people than another does not solve, for example, the rights-based problem about inequality in distributing services or satisfying these right claims. A rights framework in establishing accountability for meeting the goals and targets of such programs does not show that giving priority to one or another is the preferred solution. In short, attention to rights leaves does not set priorities among claimants to different rights and among claimants to the same rights. Accordingly, it does not set priorities among programs competing for resources, each of which arguably would improve health and satisfy of relevant rights.

One reason for our inability to resolve the conflicts among claimants within and across rights is that familiar unsolved rationing problems (see Chapter 4) arise within the various interventions. Because adolescent mothers have a mortality risk two to four times as great as that of older mothers, they are in this regard worse off than older mothers. The preventive outreach program, however, is unlikely to reach them unless a strong effort is made to reach inside their households. Such outreach is far more difficult and expensive than offering such a program to the population at large. If we give strong priority to reaching these young women, then, given resource limits, we may be unable to reach the much larger number of more accessible older mothers. Some advocates for the most vulnerable young women argue for a targeted outreach that pays less attention to households with older women of childbearing age, even if that means less overall reduction in risks. Others argue that we should aim to produce the greatest aggregate benefit, even if that means focusing very little on the hard-to-reach married adolescents. This is a moral disagreement about whether health interventions that succeed by focusing on easier-to-reach populations should be given priority over worse-off groups. There is no agreement on a distribution principle that would let us solve this problem. Because of this lack of agreement, we cannot decide which claimants have stronger claims within a rights framework.

A version of the aggregation problem also arises in deciding between the outreach prevention program or the program to increase emergency obstetric services. The obstetric services provide a very significant benefit – maternal and infant lives saved – but to a relatively few women, those who are already at the point of delivery and can get to the services readily despite geographical and other barriers. The preventive outreach program delivers a modest benefit but to much larger numbers of people in the form of some family planning services, some education about the importance of trained birth attendants, and more difficult-to-quantify reductions in the risk of maternal or infant mortality. Suppose we assume that the preventive program will not save as many lives as the surgical program in the short term, although it delivers in total a greater aggregate health benefit to the population over time than the increase in expensive obstetric services. Some would say that we should not allow that aggregation of modest benefits to many people in the preventive program to outweigh the significant benefits to a few people with the surgery. Others claim that we should put our resources where they produce the greatest aggregate health benefit and therefore favor the preventive program (we are supposing). Here too there is a fundamental moral disagreement, and we have no consensus on distributive principles to guide us. Therefore, we also cannot settle the conflict among those with competing right claims.

Finally, consider the issue about the location of treatment facilities that was raised in criticizing the emergency obstetric services. If these services are based in existing urban facilities that are already well established, we can immediately reach more people and save more lives than if we locate some of these facilities in more remote areas. A best-outcome approach would insist on locating them where more people can readily reach them, even if these are the same people who are already better served by those hospitals. But locating some facilities in more remote areas gives others a fair chance at a significant benefit, even if many women who try to reach those facilities may die and, at a minimum, must travel on much harder routes and may be in worse shape than the women who have easier access to urban health centers. How should we balance the demand that we give rural women a fair chance at a significant benefit against the competing view that we should favor getting a best/immediate outcome, even if this means that rural women have no chance at any benefit? This problem too involves moral disagreement and, as with the others, there is no consensus on moral principles that lets us resolve the dispute. Consequently, we also cannot resolve the conflict among rights claims.

Versions of these unsolved distributive problems arise in other comparisons across the proposed interventions. Because no quality services are available in peripheral centers, many communities lack trust. Because cultural attitudes are entrenched, many women may prefer traditional birth attendants to the promise of skilled ones. Consequently, many of the most vulnerable or worst-off subgroups may be hardest to persuade to use these services even if they are made available. The problem is thus similar to the one in the prevention program. Similarly, tightening the law on early marriage and enforcing it better might deliver an important benefit to a huge proportion of women. Perhaps over time, many more women would be saved by these measures than by the availability of emergency obstetric services, but the benefit is not as immediate and direct as saving lives outright by surgery. As a result, a version of the aggregation problem arises here as well, and it also infects the competing rights claims.

The winners and losers created by priority-setting choices all have right claims and claims of distributive fairness on their side. Arguably, the distributive problems just identified help explain why it is not easy to decide which claimants to different rights or even to the same right should be given priority. Neither appeals to human rights nor the appeal to general principles of distributive justice can help us agree on how to resolve these claims in setting priorities.

ACCOUNTABILITY FOR REASONABLENESS: A SOLUTION

The priority-setting problem in the human rights approach can be solved by accountability for reasonableness, the same account of fair process that addresses the priority-setting problems in just health (Chapter 4). In both contexts, we face underlying ethical disagreements, not just a lack of information or complex empirical considerations. Both human rights and distributive justice approaches focus on individuals and groups with claims to goods and outcomes that a purely maximizing strategy for pursuing population health or well-being ignores. Both human rights and distributive justice approaches attend to equity in the context of the equity–efficiency trade-offs that abound in priority setting. In both cases, accountability for reasonableness provides a way of arriving at decisions that stakeholders – both government officials and others affected by the decisions – consider fair, given the presence of underlying moral concerns, so priority setting is seen as legitimate.

Since the key elements of accountability for reasonableness are described in Chapters 4 and applied in Chapter 10 and 11, I shall not review them here. Instead, I shall concentrate on some points that are most relevant to applying this account to priority setting within a human rights approach. The points made here are in response to some objections aimed at showing that the appeal to the account is not necessary or, if it is, it is already accommodated within a human rights approach.

First, consider the objection that we do not need to appeal to fair, deliberative process because the framework of human rights, unlike general principles of distributive justice, can yield specific priorities when properly used. That is, if we just bring people together and if they reason from a human rights perspective, a unique proposal about how to improve health will emerge by consensus. Were this objection sound, the difficulties we found in setting priorities in our hypothetical case would not arise. Because the case was developed to represent a generic problem, it shows that the specific human rights that bear on health are all general, and can be realized to different degrees and differently for different subgroups. The resulting trade-offs among right claims that occur when we pursue one set of priorities rather than another are trade-offs about which reasonable people will disagree.

A second objection is that we do not need accountability for reasonableness because we already have accountability through the political process. Governments, after all, are key parties to the negotiation about priorities in a rights-based approach, along with rights advocates and other civic advocacy groups. Consequently, the public, through democratic processes, can elect other officials if it does not accept the fairness or legitimacy of specific choices about how to improve health. This objection strongly resembles an objection considered in Chapter 9 to viewing health reforms as social experiments in need of special ethical and scientific reviews. There I replied that ethical and scientific reviews of social experiments can only make political accountability more effective, since they hold up to a clear, evidence-based light the terms of the experiment and its outcome. Similarly, accountability for reasonableness enhances political accountability for the results of efforts to improve health in a rights-based approach. It enhances public learning about human rights because it makes the grounds for decisions more transparent; broadens the search for relevant reasons by including appropriate stakeholders; and requires the proper iterative airing of evidence and arguments, including mechanisms for listening to objections and appeals and revising decisions over time. It improves public understanding about the choices that must be made in order to realize these rights more effectively under resource constraints. Ultimately, there should be an improvement in political accountability, not a substitute for it.

The role of stakeholders in vetting relevant reasons demands some comment.[7] It is important that the deliberative process not deteriorate into mere

---

[7] I noted in Chapters 4 and 10 that including a broad range of stakeholders improves the deliberative process, even if it does not make it more democratic.

lobbying for specific interests. Participants have to be won to the idea that the deliberation has a common goal – progressive realization of a right to health under resource constraints. Stakeholders speak for people who have legitimate but competing rights-based claims, not just self-interested desires. They must look for priorities that respect those claims. In effect, they seek a *common or public good* that all engaged in the priority-setting process must keep in mind. Just how to keep the public good in mind rather than the competing interests is a political problem of commitment that may have no general solution.

The conditions imposed on fair process for priority setting have a strong theoretical rationale, based on both procedural justice and democratic theory, but they are not by any means utopian. In earlier chapters, I noted that elements of the recommended process are already found in a wide variety of settings, ranging from NICE in the United Kingdom to Mexico and Malawi. Nevertheless, further reassurance may be necessary to show that these features are familiar to those advocating a human rights approach.

Fair Process in a Rights-Based Approach

Accountability for reasonableness provides a systematic rationale for key elements of fair process in what is commonly thought to be part of a rights-based approach. The rights-based approach thus emphasizes transparency, the gathering of appropriate evidence for an analysis of options to improve the realization of rights that impact on health, stakeholder involvement in negotiations about the goals and targets of these options, and insistence on government accountability for implementing the resulting reforms. These central elements of the rights-based approach fit well with the rationale of accountability for reasonableness, for they address the underlying moral disagreements among reasonable people in these negotiations. To see the compatibility of these elements more clearly, compare the key requirements of fair process (see Chapter 4) to those of a rights-based approach.

The publicity *condition* in accountability for reasonableness, which calls for public access to the rationales for priority-setting decisions, simply makes concrete forms of transparency and accountability already acknowledged as key components of a rights-based approach. A rights-based approach requires transparency about what interventions are on the table for discussion; it also seeks transparency about the rationale used to give priority to an area of focus. A rights-based approach further endorses the importance of publicity by insisting on directly informing affected communities of the criteria used in selecting goals and targets and the mechanisms in place to ensure government accountability (Asher 2004).

The *relevance requirement* assures that stakeholders agree on what kinds of reasons are relevant to setting priorities. This requirement corresponds to the emphasis on the participation of affected communities in a rights-based approach. Further, the vetting of various reasons and arguments in order to include all those affected by a decision, including vulnerable groups whose rights are most threatened, is familiar ground to rights activists. The search for relevance also involves a careful gathering of evidence and arguments – just the sort of analysis of the context required by a human rights approach. The rights-based approach supplements this condition by setting out specific criteria to consider in deciding on policy. For example, determination of the accessibility, availability, acceptability, and quality of the proposed intervention, as well as a focus on nondiscrimination, helps bring to the fore specific criteria important for determining relevance (CESCR 2000).

The *revisability* condition requires ongoing monitoring and evaluation of the impact of policies so that decisions can be revised in the light of new evidence and arguments. This condition fits well with the emphasis that a rights-based approach places on setting goals and targets and monitoring the effectiveness of implementation. The evidence base that results is important in establishing government accountability for the goals and targets of reforms; it also provides a basis for reassessment of tactics.

Although these key elements of accountability for reasonableness may be present in typical human rights efforts to improve health, they are not integrated into an explicit process of priority setting. What accountability for reasonableness makes explicit is the reasonable moral disagreement people will have about priorities among claimants to the same rights and to different rights that impact on health. The explicit process it establishes provides a way to achieve legitimacy in resolving these disagreements. It clarifies the conditions under which negotiations with government officials take place and so goes beyond the question of who has moral authority to the issue of how that authority is exercised. Accountability for reasonableness provides the justification for integrating these elements into an explicit, fair process for setting priorities. A human rights approach contributes legal accountability and established criteria to be debated within the process itself.

Progressive Realization Clarified

Wedding accountability for reasonableness to a rights-based approach provides a way to respond to two criticisms of the concept of progressive realization. Progressive realization, it might be argued, provides a way of hiding government unwillingness to improve health behind claims about unfortunate resource limitations. But government foot-dragging, rather than real obstacles to improved health, may in some cases explain why realization has not progressed as far as it should. On what basis can we say that progress is unacceptably slow and could have been better? Progressive realization can also seem unworkably vague: The actual content of the right to health is not specified except as the set of entitlements that emerge from negotiated attempts to improve health.[8] But there is no way to document that the adopted programs, including their negotiated targets, deliver more or fewer entitlements than some other alternative. The vagueness lies in giving us no way to determine better from worse alternatives. These charges could be made either by human rights advocates or by their critics.

Of course, there is no absolute procedural guarantee against governments hiding unwillingness to improve health behind claims about limited resources. Nevertheless, accountability for reasonableness requires the careful collection of evidence for interventions, the thorough review of arguments for establishing particular priorities, the involvement of all relevent stakeholders in the process, and transparency for all aspects of the process, including the rationales for the priorities adopted. By combining these features – which are already embraced by a human rights approach – into a coherent framework for making priority setting explicit, it provides a basis for identifying and exposing true cases of government unwillingness to promote the right to health. It even provides assessment mechanisms for testing whether government is foot-dragging in the implementation of its agreements.[9] All of these measures provide as much protection against dissimulation as possible. With them in place, progressive realization should not serve as a smokescreen.

The same measures, however, undercut the charge of vagueness. With accountability for reasonableness in place, there is no vagueness about what the outcome of an effort to improve population health and its distribution through a human rights approach would require. Moreover, since the rationale for the priorities selected includes a justification for not favoring alternatives, there is no room for vagueness to cloud what progressive realization means. The goals and targets that are agreed to, with the assurance that these will be monitored and progress evaluated, determine what set of entitlements will emerge from a specific effort to realizing a right to health.

Considerable work by rights practioners is underway to develop appropriate monitoring and evaluation tools that track progress toward the improvement of health or the realization of other rights. Thus, the Committee on Economic, Social, and Cultural Rights (CESCR 2000) called for setting benchmarks for the realization of various rights; the benchmarks involve norms of attainment that are agreed upon for the circumstances. An example might be a benchmark rate of 80 percent immunization with some

---

8 Remember that in Chapter 5, I say that the content of a right is given by the entitlements it includes.

9 Assessment mechanisms that also measure the capacity for improving health allow praise of government efforts, if praise is earned. The Benchmarks of Fairness (see Chapter 9) can be used as such an assessment tool before implementing a reform and as a monitoring and evaluation tool once reforms are put in place.

basic vaccines.[10] Of course, these norms presuppose an appropriate set of indicators that measure, qualitatively or quantitatively, the degree to which relevant outcomes or processes that bear on each right are attained (cf. Windfur 2006).

To select appropriate indicators, we must do a conceptual and normative analysis of the specific rights, identifying the various dimensions for assessing their realization. For example, a right to life might include such dimensions as "arbitrary deprivation of life," "disappearance of individuals," "health and nutrition," and "death penalty," and rates of each might be measured (Background paper 2006). The resulting proposal for a framework for an assessment and perhaps also a monitoring tool resembles in purpose and structure the Benchmarks of Fairness discussed in Chapter 9. A human rights framework replaces the Benchmarks' ethical framework that integrates concerns about equity, accountability, and efficiency, but the careful selection of criteria and subcriteria and indicators to measure their degree of satisfaction is quite similar. The human rights monitoring tool that is developed can document specific aspects of the progressive realization of a right to health after a program aimed at improving population health has been instituted. If it includes normative benchmarking, it may also help to respond to worries about government foot-dragging or lack of will.

To respond fully to the concerns about vagueness and government lack of will, however, the assessments must be informed by the account of priority setting embodied in accountability for reasonableness. We need to know that the program priorities selected are justifiable in light of the alternatives and in the face of ethical disagreements about which claimants to rights should have priority over others. This core matter of resolving reasonable disagreements under conditions that establish legitimacy is not addressed by a monitoring and evaluation tool that simply measures progress toward human rights goals. We must know that the programs in place have justifiable priorities compared to alternatives, and we cannot know this simply by measuring progress through relevant indicators. Rather, the tool must include ways of assessing the process by which priorities were set; it has to show us that the program being followed – whose progress is being evaluated – is itself the result of a decision process that is legitimate and fair to different rights claimants. Thus, the Benchmarks of Fairness include accountability for reasonableness as a requirement for resource allocation decisions, and appropriate criteria and indicators would have to be included that monitor and evaluate this aspect of the reform effort. A similar provision should be included in tools for monitoring and evaluating the progressive realization of human rights after reform efforts have been instituted.

---

[10] There is some controversy among Human rights proponents about whether the 80 percent figure is too low to use as a benchmark. See also *International Human Rights Instruments* (2006).

To conclude, I emphasize a point made earlier. The specific content of a right to health – the entitlements it includes – cannot be specified independently of the context in a given state with given resource limits and health needs. Determining those entitlements is exactly the task that is undertaken when an effort is made to improve health by appealing to a right to health. That task is complex, as we have seen. Accountability for reasonableness provides a coherent rationale for a process whose key elements are already embodied in much thinking and practice about a human rights approach to health. It adds legitimacy to the process of specifying the content of the right to health at any given time and in any given setting – at any given degree of realization. It does this in high-income countries when it is used to address limit setting in well-functioning health systems. It plays the same role in low-income countries where the realization of a right to health is much further from its goal. In both settings, it should clarify what we can truly expect from a right to health, moral or human.

13

International Health Inequalities and Global Justice

A Concluding Challenge

Disturbing international inequalities in health abound. Life expectancy in Swaziland is half that in Japan.[1] A child unfortunate enough to be born in Angola has seventy-three times as great a chance of dying before age five as a child born in Norway.[2] A mother giving birth in southern sub-Saharan Africa has 100 times as great a chance of dying in labor as one birthing in an industrialized country.[3] For every mile one travels outward toward the Maryland suburbs from downtown Washington, DC, on its underground rail system, life expectancy rises by a year – reflecting the race and class inequities in American health.[4] Are the glaring, even larger, international health inequalities also unjust?

All of us no doubt think that they are grossly unfortunate. Many of us think that they are unfair or unjust. Why should some people be at such a health disadvantage through no fault of their own, losers in a natural and social lottery assigning them birth in an unhealthy place? Others of us are troubled by the absence of the kinds of human relationships that ordinarily give rise to the claims of egalitarian justice that we make on each other – for example, being fellow citizens or even interacting in a cooperative scheme. Who has obligations of justice to reduce these international inequalities? And do those obligations hold regardless of how the inequalities came about? What institutions are accountable for addressing them?

My account of just health, alas, gives us no simple or straightforward answers to these important questions about global justice. Some will see

---

[1] 40 vs 80+ years. Available at http://www.os-connect.com/pop/p1.asp?whichpage=10&pagesize=20&sort=Country.

[2] State of the World's Children (2000), available at http://www.unicef.org/sowc00/stat2.htm; accessed August 23, 2005.

[3] See WHO/UNICEF/UNFPA (2005), http://www.childinfo.org/areas/maternal/mortality; accessed May 13, 2007.

[4] Michael Marmot, presentation at the Harvard School of Public Health, 2006.

that as a serious shortcoming, perhaps insisting that an adequate account of justice and health must apply uniformly to all citizens of the world or even the cosmos. Others are less troubled by the silence of my account because they reject the idea that justice can apply to people regardless of their relationships to each other. For them justice is fundamentally relational – indeed, it depends on the relationship of being fellow citizens in a state – and not cosmopolitan.

My task in this chapter is to point, in a very preliminary way, to a relatively unexplored middle ground where I hope it is possible to clarify what kinds of international obligations of justice exist. This effort, however, takes us into relatively unexamined territory. Unlike the applications of just health described in Part III, where I hope I have suggested some of the power of the integrated theory developed earlier, in this concluding chapter I must be much more tentative about how to map this terrain. Though it is traditional for concluding chapters confidently to wrap things up, to look proudly backward over the route taken, I think it more important to point forward to a challenging new area of work. Just health, I shall argue, has global dimensions, but plotting them in more detail than I can suggest here is a future project we must all undertake.

WHEN ARE INTERNATIONAL INEQUALITIES IN HEALTH UNJUST?

Health inequalities between social groups, we saw in Chapter 3, count as unjust or unfair when they result from an unjust distribution of the socially controllable factors that affect population health and its distribution. We used Rawls's account of justice as fairness to describe an ideally just distribution of the socially controllable factors. Specifically, Rawls's principles of justice as fairness assure equal basic liberties and the worth of political participation rights; assure fair equality of opportunity through public education, early childhood supports, and appropriate public health and medical services; and constrain socioeconomic inequalities in ways that make the worst-off groups as well off as possible. Together, this distribution of the key determinants of population health would significantly flatten the socioeconomic gradient of health and would minimize various inequities in health, including race and gender inequities.

From this ideal perspective, we see that there are indeed many health inequities – by race and ethnicity, by class and caste, and by gender – in many countries, both developed and developing. At the same time, not all health inequalities between social groups count as inequities. For example, the health inequality that results when a religious or ethnic group achieves better health outcomes than other demographic groups because of special dietary or restrictive sexual practices would not count as an inequity if appropriate health education were available to the other groups.

This account tells us when health inequalities between groups in a given society are unjust, ignoring inequalities between different societies. It tells us what we as fellow citizens owe each other in promoting and protecting health, but not what other societies owe, if anything, in terms of improving population health in less healthy societies. The account, for example, fails to address this issue: Suppose that countries A and B each do the best they can to distribute the socially controllable factors affecting health fairly, and, as a result, there are no subgroup inequities within them. Nevertheless, health outcomes are unequal between A and B because A has more resources to devote to population health. Is the resulting international inequality in health a matter of justice? Suppose that we vary the case: Now B, whether or not it has resources comparable to those of A, fails to protect its population health as best it can, leading again to population health worse than A's. Is the resulting health inequality a matter of international justice? Our account of just health informs us about intrasocietal obligations to eliminate health inequities, but it is silent about important questions of international justice.

Recasting the problem as one of human rights, specifically a human right to health and health care,[5] does not help us answer these questions about international justice for two reasons. First, the international legal obligation to secure a human right to health for a population falls primarily on each state for its own population, as we saw in Chapter 12. Although international human rights agreements and proclamations also posit international obligations to assist other states in realizing human rights (CESCR 2000), the international obligations cannot become primary in the human right to health and health care. External forces cannot assure population health across national boundaries in the same way they might intervene to prevent the violation of some other rights, even when they can afford some assistance. Domestic responsibility has primacy because assuring a right to "the highest attainable level of physical and mental health" requires countries to secure a broad cluster of rights that impact on health by establishing legal structures and other institutions that properly distribute the socially controllable factors affecting health. Thus, there is considerable practical agreement about where accountability lies for population health between a human rights approach and our account of just health (as we saw in Chapter 12), even if the human rights approach is explicit about intentional obligation to promote the realization of these rights.

Second, even when a right to health is secured to the degree possible in different states, health inequalities between them may still exist. Since conditions do not always permit everything to be done to secure a right in one country that may be feasible in another, the right to health and health care is viewed as progressively realizable (UNCHR 2003/28). Reasonable people

---

5 The right is affirmed inter alia, in article 25, paragraph 1, of the Universal Declaration of Human Rights, article 12 of the International Covenant on Economic, Social and Cultural Rights and article 24 of the Convention on the Rights of the Child. See http://www.unhchr.ch/Huridocda/Huridoca.nsf/TestFrame/267fa9369338eca7c1256d1e0036a014?Opendocument; accessed August 23, 2005.

may disagree about how best to satisfy this right, given the trade-offs priority setting in health involves (see Chapter 12). Consequently, some inequalities may fall within the range of reasonable efforts at progressive realization of the right to health. In addition, because of their unequal resources, different states may achieve unequal health outcomes while still securing the right to health and health care for their populations. Arguments that depend on appeals to human rights cannot tell us whether these inequalities are unjust and remain silent on what obligations better-off states have to address these inequalities.

Nearly all people recognize some international humanitarian obligations of individuals and states to assist those facing disease and premature death, wherever they are. However, there is substantial philosophical disagreement, even among egalitarian liberals, about whether there are also international obligations of *justice* to reduce these inequalities and to better protect the right to health of those whose societies fail to protect them adequately. Nagel (2005), who affirms these humanitarian obligations, argues that socioeconomic justice, which presumably includes the just distribution of health, applies only when people are related to each other as fellow citizens of a state. Specifically, concerns about equality are raised within states by the dual nature of individuals both as coerced subjects and as agents in whose name coercive laws are made. Rawls (1999) also did not include international obligations to assure a right to health on the list of human rights that liberal and decent societies have international obligations of justice to protect.

This "statist" view encounters a strong counterintuition. Remember the child who is so much more likely to die before age five in Angola than the one in Norway, or the sub-Saharan African mother who is 100 times more likely to die in childbirth than one in any industrialized country. Many of us think that there is something not just unfortunate and deserving of humanitarian assistance, but something unfair about the gross inequality.

Those who claim that gross health inequalities are unjust have quite different, incompatible ways of justifying that view. For example, those who believe that any disadvantage that people suffer through no fault or choice of their own is unjust (see Chapter 2) would assert that the Angolan child's disadvantage is therefore unjust. The underlying principle of justice is applied to individuals wherever they live and regardless of their relationships to others – contrary to the Rawls–Nagel account, which applies principles of justice to the basic structure of a shared society. The disadvantage of the Angolan child might also be thought unjust by those who, like Rawls or Nagel, think that principles of justice are "relational" and apply only to a basic social structure that people share, but who, unlike Rawls or Nagel, believe that we already live in a world where international agencies and rule-making bodies provide a strong global basic structure for international justice developed perhaps through a social contract involving representatives of relevant groups globally (Beitz 1979, 2000). Fair terms of cooperation involving that structure would, some argue, reject arrangements that failed to make children in low-income countries as well off as they could be. Clearly, there may be more agreement about some specific judgments of injustice than there is on the justification for those judgments or on broader theoretical issues.

I shall briefly examine two ways of trying to break the stalemate between the statist and cosmopolitan views. One approach aims for a minimalist (though cosmopolitan) strategy that focuses on an international obligation of justice to avoid "harming" people by causing "deficits" in satisfying their human rights (Pogge 2002, 2005b). This view is minimalist in the sense that people may agree on negative duties not to harm even if they disagree about positive duties to aid. This approach handles some international health issues better than others, and to identify its limitations more clearly, I shall distinguish various sources of international health inequalities, some of which are not addressed by negative duties. A more promising (relational justice) approach, which I can only briefly illustrate, requires that we work out a more intermediary conception of justice appropriate to evolving international institutions and rule-making bodies, leaving it open just how central issues of equality would be in such a context (Cohen and Sable 2006). Properly developed, such an approach may address more of the sources of international health inequalities.

HARMS TO HEALTH: A MINIMALIST STRATEGY

If wealthy countries engage in a practice or policy – or impose an institutional order – that foreseeably makes the health of those in poorer countries worse than it would otherwise be – specifically, making it harder than it would otherwise be to realize a human right to health or health care – then, Pogge (2005b) argues, it is harming that population by creating this deficit in human rights. Since this harm is defined relative to an internationally recognized standard of justice, the protection of human rights, Pogge concludes that imposing the harm is unjust. Moreover, if there is a foreseeable alternative institutional order that would reasonably avoid the deficit in human rights, there is an international obligation of justice to provide it.

It is not clear how the baseline for measuring harm is specified. When is there a deficit in a human right to health? Whenever a country fails to meet the levels of health provided, say, by Japan, which has the highest life expectancy? Or is there some other unspecified standard? Consider two examples.

The Brain Drain of Health Personnel

The brain drain of health personnel from low-income to OECD countries may exemplify Pogge's concerns. Rich countries have harmed health in poorer ones by solving their own labor shortages of trained health care personnel by actively and passively attracting immigrants from poorer countries. In developed countries such as New Zealand, the United Kingdom, the United States, Australia, and Canada, 23–34 percent of physicians are foreign-trained. In 2002, the National Health Service in the United Kingdom reported that 30,000 nurses, some 8.4 percent of all nurses, were foreign-trained.

The situation that results in developing countries is dire. Over 60 percent of the doctors trained in Ghana in the 1980s emigrated overseas (WHO 2004). In 2002 in Ghana, 47 percent of physicians' posts and 57 percent of registered nursing positions were unfilled. Some 7,000 expatriate South African nurses work in OECD countries, while there are 32,000 public health nursing vacancies in South Africa (Alkire and Chen 2004). Whereas there are 188 physicians per 100,000 population in the United States, there are only 1 or 2 per 100,000 in large parts of Africa. The brain drain does not cause all of the inequality in health workers, but it significantly contributes to it.

International efforts to reduce poverty, lower mortality rates, and treat HIV/AIDS patients – the Millennium Development Goals (MDG) agreed upon in 2000 – are all threatened by the loss of health personnel in sub-Saharan Africa. An editorial in the *Bulletin of the World Health Organization* points out that the MDG goals of reducing mortality rates for infants, mothers, and children under five require 1 million additional skilled health workers in the region (Chen and Hanvoravongchai 2005). The global effort to scale up ARTs poses a grave threat to fragile health systems, for its influx of funds – hardly a bad thing in itself – may drain skilled personnel away from primary care systems that already are greatly understaffed (see Chapter 10).

What about causes? There is both a "push" from poor working conditions and opportunities in low-income countries and a "pull" from more attractive conditions elsewhere. Is this simply "the market" at work, backed by a "right to migrate"?

Pogge's argument about an international institutional order has a more specific grip than the vague appeal to a market. When economic conditions worsened in various developing countries in the 1980s, international lenders such as the WB and the IMF insisted that these countries severely cut back their publicly funded health systems and take other steps to reduce deficit spending (see Chapter 9). In Cameroon in the 1990s, for example, measures included suspending health worker recruitment, mandatory retirement at age fifty or fifty-five, suspension of promotions, and reduction of benefits. The health sector budget shrank from 4.8 percent in 1993 to 2.4 percent in 1999 even while the private health sector grew (Liese et al. 2004). As a result, public sector health workers shifted to the private sector and others joined the international brain drain. Cost cutting imposed on the country led to cuts in the training of health workers, increasing the shortage. Another consequence of salary cuts was an increase in under-the-table payments to secure domestic treatment and an increase in "shadow providers" who collected public salaries but practiced privately during public sector hours. The international institutional order thus increased the push and at the same time harmed the health system in various ways.

The pull attracting health workers to OECD countries is also not just diffuse economic demand. Targeted recruiting by developed countries is so intensive that it has stripped whole nursing classes away from some universities in the South Asia and Africa. In 2000, the Labour government in the United Kingdom set a target of adding 20,000 nurses to the National Health Service by 2004. It achieved the goal by 2002, absorbing 13,000 foreign nurses and 4,000 doctors. Recruitment from EU countries was flat (many of these countries also face shortages as their population age) but immigration from developing countries continued, despite an effort to frame a policy of ethical recruitment (Deeming 2004). Arguably, even if there were a diffuse economic pull, in the absence of active recruiting the harm would be much less.

The remedy for this harm is not a prohibition on migration, which is protected by various human rights. The United Kingdom has recently announced a tougher code to restrict recruitment from 150 developing countries. In addition, it has made a US$100 million contribution to the Malawi health system aimed at creating better conditions for retaining health personnel there. The United Kingdom has thus taken two steps to reduce both the push and the pull behind the brain drain. Other countries have not followed suit.

International Property Rights and Access to Drugs

The minimalist strategy becomes harder to apply in a clear way to other international health issues. The problem of international property rights and the incentives they create goes beyond the issue of access to existing drugs, such as the antiretroviral cocktails that have been the focus of attention in recent years.[6] Big Pharma has long been criticized for a research and development bias against drugs needed in developing countries. Indeed, it has responded to existing incentives by concentrating on "blockbuster" drugs for wealthier markets, including many "me too" drugs that marginally improve on the effectiveness of older drugs or reduce their side effects slightly. Funding

---

[6] Patent holders on antiretroviral drugs led a fight, until recently, to restrict access to generic versions of their drugs. The result was direct harm to those who might have benefited from antiretrovirals and died instead. Still, these generics that do save other lives would not have emerged without the incentives created by the existing patent system – or so the dominant view of intellectual property maintains.

the research needed to develop a vaccine against malaria, for example, has fallen to private foundations.

Do intellectual property rights and the incentive structures they support create a foreseeable deficit in the right to health that can be reasonably avoided? Pogge (2005b) argues that they do. Nevertheless, many drugs developed by Big Pharma under existing property right protections have become widely used as generics in "essential drug" formularies in developing countries. Health outcomes in those countries are much better than they would be without such drugs. Since many of these drugs would not have been produced in the absence of property right protections, people are not worse off than they would be in a completely free market with no temporary monopolies on products.

Arguably, however, different property right protections and different incentive schemes would make people in these poor countries with poor markets better off than they currently are. Which schemes should we select? Pogge (2005a) proposes that we revise incentives for drug development by establishing a tax-based fund in developed countries that would reward drug companies in proportion to the impact of their products on the global burden of disease. For example, drugs that meet needs in poor countries with very high burdens of disease would yield greater payment to drug companies, even if the drugs are disseminated at a cost close to the marginal cost of production. The tax, Pogge admits, would be hard to establish, but it would be offset in rich countries by lower drug prices. The program could be limited to essential drugs, leaving existing incentives in place for other drugs. Even so, the tax and thus the incentives could vary considerably, presumably with varying consequences for the global burden of disease. How do we decide what to use as a baseline in measuring a deficit in the right to health? Pogge does not tell us.

Leaving aside the problem of vagueness, Pogge's proposal cannot be justified by appealing to the "no-harm" principle alone. The proposed incentive fund would better help to realize human rights to health, as Pogge argues, but "not optimally helping" is not the same as "harming," and so the justification has shifted. There may be good reasons for an account of international justice to consider the interests of those affected by current property right protections more carefully than those agreements now do, but that takes us into more contested terrain than the minimalist strategy.

International harming is complex in several ways. The harms are often not deliberate; sometimes benefits were arguably intended. Harms are often mixed with benefits. In any case, great care must be taken to describe the baseline in measuring harm. Such a complex story about motivations, intentions, and effects might seem to weaken the straightforward appeal of the minimalist strategy, but the complexity does not undermine the view that we have obligations of justice to avoid harming health.

WHERE DO INTERNATIONAL HEALTH INEQUALITIES COME FROM?

Pogge (2005a) emphasizes that 18 million premature, preventable deaths are associated with global poverty. It is tempting, then, to infer that country wealth determines population health and that if rich countries help to keep poor countries poor, they thus harm the health of those populations. If this inference is sound, it gives the minimalist strategy considerable power in addressing international health inequalities. Unfortunately, the inference is not sound, since the relationship between country wealth and country health is more complex than the inference presupposes – as we saw in Chapter 3. We need to examine the sources of international health inequalities more systematically.

We can divide the sources of international health inequalities[7] into three categories:

1. *Those that result from domestic injustice in distributing the socially controllable factors determining population health and its distribution.* These include inequalities by race, caste, ethnicity, religion, gender, or geography in the distribution of the determinants of health. Also included are failure to fund the health sector adequately (relative to capacity), including intersectoral public health measures, immunizations, and comprehensive community-based primary care, and misallocation of resources – for example, diverting funds from public health and primary care to hospitals serving the best-off groups in response to their demand and their greater political power (see Chapter 9 for further discussion of fairness in the health sector).

2. *Those that result from international inequalities in other conditions that affect health.* These include inequalities in natural conditions, such as poor natural resources, including arable land, or susceptibility to droughts and floods, or disease vectors, such as mosquitoes carrying malaria or dengue. They also include socially produced inequalities, such as significant inequalities in capital, in human capital, and in political culture.

3. *Those that result from international practices – institutions, rule-making bodies, treaties – that harm the health of some countries.* The harms can be direct, as in the brain drain of health workers, or more indirect, as in failures to build worker health and safety protections into international trade agreements, or through international loans or other means that may perpetuate poverty.

[7] Not all international health inequalities plausibly raise questions about injustice, just as not all domestic inequalities between groups raise those questions. For example, religious or ethnic differences in lifestyle (diet, sexual practices, social cohesiveness) might give rise domestically and internationally to health inequalities that we would not consider unjust.

These sources of inequality are not exclusive. Some international practices (category 3) may help create the social inequalities in category 2 that in turn increase health inequalities; they may also make it more difficult for states to distribute the determinants of health in a just way (category 1). Some of the inequalities in category 2 may also contribute to the injustices of category 1. The minimalist strategy would have great scope if category 3 sources dominated categories 1 and 2, but this seems unlikely. Only more robust accounts of international justice can address the broader sources of inequality.

To see why the kinds of inequalities referred to in category 2 are not the only problems of international inequalities in health, return to an issue raised in Chapter 3: How much health inequality across countries is simply the result of wealth inequality? Even if we do not believe that all international inequalities in wealth are unjust, we might believe that some are, and if wealth inequalities then cause health inequalities, we would have reason to judge the resulting health inequalities unjust in at least some cases. Indeed, if wealthy countries harm poor ones by sustaining their poverty through various international practices, and if poverty clearly causes poor national health, then the minimalist strategy may cover a significant part of the terrain of health inequality. Indeed, we saw in Chapter 3 (see Figure 3.1) that the wealth of a country affects aggregate measures of health, at least up to a moderate level of aggregate wealth, say $6,000 to $8,000 GDPpc. Above that level, aggregate wealth has little influence on aggregate health. This may be some evidence that international inequalities in wealth contribute to international health inequalities, and to the extent that wealthy countries cause or sustain that inequality, the minimalist strategy obtains a grip on the problem.

But even more striking than the fact that great wealth is not needed for great health is the variation in life expectancy both above and below that middle-income figure. Some poor countries, with a GDPpc less than $3,000, such as Cuba, or the even poorer state of Kerala in southern India, with a GDPpc around $1,000, have health outcomes rivaling those of wealthy ones. Among the wealthiest countries, there are also significant differences in life expectancy.

In Chapter 3, we concluded from these facts that policy matters greatly: What is done with national resources explains much of the wide variation across countries that are equally rich or equally poor. Cuba invests great effort in public health, including ecologically sound environmental policies, as well as in basic education. It invests heavily in training health personnel (its physician/population ratio is comparable to that of the United States), and it sends physicians to worse-off countries. Indeed, it does so despite U.S. economic and travel sanctions intended to undermine its government by inflicting economic harm.

Cuba's success in health outcomes despite the harms imposed by the United States does not show that other international practices do not help produce poor health outcomes elsewhere. But the Cuban example shows how hard it is to specify the baseline in measuring harm. The minimalist strategy assumes that international practices that make a country poorer than it would otherwise be would thus make it less healthy than otherwise. But although international practices may make a country poorer than it would otherwise be, a determined public policy may achieve much better health outcomes than is typical for poor countries. The harm to health can be specified only by assuming that no good health policy is put in place – but why that assumption holds when it does may have nothing to do with the economic harm.

Kerala, like Cuba, also invests heavily in basic education, achieving high literacy rates even for poor women, as well as in public health and primary care. The positive treatment of women contrasts dramatically with practices in many other areas of India and South Asia in general. In Kerala, it is popularly believed that the lack of gender bias in education, and in reproductive and marriage rights, is the result of a left-wing government, but the story is more complex. Kerala, in contrast to the rest of India, had a history of matrilineal property transmission for 2,000 years. As a result, women could not be discounted, as in many other states of India. Its cultural tradition provided a base for a more egalitarian social policy. Given a culture in which women retain significant autonomy and power, both within and outside the home, more egalitarian education and control over reproduction are realistic social goals, and both contribute significantly to population health. Though Kerala, unlike Cuba, was not the victim of focused antagonism, its superior health outcomes were achieved despite a long period of slow economic growth. To the extent that the slow growth resulted from a lack of foreign investment prompted by fears of its left-wing government, we have an even stronger counterexample to the assumption that externally caused economic harm inevitably produces lower health outcomes.

Domestic social policy and social history matter in wealthy countries also. Many industrialized countries have better aggregate health outcomes than the United States, even though the United States spends 50 percent more on health care than nearly any other country. The better outcomes result largely from health-promoting policies: universal health care coverage, stronger protections against poverty and unemployment, better child care, more leisure, and better enforcement of workplace health and safety laws. Some of the difference in outcome is a result of the much more diverse U.S. population, both ethnically (and racially) and geographically. The social inequalities often associated with such diversity contribute to the lower aggregate health outcomes in the United States, though it would be hard to quantify them. Better policy, as in the other industrialized countries, might mitigate these effects, but again, we cannot say how much.

One key factor contributing to the poorer health outcomes in the United States compared to other wealthy countries is the history of U.S. racism, legally supported in the American South until forty years ago. Racism played an important role in dividing the working classes so that they could not pursue common interests, as workers' political movements did in Europe. This not only partly explains the absence of more egalitarian and health-promoting public policies in the United States, but it also explains some of the ongoing inequalities that better policies alone might not be able to eliminate (Kawachi et al. 2005). Even in a wealthy country, then, cultural practices that produce health inequalities both inside and outside the health system contribute to international health inequalities. One reason the United States performs less well on standard aggregate measures of health than most other industrialized countries is its homegrown production of race (and class) health disparities.

Gender bias in other regions contributes to international health inequalities the way racism has in the United States. In Chapter 11 we noted the health impact of cultural and legal policies that disempower women in sub-Saharan Africa and South Asia. Racism in the United States and gender inequality in Africa and Asia illustrate one reason that category 2 and category 3 sources of health inequality cannot cover the terrain of international health inequalities. These domestic practices arise independently of the level of country wealth and of international agreements, institutions, or practices that may contribute in other ways to health inequalities.

Of course, racism and gender bias are not the only ways in which domestic injustice can contribute to international health inequalities. Internal demands on scarce resources by politically and economically more powerful, better-off groups may distort policy in ways that leave worse-off groups more vulnerable to health risks and less able to access remedies. Wealthy landowners and industrialists may have so much political power that they can resist efforts to tax them, leading to underfunded public health systems. Domestic injustice in the distribution of the determinants of health contributes significantly to international inequalities in health, and we probably cannot explain away all domestic responsibility for the injustice by pointing to the additional contributions of some international practices.

In short, good health policy even in poor countries can yield excellent population health, and poor health policy even in wealthy countries, like the United States, can produce worse-than-expected performance. Together these observations count as evidence in favor of a point that many agree on, regardless of other disagreements about international obligations: Primary responsibility for realizing rights to health and health care in a population should rest with each state. The fact that some poor states can and do produce excellent population health makes this point dramatically.[8]

---

[8] In *The Law of Peoples*, Rawls (1999) claims that international inequality in wealth or income is compatible with well-ordered societies producing justice for their populations. He argues that if two well-ordered societies make different decisions about population policy, with the

Even if primary responsibility for population health rests with each state, this does not mean that the state has sole responsibility. Where we can explain why states cannot do as well as others because they have been harmed by international practices, the minimalist strategy applies. Where other international inequalities are important but cannot be attributed to international practices, there may still be room for other considerations of global justice.

Do international health inequalities that clearly result from domestic injustice constitute international injustice? Are other states or individuals in them obliged to try to reduce these inequalities as a matter of justice? For example, if the U.S. population is worse off than Norway's solely because of American domestic injustice, not attributable to category 2 or 3 sources, does this mean that there is no issue for international justice? That conclusion would seem to ignore the fact that victims of domestic injustice are still victims of injustice – at a disadvantage through no fault of their own. Does the obligation to improve their lot fall only on their own state?

What about international health inequalities that clearly result from category 2 international inequalities and not from category 3 practices? Suppose, for example, that country A is wealthier and healthier than country B. Nevertheless, B is well governed and arguably progressively realizes a right to health for its population as best it can within its resource limits. Perhaps this captures the difference between Norway or Japan and Cuba or Kerala (imagine that Kerala is a country of 30 million people, not an Indian state). Is the resulting international health inequality unjust?

Because there are significant international health inequalities that are not plausibly addressed by the minimalist strategy, we must use stronger approaches to international justice if we think they are unjust, or we must concede that these inequalities are not, after all, matters of justice.

THE NEW TERRAIN OF GLOBAL JUSTICE: WHERE THE ACTION IS

Global justice is a hotly disputed area of philosophical work in part because it is so new. Not only are the complex economic and social forces underlying globalization themselves fairly recent developments, but the international agreements, institutions, and rule-making bodies that regulate those forces are just emerging and evolving, forming a moving target for our understanding. Their powers and effects are newly grasped and felt, and moral understanding of their consequences and their potential is in its infancy. The content of a theory of global justice and the justification for it can only emerge from the work of a generation of thinkers and doers grappling

---

result that one becomes wealthier than the other over time, then the wealthier one should not have to make transfers to the other in accordance with some international difference principle aimed at making the worst off as well off as possible. Arguably, an analogous point holds for health policy and health inequalities.

with the problem. The process will involve working back and forth between judgments, based on arguments and evidence, about what is just in particular practices or decisions of the operation of international agencies or rule makers and more theoretical considerations. We need time for reflective equilibrium to do its work.

Accordingly, my modest goal here is not to provide a theory of international justice and global health inequalities, but to suggest where I think the most promising area of inquiry lies. Specifically, inquiry should focus on a middle ground between strongly statist claims that egalitarian requirements of social justice are solely the domain of the nation-state and its well-defined basic structure (Rawls 1999; Nagel 2005) and strong cosmopolitan claims that principles of justice apply to individuals globally, regardless of the relations in which they stand or the institutional structures through which they interact.[9] This intermediary ground consists of relatively recently formed and evolving international agencies, institutions, and rule-making bodies. Even if this intermediary ground is not equivalent in all its morally relevant features or functions to the basic structure of a state, some of its functions may have morally important similarities to such a basic structure. These similarities may justify seeking fair terms of cooperation for them, perhaps intermediary in content between strongly egalitarian concerns appropriate within a state and the skeptical rejection of international justice by strongly statist views (Cohen and Sabel 2006). Working out what international justice means for these international institutions, including what it means for global health, is the crucial task facing political philosophy and international politics in the next generation.

To motivate exploration of this intermediary ground, we need good reason to resist the pulls of both the cosmopolitan views and the strongly statist views that form the poles of the current debate. We also need some illustrations of what it would mean for these intermediary institutions to make decisions or implement practices that address gross international health inequalities as matters of justice. What results is not a road map of how to develop an account of international justice, let alone a blueprint of one, but at best a satellite map revealing some key features of the new terrain.

Resisting the Pull of the Cosmopolitan Intuition

Earlier, I invoked the powerful intuition that the vast gulf in life prospects between the Angolan child and the Norwegian one is not just unfortunate but unfair. Many people think that such dramatic health inequalities are

---

[9] Beitz (1979) holds a relational view, though it is global in scope, since he has argued that the emerging international institutions constitute a global basic structure, even if not a global state, that demands fair terms of cooperation. This view is distinct from the cosmopolitan individualism that is being contrasted with statism.

unjust when they occur between the rich and the poor or between ethnic or racial groups within a country because morally arbitrary contingencies, such as the luck of being born into one group rather than another, should not determine life prospects in such a fundamental way. The same contingency, however, applies to being born Angolan rather than Norwegian, and it seems no less morally arbitrary and troubling. By abstracting from all relations that might hold among people, including the institutions through which they interact and can make claims on each other, the intuition seems to support egalitarian forms of cosmopolitanism.

The support the egalitarian intuition appears to give to cosmopolitanism derives in part from theoretical considerations that carry weight in many ethical theories, including nonegalitarian ones. According to many ethical theories, persons or moral agents deserve equal respect or concern regardless of certain contingent differences between them. Equal concern or respect is, of course, a notion that is interpreted quite differently by utilitarians, who count each person equally as a locus of welfare even if they do not assure equal outcomes for each person, and by many egalitarians, who want some kind of equality of opportunity or outcomes. Whatever the differences in the content of equal respect, there is considerable theoretical agreement on what counts as the contingent or morally arbitrary differences that equal respect must ignore: mere physical distance, the color of skin, religion, gender, and ethnicity. Nationality seems to be part of the same family. The egalitarian intuition about the Angolan and Norwegian children thus draws power from the broader theoretical agreement about what generally counts as a mere contingency and therefore a morally arbitrary difference between moral agents.

The agreement about what counts as contingency and morally arbitrary difference, however, slides past a significant point of controversy. If we think of nationality as one of many traits an individual may have, it seems no less contingent than other troublesome ones, like race. In the relevant sense of "could," we could have been born into one race or another, one nationality or another. But if we think of nationality as a set of relationships in which one stands to others, and if we think that being in certain political relationships with others, including interacting through certain kinds of institutions, has moral import, then being a member of one nation rather than another may be a less morally arbitrary fact than it first seemed. Of course, showing that this political relationship has important moral implications – for example, for considerations of distributive justice – requires an argument, especially in light of the power of the view that ethical considerations apply to individuals in abstraction from these relationships. Indeed, the political view may seem plausible only in light of a theory that helps explain why this political relationship, or a range of other kinds of relationships, is so important. It would beg the question against a relational view, such as that of Rawls (1971, 1995), simply to affirm the intuition we have been discussing.

One of the strengths of a relational view such as Rawls's is that an account of the requirements of justice will have to explain how just institutions can remain stable and sustain commitment to them over time. Justice must be in this sense feasible. Indeed, principles of justice are not acceptable as such if conformance with them in a society's basic structure does not over time lead to a stable or feasible social arrangement. Strains of commitment, for example, must be tolerable, that is, less demanding than those for alternatives.

By abstracting justice from any account of the institutions that can deliver just outcomes in a sustainable way, the cosmopolitan view risks falling into hand wringing. It can lament injustice, but it has failed to set itself the task of showing that justice is a stable product of institutions structured in certain ways. Making justice a set of outcomes among individuals, abstracted from the institutional structures through which individuals cooperate, is utopian in a strong sense: We have no real description of what can produce it. Although the cosmopolitan may admit that institutions and political relationships are instrumentally important in achieving what justice requires in the treatment of individuals, just outcomes are specifiable independently of those institutions and relations. The basic structure of a nation-state, on this view, may be instrumentally necessary for achieving domestic justice, just as a global state may be instrumentally necessary for global justice. At any level, the institutions may be viewed as unjust if they fail to yield just outcomes for individuals. But cosmopolitan theory by design says nothing informative about how a commitment to justice can be sustained by any of these institutions. Nor does it allow for any variation in the concerns of justice that might be appropriate to institutions of different types.

Though none of these points constitutes a refutation of cosmopolitanism, they may move us to resist its pull and to consider seriously a relational view of justice. We then face the prospect of a pluralist world. Justice may be one thing for people who stand in the relations defined by one nation-state and another for those who are members of different nation-states and interact through other kinds of institutions globally.[10] Principles of justice that govern nation-states might then differ from those that govern intermediary institutions among such states, and both may differ from what considerations of fairness might mean to individuals in yet other associations. Justice, on this relational view, is a multilayered construction. Though we have well-developed relational accounts of justice for members of the same state (Rawls 1971, 1995), we have barely begun to think about what justice means or requires for international institutions and rule-making bodies.

[10] Blake (2002), for example, argues that liberal egalitarianism within nation-states raises questions about relative inequality, whereas global justice permits only considerations of absolute inequality.

Resisting Strongly Statist Versions of Relational Justice

An important obstacle to exploring this international space comes from one version of a relational theory of justice, a strongly statist alternative to cosmopolitanism. Nagel (2005), stimulated by Rawls's (1999) articulation of what a liberal state's foreign policy ought to include, argues that socioeconomic justice, with its concerns about equality of opportunity and economic inequality (see Chapters 2 and 3), requires that people stand in the specific relationship to each other defined by a nation-state. Within such a state, socioeconomic justice has application because the terms of fair cooperation must be justifiable, that is, acceptable, to all, since all citizens are both subject to coercion and parties to laws made in their name. Outside the state there is a moral order, but it is limited to more fundamental humanitarian obligations to assist those facing grave risks and having urgent needs; it must also not violate some fundamental human rights, and we must keep our agreements. We do not, however, have obligations of justice to distribute health fairly, or to protect equality of opportunity, or to assist other societies to become as well off as they can be in satisfying rights to health or education or political participation.

Why is it only within a state that we are obliged to mitigate or eliminate morally arbitrary inequalities and pursue social and economic justice? For Rawls, Nagel says, "What is objectionable is that we should be fellow participants in a collective enterprise of coercively imposed legal and political institutions that generates such arbitrary inequalities" (Nagel 2005: 128). We can ignore extrasocietal inequalities but not intrasocietal ones, despite the fact that both have great impact on people's lives, because there is a "a special involvement of agency or the will that is inseparable from membership in a political society" (Nagel 2005: 128) and so cannot arise internationally. This will is essential to the "dual role each member plays both as one of society's subjects and as one of those in whose name its authority is exercised" (Nagel 2005: 128).

As subjects of a state, individuals are exposed to coercively imposed rules, in contrast to the constraints imposed by voluntary cooperative enterprises for mutual advantage. The coercively imposed rules are imposed in the name of all citizens, who are putatively the authors of the rules. Consequently, they must take responsibility as authors and insist on the justifiability of the rules to all involved. In this context, the concern for arbitrary inequalities becomes a matter for all to address.

In contrast, Nagel argues, international institutions and rule-making bodies, such as the World Trade Organization (WTO), the WHO, the WB, or the IMF, do not directly coerce individuals, as states do, nor do they make rules directly in the name of individuals. Where international rules or agreements are made, as in establishing the North American Free Trade Agreement (NAFTA), they are the result of voluntary agreements or bargains made by states and are not made in the name of the citizens of those states. Since these two features are missing, Nagel concludes, the engagement of the will that holds for citizens of states is missing from international institutions. Consequently, the condition that necessitates a justification of inequalities and a mitigation of morally arbitrary inequalities is missing. More specifically, whereas (to use his examples) Nagel's relation to the New Yorker who irons his shirts is a contract mediated by a complex configuration of laws defining contracts and property rights that forms a system of social justice, trade agreements within the Americas that establish his relations with the Brazilian who grows his coffee constitute much "thinner" agreements or "pure" contracts that pursue mutual self-interest at the state level. They contain no assurance that background conditions of justice are met and give rise to no obligations to make such assurances.

Nagel rejects the idea that we might work out a "sliding scale" of obligations that falls in between state-mediated justice and the cosmopolitan view, that is, in the space in which I am proposing we work out our obligations. He simply asserts that a "sliding standard of obligation is considerably less plausible than either the cosmopolitan ... or the political ... standard" (Nagel 2005: 142). Since these international institutions "do not act in the name of all the individuals concerned, and are sustained by those individuals only through the agency of their respective governments or branches of those governments," they are missing "the characteristic [the engaged will] in virtue of which they create obligations of justice and presumptions in favor of equal consideration for all those individuals ... " (Ibid.). Nagel's plausibility claim is question begging because it merely asserts that the statist and cosmopolitan views are the only plausible alternatives

We should resist Nagel's strong statism for two reasons. First, some international institutions impose conditions in a manner that is coercive and that arguably involves the wills of those in the participant states. Second, some obligations of justice may arise in institutions that are not coercive. Cohen and Sabel (2006: 168) address the first reason by noting that when the WTO sets certain standards, there is no way for citizens of a country to opt out of their application. "Opting out is not a real option (the WTO is a 'take it or leave it' arrangement, without even the formal option of picking and choosing the parts to comply with), and given that it is not – and that everyone knows that it is not – there is a direct rule-making relationship between the global bodies and the citizens of different states." In effect, there is coercive application of rules, although by agencies not directly elected by the various citizenries. This mediated agency, however, is common within complex states and still involves rules made in the name of the citizens.

There is further evidence of the involvement of the wills of citizens in various cases where there is disagreement with the rulings of an international body. For example, protestors, both individuals and organizations, including official international workers' organizations, have demonstrated against some free trade agreements that were signed by their own nations.

The protest is against the rule-making body, not primarily their own governments for endorsing the agreements. They argue that they resent being implicated, even through the agency of their governments, in a policy they disagree with, such as the failure to include appropriate labor health and safety or environmental considerations in trade agreements. In effect, these protestors of the WTO and other associations and agreements believe there is a need to justify the terms of the agreements to all affected by them. Similarly, many Americans are embarrassed that George W. Bush's administration has refused to be part of the World Court, has walked away from international treaties to address global warming, and has tried to exempt itself from the Geneva Conventions regarding the treatment of prisoners of war. They think that the international agreements impose obligations appropriately in their name, whereas their president's unilateralism shamefully rejects what they want to uphold.

Consequently, even if Nagel is right about the characteristic by which egalitarian considerations arise within states – that is, the dual role of citizen as both subject and author of coercive rules and thus the engagement of citizens' wills – he is arguably wrong about the *scope* of institutions within which we may find functionally equivalent conditions that have the same moral import. We find examples that include coercion and that arguably engage the wills of citizens – enough to make them advocate, protest, and appeal to these organizations to consider their claims. Even if Nagel is right about what makes this dual role morally relevant, some egalitarian concerns may still be appropriate even outside the state.

We may also resist Nagel's strong statist position because obligations of justice can arise in international institutions even if they are not coercive and do not engage the will of citizens as subjects and authors in the way Nagel says is necessary. Cohen and Sabel (2006) argue that considerations of inclusion, falling short of fully equal concern or egalitarianism but still within the domain of justice, arise within a range of international institutions. Concerns about inclusion have implications for governance. If workers' organizations were suddenly excluded from the International Labor Organization (ILO), that would be seen to violate important concerns about inclusion (Cohen and Sabel 2006). Similarly, if a policy enables better-off groups or states to advance their interests and leaves worse-off groups with few or no benefits, and if significantly better benefits could be gained by the worst-off groups at little sacrifice by others, then the interests of all have not been adequately included in the institutions deliberations(Cohen and Sabel 2006). Nagel is then wrong to insist that only humanitarian concerns apply internationally.

Illustrations of Obligations of Justice in International Organizations

Cohen and Sabel (2006: 153) sketch three types of international relationships that might give rise to obligations of justice going beyond humanitarian concerns: international agencies for distributing a specific good, cooperative schemes, and some kinds of interdependency. Each may give rise to obligations of justice, such as concerns about inclusion. These may range from an obligation to give more weight to the interests of those who are worse off if it can be done at little cost to others, to obligations of equal concern, perhaps yielding far more egalitarian obligations. I shall illustrate each of these relationships and the obligations they give rise to with examples focused on key issues of global health.

The WHO plausibly illustrates the idea that institutions for distributing a particular important good, such as public health expertise and technology, must show equal concern in the distribution of that good. The organization would be considered unfair if it ignored the health of some and favored others. For example, this point about showing equal concern arises in other debates about the methodologies WHO employs. We saw (in Chapter 4) that cost-effectiveness analysis (CEA) ignores issues of equity in the distribution of health and health care. These criticisms of CEA thus challenge the unconstrained use of CEA by WHO whether it is using the methodology to determine health policy within a specific country or across countries. WHO is required by its mission of improving world health to consider equitable distribution in all contexts in which it works – within and across countries.

Concerns about equity show up in WHO's programmatic discussions as well. WHO paid attention to equity in the distribution of ARTs for HIV/AIDS (Chapter 10). WHO also sponsors a Commission on the Social Determinants of Health that has a strong focus on equity in health. Both of these examples illustrate behavior compatible with and required by the institutional charge to WHO. Either this is a misguided focus of energy for WHO, as seems to be implied by Nagel's strong statist view, or it is an implication of the obligation of justice to show equal concern that arises within institutions charged with delivering an important good – whether they operate within states or across them.

Consider now the international bodies that establish rules governing intellectual property rights, including those that are key to creating temporary monopolies over new drugs. Such a scheme is "consequential" in that it increases cooperation among the parties involved in producing an important collective good, research and development of drugs, and it does so in a way that has normatively relevant consequences (Cohen and Sabel 2006: 153: n.12). Suppose we conclude that this mutually cooperative scheme generates considerations of equal concern, or at least that it must be governed by a principle of inclusion.

We might then view favorably Pogge's (2005a) suggestion about structuring drug development incentives so that they better address the global burden of disease. Earlier, I said that Pogge's proposal could not be defended on the minimalist grounds that it avoided doing harm because of the problem of specifying the relevant human rights baseline. Now, however, we have a new basis on which to defend the justice of Pogge-style incentives. Such an incentive scheme, supplementing existing property rights or modifying them appropriately, would greatly enhance the benefits to those who generally receive no benefits for a long period of time, and it would do so at only a modest cost to those profiting from the endeavor. Minimally, it illustrates what a more inclusive policy should include; one can build into it even stronger egalitarian considerations if the cooperative scheme raises concerns about equality and not simply inclusion. Exactly what form the policy would take, or the justification for it deriving from the form of cooperative scheme involved, remains a task for further work. With these issues worked out, we might then support Pogge's incentive schemes as a way of moving some countries closer to satisfying a right to health, connecting the effort to human rights goals as he does.

Consider again the example of the brain drain of health personnel from low- and middle-income countries to wealthier ones. Nagel (2005: 130) notes that nations generally have "immunity from the need to justify to outsiders the limits on access to its territory," though this immunity is not absolute, since the human rights of asylum seekers act as a constraint. Still, the decisions different countries make about training of health personnel and about access to their territories have great mutual impact on them. There is an important interdependency affecting their well-being, specifically the health of the populations contributing and receiving health personnel. The British decision in 2000 to recruit 30,000 new nurses from developing countries rather than to try to train more British nurses greatly affected the fate of people being served by health systems in southern Africa. I noted earlier that the underfunding of salaries for African nurses and doctors, in part a legacy of Structural Adjustment Programs imposed by the IMF and the WB, but clearly continued by local governments, helps create the push factor driving these workers abroad.

Arguably, this relation of interdependence brings into play obligations of inclusion, perhaps those of equal concern, going beyond humanitarian considerations. In addition to Pogge's no-harm or minimalist approach, we thus have obligations of inclusion requiring us to consider the interests of all those in the interdependent relationship. These obligations can be translated into various policy options that address the brain drain: It may be necessary to restrict the terms of employment in receiving countries of health workers from vulnerable countries; it may be necessary to seek compensation for the lost training costs of these workers; it may be important to give aid to contributing countries in order to reduce the push factors; it may be necessary to prohibit active recruitment from vulnerable countries.

We might combine these relationships of interdependence with the relationships and obligations that arise from cooperative schemes. The International Organization for Migration, established in 1951 to help resettle displaced persons from World War II, now has 112 member states and 23 observer states. It manages various aspects of migration, providing information and technical advice, and arguably goes beyond its initial humanitarian mission. Suppose that it took on the task of developing a policy that helped to coordinate or manage the frightening health personnel brain drain.

Minimally, it might seek internationally acceptable standards for managing the flow – standards on recruitment, on compensation, on terms of work. More ambitiously, it might seek actual treaties that balanced the right to migrate with the costs to the contributing countries, countering at least some of the pull factors and even providing funds that might alleviate some of the push factors underlying the brain drain. In seeking these treaties, it might work together with the ILO, the WTO, WHO, and the UN. Such a cooperative endeavor would reflect the common interest in all countries of having adequate health personnel – and thus assuring citizens a right to health and health care – as well as the common interest in protecting the human right to dignified migration.

THE WAY FORWARD

My goal in this chapter has not been to provide a road map to a theory of international justice. Instead, I argue more modestly that there is a fertile area of emerging international institutions where the task of working out considerations of international justice lies. This is where the action is. We must move beyond a minimalist strategy that justifies only avoiding and correcting harms. How far we go toward robust egalitarian considerations is a matter to be worked out. In any case, how far we can go will depend specifically on the nature of the international relationships in which we stand. It will depend on the institutional structures that are still developing. This work in progress has barely started, but it must break out of the framing of the problem posed by the poles of statism and cosmopolitan individualism.

Earlier I posed the question "When are international inequalities in health unjust?" This chapter does not provide an answer because we remain unclear about what obligations states, international institutions, and rule-making bodies have regarding health inequalities across countries. In Chapter 4, we characterized domestic health inequalities as unjust when they arise from an unjust distribution of the socially controllable factors that determine population health and its distribution – and we illustrated the meaning of a just distribution by reference to conformance to Rawls's principles of justice as fairness. Internationally, we must explain the substance of international obligations for the various kinds of cooperative schemes, international agencies, and international rule-making bodies in order to specify when the internationally socially controllable factors affecting health are justly distributed and regulated.

My account of just health remains, then, a work in progress. I have suggested in various chapters where more work needs to be done: addressing the stability problems posed by global aging for distributive schemes (Chapter 6); developing an adequate framework for the ethical and scientific evaluation of social experiments on health (Chapter 9); improving our understanding of fair process in actual institutional settings (Chapter 10); developing quantified models of the equity–efficiency trade-offs in contexts where justice tells us that we have a reason to reduce health disparities and using those models to inform deliberation about policies for reducing health disparities (Chapter 11); improving our grasp of the institutional embodiment of accountability for reasonableness in human rights contexts (Chapter 12). The relatively novel and difficult issues of international justice addressed here add to this list. Despite the lack of closure on these matters, the account developed here provides an integrated theory that helps us see the path to pursue in promoting population health and distributing it fairly, globally as well as domestically.

References

Aaron, H. and Schwartz, W. 1984. *The Painful Prescription*. Washington, DC: Brookings Institution.

Acevedo-Garcia, D., Lochner, K. A., Osypuk, T. L., and Subramanian, S. V. 2003. Future directions in residential segregation and health research: A multilevel approach. *American Journal of Public Health* 93:2: 215–21.

Acheson, D. 1998. *Report of the Independent Inquiry into Inequalities in Health*. London: The Stationery Office.

Aday, L. A. and Andersen, R. 1975. *Development of Indices of Access to Medical Care*. Ann Arbor, MI: Health Administration Press.

Aday, L. A., Anderson, R., and Fleming, G. V. 1980. *Health Care in the U.S.: Equitable for Whom?* Beverly Hills, CA: Sage

Adler, N. E., Thomas, B., Chesney, M. A., Cohen, S., Folkman, S., Kahn, R. L., and Syme, S. L. 1994. Socioeconomic status and health: The challenge of the gradient. *American Psychologist* 49: 15–24.

Alkire, S. and Chen, L. 2004. "Medical exceptionalism" in international migration: Should doctors and nurses be treated differently?" JLI Working Paper 7–3, pp. 1–10.

Alma Ata Declaration. 1978. International Conference on Primary Health Care, Alma-Ata, USSR, September 6–12. Available at http://www.who.int/hpr/NPH/docs/declaration_almaata.pdf.

American Medical Association, Council on Ethical and Judicial Affairs. 1987. Ethical issues involved in the growing AIDS crisis. *Journal of the American Medical Association* 259: 360–1.

American Textile Manufacturers Institute et al v. Donovan, 452 U.S. 490 (1981).

Americans with Disabilities Act of 1990. September 17, 2006. Available at http://www.dol.gov/esa/regs/statutes/ofccp/ada.htm.

Anand, S., Ammar, W., Evans, T., Hasegawa, T., Kissimova-Skarbek, K., Lucas, L. A., et al. 2002. *Report of the Scientific Peer Review Group on Health System Performance Assessment*. Geneva: World Health Organization.

Anand, S. and Hanson, K. 1998. DALYs: Efficiency versus equity. *World Development* 26: 307–10.

Anand, S., Peter, F., and Sen, A. (eds.). 2004. *Public Health, Ethics, and Equity.* Oxford: Oxford University Press.

Anderson, E. 1999. What is the point of equality? *Ethics* 109: 287–337.

Annas, G. J. 1988. Legal risks and responsibilities of physicians in the AIDS epidemic. *Hastings Center Report* 18(suppl.): 26–32.

Arneson, R. 1988. Equality and equal opportunity for welfare. *Philosophical Studies* 54: 79–95.

   1999a. Against Rawlsian equality of opportunity. *Philosophical Studies* 93: 77–112.

   1999b. *Comments on From Chance to Choice.* Confernce on From Chance to Choice. San Diego: University of California.

   1999c. Debate: Equality of opportunity for welfare defended and recanted. *Journal of Political Philosophy* 7(4): 488–97.

   2002. Equality of opportunity. *Stanford Encyclopedia of Philosophy.* Available at http://www.plato.stanford.edu/entries/equal-opportunity.

Arras, J. 1988. The fragile web of responsibility: AIDS and the duty to treat. *Hastings Center Report* 18(suppl.): 10–20.

Arrow, K. 1963. Uncertainty and the welfare economics of medical care. *American Economic Review* 53: 941–73.

   1973. Some ordinalist-utilitarian notes on Rawls's theory of justice. *Journal of Philosophy* 70(9): 251.

Asher, J. 2004. *The Right to Health: A Resource Manual for NGOs.* London: Commonwealth Medical Trust.

Ashford, N. 1976. *Crisis in the Workplace: Occupational Disease and Injury.* Cambridge, MA: MIT Press.

Aubrey, W., Rettig. R. A., Farquahar, C., and Jacobson, P. D. 2006. *False Hope: Bone Marrow Transplantation for Breast Cancer.* Oxford: Oxford University Press.

Automobile Workers v. Johnson Controls, Inc. 499 US 187 (1991).

Background paper. 2006. Quantitative indicators for monitoring the implementation of human rights – a conceptual and methodological framework. Expert consultation, March 30–31.

Bagenstos, S. 2004. The Supreme Court, the Americans with Disabilities Act, and rational discrimination, *Alabama Law Review* 55: 923.

Barbeau, E. M., Krieger, N., and Mah-Jabeen, S. 2004. Working class matters: Socioeconomic disadvantage, race/ethnicity, gender, and smoking in NHIS 2000. *American Journal of Public Health* 94(2): 269–78.

Barry, B. 1989. *Theories of Justice.* London: Harvester Wheatsheaf, pp. 213–34.

Bartley, M., Blane, D., and Montgomery, S. 1997. Socioeconomic determinants of health: Health and the life course: Why safety nets matter. *British Medical Journal* 314: 1194.

Bayer, R. 1981. *Homosexuality and American Psychiatry.* New York: Basic Books.

   2003. Workers' liberty, workers' welfare: The Supreme Court speaks on the rights of disabled employees. *American Journal of Public Health* 93: 540–4

Bedau, M. A. 1992. Goal-directed systems and the good. *The Monist* 75: 34–49.

Beitz, C. R. 1979. *Political Theory and International Relations.* Princeton, NJ: Princeton, University Press.

   2000. Rawls's law of peoples. *Ethics* 110: 669–96.

Bennett, S., McPake, B., and Mills, A. (eds.). 1997. *Private Health Providers in Developing Countries: Serving the Public Interest?* London: Zed Books.

Benzeval, M., Judge, K., and Whitehead, M. (eds.). 1995. *Tackling Inequalities in Health: An Agenda for Action.* London: Kings Fund.

Berman, D. 1978. *Death on the Job.* New York: Monthly Review Press.

Berman, P. A. (ed.). 1995. Health sector reform in developing countries: Making health development sustainable. *Harvard Series on Population and International Health.* Cambridge, MA: Harvard University Press.

Berman, P. A., and Bossert, T. J. 2004. A decade of health sector reform in developing countries: What have we learned? Data for Decision Making Project Publication No. 85. Available at http://www.hsph.harvard.edu/ihsg/publication.html.

Black, D., Morris, J. N., Smith, C., Townsend, P., and Whitehead, M. 1988. *Inequalities in Health: The Black Report; The Health Divide.* London: Penguin Group.

Blake, M. 2002. Distributive justice, state coercion, and autonomy. *Philosophy and Public Affairs* 30: 3

Blendon, R. J., Kim, M., and Benson, J. M. 2001. The public versus the World Health Organization on health system performance. *Health Affairs* 20: 10–20.

Boorse, C. 1975. On the distinction between disease and illness. *Philosophy and Public Affairs* 5(1): 49–68.

　　1976. What a theory of mental health should be. *Journal of the Theory of Social Behavior* 6(1): 61–84.

　　1977. Health as a theoretical concept. *Philosophy of Science* 44: 542–73

　　1997. A rebuttal on health. In J. M. Humber and R. F. Almeder (eds.), *What Is Disease?* pp. 1–134. Totowa, NJ: Humana Press.

Bossert, T. 1998. Analyzing the decentralization of health systems in developing countries: Decision space, innovation and performance. *Social Science and Medicine* 47(10): 1513–27.

Brandt, A. M. 2007. *The Cigarette Century: The Rise, Fall, and Deadly Persistence of the Product That Defined America.* New York: Basic Books.

Brandt, R. 1979. *A Theory of the Good and the Right.* Oxford: Oxford University Press.

Braveman, P. 1999. *Monitoring Equity in Health: A Policy-Oriented Approach in Low- and Middle-Income Countries.* Geneva: World Health Organization.

Braveman, P., Starfield, B., and Geiger, H. J. 2001. World Health Report 2000; how it removes equity from the agenda for public health monitoring and policy. *British Medical Journal* 323: 678–81.

Braybrook, D. 1968. Let needs diminish that preferences may prosper. *In Studies in Moral Philosophy American Philosophical Quarterly Monograph Series, No. I.* Oxford: Blackwell.

　　1987. *Meeting Needs. Studies in Moral, Political and Legal Philosophy.* Princeton NJ: Princeton University Press.

Brennan, T. A., Leape, L. L., Laird, N. M., et al. 1991. Incidence of negligent care and adverse events in hospitalized patients. *New England Journal of Medicine* 324: 370–6.

Brock, D. 1988. Ethical Issues in recipient selection for organ transplantation. In D. Matheiu (ed.) *Organ Substitution Technology: Ethical, Legal and Public Policy Issues.* Boulder, CO: Westview Press, pp. 86–99.

　　1989. Justice, health care, and the elderly. *Philosophy and Public Affairs* 18(3): 297–312.

　　1998. Ethical issues in the development of summary measures of population health states. In Field and Gold (eds.), pp. 73–86.

2003. Separate spheres and indirect benefits *Cost-Effectiveness and Resource Allocation* 1: 4

Brock, D. and Daniels, N., 1994. Ethical foundations of the Clinton Administration's proposed health care system. *Journal of the American Medical Association* 271: 1189–96

Broome, J. 1989. *Weighing Goods.* Oxford: Oxford University Press.

Buchanan, A. 1975. Revisability and rational choice. *Canadian Journal of Philosophy* 5: 395–408.

Buchanan, A., Brock, D., Daniels, N., and Wikler, D. 2000. *From Chance to Choice: Genetics and Justice.* Cambridge: Cambridge University Press.

Calabresi, G. and Bobbit, P. 1978. *Tragic Choices.* New York: Norton.

Callahan, D. 1987. *Setting Limits: Medical Goals in an Aging Society.* New York: Simon and Schuster.

Case, A. and Deaton, A. 2003. *Broken Down by Work and Sex: How Our Health Declines.* Cambridge, MA: NBER Working Paper No. 9821.

CEDAW, Convention to Eliminate All Forms of Discrimination Against Women, 1979. Available at http://www.un.org/womenwatch/daw/cedaw.

Centers for Disease Control. 1989. Guidelines for prevention of transmission of human immunodeficiency virus and hepatitis B virus to health-care and public safety workers. *Morbidity and Mortality Weekly Report* (June 23, suppl. 6): 5–6.

CESCR, Committee on Economic, Social, and Cultural Rights. 2000. General Comment No. 14. The Right to the Highest Attainable Standard of Health (Article 12 of the International Covenant on Economic, Social, and Cultural Rights). UN doc.E/C., July 4, 2000.

Chapman, A. R. 1997. A "violations approach" to monitoring the ICESCR. *Human Rights Dialogue* 1: 10.

Chapman, A. R. and Russell, S. 1998. Violations of the right to education. Background paper submitted by the American Association for the Advancement of Science (AAAS) to the Commission on Human Rights, October 14, 1998. Available at http://www.unhchr.ch/tbs/doc.nsf/(Symbol)/373fa929ceafa80d 802566ce00544458?Opendocument. Accessed July 27, 2006.

Charen, M. 1989. My brother, the doctor, Is in danger. *New York Doctor* 2(7): 17.

Chen, L. and Hanvoravongchai, P. 2005. HIV/AIDS and human resources. *Bulletin of the World Health Organization* 83: 143–4.

Chevron U.S.A., Inc. v. Echazabal, 536 U.S. 73 (2002).

Cohen, G. A. 1989. On the currency of egalitarian justice. *Ethics* 99: 906–44.

1992. Incentives, inequality, and community in, G. Petersen (ed.), *The Tanner Lectures on Human Values, Volume Thirteen.* Salt Lake City: University of Utah Press, pp. 262–329.

1993. Equality of what? On welfare, goods, and capabilities. In Nussbaum and Sen (1993), pp. 9–29.

1995. The Pareto argument for inequality. *Social Philosophy and Policy* 12 (Winter): 160–85.

2000. *If You're an Egalitarian, How Come You're So Rich?* Cambridge, MA: Harvard University Press.

Cohen, J. 1989. Democratic equality. *Ethics* 99: 727–54.

1994. Pluralism and proceduralism. *Chicago-Kent Law Review* 69(3): 589–618.

1995. Amartya Sen: Inequality reexamined. *Journal of Philosophy* 92(5): 275–88.

1996a. Deliberative democracy. Unpublished manuscript.

1996b. Procedure and substance in deliberative democracy. In S. Benhabib, (ed.), *Democracy and Difference: Changing Boundaries of the Political.* Princeton, NJ: Princeton University Press, pp. 95–119.

2001. Taking people as they are? *Philosophy and Public Affairs* 30(4): 363–86.

2003. For a democratic society. In Freeman (2003), pp. 86–138.

Cohen, J. and Sabel, C. 2006. Extra rempublicam nulla justitia. *Philosophy and Public Affairs* 34(2): 147–75.

Coulter, A. and Ham, C. (eds.). 2000. *The Global Challenge of Health Care Rationing.* Philidelphia: Open University Press.

CSIS, Center for Strategic and International Studies. 2002. Meeting the Challenge of Global Aging. Available at http://www.csis.org/gai.

Dahlgren, G. and Whitehead, M. 1991. *Policies and Strategies to Promote Social Equity in Health.* Stockholm: Institute of Future Studies.

Daniels, N. 1975. Equal liberty and unequal worth of liberty. In N. Daniels (ed.), *Reading Rawls*, New York: Basic Books, pp. 253–81.

1978. Merit and meritocracy. *Philosophy and Public Affairs* 7(3): 206–23.

1981. What is the obligation of the medical profession in the distribution of health care? *Social Science and Medicine* 15F: 129–33.

1985. *Just Health Care.* Cambridge: Cambridge University Press.

1986. Why saying no to patients in the United States is so hard: Cost containment, justice, and provider autonomy. *New England Journal of Medicine* 314: 1381–3.

1987. The ideal advocate and limited resources. *Theoretical Medicine and Bioethics* 8(1): 69–80.

1988. *Am I My Parents' Keeper? An Essay on Justice between the Young and the Old.* New York: Oxford University Press.

1990a. Equality of what: Welfare, resources, or capabilities? *Philosophy and Phenomenological Research* 50 (suppl.): 273–96.

1990b. Insurability and the HIV epidemic: Ethical issues in underwriting. *Milbank Quarterly* 68(4): 497–526.

1991a. Duty to treat or right to refuse? *Hastings Center Report.* 21(2): 36–46.

1991b. Is the Oregon rationing plan fair? *Journal of the American Medical Association* 265(17): 2232–5.

1993. Rationing fairly: Programmatic considerations. *Bioethics* 7(2/3): 224–33.

1995. *Seeking Fair Treatment: From the AIDS Epidemic to National Health Care Reform.* New York: Oxford University Press.

1996a. *Justice and Justification: Reflective Equilibrium in Theory and Practice.* New York: Cambridge University Press.

1996b. Mental disabilities, equal opportunity and the ADA. In R. J. Bonnie and J. Monahan (eds.), *Mental Disorder, Work Disability, and the Law.* Chicago: University of Chicago Press, pp. 282–97

1998a. Distributive justice and the use of summary measures of population health status. In Institute of Medicine, *Summarizing Population Health: Directions for the Development and Application of Population Metrics.* Washington, DC: National Academy Press, pp. 58–71.

1998b. Ethics and health care reforms: A global view. In Z. Bankowski, J. H., Bryant, and J. Gallagher (eds.), *Ethics, Equity and Health Care for All.* Geneva: Council International Organizations of Medical Societies, pp. 86–94.

1998c. Kamm's moral methods. *Philosophy and Phenomenological Research* 58(4): 947–54.

1998d. Rationing medical care: A philosopher's perspective on outcomes and process. *Economics and Philosophy* 14: 27–50.

1999. Enabling democratic deliberation: How managed care organizations ought to make decisions about coverage for new technologies. In S. Macedo (ed.), *Deliberative Politics: Essays on Democracy and Disagreement.* New York: Oxford University Press, pp. 198–210.

2001. Justice, health and health care. *American Journal of Bioethics* 1(2): 3–15.

2003. Democratic equality: Rawls's complex egalitarianism. In S. Freeman, (ed.), *Companion to Rawls.* Oxford: Blackwell, pp. 241–76.

2004. How to achieve fair distribution of ARTs in "3 by 5": Fair process and legitimacy in patient selection. Geneva: World Health Organization/UNAIDS: Consultation, January 26–7.

2005. Fair process in patient selection for anti-retroviral treatment in WHO's Goal of "3 by 5." *Lancet* 366: 169–71.

2006. Toward ethical review of health system transformations. *American Journal of Public Health* 96(3): 447–51.

2007a. Equity and population health: Towards a broden bioethics agenda. *Hastings Center Reports* 36(4): 22–35.

2007b. Rescuing universal health care. *Hastings Center Report* 37(2): 3.

Daniels, N., Bryant, J., Castano, R. A., Dantes, O. G., Khan, K. S., and Pannarunothai, S. 2000. Benchmarks of fairness for health care reform: A policy tool for developing countries. *Bulletin of the World Health Organization* 78: 740–50.

Daniels, N. and Flores, W. 2004. An evidence-based approach to benchmarking fairness in health sector reform in Latin America. In F. L. Stepke (ed.), *Dialogo y Cooperacion en Salud, Diez Anos De Bioetica en la OPS.* Santiago, Chile: Organizacion Panamerica de Salud, pp. 101–14.

Daniels, N., Flores, W., Ndumbe, P., Pannarunothai, S., Bryant, J., Ngulube, T. J., and Wang, Y. 2005. An evidence-based approach to benchmarking the fairness of health sector reform in developing countries. *Bulletin of the World Health Organization*: 83(7): 534–41.

Daniels, N., Kennedy, B., and Kawachi, I. 1999. Why justice is good for our health: The social determinants of health inequalities. *Daedalus* 128(4): 215–51.

2000. *Is Inequality Bad for Our Health?* Boston: Beacon Press.

Daniels, N., Light, D., and Caplan, R. 1996. *Benchmarks of Fairness for Health Care Reform.* New York: Oxford University Press.

Daniels, N. and Sabin, J. E. 1997. Limits to health care: Fair procedures, democratic deliberation, and the legitimacy problem for insurers. *Philosophy and Public Affairs* 26: 303–50.

1998a. The ethics of accountability and the reform of managed care organizations. *Health Affairs* 17(5): 50–69.

1998b. Last-chance therapies and managed care: Pluralism, fair procedures, and legitimacy. *Hastings Center Report* 28(2): 27–41.

1999. Decisions about access to health care and accountability for reasonableness. *Journal of Urban Health* 76(2): 176–191.

2002. *Setting Limits Fairly: Can We Learn to Share Medical Resources?* New York: Oxford University Press.

Daniels, N., Sabin, J. E., and Farrow, L. 1991. Clarifying the concept of medical necessity. *Proceedings of the Group Health Institute*, pp. 693–707.

Daniels, N., Teagarden, R., and Sabin, J. E. 2003. An ethical template for pharmacy benefits. *Health Affairs* 22(1): 125–37.

Davey-Smith, G., Shipley, M. J., and Rose, G. 1990. Magnitude and causes of socioeconomic differentials in mortality. Further evidence from the Whatehall Study. *Journal of Epidemiology and Community Health* 44: 265–70.

de Beaufort, I., Hilhorst, M., and Holm, S. (eds.). 1996. *In the Eye of the Beholder: Ethics and Medical Change of Appearance.* Oslo: Scandinavian University Press.

Deaton, A. 2002a. Policy implications of the gradient of health and wealth. *Health Affairs* 21(2): 13–29.

  2002b. The convoluted story of international studies of inequality and health. *International Journal of Epidemiology* 31(3): 546–9.

Deaton, A. and Lubotsky, D. 2003. Mortality, inequality and race in American cities and states. *Social Science and Medicine* 56: 1139–53.

Deeming, C. 2004. Policy targets and ethical tensions: UK nurse recruitment. *Social Policy and Administration* 38(7): 227–92.

Department of Health. 1999. *Reducing Health Inequalities: An Action Report.* London: Department of Health.

  2003. *Tackling Health Inequalities: A Programme for Action.* London: Department of Health.

Dhaliwal, M., Okero, F. A., Schilleisoort, I., Green, C., Conway, C., and Jain, A. 2003. *A Public Health Approach for Scaling up ARV Treatment: A Toolkit for Programme Managers.* Draft Report. Zimbabwe Consutation on Scaling up Treatment for People with HIV.

Dickson, E. S. and Shepsle, K. A. 2001. Working and shirking: Equilibrium in public goods games with overlapping generations of players. *Journal of Law, Economics, and Organization* 17: 285–318.

Dolan, P., Shaw, R., Tsuchiya, A., and Williams, A. 2005. QALY maximization and people's preferences: A methodological review of the literature. *Health Economics* 14: 197–208.

D'Souza, R. M. and Bryant, J. D. 1999. Determinants of childhood mortality in slums of Karachi, Pakistan. *Journal of Health and Population in Developing Countries*, 2(1): 33–44.

Dworkin, G. 1972. Paternalism. *The Monist* 56: 64–84.

Dworkin, R. 1981a. What is Equality? Part 1: Equality of welfare. *Philosophy and Public Affairs* 10: 185–246.

  1981b. What is Equality? Part 2: Equality of resources. *Philosophy and Public Affairs* 10: 283–345.

  2000. *Sovereign Virtue: The Theory and Practice of Equality*, Cambridge, MA: Harvard University Press.

Edgar, W. 2000. Rationing health care in New Zealand – How the Public Has a Say. In A. Coulter and C. Ham (eds.), *The Global Challenge of Health Care Rationing*. Philidelphia: Open University Press, pp. 175–91.

Editorial. 2003. SARS: Health care work can be hazardous to your health. *Occupational Medicine* 53: 241–3.

Emanuel, E. 1988. Do physicians have an obligation to treat patients with AIDS? *England Journal of Medicine* 318(25): 1686–90.

1992. *The Ends of Human Life: Medical Ethics in a Liberal Polity.* Cambridge, MA: Harvard University Press.

2002. Review of setting limits fairly: Can we learn to share medical resources? *New England Journal of Medicine* 347: 953–4.

Engelhardt, H. T., Jr. 1974. Disease of masturbation: Values and the concept of disease. *Bulletin of the History of Medicine* 48(2): 234–48.

1981. Health care allocations: Responses to the unjust, the unfortunate, and the undesirable. In E. Shelp (ed.), *Justice and Health Care.* Boston: Kluwer, pp. 121–37.

Enthoven, A. 1980. *Health Plan: The Only Practical Solution to the Soaring Cost of Medical Care.* Reading, MA: Addison-Wesley.

Epstein, A. M., Ayanian, J. Z., Keogh, J. H., Noonan, S. J., Armistead, N., Cleary, P. D., Weissman, J. S., David-Kasdan, J. A., Carlson, D., Fuller, J., Marsh, D., and Conti, R. M. 2000. Racial disparities in access to renal transplantation – clinically appropriate or due to underuse or overuse? *New England Journal of Medicine* 343(21): 1537–44.

Epstein, R. A. 1988. Justice across the generations. Paper presented at the Conference on Intergenerational Justice, Austin TX.

Estlund, D. 1997. Beyond fairness and deliberation: The epistemic dimension of democratic authority. In J. Bohman and W. Rehg (eds.), *Deliberative Democracy.* Boston: MIT Press, pp. 173–204.

Evans, T., Whitehead, M., Diderichsen, F., Bhuiya, A., and Wirth, M. (eds.). 2001. *Challenging Inequities in Health: From Ethics to Action.* Oxford: Oxford University Press.

Finkelstein, B. S., Silvers J. B., and Marrero, U. 1998. Insurance coverage, physician recommendations, and access to emerging treatments: Growth hormone therapy for childhood short stature. *Journal of the American Medical Association* 279: 663–8.

Fishkin, J. 1983. *Justice, Equal Opportunity, and the Family.* New Haven, CT: Yale University Press.

Freedman, B. 1988. Health professions, codes, and the right to refuse to treat HIV-infectious patients. *Hastings Center Report* 18(suppl.): 20–5.

Freeman, S. 2003. *The Cambridge Companion to Rawls.* Cambridge: Cambridge University Press.

Frenk, J., Gonzalez-Pier, E., Gomez-Dantes, O., Lezana, M. A., and Knaul, F. M. 2006. Comprehensive reform to improve health system performance in Mexico. *Lancet* 686: 1524–34

Fried, C. 1969. *An Anatomy of Values.* Cambridge, MA: Harvard University Press.

1978. *Right and Wrong.* Cambridge, MA: Harvard University Press.

Friedman, M. 1962. *Capitalism and Freedom.* Chicago: University of Chicago Press.

Fuchs, V. R., and Emanuel, E. 2005. Health care reform: Why? What? When? *Health Affairs* 24: 6.

Gilson, W. 1997a. The lessons of user fee experience in Africa. *Health Policy Planning* 12(4): 273–85.

1997b. Implementing and evaluating health reform processes: Lessons from the literature. Major Applied Research 1, Working Paper No. 1. Washington DC: U.S. Agency for International Development, Partnerships for Health Reform Project.

Godfrey-Smith, P. 1994. A modern history theory of functions. *Nous* 28: 344–62.

Gold, M. R., Siegal, J. E., Russell, L. B., and Weinstein, M. C. 1996. *Cost-Effectiveness in Health and Medicine.* New York: Oxford University Press.

Gomez-Dantes, O., Gomez-Juaregui, J., and Inclan, C., 2004.*Salud publica de Mexico* 46:5: 399–416.

Gómez-Jauregui, P., Daniels, N., and Reichenbach, L. 2004. Cervical cancer screening program in Mexico: Equity and fairness implications. Cambridge, MA: Harvard Center for Population and Development Working Paper Series.

Gonzalez-Pier, E., Gutierrez-Delgado, C., Barraza-Lorens M., Porrqs-Cadey, R., Carjaho, N., Loncich, K., Dias, R., Kulkarni, S., Murakami, Y., Ezzati H., and Salomon J. A. 2006. Priority-setting for health interventions in Mexico's system of social protection in health. *Lancet* 268: 1608–18

Goodin, R. E. 1985. *Protecting the Vulnerable: A Re-Analysis of our Social Responsibilities.* Chicago: University of Chicago Press.

Graham, H. 2004a. Social determinants and their unequal distribution: Clarifying policy understandings. Milbank Quarterly 82(1): 101–24.

2004b. Tackling inequalities in health in England: Remedying health disadvantages, narrowing health gaps or reducing health gradients. *International Social Policy* 33(1): 115–31.

Graham, H. and Kelly, M. P. 2004.*Health Inequalities: Concepts, Frameworks, and Policy.* London: Health Development Agency, National Health Service.

Green, R. 1976. Health care and justice in contract theory perspective. In R. Veatch and R. Branson (eds.), *Ethics and Health Policy.* Cambridge, MA: Ballinger, pp. 111–26.

Gruskin, S., Ahmed, S., Ferguson, L., and UNAIDS Global Reference Group on HIV/AIDS and Human Rights. Forthcoming. Issue Paper: What constitutes a rightsdbased approach? Definitions, methods, and practices. Geneva: UNAIDS.

Gutmann, A. and Thompson, D. 1996. *Democracy and Disagreement.* Cambridge, MA: Harvard University Press.

Gwatkin, D. R. 2002. "Who would gain most from efforts to reach the millennium development goals for health? An inquiry into the possibility of progress that fails to reach the poor." Health, Nutrition and Population Discussion Paper. The World Bank, December. Available at http://www.poverty.worldbank.org/files/13920_gwatkin1202.pdf.

Hadorn, D. 1991. Setting health care priorities in Oregon: Cost-effectiveness meets the rule of rescue. *Journal of the American Medical Association* 265: 2218–25.

Ham, C. and Pickard, S. 1998. *Tragic Choices in Health Care: The Case of Child B.* London: King's Fund.

Ham, C. and Robert, G. 2003. *Reasonable Rationing: International Experience of Priority Setting in Health Care.* Maidenhead, UK: Open University Press.

Haninger, K. 2006 The role of equity weights in allocating health and medical resources, in Valuing health for public policy. Ph.D. dissertation, Harvard University, pp. 65–100.

Harrell, J. P., Hall, S., and Taliaferro, J. 2003. Physiological responses to racism and discrimination: An assessment of the evidence. *American Journal of Public Health* 93(2): 243–8.

Harris, J. 1987. QALYfying the value of life. *Journal of Medical Ethics* 13: 117–23.

Hausman, D. 2006. Valuing health. *Philosophy and Public Affairs* 34(3): 246–74.

Havighurst, C. 1971. Health maintenance organization and the market for health services. *Law and Contemporary Problems* 35: 716–95.

1974. *Regulating Health Facilities Construction.* Washington, DC: American Enterprise Institute.

1977. Health care cost-containment regulation: Prospects and an alternative. *American Journal of Law and Medicine* 3: 309–22.

Hayward, M. D. and Heron, M. 1999. Racial inequality in active life among adult americans *Demography* 36(1): 77–91.

Held, V. 1973. Reasonable progress and self-respect. *The Monist* 57: 12–27.

House, J. S. and Williams, D. R. 2000. Understanding and reducing socioeconomic and racial/ethnic disparities in health. In B. D. Smedly and S. L. Syme (eds.), *Promoting Health: Intervention Strategies from Social and Behavioral Research.* Washington, DC: National Academy of Sciences Press, pp. 81–124.

Hsin, D. H. and Macer, D. R. 2004. Heroes of SARS: Professional roles and ethics of health care workers. *Journal of Infectious Diseases* 49(3): 210–15.

ICESCR, International Covenant on Economic, Social, and Cultural Rights 1966. In Marks (2006), p. 80.

International Convention on the Elimination of All Forms of Racial Discrimination (CERD). Available at http://www.ohchr.org/english/law/cerd.htm

International Human Rights Instruments. 2006. Report on Indicators for Monitoring Compliance with International Human Rights Instruments. Geneva:

Institute of Medicine. 1999. *To Error Is Human: Building a Safer Health System.* Washington, DC: National Academies Press.

2002. *Unequal Treatment: Confronting Racial and Ethnic Disparities in Health Care.* Washington, DC: National Academies Press.

2006. Miller, W., Robinson, L. A., and Lawrence R. S. (eds.). *Valuing Health for Regulatory Cost Effectiveness Analysis.* Washington, DC: National Academies Press.

Jackson, R. and Howe, N. 1999. *Global Aging: The Challenge of the New Millennium,* CSIS and Watson Wyatt Worldwide. Available at http://www.csis.org/component/option,com_csis_pubs/task,view/id,892/type,1/.

Jha, P., Peto, R., Zatonski, W., Boreham, J., Jarvis, M. J., and Lopez, A. D. 2006. Social inequalities in male mortality, and in male mortality from smoking: Indirect estimation from national death rates in England and Wales, Poland, and North America. *Lancet* online DOI:10.1016/S0140–6736 (06)68975–7.

Johns-Manville Sales Corp. v. International Association of Machinists, Local 1609, 621 F. 2nd 759 (5th Cir., 1980).

Kakwani, N. C. 1977. Measurement of tax progressivity: An international comparison. *Economic Journal* 87(345): 71–80.

Kamm, F. 1987. The choice between people, commonsense morality, and doctors. *Bioethics* 1: 255–71.

1993. *Morality, Mortality: Death and Whom to Save from It: Volume 1.* Oxford: Oxford University Press.

Kant, I. 1785. *Fundamental Principles of the Metaphysics of Morals,* ed. Gregor, M. Cambridge: Cambridge University Press, 1996.

Kaplan, G. A., Pamuk, E. R., Lynch, J. W., Cohen, R. D., and Balfour, J. L. 1996. Inequality in income and mortality in the United States: Analysis of mortality and potential pathways. *British Medical Journal* 3(12): 999–1003.

Kass, L. R. 2002. *Life, Liberty and the Defense of Dignity: The Challenge for Bioethics.* San Francisco: Encounter Books.

Kawachi, I., Daniels, N., and Robinson, D. 2005. Health disparities by race and class: Why both matter. *Health Affairs* 24(2): 343–4.

Kawachi, I., and Kennedy, B. P. 1997. Health and social cohesion: Why care about income inequality? *British Medical Journal* 314: 1037–40.

Kawachi, I., Kennedy, B. P., Lochner, K., and Prothrow-Stith, D. 1997. Social capital, income inequality and mortality. *American Journal of Public Health* 87: 1491–8.

Kawachi, I., Kennedy, B. P., Prothrow-Stith, D., and Gupta, V. 1999. Women's status and the health of women: A view from the states. *Social Science and Medicine* 48: 21–32.

Kemp, J., Aitken, J. M., LeGrand, S., and Murale, B. L. 2003. Equity in health sector responses to HIV/AIDS in Malawi. Equinet discussion Paper Number 6. Available at http://www.equinetafrica.org.

Kennedy, B. P., Kawachi, I., Glass, R., and Prothrow-Stith, D. 1998. Income distribution, socioeconomic status, and self-rated health: A U.S. multi-level analysis. *British Medical Journal* 317: 917–21.

Klein, R. 1995. Priorities and rationing: Pragmatism or principles? *British Medical Journal* 311: 761–2.

Knaul, F. M., Arreola-Ornelas, H., Mendez-Carniado, O., Bryson-Cahn, C., Barofsky, J., Maguire, R., Miranda, M., and Sesma, S. 2006. Evidence is good for your health system: Policy reform to remedy catastrophic and impoverishing health spending in Mexico. *Lancet* 368: 1828–41).

Kotlikoff, L. J. and Burns, S. 2004. *The Coming Generational Storm.* Cambridge, MA: MIT Press.

Krieger, N. and Sidney, S. 1996. Racial discrimination and blood pressure: The CARDIA study of young black and white adults. *American Journal of Public Health* 86: 1370–8.

Kubzansky, L. D., Krieger, N., Kawachi, I., Rockhill, B., Steel, G. K., and Berkman, L. F. United States: Inequality and the burden of poor health. In Evans et al. (2001), pp. 104–21.

Liese, B., Blanchet, N., and Dussault, G., 2004. The human resource crisis in health services in Sub-Saharan Africa. *Background Paper: World Development Report 2004, Making Services Work for Poor People.* Washington, DC: The World Bank.

Lochner v. People of the State of New York, 198 U.S. 45 (1905).

Lowenson, R. 2002. Participation and accountability in health systems: The missing factor in equity? Equinet Discussion Paper, UNAIDS; Available at: http://www.equinetafrica.org.

2004. Participation and accountability in health systems: The missing factor in equity? Available at http://www.equinetafrica.org/bibl/docs/particandaccount.pdf.

Lynch, J. W., Kaplan, G. A., Pamuk, E. R., Cohen, R. D., Heck,, K. E., Balfour, J. L., and Yen, I. H. 1998. Income inequality and mortality in metropolitan areas of the United States. *American Journal of Public Health* 88: 1074–80.

MacGreggor, F. C. 1979. *After Plastic Surgery: Adaptation and Adjustment.* New York: Praeger.

Mackenbach, P. 2003. Tackling inequalities in health: The need for building a systematic evidence base. *The Journal of Epidemiology and Community Health* 57: 162

Macklin, R. 2004. Ethics and equity in access to HIV treatment – 3X5 initiative. Background Paper for the Consultation on Equitable Access to Treatment and Care for HIV/AIDS. Geneva, January 26–7 2004. Available at http://www.who.int/ethics/en/background-macklin.pdf.

Marchand, S., Wikler, D., and Landesman, B. 1998. Class, health, and justice. *Milbank Quarterly* 76: 449–68.

Marks, S. (ed.) 2006. *Health and Human Rights: Basic International Documents*, 2nd edition. Cambridge, MA: Harvard University Press.

Marmot, M. 1994. Social differentials in health within and between populations. *Daedalus* 123: 197–216.

1999. Social causes of social inequalities in health. Cambridge, MA: Harvard Center for Population and Development Studies, Working Paper Series 99.01.

2004. *The Status Syndrome: How Social Standing Affects Our Health and Longevity*. New York: Henry Holt, Times Books.

Marmot, M. G., Fuhrer, R., Ettner, S. L., Marks, N. F., Bumpass, L. L., and Ryff, C. D. 1998. Contribution of psychosocial factors to socioeconomic differences in health. *Milbank Quarterly* 76: 403–48.

Marmot, M. G., Hemingway, B. H., Brunner, E., and Stansfield, S. 1997. Contribution of job control and other risk factors to social variations in coronary heart disease incidence. *The Lancet* 350: 235–9.

Marmot, M., Shipley, M. J., and Rose, G., 1984. Inequalities in death-specific explanations of a general pattern. *The Lancet* 5: 1003–6.

Martin, D. K., Bernstein, M., and Singer, P. A. 2003. Neurosurgery patients' access to ICU beds: Priority setting in the ICU – a qualitative case study and evaluation. *Journal of Neurology, Neurosurgery and Psychiatry* 74: 1299–1303.

Martin, D. K., Hollenberg, D., MacRae, S., Madden, S., and Singer, P. A. 2003. Priority Setting in a hospital formulary: A qualitative case study. *Health Policy* 66: 295–303.

Martin, D. K., Pater, J. L., and Singer, P. A. 2001. Priority setting decisions for new cancer drugs: A qualitative study. *The Lancet* 358: 1676–81.

Martin, D. K., Shulman, K., Santiago-Sorrell, P., and Singer, P. A. 2003. Priority setting and hospital strategic planning: A qualitative case study. *Journal of Health Services Research and Policy* 8: 197–201.

McCarthy, M. 1981. A review of some normative and conceptual issues in occupational safety and health. *Boston College Environmental Affairs Law Review* 9(4): 773–814.

McCloskey, H. K. 1976. Human needs, rights and political values. *American Philosophical Quarterly* 13: 1–11.

McCoy, D. 2003. Health sector responses to HIV/AIDS and treatment access in southern Africa: Addressing equity. Equinet Discussion Paper No. 10. Available at http://www.equinetafrica.org.

McKerlie, D. 1989a. Equality and time. *Ethics.* 99: 475–91.

1989b. Justice between age groups: A comment on Norman Daniels. *Journal of Applied Philosophy* 6: 227–34.

1993. Justice between neighboring generations. In L. M. Cohen (ed.), *Justice Across Generations: What Does It Mean?* Washington, DC: Public Policy Institute, AARP, pp. 215–26.

Mechanic, D. 1997. Muddling through elegantly: Finding the proper balance in rationing. *Health Affairs* 16(5): 83–92.

2000. Managed care and the imperative for a new professional ethic. *Health Affairs*, 19(5): 100–11.

2002. Disadvantage, inequality, and social policy. *Health Affairs* 21(2): 48–59.

Mellor, J. and Milyo, J. 2002. Is exposure to income inequality a public health concern? Lagged effects of income inequality in individual and population health. *Health Services Research* 38: 1.

Menzel, P., Gold, M., Nord, E., Pinto-Prades, J. L., Richardson, J., and Ubel, P. 1999. Toward a broader view of values in cost-effectiveness analysis in health care. *Hastings Center Report* 29(3): 7–15.

Millikan, R. G. 1984. *Language, Thought, and Other Biological Categories.* Cambridge, MA: MIT Press.

Murray, C. J. L. and Evans, D. B. (eds.). 2003. *Health Systems Performance Assessment: Debates, Methods and Empiricism.* Geneva: World Health Organization.

Nagel, T. 1997. Justice and nature. *Oxford Journal of Legal Studies* 17(2): 303–21.

2005. The problem of global justice. *Philosophy and Public Affairs* 33(2): 113–47.

National AIDS Commission, Malawi. 2004. Position paper on equity in access to antiretroviral therapy (ART) in malawi. Llongwe. Available at http://www.aidsmalawi.org.mw.

National Commission on Acquired Immune Deficiency Syndrome. 1990. Report No. 3, *Personnel and Workforce.* Washington DC: pp. 1–13.

Navarro, V. 2001. Assessment of the World Health Report 2000. *The Lancet* 356: 1598–1601.

Neander, K. 1983. Abnormal psychobiology. Ph.D. thesis, La Trobe University.

1991a. Function as selected effects: The conceptual analyst's defense. *Philosophy of Science* 58: 168–84.

1991b. The teleological notion of "Function." *Australasian Journal of Philosophy* 69: 454–68.

Neugarten, B. L. 1974. Age groups in American society and the rise of the young-old. *Annals of the American Academy of Political and Social Science* 415: 189–98.

Neumann, P. J. 2004. *Using Cost-Effectiveness Analysis to Improve Health Care: Opportunities and Barriers.* New York: Oxford University Press.

NICE. 2006. Citizen's Council Report on Age. August 18, 2006. Available at http://www.nice.org.uk/page.aspx?o=101368.

Noh, S. and Kaspar, V. 2003. Perceived discrimination and depression: Moderating effects of coping, acculturation and ethnic support. *American Journal of Public Health* 93(2): 232–8.

Nord, E. 1999. *Cost Value Analysis in Health Care: Making Sense Out of QALYs.* Cambridge: Cambridge University Press.

Nozick, R. 1969. Coercion. In S. Morgenbesser, P. Suppes, and M. White (eds.), *Philosophy, Science, and Method.* New York: St. Martin's Press, pp. 440–72.

1974. *Anarchy, State, and Utopia.* New York: Basic Books.

Nuremburg Code. 1949. *Trials of War Criminals Before the Nuremberg Military Tribunals Under Control Council Law No. 10.* Washington, DC: U.S. Government Printing Office, Vol. 2, pp. 181–2.

Nussbaum, M. C. 2000. *Women and Human Development.* Cambridge: Cambridge University Press.

Nussbaum, M. C. and Sen, A. 1993. *The Quality of Life.* Oxford: Clarendon Press.

Occupational Safety and Health Act of 1970, Pub. L. No. 91–596, 84 Stat. 1590; 27 USS pp. 651–78, 1976.

Okero, F. A., Aceng, E., Madrae, E., Namagala, E., and Serotoke, J., 2003. Scaling up antiretroviral therapy: Experience in Uganda: Case Study. Geneva: World Health Organization

Ostlin, P. and Diderichsen, F. 2001. *Equity Oriented National Health Strategy for Public Health in Sweden.* Policy Learning Curve Series No. 1. Brussels: European Center for Health Policy.

Pannarunothai, S. and Faramnuayphol, P. 2006. Benchmarks of fairness for health care reform in Thailand – combining evidence with opinions of civic groups. *Southeast Asian Journal of Tropical Medicine and Public Health* 37(2): 1–9.

Pappas, G., Queen, S., Hadden, W., and Fisher, G. 1993. The increasing disparity in mortality between socioeconomic groups in the United States, 1960 and 1986. *New England Journal of Medicine* 329(2): 103–9.

Parfit, D. 1984. *Reasons and Persons.* Oxford: Oxford University Press.

　1995. Equality or priority? University of Kansas, Lindley Lecture.

　1997. Equality and priority. *Ratio* 10: 202–21.

Peterson, P. 1999. *Gray Dawn: How the Coming Age Wave Will Transform America – and the World.* New York: Three Rivers Press.

Pogge, T. W. 2002. *World Poverty and Human Rights: Cosmopolitan Responsibilities and Reforms.* Cambridge: Blackwell.

　2005a. Human rights and global health: A research program, *Metaphilosophy* 36(1/2): 182–209.

　2005b. Severe poverty as a violation of negative duties. *Ethics and International Affairs* 19(1): 55–83.

Potts, M. and Walsh, J. 2003. Tackling India's HIV epidemic: Lessons from Africa. *British Medical Journal* 326: 1389–92.

Public Sector Group. 2000. Reforming public institutions and strengthening governance: A World Bank strategy. Washington, DC: World Bank. Available at: http://www.worldbank.org/publicsector/strategy.htm.

Rawlins, M. 2005. Pharmacopolitics and deliberative democracy. *Clinical Medicine* 5(5): 471–5.

Rawls, J. 1971. *A Theory of Justice.* Cambridge, MA: Harvard University Press.

　1974. Independence of moral theory. *Proceedings and Addresses of the American Philosophical Association* 48: 5–22.

　1982a. The basic liberties and their priorities. In *The Tanner Lectures on Human Values,* vol. III. Salt Lake City: University of Utah Press.

　1982b. Social unity and the primary goods. In A. K. Sen and B. Williams (eds.), *Utilitarianism and Beyond,* Cambridge University Press. pp. 159–85.

　1993. *Political Liberalism.* New York: Columbia University Press.

　1995. *Political Liberalism (paperback ed.).* New York: Columbia University Press.

1999. *The Law of Peoples.* Cambridge, MA: Harvard University Press.

2001. *Justice as Fairness: A Restatement.* ed. Erin Kelly Cambridge, MA: Harvard University Press..

Ray, S. and Kureya, T. 2003. Zimbabwe's challenge: Equity in health sector responses to HIV and AIDS in Zimbabwe. Equinet Discussion Paper No. 9, p. 5. Available at http://www.equinetafrica.org/bibl/docs/Disgaids.pdf

Roberts, M. J., Hsiao, W., Berman, P., and Reich, M. R. 2004. *Getting Health Reform Right: A Guide to Improving Performance and Equity.* New York: Oxford University Press.

Rodwin, M. 1997. The neglected remedy: Strengthening consumer voice in managed care. *The American Prospect* 34: 45–50.

Roemer, J. 1995. Equality of opportunity, *Boston Review*, April–May. Available at http://www.bostonreview.net/BR20.2/Roemer.html.

Rosenthal, M. and Daniels, N. 2006. Beyond competition: The normative implications of consumer driven health plans. *Journal of Health Politics, Policy, and Law* 31(3): 671–85

Russell, L. 1986. *Is Prevention Better Than Cure?* Washington, DC: Brookings Institution.

Sabin, J. E. and Daniels, N. 1994. Determining "medical necessity" for mental health practice. *Hastings Center Report* 24(6): 5–13.

1999. Public sector managed behavioral health care: III: Meaningful consumer and family participation. *Psychiatric Services* 50: 883–5.

Saltman, R. 1995. Applying planned market logic to developing countries' health systems: An initial exploration. *Discussion Paper No. 4, Forum on Health Sector Reform?* Secretariat, National Health Systems and Policies Unit of Strengthening Health Services, World Health Organization.

SARS-FAQ 2003. Toronto Undergraduate Geography Society, University of Toronto. Available at http://www.disastercenter.com/Severe%20Acute%20 Respiratory%20Syndrome.htm.

Scanlon, T. M. 1975. Preference and urgency. *Journal of Philosophy* 77(19): 655–69.

1998. *What Do We Owe to Each Other?* Cambridge, MA: Belknap Press of Harvard University Press.

2003. Rawls on justification. In Freeman (2003), pp. 139–67.

Schauer, F. 1995. Giving reasons. *Stanford Law Review* 47(4): 633–59.

Schulman, K. A., Berlin, J. A., Harless, W., Kerner, J. F., Sistrunk, S., Gersh, B., Dube, R., Taleghani, C. K., Burke, J. E., Williams, S., and Eisenberg, J. M. 1999. The effect of race and sex on physician's recommendations for cardiac catheterization. *New England Journal of Medicine* 340(8): 618–26.

Schweinhart, L. J., Barnes, H. V., and Weikart, D. P. 1993. *Significant Benefits: High/Scope Project Perry Preschool Study Through Age 27.* Ypsilanti, MI: High/Scope Press.

Secretary of State for Health. 1999. *Saving Lives: Our Healthier Nation.* Cm4386. London: The Stationery Office.

Sen, A. K. 1980. Equality of what? In S. McMurrin (ed.), *The Tanner Lectures on Human Values.* Salt Lake City: University of Utah Press, pp. 197–220.

1990a. Justice: Means versus freedoms. *Philosophy & Public Affairs* 19(2): 111–21.

1990b. More than 100 million women are missing. *New York Review of Books* 37: 30

1992. *Inequality Reexamined.* Cambridge, MA: Harvard University Press.

1999. *Development as Freedom*. New York: Knopf.

2002. Why health equity? *Health Economics* 11(8): 659–66.

2004. Why health equity? In S. Anand, F. Peter, and A. Sen (eds.) *Public Health, Ethics, and Equity*. New York: Oxford University Press, pp. 21–34.

Shaw, G. B. 1906. *he Doctor's Dilemma* (Prefatory Essay: 1911); London: Penguin Edition 1946).

Sher, G. 1987. *Desert*. Princeton, NJ: Princeton University Press.

Singer, P. A., Benatar, S. R., Bernstein, M., Daar, A. S., Dickens., B., MacRae, S. K., Upshur, R. E. G., Wright, L., and Shaul, R. Z. 2003. Ethics and SARS: Lessons from Toronto. *British Medical Journal* 327:1342–4.

Singer, P. A., Martin, D. K., Giacomini, M., and Purdy, L. 2000. Priority setting for new technologies in medicine: A qualitative case study. *British Medical Journal*, 327: 1316–18.

Sloan, F., and Bentkover, J. D. 1979. *Access to Ambulatory Care and the U.S. Economy*. Lexington, MA: Lexington Books.

Smith, S. 2006. Cigarettes pack more nicotine. *Boston Globe*, August 30.

Sreenivasan, G. 2007 Health care and equality of oppertunity. *Hastings Center Report* 37(2): 21–31.

Starr, P. 1982. *The Social Transformation of American Medicine*. New York: Basic Books.

State of the World's Children, The. 2000. UNICEF. August 23, 2005. Available at http://www.unicef.org/sowcoo/stat2.htm.

Subramanian, S. V., Delgado, I., Jadue, L., Vega, J., and Kawachi, I. 2003. Income inequality and health: Multilevel analysis of Chilean communities. *Journal of Epidemiology and Community Health* 57: 844–8.

Subramanian, S. V. and Kawachi, I. 2004. Income inequality and health: What have we learned so far? *Epidemiologic Reviews* 26: 8–91.

2006. Whose health is affected by income inequality? A multilevel interaction analysis of contemporaneous and lagged effects of state income inequality on individual self-rated health in the United States. *Health and Place* 12(2): 141–56.

Sunstein, C. 1993. *The Partial Constitution*. Cambridge, MA: Harvard University Press.

Temkin, L. 1993. *Inequality*. Oxford: Oxford University Press.

Thomson, D. 1989. The welfare state and generational conflicts: Winners and losers. In P. Johnson, C. Conrad, and D. Thomson (eds.), *Workers versus Pensioners: Intergenerational Justice in an Aging World*. Manchester, UK: Manchester University Press, pp. 33–56.

Torres, M. A. 2005. The human right to health, national courts, and access to HIV/AIDS treatment: A case study from Venezuela. In S. Gruskin, M. A. Gordin, G. J. Annas, and S. P. Marks (eds.), *Perspectives on Health and Human Rights*. New York: Routledge, pp. 507–16.

Tunis, S. 2004. Why Medicare has not established criteria for coverage decisions. *New England Journal of Medicine* 350(21): 2196–8.

Tversky, A. and Kahneman, D. 1981. The framing of decisions and the psychology of choice. *Science* 21(4481): 453–8.

UN Commission on Human Rights 2003. Resolution 2003/28. The right of everone to the enjoyment of the highest attainable standard of physical and mental health http://www.unhchr.ch/Huridocda/Huridoca.nsf/TestFrame/267 fa9369338eca7c1256dleoo36ao14?opendocument.

UNFPA, UNAIDS, and UNIFEM. 2004. *Women and HIV/AIDS: Confronting the Crisis*, 1–10, 51–6. New York and Geneva: UNAIDS, UNFPA, UNIFEM. http://www.unfpa.org/upload/lib_pub_file/308_filename_women_aids1.pdf.

UNICEF Statistics: Maternal Mortality. May 2006. UNICEF. August 2005, 23. Available at http//www.childinfo.org/areas/maternalmortality.

United States National Commission for the Protection of Human Subjects of Biomedical and Behavioral Research. 1979. *The Belmont Report: Ethical Principles and Guidelines for the Protection of Human Subjects of Research*. April 18. Bethesda, MD: U.S. Government Printing Office.

University of Toronto Joint Center for Bioethics 2005. Stand guard for thee. Available at http://www.utoronto.ca/jcb/home/documents/pandemic.pdf.

Van Ryn, M. 2002. Research on the provider contribution to race/ethnicity disparities in medical care. *Medical Care* 40(1): 140–51.

Van Ryn, M. and Burke, J. 2000. The effect of patient race and socio-economic status on physicians' perceptions of patients. *Social Science and Medicine* 50: 813–28.

Veatch, R. 1988. Justice and the economics of terminal illness. *Hastings Center Report* 18(4): 33–40.

Villerme, L. 1840. *Tableau d'Etat Physique et Moral des Ouvriers*, vol. 2. Paris: Renouard. Cited in B. G. Link, M. E. Northridge, J. C. Phelan, and M. L. Ganz, Social epidemiology and the fundamental cause concept: On the structuring of effective cancer screens by socioeconomic status. *Milbank Quarterly* 76 (1998): 375–402.

Wakefield, J. C. 1992. The concept of mental disorder. On the boundary between biological facts and social values. *American Psychologist* 47: 373–88.

    1997a. Diagnosing DSM-IV, Part 1: DSM-IV and the concept of mental disorder. *Behavior Research and Therapy* 35: 633–50.

    1997b. When is development disordered? Developmental psychopathology and the harmful dysfunction analysis of mental disorder. *Development and Psychopathology* 9: 269–90.

    1999. Mental disorder as a black box essentialist concept. *Journal of Abnormal Psychology* 108: 465–72.

Wallace, P. 2001. *Agequake: Riding the Demographic Rollercoaster Shaking Business, Finance and Our World*. London: Nicolas Brealey.

Walzer, M. 1983a. *Spheres of Justice: A Defense of Pluralism and Equality*. New York: Basic Books.

    1983b. Spheres of justice: An exchange. *New York Review of Books*, pp. 4–5.

Wertheimer, A. 1987. *Coercion*. Princeton, NJ: Princeton University Press.

    1996. *Exploitation*. Princeton, NJ: Princeton University Press.

Whitehead, M. 1992. The concepts and principles of equity and health. *International Journal of Health Services* 22: 429–45.

Wiggins, D. 1988. *Needs, Values, Truth: Essays in the Philosophy of Value*. Oxford: Blackwell.

Wikler, D. 1978. Persuasion and coercion for health: Issues in government efforts to change lifestyle. *Milbank Memorial Fund Quarterly: Health and Society* 56(3): 303–38.

Wilkinson, R. G. 1992. Income distribution and life expectancy. *British Medical Journal* 304: 165–8.

Williams, A. (Andrew) 1995. The revisionist difference principle. *Canadian Journal of Philosophy* 25: 257–82.

Williams, A. (Allan) 1997. Intergenerational equity: An exploration of the fair innings argument. *Health Economics* 6: 117–32.

Williams, B. 1973. A critique of utilitarianism. In J. C. C. Smart, and B. Williams (eds.), *Utilitarianism: For and Against*, Cambridge: Cambridge University Press, pp. 17–150.

Williams, D. R., Neighbors, H. W., and Jackson, J. S. 2003. Racial/ethnic discrimination and health: Findings from community studies. *American Journal of Public Health*, 93: 200–8.

Windfur, M. 2006. Rights based monitoring – lessons to be learned from the work on indicators for the right to adequate food. Indicators, Benchmarks, Scoping Assessement (IBSA). Presentation in Mannheim, Germany.

World Health Organization. 2000. *The World Health Report 2000: Health Systems: Improving Performance*. Geneva: World Health Organization.

2003a. Epidemic and pandemic alert and response. September 17, 2006. available at http://www.who.int/csr/sars/country/2003_07_11/en/index.html.

2003b. Report of the 3 by 5 mission to Zambia on scaling up antiretroviral treatment as part of the global emergency response to HIV/AIDS, Geneva: World Health Organization.

2003c. Scaling up antiretroviral therapy in resource-limited settings: Treatment guidelines for a public health approach. Available at http://www.who.int/3by5/publications/documents/arv_guidelines/en/index.html.

2004. *Recruitment of Health Workers from the Developing World*. Geneva: World Health Organization.

2006a. Equity and fair process in scaling up antiretroviral treatments: Potentials and challenges in the United Republic of Tanzania. Available at http://www.who.int/ethics/Equity%20and%20Fair%20Practice%20in%20RT_Tanzania.pdf.

2006b. *World Health Report 2006. Working Together for Health*. Geneva: World Health Organization.

World Health Organization Europe. 1999. *Health 21: The Health for All Policy Framework for the WHO European Region*. Copenhagen: World Health Organization Regional Office for Europe.

2002. *The European Health Report 2002*. Copenhagen: World Health Organization Regional Office for Europe.

World Health Organization/UNAIDS 2004. Guidance on ethics and equitable access to HIV treatment and care for HIV/AIDS. Geneva: World Health Organization/UNAIDS. Available at http://www.data.unaids.org/Publications/External-Documents/WHO_Ethics-Equity HIV_en.pdf.

World Health Organisation/UNICEF/UNFPA. 2005 Maternal Mortality in 2004 – Estimates Developed by WHO. UNICEF, and UNFPA. Available at http://www.childinfo.org/areas/maternalmortality.

World Medical Association. 1964. Ethical Principles for Medical Research Involving Human Subjects. Adopted by the 18th WMA General Assembly, Helsinki, Finland, June 1964 and amended by the 29th WMA General Assembly, Tokyo, Japan, October 1975; 35th WMA General Assembly, Venice, Italy, October 1983; 41st WMA General Assembly, Hong Kong, September 1989; 48th WMA General Assembly, Somerset West, Republic of South Africa, October 1996; and

52nd WMA General Assembly, Edinburgh, Scotland, October 2000. Available at http://www.wma.net/e/policy/b3.htm.

Wright, L. 1973. Functions. *Philosophical Review* 83: 139–68. Reprinted in Sober, E. (ed.). 1984. *Conceptual Issues in Evolutionary Biology*. Cambridge, MA: Harvard University Press.

Zimmerman, D. 1981. Coercive wage offers. *Philosophy and Public Affairs* 10(2): 121–45.

Zuger, A. and Miles, S. M. 1987. Physicians, AIDS, and occupational risk. *Journal of the American Medical Association* 258(14): 1924–28.

40 vs. 80+ years. People facts and figures: Life expectancy. 2005. August 23, 2005. Available at http://www.osconnect.com/pop/p1.asp?whichpage=10&pagesize=20&sort=Country.

Index

HIV/AIDS (*cont.*)
  UNAIDS, 274n1, 275, 283–91
  See also ARTs (antiretroviral
    treatments)
Hollenberg, D., 138
homosexuality, 40
hospital stays, length of,
  26
House, J.S., 301
household income, 85–6
Howe, N., 164
Hsin, D. H., 227
human rights and priority setting
  accountability for reasonableness,
    326–32
  fair processes, 328–9
  generic illustration of, 320–6
  international health inequalities,
    333–7, 352–4
  vs. legal rights, 316
  moral rights to health/health care,
    316–20
  progressive realization of right to
    health, 318–20, 329–32
  rights-based approach to health,
    313–16, 320–6
  Universal Declaration of Human
    Rights, 316n4, 335n5

ice breakers, 133n16
ICESCR (International Covenant on
  Economic, Social, and Cultural
  Rights), 314
Ideal Advocates, 234, 236–8
illness, 13, 21, 24
income
  fair shares, 31–2
  household, 85–6
  as primary good, 56
  relative, and health, 85–8
index of primary social goods, 47–51,
  56–7, 94, 96, 98–9
India, Kerala, 342–3, 345
individual SES and health, 84–5

inequalities
  allowed by Difference Principle,
    54, 55, 58
  cross-national evidence on health,
    83–4
  flattening SES gradients of health,
    95–7
  individual SES and health, 84–5
  international, 334–7
  pathways linking social inequalities
    to health inequalities, 88–9
  Rawls on allowable, 92–5
  relative income and health, 85–8
  residual, just or unjust, 97–100
  social determinants of, *see* social
    determinants of health
  See also health inequalities
infertility and normal functioning,
  59
injustice of health inequalities and
  Focal Questions, 11, 21–4, 27,
  79. *See also* health inequalities;
  international health inequalities
Institute of Medicine (IOM), 114,
  117n9, 123, 191, 234, 297
institutions, sustainability, 166–8
intellectual property rights, 339n6,
  340, 352
*International Association of Machinists,
  Local 1609, Johns-Manville Sales
  Corp. v.*, 196n5
international health inequalities
  brain drain of health personnel,
    337–9
  cosmopolitanism, 346–8
  global justice, 345–54
  harms to health and minimalist
    strategy, 337–40
  injustice of, 334–7
  introduction, 333–4
  justice in international
    organizations, 351–4
  property rights and access to drugs,
    339–40